*Jewish High Society in
Old Regime Berlin*

DEBORAH HERTZ | *Jewish High Society in Old Regime Berlin*

Yale University Press
New Haven and London

Chapter 7 is reproduced from "Seductive Con-
version in Berlin" in Todd Endelman, ed., *Jewish
Apostasy in the Modern World*, by permission of
Holmes & Meier Publishers, Inc.

Designed by Jo Aerne
and set in Galliard type by Graphic Composition, Inc. Athens, Ga. Printed in the United
States of America by Halliday Lithograph Cor-
poration, West Hanover, Mass.

Library of Congress Cataloging-in-Publication Data
Hertz, Deborah
Jewish high society in Old Regime Berlin /
Deborah Hertz.
    p. cm.
Bibliography: p.
Includes index.
ISBN 0-300-03775-9 (alk. paper)
1. Jews—Berlin (Germany)—Intellectual life. 2.
Salons—Berlin (Germany)—History—18th cen-
tury. 3. Women, Jewish—Berlin (Germany)—
History—18th century. 4. Jews—Berlin (Ger-
many)—History—18th century. 5. Berlin (Ger-
many)—Ethnic relations. I. Title
DS135.G4B4524 1988
943.1'55004924—dc19   87–16003
                                              CIP

10   9   8   7   6   5   4   3   2   1

For Noah's Grandparents

Contents

List of Illustrations   ix

List of Figures   xi

Preface   xiii

List of Abbreviations   xv

ONE | Introduction: Why Salons?   1

TWO | Social Structure   23

THREE | The Male Intelligentsia   48

FOUR | Public Leisure and the Rise of Salons   75

FIVE | Salon Men   119

SIX | Salon Women   156

SEVEN | Seductive Conversion and Romantic

Intermarriage   204

EIGHT | The Decline of Salons   251

Bibliographic Note   287

Index   293

Illustrations

Rahel Levin. Rahel Varnhagen, Portrait by an Unknown. Courtesy of the Leo Baeck Institute, New York.

Amalie Beer. By Carl Kretschmar. Beer-Meyerbeer Collection. Courtesy of the Leo Baeck Institute, New York.

Henriette Herz. By Anna Dorothea Therbusch. Staatliche Museen Preussicher Kulturbesitz, Nationalgalerie Berlin (West).

Rebecca Friedländer. Varnhagen–Frohberg Correspondence, Varnhagen Collection, Jagiellonian Library, Crakow.

Dorothea Mendelssohn Veit. From Margareta Hiemenz, *Dorothea v. Schlegel* (Freiburg im Breisgau, 1911).

Friedrich Gentz. From Kurt Fervers, *Berliner Salons* (Munich, 1940.)

Moses Mendelssohns Examen am Berliner Thor zu Potzdam. By Daniel Chodowiecki, 1792. Bildarchiv Preussischer Kulturbesitz, Berlin.

King Frederick William III and Queen Louise. By F. W. Nettling, 1798. Berlin Museum (West).

Gustav von Brinkmann. By Maria Röhl, 1835. Königliche Bibliothek, Stockholm.

"The Abrahamson Salon." By Gottfried Schadow. From Hans Ostwald, *Kultur- und Sittengeschichte Berlin* (Berlin, 1924).

Caffée Clatché. By W. Chodowiecki, 1800. From Hans Ostwald, *Kultur- und Sittengeschichte Berlin* (Berlin, 1924).

David Friedländer. Bildarchiv d. Öst. Nationalbibliothek, Vienna. Courtesy of the Leo Baeck Institute, New York.

Markus Herz. From Kurt Fervers, *Berliner Salons* (Munich, 1940).

Friedrich Schleiermacher. From Kurt Fervers, *Berliner Salons* (Munich, 1940).

Achim von Arnim. From Margarete Susman, *Frauen der Romantik* (Jena, 1929).

David Koreff. By Wilhelm Hensel. Hensel Collection. Courtesy of the Leo Baeck Institute, New York.

Julius Hitzig. By Franz Krüger; engraving by Joseph Leudner; lithograph by Meyer, 1837. Märkisches Museum, Berlin. Courtesy of the Leo Baeck Institute, New York.

Ludwig Robert. By Wilhelm Hensel. Hensel Collection. Courtesy of the Leo Baeck Institute, New York.

Salomon Maimon. By W. Arndt, 1800. Schwadron Collection, Jewish National and University Library, Jerusalem. Courtesy of the Leo Baeck Institute, New York.

Dorothea von Courland. Engraving by Scheffner from a painting by Schröder. Friedrich Schiller University, Jena.

Friedrich Schlegel. By Joh. Veit. From Margarete Susman, *Frauen der Romantik* (Jena, 1929).

Rebecca Itzig Ephraim. Itzig Poetry Album. Courtesy of the Leo Baeck Institute, New York.

Karl August Varnhagen von Ense. By Wilhelm Hensel. Hensel Collection. Courtesy of the Leo Baeck Institute, New York.

Wilhelm von Humboldt. Bildarchiv Preussischer Kulturbesitz, Berlin.

Contemporary Satires of Salon Jews. From Edward Fuchs, *Die Juden in der Karikatur* (Munich, 1921).

Figures

1. Number of Intellectuals per German City in 1806
2. Estate and Income Distribution of Berlin and Berlin's Male Intelligentsia in 1800
3. Income Distribution among Noble, Commoner, and Jewish Intellectuals in Berlin
4. Estate of Birth of Berlin Intellectuals by Employment
5. Proportion of Nobles and Upwardly Mobile Men among Berlin Intellectuals by Occupation
6. Age of Berlin Intellectuals by Employment
7. The Berlin Intelligentsia by Occupation
8. Estate and Gender of Salon Participations
9. Occupations of Berlin Intellectuals, Club Intellectuals, and Salon Men
10. Age of Berlin Intellectuals, Club Intellectuals, and Salon Men
11. Jewish Salon Women in Berlin
12. Conversions in Berlin, 1700–1850
13. Jewish Converts in Berlin per 3,000 Jewish Residents of Berlin, 1750–1850
14. Age of Converts in Berlin, 1770–99
15. Male and Female Jewish Converts in Berlin, 1750–1850
16. Age by Gender of Converts in Berlin, 1770–99
17. Social Origin of Converts by Decade
18. Converted Jewish Outmarriers, 1800–46
19. Female and Male Conversion and Intermarriage in Berlin, 1800–46

Preface

I knew that I had found an intellectual home in the Jewish salons of eighteenth-century Berlin during the winter of 1972–73, my second year of graduate school, when I happened upon G. P. Gooch's essay on the Berlin *salonières* in his *Germany during the French Revolution*. I was already familiar with Hannah Arendt's biography of Rahel Varnhagen, and it occurred to me that there might be a dissertation topic here. But a Ph.D. thesis in women's history? For that I was only tentatively ready. In 1972, women's history did not seem weighty and ponderous enough for a dissertation, even though my adviser, Professor Otto Pflanze, tried to talk me into it. Gradually, the whole endeavor seduced me, and I came to see that reconstructing the Berlin salons was a perfect project on which I could focus my three central historical interests. The Berlin salons were an intellectual institution with a definite, if still mysterious social history; they were led by marginal Jewish intellectuals in the era of emancipation; and they were also very much a female intellectual institution. Perhaps pretentiously, I came to feel that the salons needed me, that I had been born in order to write this book.

In the thirteen years that have passed since that Minneapolis winter, many individuals and institutions have helped me along. Professor Pflanze, above all, was always encouraging and exacting. The Germanistic Society of America, the Fulbright Commission, the National Foundation for Jewish Culture, and the Memorial Foundation for Jewish Culture all made possible my dissertation work at the Free University in West Berlin during 1975–77. The Goethe-Schiller Archive in Weimar, the Rare Manuscript Collection of the Schiller University in Jena, and the Evangelisches Zentralarchiv in West Berlin generously opened their collections to me. Beginning in 1977, the staff of the Leo Baeck Institute in New York was consistently helpful, sharing research tips and precious documents. The German Academic Exchange Service funded a 1979 visit to the Evangelisches Zentralarchiv in West Berlin, where I coded conversion records for computer analysis. Colleagues in the history department of the University of Minnesota, Pittsburg State University in Kansas, and the State University of New York at Binghamton provided congenial work settings and high intellectual expectations.

Once installed at Binghamton in 1980, additional help came my way. The SUNY Research Foundation paid for more coding of conversion records in 1980. A Deans' Research Leave in the fall of 1983 gave me time to write, as did an Andrew Mellon Faculty Fellowship at Harvard University in 1984–85. Through it all, the staff of the SUNY-Binghamton Manuscript Center cheerfully typed draft after draft after draft of the manuscript. Charles Grench of the Yale University Press smoothed the book's entry on to the printed page. Many friends and colleagues talked to me endlessly about the book and patiently read chapters. My sisters in the German Women's History Study Group in New York have been an especially enduring source of intellectual comradeship.

But it was my family, especially Martin, who pulled me through.

Montrose, Pennsylvania
September 1986

Abbreviations

ALBI   Archives of the Leo Baeck Institute, New York, New York

ADB   *Allgemeine Deutsche Biographie* (Leipzig, 1893)

GSA   Goethe Schiller Archive, Weimar, German Democratic Republic

JPM   *Jahrbücher der preussischen Monarchie unter Friedrich Wilhelm III*

LBIYB   *Leo Baeck Institute Year Book*

NDB   *Neue Deutsche Biographie* (Berlin, 1959)

EZA   Evangelisches Zentralarchiv, West Berlin

ONE | *Introduction: Why Salons?*

The Rahelzeit

One day, while choosing the illustrations for this book, I overheard an archivist describing my topic to a colleague. "She works on the *Rahel-zeit*," he explained. His offhand label for the period was a large illumination for me, too immersed in this past to see it from afar. I suddenly realized: it is not all that rare for Germans to carve up their history by reference to individuals. One readily thinks of how the names of King Frederick the Great, Otto von Bismarck, or Adolf Hitler dominate the historiography of their eras. But it is unusual that a key figure for an era should be female, Jewish, and lacking in either political power or intellectual achievement. That the years between 1780 and 1806, central years in Germany's intellectual legacy, should be referred to by the name of a Jewish woman tells much about what was distinctive in this era. At that time and in that place it was possible to become famous without being a gentile or a man, without a title, civil rights, or a public position, and without publishing one's words. To discover just why this should have been the case for Rahel Varnhagen and a handful of her Jewish women friends is the purpose of this book.

Rahel Varnhagen's popularity with Berlin's most elegant coterie of early romantic intellectuals began in the 1790s, while she was still Mademoiselle Levin, a wealthy single Jewish woman in her twenties living in the attic apartment of her family's grand home in the center of Berlin. Since her youth she had enjoyed the acquaintance of a few prominent gentiles. As a child she had seen such persons from afar when playing at her friend Brendel Mendelssohn's house, whose father, Moses, was Europe's most esteemed and sought-after Jewish intellectual. Her own father, a jewelry merchant with connections at court, had invited home to dinner actors and nobles to whom he loaned money. Yet as a teenager in the 1780s his daughter Rahel had felt like a schlemiehl, a nobody, when men like Alexander and Wilhelm von Humbolt and their friends gathered at the family dinner table.

But slowly Mademoiselle Levin made her way into the very center of the Humboldts' social universe—most fundamentally by deciding to cut her ties to the Jewish community through refusing to marry the Jewish businessmen suggested by her family. Instead she worked at improving her German and her French, read assiduously, and hired a tutor to learn mathematics. Her social independence and mastery of secular languages and skills came to her advantage in her early twenties, when she met foreign diplomats and déclassé noblewomen while summering at Bohemian spas. These new friends found her exotic, charming, and soulful, and brought along their courtly friends to visit her in the city on winter evenings after the theater. This friendship circle eventually grew to become Rahel Levin's salon.

In different ways, Mademoiselle Levin's childhood friends also found their way to notoriety in Berlin's high society. Although Moses Mendelssohn's daughter Brendel had married a Jewish businessman chosen by her father when she was nineteen, she too was able to construct a secular life for herself. She changed her name from Brendel to Dorothea, kept up with the current literary scene, and organized a Reading Society in her home on Thursday evenings. In 1798, at the age of thirty-four, she met Friedrich Schlegel, who was just then becoming famous as a literary critic, at the home of a Jewish friend. Dorothea quickly fell in love, abandoned her Jewish husband and their two sons, and spent the rest of her difficult life with Schlegel. A second childhood playmate at the Mendelssohn home was Henriette de Lemos, the daughter of a wealthy Portuguese physician in Berlin, who was said to be so pretty that young officers interfered with her daily walks to school, so captivating that Princess Anna Amalia, the sister of Frederick the Great, asked to be invited to a Jewish holiday celebration at the de Lemos home just to see Henriette in her white dress. She was engaged when only twelve to Markus Herz, a Jewish physician twice her age, and in 1780 Henriette and her husband began entertaining lavishly at a large double salon that grew out of Markus's evening lecture course in natural science. In one room he performed physics experiments while in another Henriette led discussions on the newest romantic poetry, plays, and novels.

Rahel Levin, Dorothea Mendelssohn, and Henriette Herz were the most famous Jewish women of their time in Berlin, known far and wide among European intellectuals for their cultivated tastes and their intimate friendships with prominent gentiles. A number of other Jewish women in Berlin also conquered high culture and high society: Amalie Beer, a sensual beauty who frequently traveled to Italy, was happiest when her palatial home was filled with guests from morning to night, while Philippine Cohen's guests often spent the afternoons in her garden composing character sketches of each other and reading them aloud. The two Meyer sisters both began with early arranged marriages to Jewish businessmen and ended by converting to Christianity and marryingno-blemen. Sara Levy, a daughter of the powerful Itzig family, remained married to an important Jewish banker and entertained diplomats and visiting French intellectuals for decades in her home in the city's poshest neighborhood. Rebecca Solomon, who married into the important Friedländer family at nineteen and divorced at twenty-three, spent her time writing novels and long letters while searching for a noble husband.

The cultural and social successes of this group of Jewish women made the Rahelzeit a lively epoch in Berlin. During the quarter century between 1780 and 1806 the city's Jewish salons caused a stir at home and abroad. Visitors from across Europe hailed the swift assimilation accomplished by the Jewish *salonières,* whose social prominence was achieved at a time when the majority of central and eastern European Jews were still poor peddlers and traders, living in small villages, speaking Yiddish, and following a traditional way of life. Surely here, in the drawing rooms of Berlin's rich and sophisticated Jewish women, was to be found the realization of the dream of emancipation that was just then being proposed by avant-garde intellectuals. French Jewry may have been the first Jewish community in Europe to achieve authentic political emancipation in the course of the French Revolution. But it was in Germany, specifically in Berlin, that a Jewish community achieved the social glory represented by entertaining and even marrying the cream of gentile society. Nor was it only the Berlin Jewish women's role in promoting Jewish social emancipation that captivated observers of the Berlin scene. That their guests included both commoners and nobles was heralded by prominent visitors as a significant achievement in a land famous for its rigid social structure. When the French salonière Madame de Staël visited Berlin in 1804, she found it easier to gracefully entertain princes alongside humble writers than elsewhere in Germany.[1]

The public happiness created by the Jewish salonières was based on defiance of the traditional boundaries separating noble from commoner,

---

1. De Staël's discussion of her problems in Berlin are discussed in her letter of April 1, 1804, published in Alfred Götze, ed., *Ein Fremder Gast: Frau von Staël in Deutschland 1803–04* (Jena, 1928), 41.

Rahel Levin

Amalie Beer

Henriette Herz

Rebecca Friedländer

Dorothea Mendelssohn Veit

gentile from Jew, man from woman. The public happiness achieved in these salons was a real-life enactment of the ideal of *Bildung* so often discussed at the time. Bildung encompassed education, refinement, the development of character; Bildung was what commoners could work at to become noble "in spirit"; it was what Jews could work at to become more like the gentiles. But the cultivated happiness achieved in the salons was to have a short life. Although a few salons survived after 1806, both Jewish women's leadership in salon culture and the importance of the salon as an institution declined radically after Napoleon conquered Prussia in that fateful year. For the next decade Berlin was either directly or indirectly under foreign rule. As opposition to French domination festered, the city's increasingly patriotic intelligentsia came to oppose the values so crucial to the formation of salons. Imitation of the French nobility, sexual license, friendships between commoners and nobles, and the open display of Jewish wealth and culture all became deeply controversial. As Rahel Levin later lamented: "where are our days, when we were all together! They went under in the year '06. Went under like a ship: containing the loveliest goods of life, the loveliest pleasures."[2]

The Historians

The passage of years accentuated how distinctive the Berlin salons had been in both space and time. Nineteenth-century chroniclers emphasized that Berlin was the only city in Germany where salons appeared in the last decades of the eighteenth century. To be sure, these historians admitted that women had led intellectual "social circles" elsewhere in Germany in this epoch, especially in the university towns of Göttingen and Jena. But the Berlin women were considered to have been more "culturally stimulating" and their salons more "socially diverse" than the literary circles that appeared in other German cities.[3] Historians also pointed to the extreme heterogeneity of salon society in Berlin. "Representatives" of "all classes" were said to have met in the Berlin salons, and this social and religious integration was, moreover, considered "unprecedented" in

2. For a recent discussion of the role of *Bildung* in German-Jewish history see George Mosse, *German Jews beyond Judaism* (Bloomington and Cincinnati, 1985), 4. Rahel Varnhagen's lament in 1806 is quoted in translation from Hannah Arendt, *Rahel Varnhagen: The Life of a Jewess* (London, 1957; rpt., New York, 1974), 99.

3. See Fritz Giese, *Der romantische Charakter: Die Entwicklung des Androgynenproblems in der Frühromantik* (Langensalza, 1919), 124. See also Barbara Duden, "Salons," State Examination Thesis, Dept. of German, Free University of Berlin, 1973, 8. The two works in English devoted solely to the Berlin salons are Bertha Meyer, *Salon Sketches* (New York, 1938) and Mary Hargrave, *Some German Women and Their Salons* (London, n.d.).

the German past. It was also asserted that these salons had no successors: a wide range of historians agreed that the "blossoming" of Berlin society in salons was "never achieved again" and had been altogether "unique."[4] The theme of uniqueness had special implications for women because the salon was a rare opportunity for public female power; Ingeborg Drewitz proclaimed the salons as the first "high point" in the emancipation of German women.[5] For G. P. Gooch, the salons were literally the only high point, since "the Berlin salons gave women a share in the making of public opinion which they would never again enjoy in Germany."[6] But not all historians have been unequivocally proud of the salonières' achievements. Some have criticized them for their mastery of oral rather than written high culture and accused them of being merely muses for men rather than creators of their own literary universe.[7]

The Jewish identity of the salonières has also been problematic in the historiography. Although Jewish success at hosting salons declined radically after 1806, some aspects of the Jewish role in salon society continued well into the nineteenth century and after. Conversion to Christianity, intermarriage, and participation in avant-garde high culture were all traditions that remained popular with Jewish Germans until the Holocaust. As one of the first generations to assimilate in these ways, the Berlin salonières have been either praised or blamed, depending on the observer's stance toward assimilation. Those who praised the Jewish salonières were mainly mid-nineteenth-century gentile literary critics like Rahel Levin's husband Karl August Varnhagen von Ense—men who admired the salonières because they were so attractive to the glamorous male intellectuals of their day and who were so enthusiastic about Jewish assimilation that they usually neglected to mention that the salonières were Jewish. No doubt this key fact was omitted out of fear that such emphasis would diminish the women's significance with readers less philosemitic than themselves.[8]

---

4. The social heterogeneity of salon society in Berlin was emphasized by Arendt, *Rahel Varnhagen,* 30, and Karl Hillebrand, "Die Berliner Gesellschaft in den Jahren 1789–1815," in *Unbekannte Essays,* Uhde Bernays, ed. (Bern, 1955), 25. For claims about the chronological uniqueness of the salons see also Margarete Susman, *Frauen in der Romantik* (Cologne, 1960), 43; Hillebrand, "Die Berliner Gesellschaft," 25; Hans Karl Krüger, *Berliner Romantik und Berliner Judentum* (Bonn, 1939), 51; Bertha Badt-Strauss, ed., *Menschen Untereinander von Rahel Varnhagen* (Berlin, 1928), 57.

5. Ingeborg Drewitz, *Berliner Salons: Gesellschaft und Literatur zwischen Aufklärung und Industriezeitalter* (Berlin, 1965), 19.

6. G. P. Gooch, *Germany and the French Revolution* (London, 1920), 354.

7. See for instance Lily Braun, *Die Frauenfrage* (Leipzig, 1901), 59ff. For a more recent, balanced interpretation, see Dale Spender, *Women of Ideas* (London, 1982), 80–81.

8. Throughout this book I use the word *philosemitic* to mean views more positive to-

Jewish historians, on the other hand, who have tended to be Jewish nationalists of one kind or another, generally decried rather than applauded the salonières, even if they could not altogether escape the significance of the salonières' social glory for Jewish history. Thus it was asserted that these salons constituted "the first time an entire Jewish sector forged real bonds with German society," bonds which "brought Jew and Christian closer" than in any other European country during the eighteenth century.[9] But it was precisely the women's success at assimilation that so disturbed Jewish historians. The integration in salons was judged to have been "decadent," of an "unwholesome quality." Henrich Graetz disapproved so strongly of the salon women's behavior that he claimed the women did Judaism a service by converting.[10] Blame has been placed on the salonières not only because they converted, but also for the supposed effect of their conversions on Jews outside salon society. Several Jewish historians blamed the small group of salonières for initiating a "wave" of conversion in Berlin. The incidence of conversion in Berlin was described as a "mania," a "flood," or an "epidemic" that left Berlin Jewry "bordering on dissolution." Contemporary worries that only a small proportion of the Jewish families in Berlin were left "untouched" by the "epidemic" twenty years after its onset in the 1780s were cited to dramatize the pervasiveness of conversion in these years.[11]

Thus any pride Jewish historians had in the salonières' social feat so early in the fight for emancipation was marred by their dismay at the women's tendency to leave Judaism. Theirs was declared to have been a "dangerous experiment" which "unleashed" "assimilatory forces" that

---

ward Jews and Judaism than were typical for the era. I by no means intend to suggest that such views were authentically positive toward Jews. For examples of praise for the salonières in this spirit see Karl August Varnhagen von Ense, *Denkwürdigkeiten und vermischte Schriften*, 5 vols. (Leipzig, 1873) vol. 2, chap. 2, or Edward Schmidt-Weissenfels, *Rahel und ihre Zeit* (Leipzig, 1857). Such sentiments were often mocked, both at the time and later; see for instance Kurt Fervers's judgment that Varnhagen was a "Jewish apprentice," in his *Berliner Salons: Die Geschichte einer grossen Verschwörung* (Munich, 1940), 18.

9. See Adolf Leschnitzer, *The Magic Background of Modern Anti-semitism: An Analysis of the German-Jewish Relationship* (New York, 1956), 14.

10. These quotes are from Raphael Mahler, *A History of Modern Jewry, 1780–1815* (London, 1971), xxi; H. G. Adler, *The Jews in Germany from the Enlightenment to National Socialism* (Notre Dame, 1969), 53, and H. Graetz, *History of the Jews* (Philadelphia, 1894) vol. 4, 425.

11. See S. M. Dubnow, *Die neueste Geschichte des jüdischen Volkes* (Berlin, 1920), vol. 1, 202; Mahler, *A History of Modern Jewry*, 150; Heinz Mosche Graupe, *Die Enstehung des modernen Judentums: Geistesgeschichte der deutschen Juden 1650–1942* (Hamburg, 1969), 155; Dubnow, *Die neueste Geschichte*, 197; Arthur Ruppin, *The Jews in the Modern World* (London, 1934; rpt. New York, 1973), 328; N. Samter, *Judentaufen im neunzehnten Jahrhundert* (Berlin, 1906), 4; Adler, *The Jews in Germany*, 24.

"raged with undiminished intensity" throughout the nineteenth and twentieth centuries.[12] Even a recent Jewish historian not altogether unfriendly to assimilation, Walter Laquer, has found the salonières to have been problematic models because of a "great deal of affectation in the exalted conversation and in the letters exchanged, an artificial ardour, a sensibility that did not always ring true." He concluded that although the salonières' "libertinism struck their contemporaries and the succeeding generation as very wicked . . . , today it all seems naive and tedious."[13]

The Jewish historians' disdain for the salonières was largely shared by German historians, although for them the ill effects of salon life were visited on the gentile community. Heinrich von Treitschke, for instance, had harsh words both for the growing role of the Jewish literary intelligentsia in general and for Rahel Levin in particular. For Treitschke, the problem was that Jewish intellectuals of the period "boldly insisted on the display of Jewish peculiarities, while simultaneously demanding respect as spokesmen of German public opinion. These Jews without a country, vaunting themselves as a nation within the nation, exercised upon the still inchoate national self-esteem of the Germans an influence no less disturbing and disintegrating than similar Jews had exercised of old upon the declining nations of the Roman Empire." As for Rahel Levin, she was a "dilettantist adept and demi-artist" full of "artificial ecstasy"; "everything about her breathed the restless weltschmerz of a noble but profoundly unsatisfied feminine nature."[14] Nazi historians took special pains to condemn the salonières in a tone that was exaggerated and paranoid: "scholars, artists and writers had to traffic with Jews if they wanted access to the intellectual life of the nation." Salon Jews had "nearly unlimited domination in the cultural arena," and, "Jewish cultural influence in Germany has its beginnings in these salons."[15]

Unfortunately, historians' eagerness to praise or blame the salonières has not been matched by the rigor needed to explain why these salons appeared and disappeared when and where they did. During the nineteenth century the salon was a popular topic for lavish—if superficial—

12. A sensitive discussion of Jewish historians' ambivalences can be found in Maximilian Stein's "Paul Heyse und die Berliner Salons," in his *Vorträge und Ansprachen* (Frankfurt a.M., 1932). Unambiguous condemnations of the Jewish salonières are seen in Heinrich Graetz, *Geschichte der Juden* (Leipzig, 1900), vol. 16, 160, and Solomon Liptzin, *Germany's Stepchildren* (New York, 1944), 26.

13. Walter Laqueur, *A History of Zionism* (New York, 1972), 10.

14. The first quote is from Heinrich von Treitschke, *History of Germany in the Nineteenth Century* (London, 1915–19; rpt. New York, 1968) vol. 4, 556; the second is from Gordon Craig, ed., Heinrich von Treitschke's *History of Germany in the Nineteenth Century* (Chicago and London, 1975), 279.

15. Krüger, *Berliner Romantik*, 51; Fervers, *Berliner Salons*, 8 and 9.

treatments, but the authors of such books tended to repeat the same anecdotes and rarely bothered to go digging for new primary sources. Some purported explanations—that salons flourished because of the "general social situation," or that they were a mere "chance constellation in an era of social transition"—are too vague to be helpful.[16] Chance does play a role in history, but it is inadequate as the sole explanation for the appearance and disappearance of an institution as intricate as salons.

All the plausible explanations for why the Berlin salons flourished in the last years of Prussia's "old regime," which ended in 1806, build their case on how salons met the needs of the city's nobility, Jewish community, or intelligentsia. Historians have thus focused on the Prussian nobles living in Berlin, who were thought to have sought luxury, elegance, cosmopolitan ways, and intellectual excitement in Jewish homes which they could not find elsewhere in the city. In one formulation, nobles and commoners are considered to have somehow "needed" to socialize together but to have been prevented from doing so by the nobility's taboo on either visiting or entertaining downward on the social hierarchy. Wealthy Jews, however, were so distant from even the bottom of the gentile social structure that it was exotic rather than déclassé for nobles to visit them. Accordingly, nobles found both intellectual titillation and connections with commoners on the "neutral" territory of wealthy Jewish homes.[17]

A second explanation pursued by other scholars suggests that more was involved in the Jewish salons than simply Jewish distance from the established ranking system. One Nazi historian, for instance, accounted for Jewish salon participation very simply: the wealth of the Jewish community "caused" its cultural achievements, which were "conspiratorily" used to attract visitors to their salons. Salon success was thus made possible by Jewish wealth and was in turn a step in the Jewish struggle to achieve "political domination."[18] A less conspiratorial explanation focused on Jewish "intellectual marginality," which resulted in Jews' adopting progressive ideas. Jewish marginality originated, in this view, in the exclusion of Jews from all gentile social classes; the gap between proclamations that Jews should be equal and their very real oppression also marginalized them. The Jewish fight for political equality thus "caused"

16. For the first claim see Herbert Scurla, *Rahel Varnhagen: Die grosse Frauengestalt der deutschen Romantik* (Düsseldorf, 1978), 84 [original title: *Begegnung mit Rahel* (East Berlin, 1962)]. The second claim was made by Arendt, *Rahel Varnhagen*, 46.

17. On the needs of the Berlin nobility see Krüger, *Berliner Romantik*, 51. A typical "neutral turf" explanation can be found in Heinz Moshe Graupe, *The Rise of Modern Judaism: An Intellectual History of German Jewry, 1650–1942* (Huntington, N.Y., 1978), 134.

18. Fervers, *Berliner Salons*, 18.

all their abilities to be "set free."[19] Since it was Jewish women who hosted the salons, historians naturally focused on the special qualities of Jewish women in Berlin in their attempts to explain the salons. This was generally taken care of easily. The Jewish women in Berlin were simply said to be "more cultured" and "better educated" than their gentile counterparts in other German cities, without a hint as to just why this should have been the case.[20]

In addition to the nobles' search for literate distraction and the power of Jewish wealth, a third way to explain the salons is by pointing to the needs of local intellectuals. In one version, the enlightened intellectuals in Berlin had a passion for "ideas in themselves," and visiting Jewish homes was a public way to demonstrate emancipated ideas.[21] Others turn to intellectuals' material needs. After the demise of court patronage, but preceding the full maturity of the publishing industry, European cities are thought to have experienced a "vacuum" of intellectual institutions. By participating in salons, publishers, patrons, and readers helped authors both to create and to distribute their work. The sorry state of Berlin's intellectual institutions in the late eighteenth century may well have made its intelligentsia particularly needy, for the city lacked a university, a parliament, generous noble patronage, or even an important publishing industry.[22] Salons thus appeared on the scene because they were functionally necessary to meet the institutional needs of Berlin's intelligentsia.

At first glance, these three explanatory sketches do seem to fit together in a tidy fashion. Intellectuals needed to meet readers, patrons, and publishers, while urban nobles sought cultivated conversation with the déclassé. This they found at wealthy Jewish homes whose women were simultaneously socially neutral and intellectually avant-garde. But worries about the adequacy of this three-part analysis eventually surfaced. The reasons that supposedly motivated intellectuals or nobles to attend

---

19. Drewitz, *Berliner Salons,* 19.

20. Hargrave, *Some German Women,* 5, and M. Kayserling, *Die jüdischen Frauen in der Geschichte, Literatur und Kunst* (Leipzig, 1879), 198.

21. This phrase is from Hargrave, *Some German Women,* 53. A participant in the salons, Sara Meyer, also stressed the role of ideas and particular intellectuals in causing the salons: "the spirit of the eighteenth century, the rule of Frederick the Great, the soil of Berlin, and the decisive activity of Moses Mendelssohn and Lessing were all necessary in order to cause such a heyday." Her analysis, translated by me, was cited by Varnhagen von Ense in his *Ausgewählte Schriften* (Leipzig, 1871–76), vol. 19, 75.

22. Karl Mannheim, "The Problem of the Intelligentsia: An Inquiry into Its Past and Present Role," in his *Essays in the Sociology of Culture* (Londong, 1956), 137; Mannheim's account of salons borrows liberally from Chauncey Tinker, *The Salon and English Letters* (New York, 1915). For an argument of this sort specific to Berlin see Scurla, *Rahel Varnhagen,* 53 and 86.

salons were, as usual in German history, too idealized. Would intellectuals or nobles really have deigned to visit Jews in Berlin when such behavior was so infrequent among their predecessors in Germany and their counterparts elsewhere in Europe, solely for animated conversation or to demonstrate their progressive sentiments? Granted, Berlin was an important center for the creation and dissemination of Enlightenment ideas,[23] but ironically the salons flourished just at the end of the Enlightenment era. Their heyday in the 1790s coincided instead with the beginning of early romanticism. And many romantic intellectuals, even some who attended salons, had tortured and problematic if not blatantly anti-semitic attitudes. If progressive ideology was no clear-cut cause of salon attendance, perhaps these men had motivations of a crasser nature? Since, in the eyes of some, visits to Jewish homes surely cost gentile visitors a loss of status, might gentile guests have found compensatory economic gain by visiting Jewish homes?

The longer I pondered why salons had appeared in Berlin, the more plagued I came to be with the three most common ways to account for this fascinating episode. The Jewish salonières in Berlin presided over a socially, religiously, and gender-mixed coterie distinctive in Germany both at the time and across time. All the stories about these salons suggested that these women had accomplished a triple feat by emancipating themselves from their traditional patriarchal families, helping to create high culture in a crucially creative era, and, in the process, forging bonds across classes, religious groups, and the two sexes. This triple feat was all the more remarkable because salons were incongruous in three larger historical stories. First, salons were an anomalous episode in German social history. The German social structure remained more rigid and caste-like than elsewhere in Europe up to the twentieth century. If cross-class mixing was ever to take place in Germany, why did it occur so early, when social groups were still rigidly contained within ascribed estate boundaries? Second, salons in Berlin were anomalous in the context of German-Jewish history. Jewish Germans did not receive all the rights of citizens until 1871. Throughout the nineteenth and well into the twentieth century, even the wealthiest Jews rarely socialized gracefully with equally rich gentiles.[24] The Berlin salons were the fulfillment of the assimilationist dream in miniature. Yet how to account for the timing of-

23. For a survey of recent historiography on the Enlightenment in northern Germany see Joachim Whaley, "The Protestant Enlightenment in Germany," in *The Enlightenment in National Context*, Roy Porter and Mwkulas Teich, eds. (Cambridge, England, 1981), 106–17.

24. See for example Fritz Stern's description of Gerson Bleichröder's troubles of this sort in his *Gold and Iron: Bismarck, Bleichröder, and the Building of the German Empire* (New York, 1979).

their appearance on the historical stage? Why did they emerge during the very first chapter in the slow movement for Jewish emancipation? Third, the Berlin salons also seemed incongruous in the history of Jewish women. Throughout the early modern and modern period, Jewish women, not just in eastern Europe, tended to be loyal to faith and family rather than the "deserters of their faith" that the Berlin salonières were reputed to have been.[25]

My confusion about the place of the Berlin salons in these three larger historical contexts was not the only problem, for there remained several mysteries about the history of the salon as an institution. The word *salon* came into use to describe a public room that began to appear in wealthy European homes between the sixteenth and the eighteenth centuries as the "great hall," which had been the center of medieval family life, gradually lost its private character and the four-poster beds were moved into separate rooms. The great hall, now called the salon, was a lavishly decorated public space where the piano was played, feasts served, and guests received.[26] A second meaning of *salon* was a special kind of social event that regularly occurred in some of these reception rooms. In this second sense, salons were a social gathering organized by the lady of the house, who orchestrated the intellectual discourses that characterized salon socializing.[27]

Salon gatherings are best understood as a specific kind of "society" affair. In past centuries, the term *society* referred, unlike contemporary usage, not to a "body of individuals living as members of a community" but to a special group within a community, namely the "fashionable and the wealthy."[28] What transpired when members of society socialized to-

---

25. See for example chap. 2 of Carlotte Baum, Paula Hyman, and Sonya Michel, *The Jewish Woman in America* (New York, 1975). This generalization also seems to hold for Jewish women in Germany during both an earlier and a later period. See *The Memoirs of Glückel of Hameln*, Martin Lowenthal, trans. (New York, 1977), and Marion A. Kaplan, *The Jewish Feminist Movement in Germany* (Westport, Conn., 1979), chap. 1.

26. Fernand Braudel, *The Structures of Everyday Life*, vol. 1: *The Limits of the Possible* (New York, 1981), 308.

27. In constructing this altogether modest definition of the salon I profited from other definitions which have been suggested. See English Showalter, Jr., "Madame de Graffigny and Her Salon," *Studies in Eighteenth-Century German Culture* 6 (1977), 377–92, at 378, and Barabara Corrado Pope, "Revolution and Retreat: Upper-Class French Women after 1789," in *Women, War, and Revolution*, C. R. Berkin and C. M. Lovett, eds. (New York, 1980), 215–36, at 216. Carolyn Lougee's unpublished comment at a panel on salons at the 1978 Berkshires Conference on the History of Women held at Mount Holyoke College was also useful.

28. Both the definitions are listed for *society* in the *Random House Dictionary* (New York, 1978), 846. For a useful discussion of the changing meaning of this and other key eighteenth-century terms see Raymond Williams, *Marxism and Literature* (New York, 1977).

gether was so all-important that those who belonged to society in France referred to themselves as *"le Monde"*—literally "the world."[29] Because society gatherings usually included members of families belonging to different estates and employed in different occupations—the top landowners, officials, and financiers (and their wives and daughters)—these events were as crucial in the making of social history as they were in the lives of their lucky participants. Status, wealth, bureaucratic patronage, and even daughters were exchanged at these gatherings in an era when male mobility was blocked by caste systems of privilege. When society gatherings were also open to intellectuals and organized by a woman with intellectual skills and ambitions, they were called salons.

The combination of social structural ingredients that encouraged the formation of salons seems to have peaked in particular periods in the Western past. Peace, prosperity, urban life, luxury spending, and the interest of the powerful in high culture all seem to have been associated with salons. Gatherings with the characteristics of salons have been located as early as classical Greece and the twelfth-century French courts,[30] but beginning with the Renaissance in the fifteenth century, they seem to have become less episodic, especially at Italian and French courts. During the seventeenth and eighteenth centuries Paris became the salons' premier city, where they thrived more continuously throughout the decades than in any other European city. The social functions performed by one cluster of Parisian salons, the *précieuse* or "precious" salons of the late seventeenth century, have been meticulously reconstructed by Carolyn Lougee, who asked why these women were attacked by Molière and other male intellectuals as precious, pretentious, and ignorant all at the same time. Her investigation of the social mobility achieved by salon women through upwardly mobile marriages showed that the hostility of male intellectuals was triggered more by social than by gender conflict. The "precious" salons' function was to legitimize and polish the daughters of wealthy robe noblemen who had married up into sword noble families possessing higher status.[31]

29. Pope, "Revolution and Retreat," 216.

30. See Sarah Pomeroy, *Goddesses, Whores, Wives, and Slaves: Women in Classical Antiquity* (New York, 1976). For discussions of various medieval and Renaissance salons see Mannheim, "The Problem of the Intelligentsia"; Valerian Tornius, *Salons: Pictures of Society through Five Centuries* (New York, 1929); L. Charles Keating, *Studies on the Literary Salon in France, 1550–1615* (Cambridge, Mass., 1971). For a primary-source glimpse at events in Renaissance Italy that might be called salons see Baldesar Castiglione, *The Book of the Courtier*, Charles S. Singleton, trans. (Garden City, 1959).

31. Carolyn Lougee, *Le Paradis des Femmes: Women, Salons, and Social Stratification in Seventeenth-Century France* (Princeton, 1976). Another, quite different sort of study of the same salons is Anne Backer's *Precious Women: A Feminist Phenomenon in the Age of Louis*

In the ensuing half century, the social and cultural power of the Parisian salons was challenged by Louis XIV's policy of centralizing noble sociability at the court of Versailles, but by the third quarter of the eighteenth century, French patronage and intellectual life were less centered at the court and again concentrated in Paris. Indeed, the Enlightenment era was the heyday of the Parisian salons, which had become diverse and specialized. Some met in convents, and at least two were hosted by men. Mondays at one home were reserved for literary stars and Wednesdays for the politically influential. Wealthy women were eager to try their hand at opening salons—so eager that failure was said to distress them more than the loss of a lover.[32] But the balance between the social and intellectual functions of salons continued to worry some male intellectuals like Jean-Jacques Rousseau, who took up Molière's derision of the seventeenth-century "precious" salon women, attacking their eighteenth-century successors for their pretension and lack of intellectual seriousness. Despite his superior attitude, Rousseau's own behavior—he did, after all, read drafts of his works in salons—was a fitting tribute to the indispensable role Parisian salons played in the patronage and publicity of avant-garde intellectual creation in the Enlightenment years.[33]

Outside of Paris, the two most important clusters of salons in the late eighteenth century were those that now appeared in London and in several central European cities. The London gatherings were called "bluestocking" salons because of their intellectual seriousness: blue stockings were daytime apparel, and a hostess's reminder to wear them meant rigorous discussion of intellectual matters was on the agenda. Bluestocking women in London were better educated and more inclined to publish their writing than were the Parisian salonières, and their salons, moreover, often excluded men.[34] In the late eighteenth century salons also

XIV (New York, 1979). For an earlier monograph which traces French salons through two centuries see Roger Picard, *Les Salons Littéraires et la Société Française, 1610–1789* (Paris, 1943, and New York, 1946).

32. On the atmosphere at the Versailles court during the early eighteenth century see W. H. Lewis, *The Splendid Century: Life in the France of Louis XIV* (Garden City, 1954), or Norbert Elias, *Die höfische Gesellschaft* (Neuwied, 1975). For details about the Enlightenment salons in Paris see E. L. A. and J. A. Goncourt, *The Woman of the Eighteenth Century* (London, 1925); Helen Clergue, *The Salon: A Study of French Society and Personalities in the Eighteenth Century* (New York, 1907); on d'Holbach's males-only salon see Alan Charles Kors, *D'Holbach's Coterie: An Enlightenment in Paris* (Princeton, 1976).

33. On Rousseau's views on women see Abby Kleinbaum, "Women in the Age of Light," in *Becoming Visible: Women in European History*, Renate Bridenthal and Claudia Koonz, eds. (Boston, 1977), 217–35.

34. See Evelyn Bodek, "*Salonières* and Bluestockings: Educated Obsolescence or Germinating Feminism?" *Feminist Studies* 3 (1976), 185–99.

appeared for the first time east of Paris, in the major towns of German-speaking central Europe; the Berlin salons were part of this wider trend. Vienna had three salons before and even more salons during the Vienna Congress (1814–15). Gatherings labeled salons have also been located in Potsdam, Jena, Heidelberg, Darmstadt, Leipzig, and Weimar during the last two decades of the eighteenth century. More than their French and English counterparts, central European salons in this era tended to meet at princely courts, suggesting that they were still at a stage through which French and English salons had already passed.[35]

Even this brief survey shows that the salon was an institution which flourished in different settings and performed a variety of social and intellectual functions.[36] The spectrum of gatherings called salons either by contemporaries or retrospectively by historians was a wide one. Salons almost always met in homes, although the home was at times the court where the ruling family lived, in which case the salon's location was also the public seat of political power. Salons were usually organized by wealthy married women, but sometimes a man was the host. Johann Wolfgang von Goethe in Weimar and Baron D'Holbach in Paris, for example, hosted informal intellectual gatherings that resembled the events called salons elsewhere. There were also unmarried salonières and salonières too poor to serve anything but tea and cookies. Not only did the locations and hosts for salons vary considerably; salons are also difficult to define with precision because they were simultaneously social *and* intellectual events. Whereas some salons provided a workaday at-

---

35. Two general histories of the salon which presume that the only central European salons of the era were in Berlin are Louis Batibfol, *The Great Literary Salons* (London, 1930) and Evelyn Beatrice Hall, *The Women of the Salons* (rpt., New York, 1969). But research shows that other central European cities also had salons. Discussions of salons in Vienna can be found in Hilde Spiel, *Fanny von Arnstein, oder Die Emanzipation: Ein Frauenleben an der Zeitwende, 1758–1818* (Frankfurt a.M., 1962). Spiel also has two essays on central European salons in Peter Quennell, ed., *Affairs of the Mind: The Salon in Europe and America from the Eighteenth to the Twentieth Century* (Washington, D.C., 1980): "Rahel Varnhagen," 13–22, and "Fanny von Arnstein," 47–56. Frederick II's "Round Table of Philosophy" at his palace in Potsdam is classified as a salon in Tornius, *Salons*, 206ff. Caroline Schlegel's Jena gatherings were classified as a salon in the compact but detailed article "Der Salon," in *Lexikon der Frau* (Zurich, 1954), vol. 2, 1129–30. Darmstadt as city of salons is discussed in Tornius, *Salons*, 224. Tornius discusses two Weimar salons on pp. 252 and 259; a salon in Bern was noted in *Lexikon der Frau*, vol. 2, 1130. Silvia Bovenschen, *Die imaginierte Weiblichkeit: Exemplarische Untersuchungen zu kulturgeschichtlichen und literarischen Präsentationsformen des Weiblichen* (Frankfurt a.M., 1979), suggests that Christiana Mariane von Ziegler hosted Germany's first salon in Leipzig, on p. 138.

36. See Isser Woloch, *Eighteenth-Century Europe: Tradition and Progress, 1715–1789*, (New York, 1982), 183–94, and Jürgen Habermas, *Die Strukturwandel der Öffentlichkeit* (Neuwied and Berlin, 1974).

mosphere in which rough drafts were read aloud for criticism and new plays and books evaluated, others were known mainly for sparkling conversation, elegant dinners, and musical performances.

Salons elude definition in other ways as well. Take the issue of whether salons were a public or a private institution. Most salons took place in private homes. Yet what went on there was known to a wider public. In this sense salons were more characteristic of the medieval than of the modern age, insofar as the public, and therefore publicity, came into some homes at specific times during the day or the year. That the home could be a public as well as a private place was obviously one reason why salons were organized by women. The synthesis of the private and the public in salons was also evident in the curious, bygone way that guests arrived at the door. Salon history can make modern intellectuals nostalgic, because salons were exclusive occasions for which invitations were not issued. Salon participants were often famous and salon connections very useful. Many more would have liked to come than did, but they stayed away because they lacked an entrée. To us now this is quite confusing: how could a social event be at once voluntary and unrestricted, yet remain small and elite?

The more I pondered the wide variety of events labeled by others as salons and the mysterious, antiquated self-selection process of recruitment of salon guests, the more troubled I became about how it was that salons had come to exist at all. That social institutions like salons should ever have appeared in preindustrial Europe, even intermittently, came to seem quite odd. It was odd that private drawing rooms should have been public places, odd that in an age when women were excluded from educational and civic institutions, even wives of rich and powerful men should lead intellectual discussions among the most learned men of their cities. It was odd that men and women should have had important intellectual exchanges during centuries when the two sexes generally had little to say to each other and few public places in which to say it. The mixture of male guests was also odd. Some male guests were powerful officials, financiers, or landowners; others possessed only their wit, their reputations as writers, and the will to move up in the world. That the rich and powerful should have deigned to socialize in intimate face-to-face gatherings with impoverished writers demands an explanation. The "institutional vacuum" interpretation, upon reflection, was not sufficient to quiet this set of worries. The vacuum that followed the decline of princely patronage and preceded the rise of the publishing industry surely could have been met without the aid of women organizing learned discourses in their drawing rooms. That women were not functionally required to fill the institutional vacuum is the conclusion which must be drawn from-

contrasting English and French intellectual institutions during the eighteenth century. London was awash in coffee houses, dinner clubs, and reading societies, all open mainly to men; Paris, in contrast, was dense in salons.[37] An enormous variety of transitional intellectual institutions bridged the gap between patronage and publishers, but only one, the salon, did so under female leadership.

These perplexities about the history of the salon as an institution were all the more disquieting, given that the unsettling chronological position of the Berlin salons seemed to constitute a sharp challenge to established assumptions about continuity and progress in German history. It has long been thought that neither Jews nor women were free or powerful in the German past. So the notion that even a miniature bastion of female and Jewish cultural power could have existed so early in Germany came to be as conceptually troubling as it was pleasing.

This book is the record of my attempt to understand salons in general and the Berlin salons in particular. Not seen as an important mystery hitherto, this transient social formation became an important mystery for me. Yet how to ferret out the information which would answer my questions was not clear at the outset of the project. Like other social history puzzles, salons were more akin to a process than to the standard, well-recorded events which have long been the staple of traditional history. Transposing the distinction between process and event into the context of intellectual history, salons were "cultural practices," whereas the publication of books or student registrations at universities were intellectual events.[38] Yet cultural practices are much more elusive than the processes generally reconstructed by social historians. For episodes in demographic or economic history, there is often some previously untapped sources in an archive waiting to be counted and tallied up. But primary sources useful in charting salon society are much harder to define and to discover. For much about the salon as an institution and about specific salons lies deep below the surface of our inherited records of the past. No local police, universities, or publishers made it their business to document salon life. And for all of the marvelous chattiness of eighteenth-century correspondences, letters between salon participants often assumed rather than discussed the details of how salons functioned on a day-to-day level.

The research design of the book has been constructed to compensate

37. See Woloch, *Eighteenth-Century Europe*, 183–94.
38. For an insightful discussion of cultural practices see Williams, *Marxism and Literature*, 47.

for this fundamental absence of first-person narrative descriptions of salon life. But the book's structure also has another, more fundamental
justification in my intention to write a social history of the Berlin salons.
For nothing less than a systematic social history is required in order to
go beyond the typical portrayal of a few famous salonière personalities
and their even more famous male guests, to go beyond the generalizations that persons of "all classes" mixed in salons. The central, overriding
question of the book is: who came to the Berlin salons, and why? To
reconstruct who came to salons and how the city's social structure affected their presence in salons involves the typical historian's project of
trying to know more, or differently, about some aspect of the participants' lives than they themselves could know at the time. My aim was
thus to turn the absence of direct primary evidence describing salon life
into a virtue, forcing the project to take on a deliberately external perspective. And by answering this question for the Berlin case, my puzzles
about the larger mysteries about the salon as an institution would surely
be solved as well.

The centerpiece of the source material used to answer the question of
who came to salons and why is a collective biography of 417 female and
male intellectuals who lived in Berlin in 1780 and 1806 who had the skills
so useful in salon society. The names, birthdates, father's occupation,
intellectual's own occupation, and leisure activities of the 417 have been
reconstructed from biographies, memoirs, letters, and biographical dictionaries. One hundred persons, just under a quarter of the 417 intellectuals, attended at least one salon in these twenty-six years. The point of
the book is to show how the social origins, occupations, friendships, love
affairs, and intellectual work of the hundred guests propelled them and
did not the other 317 intellectuals into salons.

But to say that the one hundred guests were an idiosyncratic mix
makes no sense without reconstructing the larger social structures which
determined their lives. Dramatic changes in Berlin's social structure came
to pass in the last half of the eighteenth century which created new alliances between groups with altered amounts of money, power, and status.
A specific pattern of downward and upward mobility made salons possible by creating a new sort of person whose needs could be met in salons. Social classes based on common economic and professional
achievements had hardly begun to form by the close of the century. Rising land prices, high fertility, urbanization, and inadequate education
polarized the Prussian nobility; as a result, some nobles came to be rich
in status but poor in cash. Meanwhile, the monarchy adhered to a rigid
mercantilism, was unwilling to sell bureaucratic offices, and tried to promote industry without making any gentile commoners rich. These poli-

cies all hindered the formation of a gentile bourgeoisie able to compete for social dominance even with a wounded nobility. The large elite of the tiny Jewish community, instead, increasingly came to play the role of a surrogate bourgeoisie during the eighteenth century.

As many noble fortunes sank and some commoner fortunes rose, noble and commoner men came to share intellectual interests and intellectual work. And although Berlin had no university and was not Germany's leading publishing center, the city nevertheless managed to attract both accomplished and aspiring intellectuals. In Berlin they found employment as tutors, as professors at gymnasia and knightly academies, as private lecturers, and especially, as state officials. Through this education and this employment, a significant number of commoner intellectuals born into poverty achieved significant upward mobility.

But there was more to life in Berlin than managing one's landed estate, founding banking houses, and looking for publishers. There was the theater, promenades in the Thiergarten park, sitting in cafes with friends, listening to lectures and having dinner with visiting scholars. Public leisure opportunities, including salons, provided Berliners with a chance to enjoy themselves while making friends with those born into different estates and employed in different institutions. Affiliation with salon society both presumed and in turn affected their participants' social mobility. Friendships across estates and income groups aided the men's careers, their intellectual work, and their very participation in salons. Noble visitors to salons lent decisive prestige to the Jewish women whose homes they visited. We need to discover why so many noble men became serious intellectuals in the first place, and then how their intellectual interests ledthem into salon society. If nobles saw themselves as "slumming" in salons, for others born far down the social scale, participation in salon society was a glittering prize. The friendships of the Jewish women were also crucial in the making of salon society. Their intimates included noble women, actresses, and other Jewish women who had also embarked on the arduous project of distancing themselves from community and custom. For contrary to established opinion, the Jewish salon women did not assimilate as token individuals. Rather, they traveled the journey away from Jewishness as a small group knitted together by their family ties, by their common predicament of a chosen but painful marginality, and by their common passion for the literary life. Yet neither for the Jewish nor for the gentile salon women was the passion for literature very frequently expressed in published form.

But if literature was not a way for very many salon women to improve their social position, marriage definitely was. Most salon participants were in their twenties or thirties, and many had incomes either higher or lower than the norm for their ascribed status. Nobles were too poor, Jews too rich. Central to the ethos of salon culture, moreover, was imitation of the French nobility's relaxed sensuality. Salons thus became an arena for exotic romantic entanglements which often resulted in misalliances, almost always involving divorced and converted Jewish women. To learn how their Jewish husbands came to lose their wives, we unearth the role that economic need on the gentile side, and wealth on the Jewish side, played in motivating the misalliances.

The task of the central chapters is to show the variety of ties which held salon society together. In the final chapter I turn to the group's disintegration, which really began in the heyday of salon culture. Ironically, many prestigious gentile salon guests had ambiguous attitudes toward their Jewish hosts even while they flattered them with their visits. The antisemitic pamphlets which began to appear in Berlin in 1803 show that it was the success of the Jewish salonières which contributed to increasing antisemitism among the city's intelligentsia. The patriotic reaction to the French occupation only exacerbated the antisemitism that salons themselves had provoked. The double bind was that the successes of the Jewish salonières provoked a new, anti-assimilationist antisemitism which eventually undermined the salons.

The social and institutional needs met in the Berlin salons of this epoch did not appear in exactly the same constellation either in other German cities in the eighteenth century or in later decades in Berlin. In this sense, previous historians' ardent conviction that the salons of eighteenth-century Berlin were both geographically and chronologically unique was really on the mark. By reconstructing precisely why it was that the salons appeared then and there, I aim to dissociate the unique from the random, and tell the story of how a special moment in German history could be utterly logical, even if all too fleeting.

TWO | *Social Structure*

Prussian Contradictions

Visitors to Berlin two hundred years ago tended to wax enthusiastic about the scenery in their published impressions. They delighted in the new stone palaces and the new opera house on Unter den Linden, in the smartly attired promenaders on the grand broad thoroughfare and in the Thiergarten park—all of which they took to be evidence of a prosperous city.[1] Many observers who lived year-round in Berlin joined the chorus of praise. More concerned with social relations than with architecture, some local writers sketched a rosy picture of societal harmony where the nobility was "loved and respected" by their social inferiors; after all, nobles indulged in the same vices and entertainments as did the burghers. The wealthy in Berlin were thought to be less concerned with clothing displays than elsewhere in Germany, and any admission that there was a class of "rich idlers" was qualified by emphasizing that the "idler class" was "insignificant in size."[2] Local commentators extolled the social egalitarianism they experienced in Berlin: social life there was literally "open to all," whatever their social position, and social gatherings were "more mixed" and less "title-oriented" than in Germany's merchant cities.[3] Even when it was admitted that some clubs in Berlin were visited

1. (Wolf Davidson), *Briefe über Berlin* (Berlin, 1798), 1, as cited in Franz Eyssenhardt, *Berlin im Jahre 1786* (Leipzig, 1886), 51, and Anon., *Schattenriss von Berlin* (Amsterdam, 1788), 4.

2. J. D. F. Rumpf, *Neuester Wegweiser durch die königlichen preussischen Staaten* (Berlin, 1793), 142, as cited in Eyssenhardt, *Berlin*, 82 and 88.

3. (Johannes Pezzl), *Faustin oder das philosophische Jahrhundert* (1785), 577, as cited in Eyssenhardt, *Berlin*, 57.

only by exclusive cliques, at least it could be said that "everyone" visited one club or another."[4]

Not all observers were so satisfied that the city's aesthetic or social life was entirely what it seemed on the surface. A more cynical view was that much that "seemed to glitter" was actually "poverty covered with a sparkling varnish."[5] George Forster declared glumly after his visit in 1779 that "the exterior [of this great city] is much more beautiful, the life within much more dark than I had pictured it. Berlin is certainly one of the handsomest cities in Europe. But the inhabitants!"[6] Fine-looking homes were, on closer inspection, often dreadfully overcrowded. The broad thoroughfares lined with grand stone palaces were poorly lit at night and hopelessly muddy in the spring. Anyone who ventured out to the new suburbs that had sprung up outside the walls of the city met with some nasty sights, chief among them the army barracks. One observer lamented that among the numerous soldiers and their families garrisoned were too many "rude youths," that Berlin had more of these "distressing characters" than "anywhere else in the world."[7]

Critics were as troubled by the similarities of behavior across the social hierarchy as satisfied commentators were delighted by them. As early as 1760, the queen's chamberlain, Count von Lehndorff, regretted that the nobility no longer had a monopoly on conspicuous consumption.[8] The promenading lanes in the Thiergarten park, which gave Jewish women a chance to mix with gentile men, were also a source of displeasure. "Truly prominent" persons complained about the difficulty they had avoiding the pretentious Jewish women and the "dandies who buzzed about them" at select promenades.[9] Jewish women were by no means the only Berliners whose behavior was attacked for blurring traditional social gradations. Women who imitated their superiors were accused of forcing their families to spend too much on luxury items; some speculated that the result of this extravagance was the ruin of many marriages. Husbands earning eight hundred taler a year protested that they could not afford the hoop skirts, silk clothing, and parlors proposed by their wives.

4. Eyssenhardt, *Berlin*, 58.

5. *Schattenriss*, 142.

6. George Forster, *Sämmtliche Schriften*, vol. 7, (Leipzig, 1843), 112, as cited in Karl Bruhns, *Life of Alexander von Humboldt* (London, 1873), vol. 1, 36.

7. *Schattenriss*, 106.

8. Lehndorff's *Tagebücher*, 432, as cited in Frederick Marquardt's "The Manual Workers in the Social Order in Berlin under the Old Regime," Ph.D. diss., University of California, Berkeley, 1973, 390.

9. *Schattenriss*, 108.

"Mere" wig-makers and tailors also dared to wear the embroidered and braided clothing once worn only by those they served.[10]

The excited commentary that began to appear in print in the last two decades of the eighteenth century praising or decrying the blurring of social gradations in Berlin reflected the dramatic consequences of a deeply contradictory state policy. The central aim of Prussian rulers in the seventeenth and eighteenth centuries had been to transform Prussia into a European-class power—a large and complex task, given the meager geographical and social resources at the state's disposal. Before it was completed by King Frederick the Great (1740–86), significant territories had been won in war and an enormous army and an efficient civil service had painstakingly been constructed. The kings' religious tolerance made possible a flexible immigration policy that also stimulated Prussia's rise. To promote industry, Huguenot artisans persecuted in France were welcomed into Prussia in 1685. To promote trade and capital formation, wealthy Jews expelled from Vienna in 1671 were also invited to settle in Prussia. Yet these same activist monarchs, innovators at constructing the institutions necessary to put Prussia on the map, were passionately committed to maintaining an ancient social structure, the lynchpin of which was the nobility's absolute monopoly on land ownership. The tension between activist innovation and social rigidity was central to Prussian policy in these two centuries. Ironically, it was precisely this contradiction between innovation and conservatism, not innovation alone, which created the geographical and social mobility that eventually made salons possible in the last two decades of the eighteenth century. The diversity of the guests at salons reflected the extraordinary heterogeneity of Berlin's elite, and this heterogeneity was largely a result of the state's contradictory policies.

For if Berlin had not been the court city for such an activist monarchy, fewer foreign and domestic officials would have found a home there. If the monarchy had not made service in the army and the civil service attractive to the nobility, the previously provincial and rural Prussian Junkers would not have moved to Berlin in the first place. If the elector had not invited Huguenots into Prussia, the French language, French fashions, French ideas, and French educational styles would not have been diffused in the capital city. If the Viennese Jewish families had not been invited to settle in Prussia, their descendents, the sophisticated Jewish salonières, would not have been in Berlin to host the salons. If the monarchy and the nobility had not begun to care about the life of the

10. Marquardt, "The Manual Workers," 409.

mind, up-and-coming young writers would not have flocked to the city for employment as tutors, clerks, itinerant lecturers, freelance writers, booksellers, and publishers.

During the same years when nobles, Huguenots, Jews, and intellectuals moved to Berlin, thereby allowing salon society to coalesce, Prussia and Berlin were both experiencing booming population growth. At the-beginning of the eighteenth century, the tiny capital of the poor and obscure Electorate of Brandenburg-Prussia was not a town anyone deemed worthy of much published commentary. In 1700, Prussia was still recovering from the devastation of the Thirty Years' War; its capital, Berlin, had a mere 24,000 inhabitants. But with political power came territory and numbers. The Electorate of Brandenburg-Prussia was upgraded to the status of Kingdom of Prussia. The new state vastly expanded its lands through war and annexation. With his victory over Austria's Empress Maria Theresa in 1740, Frederick the Great gained Silesia; triumph in the Seven Year's War brought Prussia Saxony. And Prussia's share in the three partitions of Poland vastly expanded her eastern territories. As a result of immigration, war, and annexation, the size of the Prussian population more than doubled in a half century, growing from two-and-one-half million in 1740 to five-and-one-half million by 1786.[11] Berlin's population growth in the same century was even more dramatic, multiplying six-fold between 1700 and 1800.[12] In an epoch when a host of second-string European cities were also growing rapidly and breaking the 100,000 mark, Berlin grew more rapidly than any other city in central Europe. By the end of the century it had 172,000 residents, making it the largest city in the Germanic territories. Within central Europe as a whole, Berlin was second in size only to Vienna.[13]

Why did Berlin grow so fast? Until the last years of the century, high urban birth rates were not an important factor, for like all European cities in preindustrial times Berlin's mortality rate was higher than its birth rate. Emigration from the more populous countryside replaced the urban residents killed off by the city's dirt, disease, and overcrowding more quickly than urban deaths could be replaced by urban births. For once, the kings were not to blame. Indeed, throughout the seventeenth and eighteenth centuries, Prussian rulers had been trying to lower the city's death rate by making Berlin a cleaner place to live. City officials struggled

11. Henri Brunschwig, *Enlightenment and Romanticism in Eighteenth-Century Prussia* (rpt. Chicago, 1974), 102, gives the figures 2,240,000 for 1740 and 5,430,000 for 1786. The exact percentage growth for this period was 59 percent.

12. H. Kiesel and P. Münch, *Gesellschaft und Literatur im 18. Jahrhundert: Voraussetzungen und Entstehung des literarischen Markts in Deutschland* (Munich, 1977), 15.

13. See Woloch, *Eighteenth-Century Europe*, 91–92.

to enforce legislation that forbade lodging pigpens in front of homes, casting rubbish into the market square, and emptying "night pans" into the street.[14] By the 1770s, state efforts to reform the dirty habits of Berliners must have begun to pay off, for the city's birth rate finally overtook its death rate. By the time of Frederick the Great's death in 1786, the surging population resulting from both the improved health of city life and rural immigration caused a severe housing shortage. Additions were made to many existing two- and three-story buildings, and some were replaced by new four-story buildings.[15]

Berlin also grew because it was a court city. Like other Germanprinces, the Hohenzollern dynasty in Prussia succeeded in breaking the power of the local guild and merchant towns. But court cities flourished just as trade cities declined. The court cities of Vienna, Berlin, Dresden, Munich, and Mannheim all grew by at least 100 percent during the century; their mean rate of increase was 340 percent. Independent trade cities grew much less robustly or actually shrank. Thus Nuremberg's population fell by 33 percent, and Hamburg, Frankfurt am Main, and Leipzig grew only by an average rate of 52 percent.[16] Court cities grew quickly because the administrative needs of the state and the imposing displays of the courts drew officials and would-be courtiers into the capitals. Clerks, secretaries, tutors, domestic servants, shopkeepers, and artisans moved to court cities to serve the officials and the courtiers. The greater the size of the state and the more activist its policies, the larger its bureaucracy tended to be, and thus the larger its court city was. But why did Berlin grow so much faster than the other court cities in central Europe? One reason was that Berlin was the central garrison town for the unusually large Prussian army, another that as Berlin came to be a manufacturing and an educational center, it also became a magnet for laborers and for intellectuals.

The institutional consequences of state policies thus made Berlin a fast-growing and an unusually heterogeneous capital city in the German context. The other major German cities in the early modern centuries usually had only one major economic function and thus one major elite. The Hanseatic towns—Lübeck, Hamburg, Bremen—specialized in

14. Reinhold August Dorwart, *The Prussian Welfare State before 1740* (Cambridge, Mass., 1971), 87–88.

15. Gordon Craig, *The Germans* (New York, 1982), 269.

16. These calculations use the population figures provided by Kiesel and Munch, *Gesellschaft*, 15. For a discussion of the court cities' growth see Helmut Böhme, *Prolegomena zu einer Sozial- und Wirtschaftsgeschichte Deutschlands im 19. und 20. Jahrhundert* (Frankfurt a. M., 1968). For a comparative analysis see Etiene François, *Koblenz im 18. Jahrhundert* (Göttingen, 1982).

long-distance trade. The imperial cities—Frankfurt am Main, Nurem-berg, Augsburg—specialized in the production and sale of artisan prod-ucts. Other towns, like Göttingen and Leipzig, were distinctive because they possessed major universities or publishing houses. The elite of court cities other than Berlin—Munich, Dresden, Mannheim—was composed mainly of state officials. That Berlin had officials and financiers as well as a sizable intelligentsia made it special.

But before 1780, Berlin's heterogeneity was abstract and frozen. Each estate or religious minority or occupational group tended to work, so-cialize, and marry within its own circle of families. Sometimes this intra-group marriage, called endogamy, was explicitly a law of the state. Noblemen, for instance, needed the crown's permission to marry a com-moner. Unconverted Jews and Christians could not intermarry, because civil marriage did not yet exist. In other cases, like that of the officials, a common educational process and a common income level led to caste-like behavior. The endogamous pattern indicates that the monarchy was successful in preserving the old social structure. A tiny imported Jewish bourgeoisie dominated the mercantile sector and effected improvements in banking, trade, and manufacturing without making any gentile com-moners rich. In this fashion the monarchy attempted to promote Prus-sia's economic development without allowing any competition within the gentile social structure that would threaten the domination of the nobility. As long as land ownership remained the most profitable enter-prise in the economy and as long as it was open only to nobles, the nobility's unique status would have a secure financial basis. If the only comparable wealthy group in the society—the Jews—was socially de-spised, legally and politically disenfranchised, and constrained within tight caste restrictions, then economic development would not conflict with social stability.

But the monarchs' twin goals of development and stability became less and less compatible toward the close of the eighteenth century. Salons would never have come to pass if individuals born into diverse estates did not experience needs very different from those of their parents. A new mobility began to dissolve the old estate barriers in the last decades of the eighteenth century as the tightest caste in the city began to expe-rience grave problems that threatened its survival as an estate.

The Nobility

Across the centuries, the Prussian nobility (also called the Junkers) ex-hibited a remarkable instinct for survival and enjoyed the full backing of the monarchy until its demise in 1918. This monarchy, moreover, was more powerful at home than most dynasties to the west, and almost as influential abroad as the leading European states. The Junkers' hardiness derived in great part from their extraordinarily graceful transition from a particular kind of feudalism to a particular kind of capitalism. From the sixteenth century onward, the Junkers slowly acquired the means to organize and greatly profit from the production and sale of grain on the world market. Even after crucial aspects of serfdom were abolished in 1807, the elite of the Prussian nobility retained exclusive use of a landless rural labor force, dominance in the prosperous agricultural sector, and strong influence over the monarchy, which granted them privileged access to prestigious posts in the army and the civil service.

To be sure, most Junkers lacked the spectacular wealth of some English absentee noble landlords, and as everyone was well aware—some painfully so—they had little of the cultural polish of their courtly French counterparts.[17] But neither great wealth nor cultural polish were crucial in the long run. On the contrary, the very modesty of their situation also made it sturdy. First of all, unlike many of their English and French counterparts, most Junkers continued to manage their own estates and did not become absentee landlords. The land continued to be farmed and owned primarily by nobles. Their economic domination of the peasantry was reinforced by their legal and military authority over the peasants. Nor were their most important privileges challenged by the peasantry or the monarchy throughout the nineteenth century. As long as their grain remained cheaper at home and abroad than grain grown elsewhere, agriculture in eastern Prussia remained a crucial growth sector within central Europe. Paradoxically, of course, the very success of grain production in Prussia retarded industrialization. But this was not always clear at the time. For much of the nineteenth century, Prussian monarchs as well as Prussian bureaucrats were justified in thinking that what was good for the nobility was also good for Prussian economic development. Yet none of the long-range economic success of the Junkers could have been foreseen during the eighteenth century. The social and political durability of noble power in Prussia was by no means an inevitable development. The crucial turning point in the Junker transition from feudalism to capitalism took place between 1775 and 1825, when the nobility's hold on power was in jeopardy. In order to understand why some young noble men visited, courted, and even sometimes married the daughters

---

17. Fritz Stern, "Prussia," in *European Landed Elites in the Nineteenth Century,* ed. David Spring (Baltimore and London, 1977). On the comparison to the English landlords see Hanna Schissler, "The Junkers: Notes on the Social and Historical Significance of the Agrarian Elite in Prussia," in Robert Moeller, ed., *Peasants and Lords in Modern Germany* (Boston, 1986) (this article is a revised version of the article cited in note 24 below).

and ex-wives of Jewish financiers in these years, we must inspect the crisis of the nobility at the turn of the century.

The noble dilemma was in part a consequence of changing demography. Rapid population growth pushed on the food supply during the second half of the eighteenth century, demand outstripped supply, and in Germany grain prices rose above industrial prices for the first time since the Thirty Years' War. Skyrocketing grain prices were also a consequence of the decline in agriculture in England, where completion of the enclosure process and movement of textile production out of cottages and into factories led to reliance on Prussian rye and barley. The rise in grain prices was, in turn, reflected in a rise in the going price of Prussian land. In addition to population growth and increasing exports, a third cause for higher grain and land prices was the desire of wealthy commoners, mainly in Berlin, to invest their capital in land rather than in manufacturing. Although commoners were prohibited by law from buying land, they increasingly did so illegally. Land in Prussia became a commodity for speculation and boom profits.[18]

In spite of these favorable economic developments, it was not clear at the time that state policies, inheritance patterns, or fertility rates would allow the nobility to utilize the favorable developments to their own advantage. By the closing decades of the eighteenth century, east Prussian grain was being sold at home, to the state's grain magazines, and abroad, to England, via Dutch merchants. In order to increase their profits on the foreign sales, the Junkers needed a reduction in the heavy

18. My portrait of the Prussian nobility on these pages is drawn from the following general works: Paul Bainroch, "Agriculture and the Industrial Revolution," in *The Fontana Economic History of Europe*, vol. 3, ed. Carlo M. Cipolla (London, 1973), 452–506; Barrington Moore, *The Social Basis of Democracy and Dictatorship* (Boston, 1966); Robert Brenner, "Agrarian Class Structure and Economic Development in Pre-Industrial Europe," *Past and Present*, 70 (February 1976), 30–75; A. Goodwin, *The European Nobility in the Eighteenth Century* (London, 1953).

For the German and Prussian nobilities I have relied on F. L. Carsten, *The Origin of Prussia* (Oxford, 1954); Günter Birtsch, "Zur sozialen und politischen Rolle des deutschen, vornehmlich preussischen Adels am Ende des 18. Jahrhunderts," in *Der Adel vor der Revolution*, Rudolf Vierhaus, ed. (Göttingen, 1971), 77–95; Otto Hintze, "The Hohenzollern and the Nobility," recently translated in Felix Gilbert, ed., *The Historical Essays of Otto Hintze* (New York, 1975); Uwe-Jens Heuer, *Allgemeines Landrecht und Klassenkampf: Die Auseinandersetzungen um die Prinzipien des ALR am Ende des 18. Jh. als Ausdruck der Krise des Feudalsystems in Preussen* (East Berlin, 1960); Gerd Heinrich, "Der Adel in Brandenburg-Preussen," in *Deutscher Adel 1555–1740*, ed. Hellmuth Rössler (Darmstadt, 1965), 259–314; and W. Görlitz, *Die Junker: Adel und Bauer im deutschen Osten* (Glücksberg, 1957). The classic work remains the indispensable book by Hans Rosenberg, *Bureaucracy, Aristocracy, Autocracy: The Prussian Experience, 1660–1815* (Cambridge, Mass., 1958).

mercantilist duties on exports. By 1790 this problem was alleviated, for as mercantilism became less severe under Frederick William II, duties on the export of grain were sharply reduced. The nobility also needed large estates and large amounts of capital in order to carry out the innovations necessary to export grain for profit. Here they faced a major problem. Many families had neither large estates nor much capital, and these two difficulties exacerbated each other. The absence of primogeniture encouraged the subdivision of estates, since all sons had an equal claim on the land. And lack of capital was an incentive to give in to the pressure to sell subdivided estates. High fertility due to good nutrition and a rapid decrease in "positive checks" on mortality like wars and epidemics led to large noble families, with all of the progeny demanding an inheritance. As a Protestant land, Prussia lacked convents where unmarried daughters clamoring for dowries might be removed from the marriage market. More daughters marrying meant more dowries. Booming land values were thus an incentive to gain cash by selling the increasingly small plots to the highest bidder.

The resulting noble alienation from the land was accelerated by sending sons into the army and the civil service, a practice that was consolidated by a noble pact with the crown in the mid-seventeenth century and intended to alleviate the pressure of many progeny demanding land or cash. But several kinks turned up in this system a century later. First, the increasing difficulties of settling noble sons on the land meant that more and more of them came to the city in search of a post in the bureaucracy or military. But just when the noble need for offices grew, the number of qualified commoner applicants increased greatly. Nobles could not use liquid capital to stop this development, even if they had possessed it. The Prussian bureaucracy had always been more meritocratic than venal: offices were not for sale. Noble army officers were an especially penurious lot, infrequently earning enough to marry and live in the proper style. When they did manage to do so, their daughters had difficulty amassing a dowry that would allow them to live nobly as well.[19]

Frederick the Great, sensitive to the nobility's mounting problems, reversed his father's practice of awarding high posts to commoners and reserved more posts for nobles. Nevertheless, the noble exodus from the land was not matched with sufficient employment opportunities in the city. A full third of the noble families in Brandenburg (the province

19. Fritz Redlich, *The German Military Enterpriser and His Work Force*, Beiheft 47–48 of the *Vierteljahrschrift für Sozial- und Wirtschaftsgeschichte* (Wiesbaden, 1964), part 3, 169, and Fritz Martiny, *Die Adelsfrage im Preussen vor 1806*, Beiheft 35 of the *Vierteljahrsheft für Sozial- und Wirtschaftsgeschichte* (Stuttgart, 1936), 84.

around Berlin) lived exclusively from urban occupations by the end of the century.[20] They and their rural cousins who regularly visited Berlin developed an expensive courtier lifestyle, which was yet another reason for nobles to sell off small sections of their landed estates. It was a vicious cycle. Lack of sufficient official posts and city living combined to increase the cost of living just when it was tempting to abandon the land, the only long-term source of wealth. Something had to be done. True, the only voices calling into question the nobility's right to survive as a closed estate were quiet ones published in the journals, never noisy cries in thestreets or in the fields.[21] But the economic situation was serious. Only a third of the noble families lived exclusively from income from their landed estates. Over a tenth of the estates were owned by commoners, while an estimated half of the worth of officially nobly owned estates was endebted to commoners.[22] The short-range benefits of subdivision and sale in a boom land market blinded members of this lucky estate to the long-run consequences of these practices.

Until his death in 1786, Frederick the Great tried to help. The king was willing to risk the repercussions of angry writers and bureaucrats unhappy with increased noble domination of the top positions in the administration and the army. But even this bureaucratic preference for nobles was no longer an adequate stopgap. The solution had to address what was awry in the noble position in the countryside. Only then could the nobility possess a source of permanent high profits, maintain their size and relative economic homogeneity, and retain maximum control over the rural labor force. The two mechanisms of salvation provided by Frederick the Great and his two eighteenth-century successors did not succeed immediately. The first was the establishment of family trusts (*Fideicommisse*) to prohibit subdivision of the estate among future generations. This practice was, however, slow to catch on, precisely because of the attraction of paying off urban debts by selling small pieces of land at high prices.

The second mechanism the crown offered to save the nobility was intended to close the loophole that permitted commoners to buy noble estates de facto. Given the structural weakness of the industrial sector,

20. Reinhard Koselleck, *Preussen zwischen Reform und Revolution: Allgemeines Landrecht, Verwaltung und soziale Bewegung von 1791 bis 1848* (Stuttgart, 1967), 78, and Brunschwig, *Enlightenment and Romanticism,* 55.
21. See Klaus Epstein, *The Genesis of German Conservatism* (Princeton, 1966) chap. 4, for a detailed discussion.
22. The first estimate was made by Görlitz, *Die Junker,* 158; the second by Martiny, *Die Adelsfrage,* 30. Brunschwig, *Enlightenment and Romanticism,* 54, claims that 13 percent of the noble estates in the Kurmark region around Berlin were owned by commoners.

there was only so much that could be done about this situation: Germany was not England.[23] Neither cottage industries nor luxury manufactories were secure investments for surplus commoner capital. If commoners had been allowed to continue to purchase noble land during the early nineteenth century at the same rate as in the last quarter of the eighteenth, this illegal but growing practice would have ended the noble monopoly on the land. To plug this hole and yet allow commoners to invest in grain production, a credit bank (*Landschaft*) was established in 1793.[24] The nobility was to put up its collective estates as collateral and receive what were in essence "commoner" loans on their mortgaged land. The commoners would receive high interest for their loans, more money would be available to invest in innovations to expand agricultural production, but no commoners would henceforth be even the unofficial owners of landed estates. State efforts to persuade them notwithstanding, Prussian nobles tended to be as slow to take advantage of the credit bank as they were to entail their estates. They feared putting their lands up as security. Slowly they came to see that without participation in the credit bank they would eventually go under as a group.

"Going under as a group" essentially meant losing the tight fit between the nobility's position on both the ascriptive and achievement hierarchies. Adult male members of the noble estate, as landowners or high officials, had once been almost exclusively in the highest income group. At the same time, this highest income group included mainly nobles. This tight fit was, of course, characteristic of an estate society. Each closed order had a social function and a level of wealth unique to itself. But the fit between being noble and being in the upper-income strata became less tight as the century progressed. That was just the trouble. The crisis of the agricultural economy impoverished small landowners while allowing commoners to intrude on the noble monopoly of land-ownership, and there was stiffer commoner competition for offices once considered noble preserves. The growing educational apparatus and the emergence of a commercial elite meant that the highest income group was no longer exclusively filled with noble landowners and officials. In short, birth was less often a sufficient condition for living the way nobles were meant to live.

But the nobility did not die. After a series of structural reforms exe-

23. I am indebted here to the provocative volume by David Blackbourne and Geoff Eley, *The Peculiarities of German History: Bourgeois Society and Politics in Nineteenth-Century Germany* (New York, 1984).

24. See Hanna Schissler, "Die Junker," in *Preussen im Rückblick,* H.-J. Puhle and H.-U. Wehler, eds. (Göttingen, 1980), 89–122, at 96. A revised, English version of this essay is cited in note 17 above.

cuted between 1807 and 1813, a smaller, healthier nobility survived and even flourished during the nineteenth century. First, nobles eventually gained more real control over their labor force even though they lost some legal controls over the peasantry. Key aspects of serfdom were abolished, which was in fact useful for noble landowners. For even if wages had to be paid, a geographically mobile peasantry that could be dismissed out of season was cheaper than year-round responsibility for the upkeep of serfs. Second, after the reform era those nobles who were also landlords tended to have larger estates than was often the case in the late eighteenth century. Nobles better endowed with land bought out the "cabbage Junkers," the impoverished nobles. Third, ex-serfs were now able to convert their labor services into money payments to the landlord. This eased the smaller group of larger landlords' lack of capital. Finally, since another impediment to noble survival was the glut of sons without a secure position on land or in the city, the reforms were beneficial insofar as they allowed nobles to practice "commoner" occupations previously forbidden them.

A further—potentially perilous—reform allowed commoners to legally buy noble estates after 1807. This new practice could easily have become a new impediment to noble survival, but did not, for several reasons. Throughout the nineteenth century, the proportion of non-noble landowners was kept to a fifth of the total.[25] Commoners rarely received the local legal powers over the peasantry normally retained only by noble landowners, and the monarchy, moreover, was tightfisted in the sale of noble titles. Unlike the Hapsburgs, the Hohenzollerns generally preferred to keep the government solvent by taxing the residents rather than by selling titles. This, too, helped the surviving nobles maintain their social and legal hegemony over other landowners.

At the same time, the newly legal infusion of commoner capital into agriculture by buying estates helped make grain production more efficient. By 1820, the Prussian landowners entered into an epoch of prosperity that was to last for a crucial half-century. When Prussian grain began to face stiff competition during the last third of the nineteenth century, help from the state was urgently demanded, in the form of protectionism. With some difficulty, the landowners received this help. The cost of their victory to the economic and political development of modern Germany is a tale that has been told elsewhere.[26] The point for our

25. Schissler, "Die Junker," 113. Much of my analysis in these paragraphs is derived from reading this extremely useful article. See also Robert M. Berdahl, "Preussischer Adel: Paternalismus als Herrschaftssystem," in *Preussen im Rückblick*, Puhle and Wehler, eds., 123–45.

26. A rigorous account of the long-term economic background of Otto von Bismarck's

story is that the quarter century before 1806 was a fluid, decisive time for the Prussian nobility. More nobles flocked to the city and were exposed to new values, new ideas, new friends. The ideological and social upheavals they experienced in the city increased the likelihood that they would gravitate into Jewish salon society. And in a complicated way, financial woes also played a role in the noble tendency to visit salons and eventually to marry the Jewish women they met there. For Berlin's Jewish community was the only estate in a position to help the many nobles in Berlin committed to a life of luxury without the proceeds to sustain their indulgences.

The Jewish Community

In their sizes, lavish lifestyles, and marriage patterns, the noble and the Jewish estates during the last quarter of the eighteenth century bore an uncanny resemblance to each other. This in itself was an unusual development. When resemblance blossomed into personal intimacy between even a handful of nobles and Jews, it was logical that many eyes in Europe would turn their gaze to the glamorous "social splendor" enjoyed by Berlin Jewry. Rahel Levin wrote her family from Paris in 1801 that "being from Berlin and a Jew really gives one a kind of *coutenance* even here."[27] The Berlin Jews had something to boast about, at least when abroad.

The similarities between the two estates which began to appear in the course of the century made possible the friendships between individual nobles and Jews that would come to pass in later years. First of all, both groups were tiny. There were never many more or less than 3,500 Jews in Berlin between 1770 and 1800, well under 2 percent of the city's population.[28] The noble proportion of the city was probably also around 2 percent.[29] The size of the two groups, moreover, remained rather consistent

adoption of a protectionist policy in 1880 is Frank B. Tipton's *Regional Variations in the Economic Development of Germany* (Middletown, Conn., 1976). For the story of how the landowners' victory in achieving a protectionist policy helped cause Nazism see David Abraham, *The Collapse of the Weimar Republic* (Princeton, 1981).

27. *Rahel: Ein Buch des Andenkens für ihre Freunde*, (Berlin, 1834), vol. 1, 237, as cited in Michael Meyer, *The Origins of the Modern Jew* (Detroit, 1967), 109.

28. See Herbert Secliger, "The Origin and Growth of the Berlin Jewish Community," *LBIYB* 3 (1968), 159–68.

29. Martiny, *Die Adelsfrage*, 8, claims that there were 20,000 noble families in Prussia in this era; if each family contained five persons, and since Prussia had 5,750,000 persons in 1783, the nobility would be 1.7 percent of the population. For a nineteenth-century estimate of the noble proportion of Berlin specifically see Gerhard Masur, *Imperial Berlin* (New York, 1971), 87.

over time, for the borders of both estates were rigid. Although many coveted noble titles, Frederick the Great awarded few for accomplishment and sold even fewer for contributions to the royal treasury. There was little incentive to leave the nobility, since few of the occupations closed to nobles provided either social esteem or financial profit. If more wanted to enter than to exit the noble estate, the reverse was true for the Jewish estate. Except for a few "return conversions" of repentent converts, conversions *into* Judaism were rare in this era. To be sure, there were some defections from the Jewish ranks. As we shall see in chapter 7, such defections did rather suddenly become popular in the last three decades of the century among key sectors of the Jewish community: the young, the rich, the women. But for Jews as well as for nobles, the trickle in or out of estates of birth remained minimal before the nineteenth century.

A second similarity between the two estates was that a high proportion of the landed and the liquid wealth in Prussia was in the hands of either nobles or Jews. Wealthy members of both groups, moreover, believed that it was to their economic and social advantage to spend their money on display. From our perspective, alert to the investment necessary for an economy to industrialize, they were squandering their wealth. But at the time, the impressions and connections to be made by owning stone palaces in the city, hosting lavish dinner parties, and buying silk dresses seemed well worth the expenditure.[30] Partly as a consequence of their wealth, both nobles and Jewish families lived in large and complexhouseholds. Servants, business assistants, unmarried relatives, visiting scholars, tutors, and many children filled their palatial homes on Unter den Linden and the Spandauer Strasse. Noble and Jewish households were large not only because they had the means to provide for so many employees, progeny, and extended family members; their large nuclear families were also a consequence of the adolescent ages at which their daughters married. Early marriage usually meant more children in this century. For both groups, marriages were arranged at early ages because marriage was a central way to hold and gain wealth and power. Daughters traded and married off young would be sure to be pure, and their dowries would therefore tend to go further on the marriage market.

A century earlier few would have predicted that this essentially aristocratic lifestyle could be achieved by more than a few isolated court Jewish families. Pessimism about Jewish life in Europe then was well founded, because the condition of western European Jewry had deteriorated dramatically since the late medieval period. France, England,

---

30. See Norbert Elias, *Die höfische Gesellschaft* (Neuwied, 1975), III.

Spain, and Portugal all expelled some or all of their Jewish residents between the thirteenth and the fifteenth centuries.[31] The result of these national explusions was the migration eastward of hundreds of thousands of Jews. The destination for many of them was Poland, where in the late medieval period Jews prospered as managers of noble landed estates, grain or cattle dealers, or innkeepers. Although their economic activities were more narrowly restricted to the money economy in Poland than they had been in western Europe, Poland nevertheless offered Jews an opportunity for large, unrestricted settlement and thus for explosive demographic growth.

The situation worsened for central as well as for western European Jewry in the late medieval era, especially in the years between 1490 and 1570. Across the German-speaking territories, city councils, princes, and emperors were besieged by complaints from gentile craftsmen and merchants that Jewish business practices already had or would soon undermine their livelihood. But even if these rulers wanted to expel resident Jews or stop Jewish immigration from the west, the territories of central Europe were simply too decentralized for national expulsion to be feasible. Instead, local expulsion from large cities where artisans and shopkeepers feared Jewish competition was the typical central European practice. Jews were forced to leave many cities where they had been active in handicraft production as well as in intraregional trade. As a result, by the seventeenth century Jews in the Germanic states were scattered over a greater number of smaller towns than previously. Village Jews served the exchange needs of the surrounding countryside as cattle traders, peddlers, hawkers, moneychangers, moneylenders, and innkeepers. They were rarely found in court cities in this era. A prince could, after all, meet his need for credit by dealing with Jewish financiers in nearby trade cities or with a tiny circle he allowed to settle near the court.[32] The only large

---

31. I have relied upon the general histories of European Jewry covering the late medieval period, including Heinrich Graetz, *History of the Jews,* 5 vols. (London, 1891–92); Salo Baron, *A Social and Religious History of the Jews,* 3 vols. (New York, 1937); Raphael Strauss, *Die Juden in Wirtschaft und Gesellschaft* (Frankfurt, 1964); Uriah Zevi Engelman, *The Rise of the Jew in the Western World: A Social and Economic History of the Jewish People of Europe* (New York, 1944, rpt. 1973); Howard M. Sachar, *The Course of Modern Jewish History* (Cleveland, 1958); Nachum Gross, ed., *Economic History of the Jews* (New York, 1975). The single most useful volume came to my attention at the end: Jonathan Israel, *European Jewry in the Age of Mercantilism, 1550–1750* (Oxford, 1985).

32. Works used here on the court Jew include Selma Stern, *The Court Jew: A Contribution to the History of the Period of Absolutism in Central Europe* (Philadelphia, 1950); F. L. Carsten, "The Court Jews: A Prelude to Emancipation," *LBYIB* 3 (1958), 140–58; and Heinrich Schnee, *Die Hoffinanz und der moderne Staat,* vol. 1: *Die Institution des Hoffaktorentums in Brandenburg-Preussen* (Berlin, 1953). A stimulating interpretation of the ambivalent po-

trade city that allowed continuous Jewish residence was Frankfurt am Main, but even there, local laws squeezed the Jews out of handicraft production and ever more tightly into trade and money exchange. Indeed, wherever they lived in Germany, Jews were increasingly restricted in their choice of neighborhood as well as occupation, and taxed more heavily than in the past.

The central European pattern of local expulsions continued into the last third of the seventeenth century, when the Viennese Jewish community was expelled in 1670. The Prussian Great Elector's invitation to some of the richest of these families to settle in Prussia reversed a century-long ban on Jewish residence in Berlin. Previously, Jews had lived continuously in the Electorate of Brandenburg (the province around Berlin) for almost five hundred years. But this long epoch of tolerance had ended in the sixteenth century. In 1446, 1510, and again in 1571 there were violent popular explosions against the Berlin Jews, two of which ended with a burning at the stake. After the third, the remaining Jewish community was expelled from the city.[33]

Frederick William's decision to invite the Viennese families into Prussia was not motivated by philosemitism, for he and his successors shared a vivid and often expressed personal dislike for Jews. Rather, the Great Elector was sure that importing carefully selected wealthy Jews would be useful in increasing the power of Prussia: the Berlin Jews were to be the golden goose that was to lay golden eggs.[34] This was a typical Prussian decision, insofar as its activist rulers were ready to flout convention if doing so would create a financially strong, militarily successful, and self-sufficient state. Just as the Huguenot artisans were to set Prussia on its way to autarky in silk production, the Viennese financiers would supply the liquid capital and the foreign connections required to feed and clothe the army, make personal loans to the court and to courtiers, mint new coins and distribute devalued ones, and even finance new manufactories.

The Prussian decision may have been a bold one, but it was not entirely out of step with the changing times. Vienna itself welcomed Jews back into the Hapsburg capital beginning in 1675. As economic and po-

---

sition of court and other privileged Jews is Hannah Arendt, "Privileged Jews," *Jewish Social Studies* 8 (1946), 3–30.

33. See Eugen Wolbe, *Geschichte der Juden in Berlin und der Mark Brandenburg* (Berlin, 1937).

34. This apt phrase was used by Dorwart, *The Prussian Welfare State*, 132. For a good analysis of the expulsion of the Viennese Jews and a summary of immigration into Prussia see S. Ettinger, "The Modern Period," in H. S. Ben-Sasson, ed., *A History of the Jewish People* (Cambridge, Mass., 1976), 755. Mary Fulbrook's *Piety and Politics: Religion and the Rise of Absolutism in England, Württemberg and Prussia* (Cambridge, England, 1983), came to my attention too late to be used here.

litical conditions worsened in Poland during the eighteenth century, the direction of migration of the preceding centuries was reversed. More and more Polish Jews, some of them quite wealthy, sought new homes in the dynamic new states just then emerging from the dwarfish territorial doldrums of the recent central European past. Some of these Polish Jews found their way to Prussia. The especially lucky ones found their way to Berlin and managed to remain there. Berlin offered specifically qualified Jews a phenomenal opportunity. It was the only court city in Germany where a good-sized Jewish community was allowed to grow; it had no formal ghetto; housing restrictions were minimal and the richest Jews lived in the poshest section of town. This court city, moreover, became a center for intra- and interregional trade, textile manufacturing, and eventually, for education and publishing. Eventually, select members of Berlin's Jewish community were allowed to enter a secular world closed to most other European Jews during the eighteenth century.

In return for their financial services, Berlin provided a tiny group of Jews the opportunity to make the huge amounts of money which were a necessary material prerequisite for acculturation and social integration. Precisely because of the distinctive opportunities possible in Berlin, many more Jews wished to live there than managed to get accepted into and remain in the city. The necessary recital of the very real persecution of the Berlin Jews should not, therefore, confuse us about how contemporaries saw the situation. For at a time and in a place where everyone was a subject of one kind or another and no one was a citizen, degrees of political persecution are difficult to measure. It was in the nature of an estate society for closed religious and social communities to pay a particular kind and amount of taxes, to be subject to the rulings of separate court systems, and to be allowed to work only in specific occupations. And it was also in the nature of an estate society for these demarcations to be enforced by law. In principle, therefore, the procedures developed in Prussia during the eighteenth century for regulating Jewish existence were not in their nature discriminatory.[35] The French and the Bohemian colonies were also subject to specific regulations. But in practice this system was worse for the Jews. The degree and kind of regulation, the sheer amount of taxes, and the occupational restrictions imposed on the Jewish community were especially onerous. Unlike other estates with parallel arrangements with the crown, the Jewish community paid far

35. On the housing restrictions discussed above see Jacob Katz, *From Prejudice to Destruction: Anti-Semitism, 1700–1933* (Cambridge, Mass., 1980), 94–95. The problem of interpreting how discriminatory corporate regulations of the Jewish community was raised by Toni Oelsner in "Three Jewish Families in Modern Germany: A Study of the Process of Emancipation," *Jewish Social Studies*, 4 (1942), 241–68.

more in duties for the most basic of rights, namely the right to be protected by the king against expulsion.

Theirs was a most anomalous position. Although they were too large a group to all be called court Jews, wealthy Berlin Jews in the eighteenth century shared with their seventeenth-century predecessors the fate of being "powerful slaves." Some of the Berlin Jews were among the richest men in central Europe. Yet unless they were lucky enough to receive dispensation from the rules, they could only enter Berlin through one gate, where they were forced to pay a tax like that paid for donkeys. Moses Mendelssohn had to entertain his prominent guests with twenty porcelain monkeys sitting on his shelves; even Mendelssohn's intellectual stature did not exempt him from having to buy these surplus products of Frederick the Great's troubled luxury industries. Because the monkeys were so overpriced, the Jews had no hope of selling them, and in many ways they symbolized the community's privileged powerlessness. As powerful slaves, too, the wealthy Berlin Jews could only maintain their anomalously "positive" position by policing their own kind. The hostel set up outside the city gates was visited regularly by the community elders, who decided which itinerant Jews could enter the city and for how long.[36]

But before a Jew could become or even serve a powerful slave, the first obstacle to be surmounted was gaining the right to reside in Prussia at all. This process became increasingly difficult during the course of the eighteenth century. Frederick William I (1713–40) and Frederick the Great successively restricted the scope of Jewish economic activity and increased the taxes imposed on the community. Beginning in 1730, Jews in Prussia were forbidden to engage in retail trade and gradually restricted to long-distance trade in luxury items, supplying the army, and minting coins. Again in 1750, the crown issued another order limiting Jewish life in Prussia in various ways: only one son could settle in Prussia and trading was limited even further. But these restrictions actually concentrated Jewish economic activity and thereby gave Jews advantages over gentile merchants. For Jews could import new goods like chocolate and coffee that other merchants were forbidden to purchase, and also engage in foreign trade with contacts from which gentile merchants were

36. See Arendt, "Privileged Jews," and also the "Antisemitism" section of her *Origins of Totalitarianism* (New York, 1951). Arendt's view of Jewish history is elaborated in a collection of her essays, *The Jew as Pariah*, Ron Feldman, ed. (New York, 1958). A graphic depiction of the hostel can be found in the autobiography of Solomon Maimon: see Moses Hadas, ed., *Solomon Maimon: An Autobiography* (New York, 1967). On Maimon see also Jakob Fromer, *Salomon Maimones Lebensgeschichte* (Munich, 1911).

excluded. In sum, in the first half of the eighteenth century much was lost, but there were compensations.[37]

The complex economic division of labor within the Jewish community was reflected in an equally complex legal categorization.[38] At the top of this legal hierarchy were three sorts of "protected" or "escorted" Jews. At the very summit were the "most" protected families, whose heads had a "general privilege" that gave themselves and their children the same rights of residency and occupation as those possessed by gentile merchants. There may have been as many as one hundred generally privileged families under Frederick the Great. Below them, on the next rung, were the 63 "ordinarily" protected families. The third kind of privileged families were the 203 "extraordinarily" protected families, who actually had fewer privileges than the "ordinarily" protected. All told, the number of all three kinds of protected families must have been somewhere near four hundred.[39] Below the protected were three sorts of unprotected Jews: the community officials, the "tolerated," and the domestic servants. The officials included rabbis, kosher butchers, cemetery caretak-

37. I am indebted to Ettinger, "The Modern Period," 754, for this summary of the situation in 1750.

38. The most comprehensive history of the Prussian Jewish community is Selma Stern, *Der Preussische Staat und die Juden*, 3 vols. (Tübingen, 1971). A recent short history, richly illustrated, is *Juden in Preussen: Ein Kapitel deutscher Geschichte*, Bildarchiv Preussischer Kulturbesitz, ed. (Harenberg, 1981). See also Henri Brunschwig's essay "The Struggle for the Emancipation of the Jews in Prussia," which is included as an appendix to his *Enlightenment and Romanticism*. For a good summary in English of the complex categorization of the Berlin community see Heinz Moshe Graupe, *The Rise of Modern Judaism: An Intellectual History of German Jewry, 1650–1942* (Huntington, N.Y., 1978), chap. 8. Jacob Jacobson, *Die Judenbürgerbücher der Stadt Berlin, 1809–51* (Berlin, 1962), 10, claims that between 1809 and 1812, 330 Berlin Jews became citizens of the city. Stefi Jersch-Wenzel describes the stiff financial requirements necessary for Jews to become citizens in her *Jüdische Bürger und kommunale Selbstverwaltung in preussischen Städten, 1808–48* (Berlin, 1967); Jersch-Wenzel also provides a detailed occupational breakdown of the Berlin Jewish community on p. 28.

39. A rough match between the legally designated elite (the 400 heard of "protected" households) and the economic elite is possible. In 1812, there were 32 bankers, 12 entrepreneurs, and 167 large-scale merchants (*Kaufmänner*) among Berlin Jewry, as cited in Jersch-Wenzel, *Jüdische Bürger*, 28. The 211 Jews with these occupations must have formed the core of the "protected" sector of the community in the previous decades.

Another way to arrive at the estimate of 700 adult males is the following: the civilian population of Berlin in 1799 (according to "Tabellen von den Küstlern, Gerwerken, Meteiers und Personen in Berlin" published in the *Jahrbücher der preussischen Monarchie unter der Regierung Friedrich Wilhelm III,* 2 (1799, 73), was 142,099. Those identified as adult males, 29,502, were 21 percent of the entire population. In order to identify the adult Jewish males I have used the figure 684, which is 21 percent of the total number of Jews in Berlin in 1798, 3421.

ers, and religious teachers, who, instead of letters of protection, merely
had residence permits that could not be passed on to their children. The
"tolerated" Jews tended to be the second and third children of the protected, as well as the children of community officials. The third sort of
unprotected Jews were the domestic servants, who were not allowed to
marry, and whose residency permits lasted only as long as their employment.

A paucity of appropriate sources makes it difficult to match the legal
divisions that stratified the community with its internal economic structure. Reconstructing the community's structure is also rendered difficult
by the complex maze of restrictions on the right to marry and to settle
children. These restrictions played havoc with the age structure, family
size, and possibly also with the sex ratio of the community. But we do
not yet know exactly how this havoc was played. Some have presumed
that because most Jewish women married in their adolescent years, Jewish nuclear families in Berlin were universally large and extended. But as
we shall see in Chapter 7, adolescent marriage was not as widespread in
late-eighteenth-century Berlin as some have assumed. The first step in
reconstructing the rough outlines of the community's social structure is
to estimate the number of adult males, those whose economic activity
defined the family's social position. If we presume that all adult males
were heads of households and that the family size of the Jewish community was a "normal" eighteenth-century mean of five, given an average
population of 3,535 between 1770 and 1799 there would have been roughly
700 adult men, one per nuclear family. The two published estimates of
the number of Jewish families in Berlin then are both somewhat lower
than this, suggesting that families had more than five members. One
historian claimed that there were 600 Jewish families in the city; other
scholars estimated that there were 450 families.[40] Using the first estimate,
600, as the denominator, the 300 to 400 wealthy protected families
would constitute almost half of the community. Using the smaller estimate, 450, the wealthy protected families would constitute as much as
two-thirds of the community.

This large elite was inevitable, given that the assortment of Jewish persons allowed to reside in Berlin was a consequence of the monarchs'
rigidly adhered-to maxim of obtaining precisely the right economic services from the smallest number of local Jews. By any measure, the Berlin
community was therefore top-heavy with rich financiers able to pay the
extensive taxes and still prosper. There was accordingly a tight fit be-

40. See Arendt, *Origins*, 16, note 6, and *A History of Modern Jewry, 1780–1815* (London,
1971), 127.

tween the protected and the wealthy, which is no surprise given the way in which "freedoms" were pegged to the ability to pay for them. The large number of wealthy Jews in Berlin was highly unusual compared to the gentile social structure in the city. The gentile elite in Berlin was definitely not larger than a tenth of the population.[41] The inflated size of the Jewish community's elite was also unusual compared to the social structure of Prussian Jewry as a whole. Only a tiny percent of Prussian Jewry at large were bankers, financiers, and entrepreneurs in 1800.[42] Nor was the size of the Jewish elite as large in other major German cities with wealthy Jewish communities. In Hamburg, the largest Jewish community in Germany, roughly 6 percent of the community was estimated to have been "wealthy," while in Frankfurt am Main the wealthy were at most a tenth of the community. In the western metropolises of London, Paris, and Amsterdam there were wealthy Jewish financiers, but in none of these three cities did the wealthy have the numerical hegemony within the community that they had in Berlin, because all three cities had large proportions of poor Jews.[43] To the east, in the northwestern sections of Poland that were Prussian between 1792 and 1807, there were no large cities, and the majority of Jewish men were poor peddlers.

But the artificially fat "goose" of Berlin Jewry did not produce its golden eggs in isolation from poorer Jewish communities elsewhere. None of the loaning, purveying, selling, or investing feats performed by the wealthy Jews in Berlin could have been executed without the aid of poor Jews who lived in small villages to the east. Both economic historians and antisemites alike have long pointed out that cooperation between Jewish financiers in various European capitals was indispensable

41. This estimate is suggested by an analysis of preindustrial social structures in Vincent Knapp, *Europe in the Era of Social Transformation* (Engelwood Cliffs, 1976), and Franklin Kopitzsch's introduction to his *Aufklärung, Absolutismus und Bürgertum in Deutschland* (Munich, 1976).

42. See Jacob Lestschinsky, "Das wirtschaftliche Schicksal des deutschen Judentums," *Schriften der Zentralwohlfahrtsstelle der deutschen Juden*, 7 (Berlin, 1932), 92, who claims that at the beginning of the nineteenth century approximately 90 percent of the German Jews as a whole belonged to the poorest parts of the German population. A parallel claim is made by Marvin Lowenthal, *The Jews of Germany: A Story of Sixteen Centuries* (Philadelphia, 1936), 225.

43. Helga Krohn, *Die Juden in Hamburg 1800–1850* (Hamburg, 1967), 29. See also M. Grunwald, *Hamburgs deutsche Juden bis zur Auflösung der Dreigemeinden* (Hamburg, 1904). On Frankfurt's Jewish community see I. Kracaver, *Geschichte der Juden in Frankfurt A.M. 1150–1824* (Frankfurt a.M. 1927), 309. On English Jewry in this era see Todd Endelman, *The Jews of Georgian England* (Philadelphia, 1979); on French Jewry see Arthur Herzberg, *The French Enlightenment and the Jews* (New York, 1968). On Amsterdam Jewry see H. Bloom, *The Economic Activities of the Jews of Amsterdam in the Seventeenth and Eighteenth Centuries* (Williamsport, Pa., 1937).

for Jewish financial success in this era. It has less frequently been noted that the international ties linking Jews in different cities were also ties *across* the Jewish social hierarchy. The brokers, peddlers, hawkers, and small-scale moneychangers and moneylenders in the east distributed devalued coins, bought raw materials, and sold manufactured ones on commission for the wealthy Jews in Berlin, and were absolutely crucial for the Berliners' economic successes. The Berlin Jewish social structure was top-heavy only because the Prussian rulers calculated that their state could benefit from trading by the rich Jewish financiers and still keep the poor Jews out of the city.

Although the Jewish elite was allowed in Berlin at the behest of the crown to serve the state, they nonetheless operated in a climate notably hostile to financial and industrial development. Indeed, historians have debated whether merchants of any religion in the late eighteenth century made a significant contribution to the industrial development of Prussia. The evidence for a somber view of the merchants' place in Prussian economic history is compelling. To be sure, the Prussian merchants' woes were mainly caused by constraints beyond their control. It was just not possible for Prussia to industrialize while the agricultural system remained feudal and while the borders between hereditary estates were legally enforced. A strict mercantilist policy ill suited to Prussian conditions only exacerbated these two fundamental impediments. The circle of a weak commercial sector's tendency to feed a capital-hungry nobility with merchant profits was a vicious one. Import of foreign manufactured products was forbidden, but domestic luxury industries were well known as a bad investment. Public banking facilities in which the public's savings could be circulated did not exist. Even hoarding cash was ill advised, since periodic devaluations of the currency led to persistent inflation.[44] Berlin's merchants did make money, by putting out raw materials to artisans, by producing supplies for the army, and by long-distance trade. But their profits often managed to seep upward into noble hands through illegal purchase of noble estates or—if that was impossible— through the purchase of land mortgage bonds. Merchant profits also seeped upwards by extensive private loans to spendthrift nobles in the city, or through payment of lavish dowries settled on daughters who married noble grooms.

Yet alongside these gloomy facts there is also a more optimistic interpretation of the role played by Berlin's merchants, Jewish and gentile

44. See Hans Motteck, *Wirtschaftsgeschichte Deutschlands* (Berlin, 1964), vol. 2, 355ff.; Hugo Rachel and Paul Wallich, *Berliner Grosskaufleute und Kapitalisten*, vol. 2: *Die Zeit des Mercantilismus, 1648–1806* (Berlin, 1938, rpt. 1967); Hugo Rachel, *Das Berliner Wirtschaftsleben im Zeitalter des Frühkapitalismus* (Berlin, 1931).

alike. One very rosy assessment goes so far as to locate the beginnings of the industrial revolution in Prussia during this half century.[45] Army-related trade and production during the Seven Years' War (1756–63) generated so much profit for French and Jewish merchant contractors that private banking firms evolved out of trade firms to organize the flow of credit and investment. The new stock exchange, which opened in 1803, was a further manifestation of the need for organized public coordination of investments. New manufactories were founded to produce necessities like wool, armaments, coins, and sugar, as well as for the production of luxuries like ribbons, velvet, silk cloth, and porcelain. Even if some banking houses and luxury manufactories went under in the first decades of the nineteenth century, they left behind a legacy of skilled workers, accelerated diffusion of new techniques, and substantial accumulated capital.

Much of the debate about how to interpret the institutional climate in which Berlin's merchants worked revolves around deciding how central the making and trading of luxury products was in the emergence of modern capitalism. Jewish merchants were central in Berlin's luxury trade; the main purchasers of luxury goods were noble members of court society and other wealthy merchants.[46] If one had the cash, buying paintings, jewelry, and precious stones made good economic sense. These were often the best investments for commoners excluded from legal purchase of land at a time when manufacturing was a risky investment. Not all of Berlin's merchants were Jewish, of course. But the most successful gentile merchants, like the Jewish ones, also tended to come from immigrant families, either Huguenot or Slavic. Some of the gentile merchants also participated in the trade in precious metals. But unlike their Jewish colleagues, gentile merchants lacked state pressure forcing them to manage the mint, and with it, the stimulus to concentrate on the long-distance trade in gold and silver. To be sure, supplying silver and minting coins were central to Prussian economic development, not a mere luxury. The growth of the commercial economy across Europe had led to a shortage of silver, and Jewish minters were indispensable suppliers of the metal.[47]

45. The most important optimist is W. O. Henderson. See his *Studies in the Economic Policy of Frederick the Great* (London, 1963), and his *The Rise of German Industrial Power, 1834–1914* (Berkeley and Los Angeles, 1975), chap. 1.

46. See Werner Sombart's *Luxury and Capitalism* (New York, 1938) and his *Jews and Modern Capitalism* (Glencoe, Ill., 1981). See also David Landes, "The Jewish Merchant: Typology and Stereotypology in Germany," *LBIYB* 19 (1974), 11–24.

47. On the numerical balance between Jewish and gentile merchants see Schnee, *Die Hoffinanz und der moderne Staat* vol. 1, 243. Schnee, notes that in 1807 there were 30 Jewish and 22 Christian bankers in Berlin. Rachel and Wallich, *Berliner Grosskaufleute und Kapitalisten*, vol. 2, note that there were 7 Jewish and 5 Christian brokers in Berlin in 1773. See also

The gentile merchants also lacked the Jewish merchants' international connections at both ends of the social hierarchy so useful in the trading of metals and coins.

When Jewish financiers opened family banking houses to circulate the profits earned in coin minting and luxury trade, they added yet another service to the crown and to the nobility. Their "private" banks continued to fill an important function in Berlin right into the first decades of the nineteenth century. Few gentile merchant families opened banking houses, and the new royal bank had too little capital to get off the ground. The capital crisis of some urban nobles deepened as the century wore on, and so beginning in the 1770s the rate of private loans from Jewish banker to impoverished noble accelerated. Since merchants had their offices in their homes, a shared enjoyment of luxuries surely made the personal interaction surrounding these loans more graceful and intimate.

Historians more pessimistic about how useful luxury manufacture and trade were for capitalist development would also find relevant evidence in the Berlin story. For the role of the Jewish "surrogate" bourgeoisie in this era is a poignant illustration of how limited the power of urban commercial capital was in undermining feudalism. Tiny merchant strata in preindustrial settings often tended to function as a closed caste within the nobility rather than truly stimulating industrialization and social mobility.[48] The Jewish elite was not, to be sure, in any way within the nobility; neither the gentile nor the Jewish merchants were united in one caste, nor was either group inside the noble estate. Still, an emphasis on the caste-like character of merchant elites under feudalism fits the Berlin case. Both the gentile and the Jewish merchants were self-enclosed castes unto themselves. Merchants of both faiths were separated by a wide social gulf from others in the highest income group, who were mainly landowners or officials, as well as from the lower orders of their same faith. Moreover, the gulf in language, family size, and spending habits which divided the gentile merchants from the Jewish merchants was equally as wide and as deep as that which loomed between each of the two merchant elites and those below them. In other words, despite the fruits of merchant labor, in the end Frederick the Great got his way. Merchants of both faiths circulated capital without causing the borders

Karoline Cauer, *Oberhofbankier und Hofbaurat: Aus der Berliner Bankgeschichte des XVIII Jh.* (Frankfurt a.M., 1968). On Jewish participation in the silver trade see Ettinger, "The Modern Period," 737.

48. See Maurice Dobb, *Studies in the Development of Capitalism* (New York, 1947), for a general argument critical of the view that the sheer presence of a small group of merchants will necessarily unravel an estate social structure.

dividing estates to collapse. The mere presence of wealthy merchants did not necessarily set off a radical transformation of a society whose social structure was essentially rigid. But given the absolutist and mercantilist constraints which shackled both rulers and society, the decision to invite in and nourish the Jewish golden goose worked rather well for Prussian development. When wealthy Jews minted and distributed coins, supplied armies with uniforms and food, loaned to nobles at profitable interest rates, and put out raw textiles to local artisans, they engaged in activities that were simultaneously good for Prussia's commercial development and profitable for themselves.

The central paradox of Jewish life in the last quarter of the eighteenth century in Berlin was that Jewish cultural and social integration could peak at breakneck speed in spite of the humiliating and extensive legal regulations. Jewish prosperity was in itself far less surprising than the cultural acculturation and social integration which this wealth made possible. Rich Jews were allowed to live in Berlin only so that they could perform specific economic functions. Had such functions not been performed successfully, it is unlikely that Jews at all, or as many Jews, would have lived then in Berlin. Wealth was surely necessary for the cultural acculturation and social integration of the Jewish elite in Berlin, but it was by no means a sufficient condition for these other, mysterious developments. We must therefore learn more about life in Berlin, because only then can the gap between necessary and sufficient be closed, with an explanation for why any members of the wealthy Jewish community in Berlin wrote important books in German, named their daughters Henriette, and had princes as guests for tea.

THREE | *The Male Intelligentsia*

Berlin, Intellectual Metropolis

In 1785, twenty-one-year-old Friedrich Gentz arrived in Berlin to begin his career in the Prussian bureaucracy. Gentz's father was a prominent state official who managed a mint in Breslau; his mother belonged to the leading Huguenot family in Berlin. Their son Friedrich had studied law at the university at Frankfurt an der Oder and completed his degree at Königsberg. The job that drew young Gentz to Berlin was the post of privy secretary, which paid a modest two hundred taler a year. But both Gentz's salary and social standing would improve over the years in Berlin, for he gradually made his way into the most prominent circles of the highest society. Luckily, he had some powerful patrons. Immanuel Kant, Gentz's professor from his Königsberg days, helped Gentz find work as a proofreader to supplement his meager income. In 1788 Christian Garve, a popular Breslau author and a friend of the Gentz family, suggested to his friend Wilhelm von Humboldt that he look up young Gentz. The two hit it off immediately, and von Humboldt's friend, the diplomat Gustav von Brinkmann, made the group an intimate threesome. In the next decade Gentz made his way into Berlin's high society. In addition to enjoying the "precarious respectability" of the Jewish salons, Gentz spent long hours with his friend Prince Louis Ferdinand at the Cafe "Stadt Paris," at a variety of local gambling tables, and at the city's elegant brothels. All this carousing caused him to go deeply into debt, since in 1792 Gentz had married but was still earning less than eight hundred taler a year. To be sure, he supplemented his salary with remuneration from publishing, since he had become a prolific author of anti-Napoleonic political essays. Eventually he would put his talents as a publicist

48

and his increasingly conservative views to use in the service of the Austrian monarchy, who rewarded him with a handsome title and a salary to match.[1]

In 1800, fifteen years after Gentz arrived in Berlin, Friedrich Buchholz, a thirty-two-year old teacher from the provinces, also made his way to the city. Born into a preacher's family in 1768 in Altruppin, Buchholz had every intention of surpassing the social station of his father, but life consistently threw up obstacles. He enrolled at the University of Halle, but poverty forced him to give up his studies when he was twenty-one. Buchholz then settled in Brandenburg, where he spent the next twelve years employed as a tutor to noble students at the local knightly academy. For this labor he was paid two hundred taler a year, by no means enough to feed his growing family. He detested the job, finding the students arrogant and bored with intellectual matters. At the age of thirty-two, in 1800, he finally quit the teaching post and left with his large family for Berlin, where he hoped to find a position in the civil service. With the idea of improving his chances, Buchholz dedicated his first book, published that year, to Herr von Köckritz, the general-adjutant of the king. But despite this obsequious act, Buchholz had little luck in his search for a position and had to support his family by freelance journalism and editing. He lamented that he lived the life of an "obscure creature," who "never stood in the good graces of the great, who never invited him to their homes."[2] Buchholz claimed to have little interest in making friends with the rich and prominent; he complained that their only question about a visiting scholar was "has he already eaten here and here?"[3] Yet at the same time, the material conditions of literary life obviously made it hard for him to completely refrain from supplicating the powerful, as seen in his dedication of the book to the general-adjutant. But for all his efforts Buchholz never did obtain an official post and never did escape the poverty he sought to avoid in his early years. Although his writing brought him neither riches, fame, nor entrée to high society, he persisted. Before he died in 1848 he had produced over a dozen books and edited a variety of important if short-lived journals.

1. On Gentz's first job see Jakob Baxa, *Friedrich von Gentz* (Vienna, 1965), 13; on Garve's role in introducing Gentz to von Humboldt see ibid., 41, note 72. On Gentz's visits to Jewish salons see Paul Sweet, *Wilhelm von Humboldt: A Biography* (Columbus, Oh., 1978), vol. I, 24.

2. For biographical information on Buchholz see Rütger Schäfer, *Friedrich Buchholz — ein vergessener Vorläufer der Soziologie* (Göppingen, 1972), 40. A short entry on Buchholz can be found in the *Neue Deutsche Biographie* (Berlin, 1953), vol. 2, 701–02.

3. On Buchholz's complaints about the rich and prominent see [Saul Ascher], *Kabinet berlinisher Charaktere* (Berlin, 1808), 14.

Friedrich Gentz

As it happened, Gentz and Buchholz were on different sides of the political fence; Buchholz defended Napoleon while Gentz opposed him. But what matters is not the men's political differences, their different backgrounds, or even their different experiences on the job market in Berlin. What matters is that men who shared nothing but their aspirations to official positions and to intellectual prominence chose Berlin as the city in which to realize their dreams. In this chapter we discover who these men were and how they fared when they came to Berlin. Only then can we understand which of them flocked to the Jewish salons, and more importantly, why.

The men whose tales are recounted here chose Berlin as the site for making careers as intellectuals just when intellectual life in Germany was acquiring a new popularity, a new level of accomplishment, and a new chance to effect social mobility. In the same years that Germany's political disunity and its antiquated social structure caused so much despair, literature provided solace. A young Friedrich Engels later summed up the contrast between Germany's social misery and her intellectual glory: literature constituted the one "fantastic exception, a glittering, wonderful appearance . . . . [it] was seen as the country's only hope for improvement. The shameful political and social century was simultaneously the-greatest epoch of German literature."[4] Others who scarcely shared Engels' political passions were equally enthusiastic. The era between Goethe and Hegel witnessed nothing less than an "expansion of forces upon which the German mind has existed ever since."[5] Lessing, Mendelssohn, Schiller, Fichte, Herder, Kant, the Schlegel brothers, and the Humboldt brothers wrote important books which changed European intellectual history. Their books were read by a rapidly growing public whose purchases and subscriptions allowed German intellectuals to refuse degrading positions in courts and in state bureaucracies. Moreover, authors and readers gathered together in reading and discussion societies, where there was space to formulate a public opinion independent of princes, bureaucracies, scientific academies, universities, and greedy publishers. German intellectuals covered vast conceptual ground, leaving behind the rationalist Enlightenment and discovering romanticism. These are the reasons to celebrate the "good old days" of eighteenth-century Germany, that bygone time when Germany was the home of brilliant poets and thinkers.

A glance at the statistics shows how swiftly participation in the life of the mind took hold in Germany during the last decades of the eighteenth century. The number of authors in Germany literally tripled, from just under 3,000 in 1760 to over 10,000 in 1800.[6] Alongside this escalation in the number of authors, the number of books and journals published doubled in the last three decades of the century. The number of bookstores in Germany grew almost fourfold between 1750 and 1801, from 101 to 473.[7] As book-fair catalogues show, books were less often written in Latin and less frequently devoted to theological or scholarly topics. Novels were the new rage. During the decade of the 1790s alone, three hun-

4. The Engels quote first appeared in a letter of Engels to Karl Kautsky, *Marx/Engels Werke* (East Berlin, 1967), vol. 37, 274; it is cited by Jürgen Kuczynski in his *Geschichte des Alltags des Deutschen Volkes 1650–1810* (East Berlin, 1981), vol. 2, 132.

5. Golo Mann, "The German Intellectual," in George B. de Huszar, ed., *The Intellectuals: A Controversial Portrait* (Glencoe, Ill., 1960), 459–70, at 459.

6. These estimates were first published by G. C. Hamburger and G. J. Meusel in their introduction to *Das gelehrte Teutschland* (Lemgo, 1796).

7. On the increase of the number of books and journals published see Johann Goldfriedrich, *Geschichte des Deutschen Buchhandels vom Beginn der Klassischen Literaturperiode bis zum Beginn der Fremdherrschaft (1740–1804)* (Leipzig, 1909; rpt. Aalen, 1970), vol. 3, 280. On the increase in the number of bookstores in Germany see F. M. Meyer, "Der deutsche Buchhandel gegen Ende des 18 und zu Anfang des 19 Jh.," *Archiv für Geschichte des deutschen Buchhandels* n.s. 7 (1882), 199–249, at 205. The seven volumes of the new series *Wolfenbütteler Schriften zur Geschichte des Buchwesens*, Paul Raabe, ed. (Wolfenbüttel, 1977–80), as well as Raabe's *Bücherlust und Lesefreuden: Beiträge zur Geschichte des Buchwesens im 18. und frühen 19. Jahrhundert* (Stuttgart, 1984), came to my attention too late to be included here.

dred novels were published each year in Germany. Altogether, this expansion of the reading public has been heralded as nothing short of a "literary revolution."[8]

This revolution was not just a matter to be measured with statistics, for the status of both intellectual institutions and of publishing intellectuals dramatically increased during the last decades of the eighteenth century. Now, for the first time in German history, men of letters began to have real standing in society. New universities, like the one at Göttingen, attracted noble students, which bestowed new prestige on university professors. Lower on the intelligentsia's occupational hierarchy, university graduates employed as schoolteachers and as preachers began to comport themselves as professionals. Teachers and preachers, like professors, took to regulating the training, recruitment, standards, and salary appropriate to their respective fields.[9] The social composition of the intellectual world also changed radically as parents in the lower and lower middle classes were increasingly able to send their sons up the social ladder. Scholarships to local Latin schools and to universities, as well as stints as tutors or teachers, could support a bright son until he received his "call" to an official or to an academic post.[10]

Yet despite the dramatic rise in the scope and status of intellectual activity, and despite the success some poor boys had in climbing onto the intellectual stage, many ultimately failed in the attempt to change-

8. See Helmut Hiller, *Zur Sozialgeschichte von Buch und Buchhandel* (Bonn, 1966), 94, for research using book-fair catalogues and on the yearly production of novels. See also Goldfriedrich, *Geschichte,* 274, on the jump in publication of novels. Rolf Engelsing suggested that the changes in the size of the reading public and the consequences of its reading habits in this period were significant enough to be called the "literary revolution" of the 1790s: *Der Bürger als Leser: Lesergeschichte in Deutschland 1500–1800* (Stuttgart, 1974), 266. See also Engelsing's *Analphabetentum und Lektüre: Zur Sozialgeschichte des Lesens in Deutschland zwischen feudaler und industrieller Gesellschaft* (Stuttgart, 1973).

9. On the success of Göttingen see Charles McClelland's "The Aristocracy and University Reform in Eighteenth-Century Germany," In Lawrence Stone, ed., *Schooling and Society: Studies in the History of Education* (Baltimore and London, 1976), as well as McClelland's *State, Society, and University in Germany, 1700–1914* (Cambridge, England, 1980). On the new prestige of men of science and letters in society see Levin Schücking, "Shifting of the Sociological Position of the Artist," in George de Huszar, ed., *The Intellectuals: A Controversial Portrait* (Glencoe, Ill., 1960).

10. A good summary of this research is Hans J. Haferkorn, "Zur Entstehung der bürgerlich-literarischen Intelligenz und des Schriftstellers in Deutschland zwischen 1750–1800," in Bernd Lutz, ed., *Deutsches Bürgertum und literarische Intelligenz 1750–1800*, a volume in the annual *Literaturwissenschaft und Sozialwissenschaften* 3 (Stuttgart, 1974), 113–239. For commentary on the "newness" of this upward mobility in the period (and a comparison of it to mobility in the Renaissance era) see Hans Gerth, *Bürgerliche Intelligenz um 1800: Zur Soziologie des deutschen Frühliberalismus* (rpt., Göttingen, 1976), 29–45.

classes by becoming intellectuals. Contemporaries worried about the "specter of an academic proletariat" and were alarmed at the new "addiction to study." Historians have tended to concur with contemporaries, agreeing that there was an "overproduction" of intellectuals in these years.[11] But the number of "overproduced" intellectuals differed from city to city, because each German city offered intellectuals a different set of employment possibilities and thus different chances to change their social position through intellectual work. Just as the social structure of German cities depended on the city's economic functions, so too the composition of each city's intelligentsia depended on that city's distinctive intellectual institutions. Figure 1 shows the distribution of intellectuals in the major German cities in 1806, at a time when trade cities shrank or grew very little, whereas court cities flourished. This new ranking of the major German cities affected the residency patterns of the intelligentsia. For a city to attract a sizable intelligentsia, it had to possess a variety of institutions where intellectuals might earn wages, royalties, or pensions. Trade cities fared poorly in this contest. Although both Frankfurt am Main and Hamburg had important publishing industries, neither city provided a home to many intellectuals. Other cities which, like Frankfurt and Hamburg, had only one intellectual institution—even a very successful one—also failed to attract a large number of intellectuals. Even Göttingen, the home of a prominent university, had only marginally more intellectuals than the two trade cities. Only if a university town had some other source of employment for intellectuals beyond the university did such towns become intellectual metropolises beckoning intellectuals from the provinces. This, at least, is suggested by the case of Leipzig, which for most of the eighteenth century was the

11. The phrases "addiction to study" and "specter of an academic proletariat" appear on p. 18 of the unpublished paper by Anthony La Vopa, "The Language of Profession: Germany in the late Eighteenth Century," presented in April 1980 at the Davis Center at Princeton University. See also La Vopa's *Prussian Schoolteachers: Profession and Office, 1763–1848* (Chapel Hill, 1980). For different analyses of the amount and causes of the "overproduction" of intellectuals see Karl Mannheim, "The Problem of the Intelligentsia: An Inquiry into its Past and Present Role," in his *Essays on the Sociology of Culture* (London, 1956), 91–166; Lenore O'Boyle, "The Problem of an Excess of Educated Men in Western Europe, 1880–1850," *Journal of Modern History* 42 (1970), 471–94, at 477; Henri Brunschwig, *Enlightenment and Romanticism in Eighteenth-Century Prussia* (Chicago, 1974) chap. 9; John Gillis, *Youth and History* (New York, 1974), 67–76, and Hans Gerth, *Bürgerliche Intelligenz*, 49. On the drop in university attendance—which, ironically enough, coincided with the surplus of intellectuals—see Franz Eulenberg, *Die Frequenz der deutschen Universitäten von ihre Gründung bis zur Gegenwart* (Leipzig, 1904). For analysis see Fritz Ringer, *Education and Society in Modern Europe* (Bloomington, 1979), 48–50.

hub of the entire German publishing industry as well as the site of a university.[12]

Berlin was a latecomer to the contest between German cities competing for intellectual glamour. It did not have a university until 1810, and its publishing industry languished until the 1780s. Court partronage was hard to come by. Prussian Junkers tended to live on their country estates, and Prussian kings did not consider high culture an appropriate investment. Frederick William I (1713–40) was an ascetic, military-minded penny-pincher, and even his son Frederick the Great, who was willing to spend millions of taler on architecture, art, and music, had nothing but disdain for any intellectual who wrote in German. Of course, the Prussian state did sponsor a few institutions that employed intellectuals. The logic of the court as the premier symbolic institution in the state necessitated funding some intellectual creation, to add luster and polish to the state's image. Some intellectual exchanges were elaborate public performances, designed as entertainment for courtly society. Even Prussian

Figure 1. Number of Intellectuals per German City in 1806

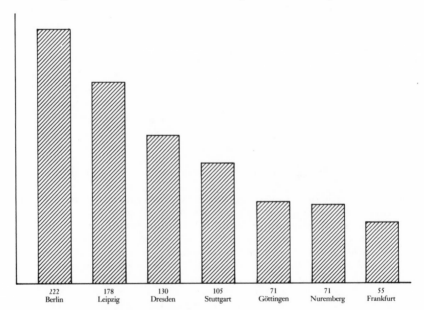

| 222 | 178 | 130 | 105 | 71 | 71 | 55 |
| Berlin | Leipzig | Dresden | Stuttgart | Göttingen | Nuremberg | Frankfurt |

Source: Franklin Kopitzsch, ed., *Aufklärung, Absolutismus und Bürgertum in Deutschland* (Munich, 1976), 61.

12. On Leipzig as an intellectual center see W. H. Bruford's *Theatre and Drama in Goethe's Germany* (London, 1950), 85.

kings believed that some intellectual glory was necessary to build a dynamic state.

Remarkably, despite the comparative modesty of courtly patronage, the slow growth of the publishing industry, and the lack of a university, by 1806 Berlin had the highest number of intellectuals of any German city. To discover which institutions employed Berlin's intellectuals, and how much social mobility this employment made possible, is the double task of this chapter. Did the city's intelligentsia suffer from an institutional vacuum which salons were uniquely equipped to fill? Did Berlin's intellectuals share a set of social needs resulting from their common mobility patterns, needs which salons were uniquely able to meet?

Upward Mobility

Answering these questions is possible only because Berlin's intellectuals left behind documents that allow us to reconstruct their career patterns. The very existence of these sources is revelatory about the conditions under which they labored. Because Germany lacked an intellectual capital city and because the institutions where intellectuals worked were so diverse, German intellectuals needed books to identify their unknown counterparts in distant cities. Biographical dictionaries were thus badly needed, and they were a popular item in eighteenth-century Germany. Guides to court personnel proliferated too, because courtiers, like intellectuals, were geographically dispersed but intensely status-conscious.[13] Biographical dictionaries of intellectuals existed to suit every taste. Some were long, multivolume productions like Hamberger and Meusel's *Das gelehrte Teutschland*; others were more selective, gossipy versions, whose authors insulted enough of their colleagues to prefer anonymity. Some guides emphasized academically affiliated intellectuals; one volume compiled by the French priest Abbé Denina concentrated on courtly intellectuals and was, appropriately, written in French.[14] Biographies, memoirs,

13. See, for example, the *Address-Kalender der königlichen Preussischen Haupt- und Residenzstadt Berlin* (Berlin, 1787) or the *Handbuch über den königlich Preussischen Hof und Staat auf das Jahr 1794* (Berlin, n.d.).

14. Abbé Denina, *La Prusse Littéraire sous Frederic II*, 3 vols. (Berlin, 1790); Friedrich Nicolai, *Beschreibung der königlichen Residenzstädte Berlin und Potsdam und aller daselbst befindlicher Merkwürdigkeiten* (Berlin), 1779); Julius Friedrich Krüppeln, C. Chr. Nentke, und Chr. Paalzow, *Büsten berlinscher Gelehrten und Künstler mit Devisen* (Leipzig, 1787). [Saul Ascher], *Kabinet berlinischer Charaktere*, gives short sketches of nineteen intellectuals; see also Friedrich Buchholz and August Ludwig Massenback, *Gallerie preussischer Charaktere* (Berlin, 1808). Two additional contemporary guides are Johann Michael Sigfried Lowe, *Bildnisse jetztlebender Berliner Gelehrten, mit Ihren Selbstbiographien* (Berlin, 1806); and also Valentin H. Schmidt and D. G. G. Mehring, *Neuestes gelehrtes Berlin* (Berlin, 1795; rpt.

letters, and literary histories have been canvassed for additional information about the intellectuals.

These sources have yielded up the names of 386 male authors who lived in Berlin for at least two years between 1780 and 1806, the quarter-century when salons flourished. In order to tailor the conceptual vocabulary to the sources, published authors are equated with intellectuals here; the term *intelligentsia* is used as the collective noun.[15] These 386 male intellectuals are not a sample of a larger group, a sample which might be a biased subsection of some larger population not investigated. To the contrary, there are good reasons to believe that these 386 are very close to being the total population of published male authors who passed through Berlin in these years.[16] To be sure, the threat of bias does come into play in another respect. Their fathers' occupations, for example, are obviously crucial for measuring the intellectuals' mobility, but those

Leipzig, 1973).

More recent guides include Elisabeth Friedrichs, *Literarische Lokalgrössen 1700 bis 1900* (Stuttgart, 1967); *Biographisches Wörterbuch zur deutschen Geschichte,* 3 vols. (Munich, 1952); Wilhelm Kosch, *Deutsches Literatur-Lexikon* (Bern, 1958). A useful volume for tracking down the social origins and educational experience of a number of intellectuals was Johann Schultze, *Adel und Bürgertum in den Deutschen Zeitschriften der lezten drei Jahrzehnte des 18. Jahrhundert, 1773–1806* (Berlin, 1925). Also useful, in spite of its Nazi perspective on the salons, was Kurt Fervers, *Berliner Salons: Die Geschichte einer grossen Verschwörung* (Munich, 1940). A recent microfilm edition of 254 biographical dictionaries covering the eighteenth and nineteenth centuries has recently been published: Bernhard Fabian, ed., *Deutsches Biographisches Archiv* (Munich, 1982–84).

15. There is an enormous range of definitions of *intellectual* and *intelligentsia*. For a lament about the conceptual disorder in the field see J. P. Nettl, "Ideas, Intelectuals, and Structures of Dissent," in Philip Rieff, ed., *On Intellectuals: Theoretical Studies, Case Studies* (Garden City, N.Y., 1969), 53. Definitions which focus on the nature of the person's employment include those used by Seymour Martin Lipset and Ralf Dahrendorf: S. M. Lipset, *Political Man* (New York, 1960), 311; Dahrendorf, *Society and Democracy in Germany* (New York, 1979), 267. L. G. Churchward also focuses his definition on employment and education but uses the term *intelligentsia* in his *The Soviet Intelligentsia* (London, 1973). A second kind of definition focuses on the particular kinds of ideas and attitudes held by intellectuals (or by the intelligentsia). See Norman Birnbaum, *Toward a Critical Sociology* (New York, 1971), 426, and Thomas Molnar, *The Decline of the Intellectual* (New York, 1961), 9. Most who use this second definition use the term *intelligentsia*: see Alexander Gella, ed., *The Intellectuals and the Intelligentsia: Theory, Method, and Case Study* (London and Beverly Hills, 1976), 9–34, and J. P. Nettl, "Ideas," 78. A critique of the latter definition can be found in the book by George Konrad and Ivan Szelenyi, *The Intellectuals on the Road to Class Power* (New York and London, 1979), 24ff.

16. By comparing the number of intellectuals I have found (386) with the number listed for Berlin in figure 1 (222), I confirm Franklin Kopitzsch's complaint (in his introduction to *Aufklärung, Absolutismus, und Bügertum in Deutschland* [Munich, 1976], 61) that Hamberger and Meusel's volumes did not include all of the publishing intellectuals because of a focus on the academic intelligentsia.

whose fathers' positions are known now tended to be the intellectuals who were famous then, since it is their stories that were deemed worthy of preservation in the biographical dictionaries. As a result, generalizations must often be limited to the not necessarily representative subgroup for which the relevant information is known.

The identification and sorting of occupations has also been somewhat problematic. Precisely because intellectual work was often part-time work, a string of posts was often listed for each author. In such cases, the position held closest to the year 1800 was selected. Rough wage rates obtained from other sources were used to place the main occupation held by the intellectuals and some of their fathers into either a lower-, a middle-, or an upper-income group.[17] (It is not assumed that these income groups bear any necessary relationship to classes. Deciding what criteria determined membership in various classes in these years is a task well beyond the aims of this book.) The intellectuals' estates of birth were easier to sort out. Those with a *von* before their last name at birth were of course tagged as noble. Jews were also usually recognizable from their names, or were identified as such in the source. Everyone else was called a commoner. Neither ennoblements nor conversions were allowed to change the intellectual's estate designation, as doing so would obscure the entire point of the exercise. The goal here is to hold steady their position on the caste system of stratification, while measuring how their becoming intellectuals affected their position on the more flexible income hierarchy.

First, a look at how Berlin's intelligentsia differed from Berlin society as a whole. It comes as no surprise to learn that they were a more privileged group than Berliners at large. The question is, how much and in what ways more privileged? As figure 2 shows, the intelligentsia included about eight times as many nobles as the city at large. Fifteen percent of the intelligentsia, but no more than 2 percent of the city population was noble. The Jewish community was an equally tiny group in the city. But unlike noble men, Jewish men barely held their own in the intelligentsia, as a mere 3 percent of all intellectuals. In its income stratification as well as its estate composition, the intelligentsia was also more privileged than were Berliners at large. To make this comparison, the intellectuals' paying jobs have been sorted on the same income hierarchy used throughout the book. Anyone employed in a position that usually paid over 600 taler yearly is in the upper income bracket; anyone with a position which

17. The employment of 122 of the 386 fathers (32 percent) has been identified. Of these, 43 percent had upper-income positions, 55 percent had middle-income posts, and 3 percent lower-income positions.

usually paid between 150 and 600 taler is in the middle income bracket; jobs paying below 150 taler are in the lower bracket. The most common upper occupations among the intellectuals were officials and professors; the most common middle occupations were preachers, teachers, and writers; the main lower occupations were tutors and students.

As figure 2 shows, half of the intellectuals were employed in upper-income positions, over a third of them held middle-income posts, and a mere 5 percent worked in lower-income jobs. We lack a precise break-down of Berlin's social structure in these years, but such estimates do exist for other central European cities.[18] In comparable cities, the upper-income strata was at most a tenth of the population, the middle-income strata included a third to two-fifths of the population, and as much as half of the city's residents were in the lower-income strata. Using these estimates for comparison, Berlin's intelligentsia had five times as many upper-income persons, slightly more middle-income persons, and many, many fewer lower-income persons than did the population of eigh-teenth-century German cities comparable to Berlin. Thus although many of Berlin's intellectuals were undoubtedly dissatisfied with their lot, the intelligentsia as a whole was a relatively privileged group.

Both Jewish and commoner intellectuals tended to have about the same occupational composition as did the intelligentsia as a whole. As shown in figure 3, only half of the Jewish or commoner intellectuals held upper-income occupations, and under 10 percent of both Jewish and commoner intellectuals held lower-income posts. This left roughly two-fifths of both Jewish and commoner intellectuals with middle-income positions. In other words, among the vast majority of commoner intel-lectuals, religion had little effect on the intellectual's social position. Al-most nine out of every ten noble intellectuals, in contrast, had upper-income occupations.

18. These estimated social strata divisions for a variety of other German cities can be found in the introduction to Köpitzsch's *Aufklärung, Absolutismus, und Bürgertum in Deutschland*, 31–32.

In order to sort the Berlin intellectuals' occupations into income strata, I have used 600 taler a year to divide the upper from the middle strata, and 150 taler a year to divide the middle from the lower strata. The professor Christoph Meiners claimed that one could not live "Standesgemäss" ("in accordance with one's rank") with less than 600 taler a year. His complaint is cited in Goldfriedrich, *Geschichte*, 94. Other information about wage levels was found in Bruford, *Germany in the Eighteenth Century*, 331; Gerth, *Bürgerliche Intelligenz*, and Bruschwig, *Enlightenment and Romanticism*, 28 and 29. According to the average wage rates for the intellectuals' occupations, upper-strata occupations included high officials and professors; middle-strata occupations included preachers, teachers, clerks, lower-level offi-cials, publishers, booksellers, journalists, and freelance writers; and lower-strata occupa-tions included tutors and students.

Figure 2. Estate and Income Distribution of Berlin and Berlin's Male Intelligentsia in 1800

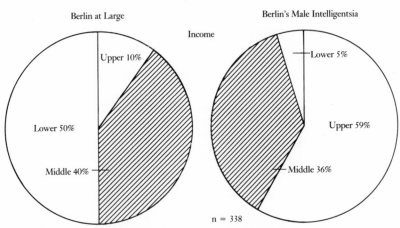

Sources: Franklin Kopitzsch, ed., *Aufklärung, Absolutismus, und Bürgertum in Deutschland* (Munich, 1976), 31–33; collective biography.

The bottom of the intelligentsia's income pyramid was thus tiny; to some degree, this conclusion is an artifact of the crude classificatory system used here. Due to the lack of individual wage rates, all preachers, teachers, clerks, and writers were assigned to the middle-income group. Yet some of the intellectuals employed in these occupations surely earned less than 150 taler yearly, and thus had the bad luck to be in the lower-income group. Still, despite the possibility that some authentically lower-income intellectuals were systematically misclassified in the middle-

Figure 3. Income Distribution among Noble, Commoner, and Jewish
Intellectuals in Berlin

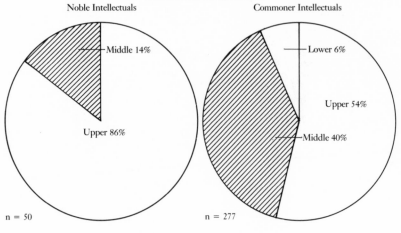

Noble Intellectuals

Middle 14%

Upper 86%

n = 50

Commoner Intellectuals

Lower 6%

Upper 54%

Middle 40%

n = 277

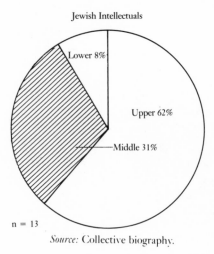

Jewish Intellectuals

Lower 8%

Upper 62%

Middle 31%

n = 13

Source: Collective biography.

income group, the true proportion of lower-income intellectuals is
unlikely to have been higher than 15 percent of the intelligentsia. If the
intellectual "proletariat" is to be equated with intellectuals who held
lower-income posts, such proletarians were not a major presence among
Berlin's intellectuals in these years.

What is fascinating is the contrast between those intellectuals at the
summit of the estate hierarchy and those intellectuals at the summit of
the income hierarchy. As in Berlin society at large, for intellectuals the

income pyramid was far less steep than was the estate pyramid. Only 15 percent of the intelligentsia was noble, but almost two-fifths had upper-income occupations. We can surmise that the 149 intellectuals with upper-income posts but no noble title had at least a mild case of status inconsistency. As officials and professors, they had achieved much and were sometimes paid accordingly. But without the noble *von*, many doors would still be closed to them. The status inconsistency caused by envy of those above was not the only conflict many intellectuals suffered. Those intellectuals who did manage to settle in Berlin and move up the income hierarchy had to live with the stress of separating from family and friends left geographically and socially behind. A comparison of the intellectuals' jobs and those held by their fathers shows that more than half of the intellectuals in the upper-income group had come up from-below. Over half of the intellectuals themselves had upper-income jobs, whereas only two-fifths of their fathers had such well-paying employment. The real amount of upward mobility among the intellectuals was undoubtedly even greater than this. This case study understates the real amount of upward mobility because the sample of fathers whose occupations are known (one-third of all fathers) is biased in favor of the socially prominent. The more obscure intellectuals and their obscure fathers are underrepresented, and it is precisely they who may well have moved up in the world. But even the mobility that has been documented is significant. To see how this upward mobility came to pass, the time has come to turn away from abstract classifications of the Berlin intellectuals and look concretely at their actual jobs.

Employment

Just under a third of Berlin's 386 intellectuals worked in the city's intellectual institutions. This in itself was quite new. It had long been possible for German intellectuals to support themselves with positions as state officials or, with less prestige, as preachers, clerks, or merchants. Intellectuals may have needed university training and intellectual skills to obtain and keep these non-intellectual posts, but they were not paid to create or to distribute knowledge. It was only as the general standard of living, exposure to education, and the size of the reading public all increased that a significant number of jobs that paid for intellectual labor per se came to exist in preindustrial European cities. The Berlin intellectuals experienced the first blossoming of employment-providing intellectual institutions during their own lifetimes. The attractiveness of this kind of work depended, of course, on where on the social hierarchy the intellectual was born. Posts at most intellectual institutions certainly rarely offered much in terms of income. Teachers, tutors, freelance writers, and booksellers only very infrequently earned more than six hundred taler a year. Professors, the highest-paid employees in an intellectual institution, earned only little more than this. Nor did employment at this level offer much of a chance to mingle with noble intellectuals. As figure 4 shows, very, very few noble intellectuals found employment in intellectual institutions. Because most of the intellectual institutions were new, it might be thought that they would be more open to marginal intellectuals. But this was by no means the case, at least for Jewish intellectuals. Only three Jewish intellectuals worked at intellectual jobs.

Professors had the only intellectual post which was at all attractive in terms of prestige and pay. As shown in figure 5, it was also the occupation

Figure 4. Estate of Birth of Berlin Intellectuals by Employment

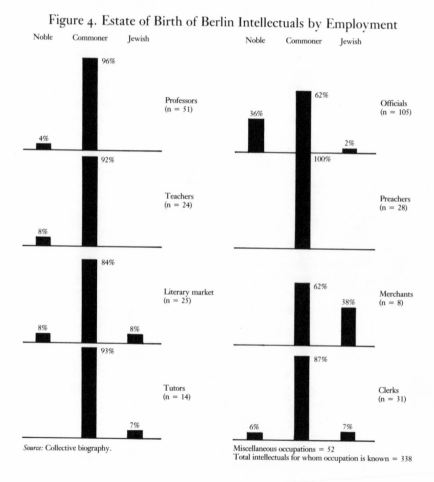

Source: Collective biography.

Miscellaneous occupations = 52
Total intellectuals for whom occupation is known = 338

which had the highest rate of arriviste intellectuals, those who had moved up out of the income group into which they were born. Almost two-thirds of the professors (whose fathers' occupations are known) had fathers with middle-income or even lower-income posts. There were fifty-two professors in Berlin, accounting for almost half of those employed in any of the city's intellectual institutions. It is logical to wonder: how could Berlin have had so many professors if it had no university? In part, the large number of professors among Berlin's intelligentsia was due to the fact that German intellectuals were a migratory breed. Professors at universities outside Berlin visited Berlin for long stretches during these twenty-six years, and so they appear in the collective biography. More importantly, the title "professor" was not synonymous with the institution "university." Professors could be affiliated with either of the two Royal Academies, or teach at a knightly academy or gymnasium. Or, as in the case of Marcus Herz, intellectuals could be awarded the title "professor" by the crown because they offered private lecture series in their own homes. The number and variety of such lecture series was impressive; twenty-one of them were offered during 1786 alone. A. W. Schlegel lectured on aesthetics in 1804; Johann Fichte delivered his famous lectures where he articulated a proud Prussian patriotism in the winter of 1806. Some lectures were graced by members of the royal family as well as by cultivated gentile ladies and Jewish men. Some lecture series sold entrance by subscription and some by single ticket. When the audience became too large, the lectures were moved into larger private homes or even sometimes to the lecture hall of the Royal Academy of Science.[19]

By voting to invite an intellectual to become a member of the Royal Academy of Science, this powerful institution could confer huge amounts of intellectual and social prestige on the lucky man. Precisely because academicians possessed so much glamour, and because the monarchy had ultimate control over its doings, Royal Academy appointments and policies tended to be a hotbed of scandal and intrigue. Until 1786, the academicians were often imported from France, and publications were also in French. Frederick the Great, after all, never mastered the German language himself, nor was he ever convinced that German was an adequate language for literature or scholarship. Take the case of Moses Mendelssohn, who won the essay contest in 1763, the same year

19. The estimate of twenty-one lectures can be found in H. P. Rickman, ed., *W. Dilthey: Selected Writings* (Cambridge, England, 1976), 71. (The volume is a selection from Dilthey's biography of Friedrich Schleiermacher.) The enormous variety of lecture topics and arrangements for lecture series can be learned from a survey of the ads in the *Vössische Zeitung* in these years.

Figure 5. Proportion of Nobles and Upwardly Mobile Men among Berlin Intellectuals by Occupation

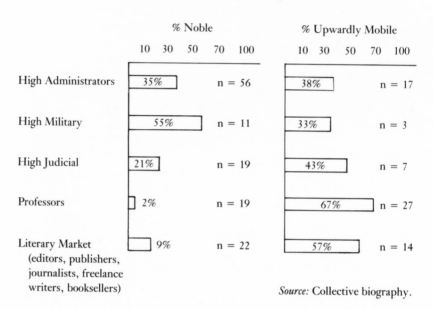

	% Noble		% Upwardly Mobile	
	10 30 50 70 100		10 30 50 70 100	
High Administrators	35%	n = 56	38%	n = 17
High Military	55%	n = 11	33%	n = 3
High Judicial	21%	n = 19	43%	n = 7
Professors	2%	n = 19	67%	n = 27
Literary Market (editors, publishers, journalists, freelance writers, booksellers)	9%	n = 22	57%	n = 14

Source: Collective biography.

that Immanuel Kant's submission came in second. If King Frederick shunned gentile German intellectuals, of course he shunned Jewish German intellectuals. He therefore vetoed Mendelssohn's election as a member of the Royal Academy, although Mendelssohn had received a unanimous vote of admission from the membership on two separate occasions. Appeals to King Frederick by prominent intellectuals were to no avail. Mendelssohn had to content himself with a subsequent invitation to visit the king at his castle in Potsdam. Daniel Chodowiecki's contemporary portrait of Mendelssohn presenting his letter of invitation to the giant-sized guards en route to his audience with the king is a poignant tribute to the ambiguity of Mendelssohn's position.[20] The enor-

20. On the Royal Academy of Science see A. Harnack, *Geschichte der Berliner Akademie der Wissenschaft* (Berlin, 1900). See also Kurt Miller, "Zur Enstehung und Wirkung des Wissenschaftlichen Akademien und Gelehrten Gesellschaften des 17. Jahrhundert," in Helmuth Rössler and Gunther Franz, eds. *Universität und Gelehrtenstand 1400–1800,* Büdinger Vorträge 1966 (Limburg/Lahn, 1970), 127–44. On the king's rejection of Mendelssohn as an Academy member see Alexander Altmann, *Moses Mendelssohn* (University, Alabama, 1973), 264–65.

Moses Mendelssohns Examen am Berliner Thor zu Potsdam

mous prestige of the Royal Academy of Science and its success in sponsoring important research in the natural sciences were two reasons why prominent intellectuals in this era questioned whether it was wise to reinvigorate the moribund Prussian universities. Another kind of institutional competitor to the university were such autonomous institutes for professional education as the Collegium Medico-Chirurgicum, the leading medical school in Germany, whose students and professors had access to a variety of modern facilities not found at any contemporary universities.[21]

Berlin professors also sold their intellectual labor power to the knightly academies and to the gymnasia. The knightly academies were a fleeting genre of educational institution. The two Berlin knightly academies were founded in 1765 and in 1791.[22] As the agricultural crisis deepened, young Prussian nobles increasingly needed a systematic education to prepare for the steep competition for official posts. Neither the content of the education nor the class of student at the public secondary schools was deemed appropriate by noble parents. The knightly academies, in contrast, offered their young charges the horsemanship, duels, and exclusive social life which would polish the young Junkers' rough edges and prepare them for life in high society. The knightly academies actually offered a rather serious intellectual fare in addition to training in the social graces. These schools pioneered in teaching modern languages, rhetoric, and history, subjects that could not be learned at most universities, which were still bound to a medieval curriculum. The eventual decline of the knightly academies in the early nineteenth century was in part due to their inability to hold onto their monopoly in modern disciplines. With Göttingen leading the way, German universities increasingly incorporated these new disciplines into their own curriculum. That innovation, and the pressure on young nobles to obtain university training as preparation for posts as high officials, both eventually drained the knightly academies of their young noble clientele.

The fact that some gymnasium instructors were given the title professor is itself good evidence for the high rank these schools had in the hierarchy of intellectual institutions during the eighteenth century. Some gymnasia were considered to be more rigorous than some universities, and a clear-cut boundary between the two kinds of institutions only emerged later, during the first decades of the nineteenth century.[23] By that time university reformers, led by Wilhelm von Humboldt, won fa-

21. See Frederic Lilge, *The Abuse of Learning: The Failure of the German University* (New York, 1948), 4.

22. A contemporary description of Berlin's knightly academies can be found in Friedrich Nicolai, *Beschreibung der königlichen Residenzstädte Berlin und Königsberg* (Berlin, 1786, rpt. 1980), 721–27.

23. On the gymnasium in eighteenth-century Germany see Karl-Ernst Jeismann, *Das preussische Gymnasiums als Schule um der Gebildeten 1787–1817*, (Stuttgart, 1974); Paul Barth, *Geschichte der Erziehung in soziologischer und geistesgeschichtlicher Bedeutung* (Leipzig, 1916); Helmut König, *Zur Geschichte der Nationalerziehung in Deutschland im letzten Drittel des 18. Jahrhundert* (East Berlin, 1960); Lenore O'Boyle, "Klassische Bildung und soziale Struktur in Deutschland 1800–1848," *Historische Zeitschrift* 207 (1968); 548–608, and Wolfgang Zorn, "Hochschule und höhere Schule in der deutschen Sozialgeschichte der Neuzeit," *Spiegel der*

vor for the view that gymnasia should be solely devoted to teaching younger boys. According to the reformers' view, modern universities should synthesize the emphasis on research offered by the Royal Academy of Science and in the professional institutes with exposure to the modern curriculum originally offered by the knightly academies. By the early nineteenth century, the reformers had triumphed, as innovative research became the defining activity of university professors. Publications thus became ever more important in the recruitment, appointments, wages, and promotion of university professors in Prussia.[24] As knightly academies disappeared and gymnasia sank to the secondary-school level, publishing became more crucial in landing a post as university professor. Prussian professors logically began to covet university appointments as the just reward for research and publication. It was their research which won the professors the right to sell their labor power lecturing students, whose direct fees to the professor were a crucial part of his income. University professorships offered another advantage: the status of noble students, who increasingly went to university, adorned their less well-born instructors.

Not all intellectuals who sold their labor power teaching were as lucky as the professors. Take, for example, the twenty-four intellectuals employed as schoolteachers. Schoolteaching at the primary or secondary level was an ancient and unpopular occupation, as it lacked both intellectual challenge and financial advantage. Since schoolteachers were usually too obscure to appear in the biographical dictionaries, their fathers' jobs, and thus their own mobility patterns, are difficult to trace. It is clear, though, as illustrated in figure 6, that schoolteachers did not tend to be any younger than the average intellectual. Teaching was therefore unlikely to have been a stepping-stone position for many Berlin intellectuals trying to move on to something better.

Tutors were usually in a much better situation than were the schoolteachers, although they may have had less money to live on. For since, as figure 7 shows, they were so young—two-thirds of the tutors were

---

Geschichte: Festgabe für Max Braubach (Münster, 1964), 320–27. Margret Kraul's *Das deutsche Gymnasium, 1780–1980* (Frankfurt a.M., 1984) came to my attention too late to be used here.

24. See R. Steven Turner, "University Reformers and Professional Scholarship in Germany, 1760–1806," in Stone, ed., *The University in Society*, vol. 2, 495–531. On von Humboldt's contribution see Sweet, *Wilhelm von Humboldt*, vol. 2, chap. 8. For a contemporary view of the issues see A. Stölzel, "Die Berliner Mittwochsgesellschaft über Aufhebung oder Reform der Universitäten (1795)," *Forschungen zur brandenburgischen und preussischen Geschichte* 2 (1889). On the founding of the university in Berlin see M. Lenz, *Geschichte der königlichen Friederich-Wilhelm-Universität* (Berlin, 1910).

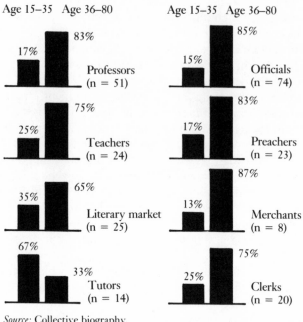

Figure 6. Age of Berlin Intellectuals by Employment

Age 15–35 Age 36–80

83% Professors (n = 51)
17%

75% Teachers (n = 24)
25%

65% Literary market (n = 25)
35%

67% Tutors (n = 14)
33%

Age 15–35 Age 36–80

85% Officials (n = 74)
15%

83% Preachers (n = 23)
17%

87% Merchants (n = 8)
13%

75% Clerks (n = 20)
25%

Source: Collective biography.

under thirty in 1800—their poverty, unlike that of the teachers, might well have been merely temporary. The tutoring profession, like knightly academies, was a transient intellectual institution characteristic of the eighteenth century. Noble or wealthy commoner parents hired tutors so that their children would not have to mix with those enrolled in the public primary or secondary schools. Some day tutors also sold lessons on an hourly basis to male students preparing for gymnasium, or to adolescent and young married women in search of cultivation. The luckier tutors lived in the homes of their employers, supervising the education of the sons, and sometimes that of the daughters too. Unfortunately, the wages of these live-in tutors over and above room and board were usually only slightly higher than those received by domestic servants. Tutors themselves frequently complained that they were treated with scarcely more respect than were the servants.[25]

25. On tutors see G. Stephen, *Die häusliche Erziehung in Deutschland während des 18. Jahrhundert* (Wiesbaden, 1891), and Franz Neuman, *Der Hofmeister: Ein Beitrag zur Geschichte der Erziehung im 18. Jahrhundert* (Halle, 1930). Some discussion on the conditions of tutor employment can also be found in W. Roessler, *Die Enstehung des modernen Erziehungswesens in Deutschland* (Stuttgart, 1961).

Yet for some tutors, this post was a pivotal, transforming appointment. Specific tutoring posts dramatically altered the fortunes of some Berlin intellectuals. Tutors are crucial in our story, because they were indispensable in the emergence of salon society in Berlin. Tutors could help salon society coalesce precisely because they themselves participated in a delicate set of social and intellectual exchanges with their young charges and their parents. On the one hand, tutors had practical favors to gain if they made a favorable impression on the head of the household. If pleased, he might one day provide recommendations for desirable appointments as preachers, professors, or officials. Since tutors hired by prominent families often also helped to manage the family's business affairs, the tutor could come to know and impress his employer's colleagues and friends directly. The lady of the house could teach him the social graces, so that he could himself later succeed in charming a woman more educated and refined than his mother was likely to have been. He was under no condition to allow himself to fall in love with his employer's wife or his daughters. Some tutors did so, of course, and the consequences were unpredictable, as we shall see later.

The tutor's dilemma was to preserve his self-respect without losing the desired patronage and the chance to be resocialized in the bosom of a prominent family. He was not, of course, allowed into their home as a favor; he was allowed to live there because he sold a service, namely his ability to distribute his own educational capital. But because tutors were generally born into a lower estate and a lower-income stratum than their employers, they had other services to offer. Tutors could introduce their young noble students to commoner intellectual celebrities by bringing their charges to local gatherings of the intelligentsia, where the young noble's mind could be opened to the fresh ideas of the moment. Noble parents, especially noble mothers, often hungered for these connections for themselves too. The heritage of noble alienation from urban life and public education meant that if nobles wanted intellectual excitement, they might have to go slumming to get it. In sum, approriate tutors managed the noble family's entrance into déclassé social territory.[26]

Many of the professors, schoolteachers, and tutors depended on their publishing income to supplement their salaries. But, as figure 8 shows, only twenty-four intellectuals, a mere 7 percent of Berlin's intelligentsia, depended exclusively for their income on the literary market as freelance writers, journalists, editors, publishers, or booksellers. These were the

26. For a description of the life of a very successful tutor in this era see the biography of the Humboldt brothers' tutor: Friederick and Paul Goldschmidt, *Das Leben des Staatsrath Kunth* (Berlin, 1888).

Figure 7. The Berlin Intelligentsia by Occupation

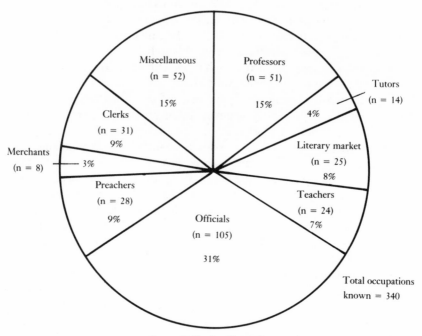

Miscellaneous
(n = 52)

15%

Professors
(n = 51)

15%

Tutors
(n = 14)

4%

Clerks
(n = 31)

9%

Merchants
(n = 8)

3%

Literary market
(n = 25)

8%

Preachers
(n = 28)

9%

Teachers
(n = 24)

7%

Officials
(n = 105)

31%

Total occupations
known = 340

Source: Collective biography.

only intellectuals whose livelihood was directly dependent on an imper-
sonal market system. They thus earned their income in a fashion completely new to the history of intellectual work. German intellectuals had
long been bitter about how difficult it was to live solely from writing.
But the existence of even a small cadre of freelancers shows that the feat
of surviving in this tenuous occupation now became possible for the first
time. It may have become possible, but it was still difficult. Full-time
writers often had to take on translating and editing work to support their
families; wives and older children were put to work as copyists. So har-
ried were the lives of the literary-market intellectuals that it comes as no
surprise to discover that their social origins were not very glamorous. As
shown in figure 5, almost two-thirds of those who worked in the literary
market were born to lower-income fathers. To be sure, this may have not
been their final resting place on the occupational ladder. Figure 6 shows
them to have been the second-youngest occupational group within the
intelligentsia. Thus a good many of the literary-market intellectuals may
have eventually climbed up to become arriviste professors or officials.

The dead writers, journalists, and editors would be angry indeed could they hear us discussing their fate on the same pages alongside the publishers and booksellers who sold their manuscripts to the public. For the authors whose labor was needed to produce books, journals, and newspapers violently disagreed with the publishers about how profits should be divided between them. Beginning in the 1770s, German writers began to complain that the publishers' and the booksellers' profits were too high, that booksellers were earning 30 to 40 percent in profit, while other merchants were satisfied with 10 percent. In their eagerness to avoid dependence on literary middlemen altogether, several prominent authors laid plans for self-publication projects and "scholars' institutes." Unfortunately but not unpredictably, lack of capital doomed the projects to eventual failure.[27]

In the far less specialized eighteenth century, the publisher and the bookseller were often one and the same person. They could well respond to the angry writers that their rate of profit was a just reward in a highly speculative industry. From the publisher's point of view, the price of paper and the honorariums paid per page were both rising at astronomical rates. The rising honorariums were obviously in the interests of the writers; it was the rise in the amount paid per page which allowed even a small group of poor authors to live solely from their publishing income. These increased costs led to ever higher prices for books. And, because of its political fragmentation, Germany, unlike England or France, had no copyright laws. As a result, illegal reprinting was widespread during the last decades of the century. Since the profit on reprinting was as high as 300 percent, this practice deprived both the author and the legal publisher of a good deal of money.[28]

The plight of the writers only adds to the impression that few of the prestigious intellectuals would have wanted to live from selling their services as professors, teachers, or tutors, or from selling their writing to the reading public. To be sure, some professors earned enough to be classified in the upper-income strata. Depending on where they taught, professors, like tutors, might have had occasion to mix socially with their

27. See Goldfriedrich, *Geschichte*, 153. For background on freelance writers in Germany in this era I have used Dieter Baumer, *Die Entstehung des deutschen Journalismus* (Munich, 1928), and Margot Lindeman, *Deutsche Presse bis 1815: Geschichte der deutschen Presse* (Berlin, 1969); for Europe as a whole, Robert Darnton, Bernard Fabian, Roy McKeen Wiles, and Paul Korshin, eds., *The Widening Circle: Essays on the Circulation of Literature in Eighteenth-Century Europe* (Philadelphia, 1976). A large reprint series which includes many contemporary titles relevant to the writing career in the era is Reinhard Wittman, ed., *Quellen zur Geschichte des Buchwesens*, 44 vols. (Munich, 1980–81).

28. Goldfriedrich, *Geschichte*, 154.

noble pupils and their parents. But in general, employment in an intellectual institution could be considered a long-term achievement of upward mobility only if one had been born into a lower- or middle-income family. Even the teachers and writers, who tended to be older than the tutors but still younger than the average intellectual, probably dreamed of getting something better. And in Berlin, where professorships were limited because there was no university, that better position was generally not to be found in any intellectual institution. It was not just a matter of avoiding jobs in which one taught or wrote for pay. There were also onerous jobs outside of the intellectual institutions which no intellectual dreamed of having. For instance, few intellectuals moved up the occupational hierarchy by becoming clerks or preachers. As figure 5 shows, the thirty-one clerks and the twenty-eight preachers tended to have the same lowly social origins as the professors, teachers, tutors, and writers. It is possible that the clerks were only temporarily trapped in the class of their fathers, since figure 6 shows them to have been somewhat younger than the average intellectual. The preachers, on the other hand, were one of the oldest groups among the intelligentsia. They were probably stuck with their lot in life, which was not an easy one. Nor would an intellectual in search of a well-paying and prestigious post dream of becoming a merchant. Not that merchants could not make a lot of money in eighteenth-century Berlin. But the commercial spirit was not much valued among German intellectuals. Since nobles stayed away from business for legal and customary reasons, if one yearned for the status enhancement and patronage to be gained by having noble colleagues, commerce was not a desirable occupation. Merchants in Berlin do not seem to have published very often; there were only eight merchants among the 386 intellectuals. The Jewish intellectuals—all thirteen of them—were well represented among the merchants, but this was not their only occupation. Some were tutors, others teachers, a few were writers; some converted Jewish intellectuals became officials.

Officialdom of one sort or another was the pot of gold craved by many, including many of Berlin's intellectuals; military office, diplomacy, and the administrative and judicial civil service were all occupations that offered both high salaries and privileged access to noble colleagues. As the bureaucracy gained more power over state policy, getting the "call" to fill one of these posts was a chance both to work for political progress and to earn enough to properly represent an exalted standing by appropriate consumption.[29] A third of the Berlin intelligentsia was employed directly

---

29. See Hubert C. Johnson, *Frederick the Great and His Officials* (New Haven and London, 1975), Werner Sombart, *Luxury and Capitalism* (New York, 1938), John Gillis, *The*

by the state as one of the four kinds of officials, making this the single most frequent occupation among the intellectuals. The chief glamour of officialdom may well have been the density of noble intellectuals working as one or another kind of official. Over half of the twelve military officer intellectuals were noble, just over half of the thirteen diplomat intellectuals were of noble birth, and over a third of the seventeen administrative bureaucrats were noble. But these numbers also show that there was room for commoners in some sections of officialdom, and not just for privileged commoners. The proportion of fathers' occupations known is not large enough to be more than suggestive. But, as figure 5 shows, a third of the officials were born into the lower or middle strata—a rate of upward mobility topped only by the professors. No wonder so many dreamed of arriving here: officialdom was at once the most prestigious occupation of Berlin intellectuals and one which allowed in a high proportion of arrivistes. Not everyone who wanted to could become an official, but enough upstarts succeeded to fuel the dreams of the others.

These numbers reconstructing the mobility of Berlin's 386 intellectuals provide an answer to the anomaly with which this chapter began. How could Berlin be home to more intellectuals than any other German city in the salon era, although it had meager courtly patronage, no university, and its publishing industry had gotten off to a slow start? The answer is that large intellectual institutions were not necessary in this era if both a bureaucracy and transitional intellectual institutions were on hand. Only a third of the intelligentsia worked in intellectual institutions of any kind. The old German tradition of doing one's creative intellectual work off the job thus continued to be important. Since half of these intellectuals who labored outside of the intellectual institutions were high officials of one kind or another, and officialdom was at once well paying, prestigious, and open to arrivistes, Berlin's bureaucracy was the central magnet for publishing authors. A large number of intellectual institutions were not, after all, indispensable to attract intellectuals into an eighteenth-century German city. Even if Berlin did not have a court like Weimar's, a university like Göttingen's, or publishing houses like Leipzig's, its lecture courses, tutoring posts, gymnasia, Royal Academy of Science, and knightly academies all attracted intellectuals into the city. Obviously, if enough transitional teaching and research institutions existed in a city that lacked a university or a flourishing publishing industry, many intel-

Prussian Bureaucracy in Crisis, 1840–1860 (Stanford, 1971), and A. Lotz, *Geschichte des deutschen Beamtentums* (Berlin, 1909), 208. C. B. A. Behrens's discussion of the Prussian bureaucracy in her *Society, Government, and the Enlightenment: The Experiences of Eighteenth-Century France and Prussia* (New York, 1985), came to my attention too late to be used here.

lectuals could still find intellectual employment by selling their intellectual skills in one way or another.

Younger intellectuals were more often lodged in middle-income posts
than older intellectuals were. Whether these younger men eventually
managed to climb into the upper strata by becoming professors or officials must remain a mystery for now. However the social structure of the
Berlin intelligentsia changed in future years, it is clear from this survey
that at the close of the eighteenth century the proportion of intellectuals
employed in the lower-income strata was tiny. There was no significant
intellectual proletariat in Berlin. Still, all was not idyllic, for the proportion of intellectuals who had to make do with middle-income occupations remained substantial. Over half of the Berlin intellectuals were born
into the middle strata, and most failed to move out of this level when
they became publishing intellectuals—an indication of blocked mobility.
Yet it would be wrong to imagine Berlin's intelligentsia as having been
exclusively populated by aspiring young men looking to move up in the
world. As we shall see, it was crucial for the formation of salons that the
agricultural crisis had caused nobles to move into the city to seek both
an education and posts in the bureaucracy, and thus to be so overrepresented among the intellectuals.

Alas, these numbers, illuminating as they are, cannot clarify what it
meant for noble officials and penniless tutors to have been "together" in
Berlin's intelligentsia. All that the 386 intellectuals necessarily shared was
the practice of spending time alone at their desks, sharpening their quills,
and moving them across expensive paper. Their cohesiveness, as depicted
thus far, was an abstract one. To capture the real flavor of the lives of the
386 intellectuals, it is necessary to move beyond description of an anonymous cluster of intellectuals who shared only the same disposition to
publish their writings. We must proceed to meet smaller, face-to-face
circles in order to locate groups in which members felt themselves consciously united for common purposes. This exploration will finally take
us to the heart of this book, the salons.

FOUR | *Public Leisure and the Rise of Salons*

Public Places for Cultivated Persons

K. W. Brumbey, an obscure preacher who was seventeen years old when Frederick the Great became king in 1740, later reflected on the changes that had occurred during Frederick's reign. Brumbey remembered that "when the king ascended to the throne, Berlin had no theater, and there were no public places at which cultivated persons could meet. Residents of almost every class were limited either to domesticity, or searched for their enjoyment in taverns, where was little cultivation to be found."[1] By the time that Frederick died in 1786, Berlin's public life had expanded and diversified greatly. Anyone with the time, the inclination, and the right clothes could stroll in the newly landscaped Thiergarten park or chat at the Pariser Platz at the end of the city's central thoroughfare, Unter den Linden. Berliners flocked to the evening market across from city hall, where the confectioners displayed "masterpieces of sugar and puff paste."[2] Tickets for the pantomime, juggling, and farcical plays at the twice-yearly town fairs were nominal.[3] It cost only a groschen to be admitted to the bottom floors of the new opera house, which was also the scene of wild, late-night masked balls during the carnival season in January and February. As long as one could afford a costume, the balls were open to the general public; the sole restriction was that only nobles

1. Brumbey's opinion is cited in the "Zweiter Brief" in the contemporary annual *Jahrbücher der preussischer Monarchie* (hereafter *JPM*) vol. 1 (1800), 171–76.

2. On the evening market see Henri Brunschwig, *Enlightenment and Romanticism in Eighteenth-Century Prussia* (Chicago, 1974), 63.

3. On the fairs see Reinhold August Dorwart, *The Prussian Welfare State before 1740* (Cambridge, Mass., 1971), 5.

could wear red costumes.[4] Once every three weeks a lottery was held at town hall, and Berliners gathered there to watch the great wheel turn and hope that their number would come up.

Other diversions open to the broad public required a bit of money. Coffeehouses and "coffee gardens" offered refreshments, billiards, and conversation.[5] Dance halls often were attached to bordellos. Male visitors could retire to a back room, order a bowl of punch or some wine, and a wink would suffice to bring them the woman of their choice. At Vauxhall, Madam Schuwitz's bordello, men of "good society" bought pleasure sold by the "top class" of Berlin's three thousand prostitutes, who reportedly indulged with their clients in "real orgies." Among Vauxhall's enthusiasts were two prominent salon guests, Wilhelm von Humboldt and Gustav von Brinkmann. In November 1790, von Humboldt wrote von Brinkman how sorry he was that von Brinkmann was not along when he and Friedrich Gentz made one of their "evening expeditions" to Vauxhall. Von Humboldt found the "elegant furnishings, the punch, and all that one values there so lovely, that one completely forgets in what kind of a house one is in."[6] A more select set of opportunities for amusing oneself was open only to the *hoffähig,* or those privileged to enter courtly society. The extended ruling family and the most important noble families who spent winters in the city were the only ones who had a sure entrée into courtly circles. They attended assemblies, receptions, concerts, hunts, and picnics at royal palaces in and around Berlin. For another circle, those who found learned and witty dialogue the most exciting diversion imaginable, Berlin offered a wide variety of more erudite leisure opportunities. There were public lectures at the Royal Academies, private lecture courses offered by prominent scholars in their homes, as well as discussion clubs and reading societies.

It was only in the last years of King Frederick's reign that a fourth kind of leisure opportunity, salons, appeared in Berlin. Salons were at once far more heterogeneous in their personnel and far more informal in their style than the leisure available in courtly or commercial settings or in the intellectual clubs. It was precisely the volatility of such a diverse group

4. On the opera in Berlin see Henry Raynor, *A Social History of Music* (New York, 1972), 293. On the carnival season see Erich Bleich, *Der Hof des König Friedrich Wilhelm III* (Berlin, 1914), vol. 3, 97. On balls at the opera house see Hans Ostwald, *Kultur- und Sittengeschichte Berlins* (Berlin, 1924), 100.

5. On the history of coffeehouses in Berlin see Ludwig Geiger, *Berlin 1688–1840: Geschichte des geistigen Lebens der preussischen Hauptstadt* (Berlin, 1893–95), vol. 2, 191.

6. On Vauxhall see Geiger, *Berlin,* vol. 1, 618. On von Humboldt's tale of life at Vauxhall see Albert Leitzmann, ed., *Wilhelm von Humboldts Briefe an Karl Gustav von Brinkman* (Leipzig, 1939).

gathering in such an intimate style that made salons such a special adventure at the time. Yet for all the social distance which eventually came to divide courtly, commercial, and club leisure experiences from the salon world, salons actually evolved out of these other three institutions.

Each of these three different settings for leisure experiences contributed in its own way to Berliners' chances to mix with those outside their estate and occupation, and thus eventually to the emergence of salons. The style of courtly leisure was important in the evolution of salons because the court set the tone for those who watched palace life from a distance. As some courtly leisure events were gradually opened to those outside courtly circles, the luxury and glamour of court life came to be shared, however vicariously, by a wider public. Then, too, the leisure available for a price at inns, theaters, and coffeehouses made possible some very heterogeneous mixing, although not on very intimate terms. The intellectual clubs, whose members met regularly to discuss books, manuscripts, and ideas, allowed for a deeper level of bonding between men born into different estates and employed in different occupations. Yet these intellectual clubs tended to exclude women, middle-income intellectuals, and Jews.

Although these three leisure opportunities did promote ties across social barriers, neither their structure nor their personnel allowed a miniature society to coalesce that was simultaneously heterogeneous and intimate. Entrance to the socializing at the court itself was strictly limited to those from old noble families. Even the court events open to to the public required expensive tickets or a high position on the occupational hierarchy. The commercial leisure institutions, on the other hand, were more accessible than the court, but provided only superficial contact among their consumers. The intellectual clubs, whose format allowed for more intimacy, were attended mainly by older, well-established gentile male intellectuals. It was only in 1780, when salons first appeared among Berliners' leisure choices, that the limited social fusion which had been achieved previously at courtly, commercial, and club events could be deepened and expanded.

Courtly Society

Court life in the seventeenth and eighteenth centuries was anomalous insofar as the royal residence served both a private and a public function. Courts were the private home of the monarch and his or her immediate family, yet they also represented the state to its subjects.[7] The court

7. For a structural analysis of European courts see Jürgen Habermas, *Strukturwandel*

nobles' "private" actions were thus public in that their assemblies, their choice of clothing, and often their sexual relationships were known far beyond the palace; the personalities and styles of the courtly retinue set the tone for the entire society. In practical ways too—by providing entertainment in operas, theaters, and museums for a tiny group of nobles who did not live in the palace—the courts founded and funded the institutions that eventually served the nation at large.

The style and tone of Prussian courts during the eighteenth century alternated between the decadent and the ascetic. The decadent style was bad for the economy but good for high culture; the ascetic regimes were good for the economy but starved high culture. During the seventeenth century, the Great Elector Frederick William concentrated on populating his territories and building up the army, disregarding culture altogether. But his son, Frederick I (1688–1713), turned instead to decoration and ceremony. It was he who maneuvered kingly status for the duchy of Prussia; his well-educated wife Queen Sophie Charlotte befriended the philosopher Gottlieb Liebniz. It was Leibniz and the queen who drew up plans for the Royal Academies of Science and of Art. In Frederick I's effort to imitate his model, Louis XIV of France, he agreed to be the patron for both Royal Academies. Some of Frederick's other imitations of the Sun King were quite comical. He went through the motions of having mistresses, although he actually preferred his wife. Frederick I's imitative expenditures—the paintings, silver, fine furniture, and new palaces at Charlottenburg and Potsdam—brought the kingdom to the brink of bankruptcy.[8]

Frederick's son Frederick William I (1713–40) turned away from the Frenchified patronage of science and art as the road to great power for Prussia, setting instead an abstemonious, orderly, and military tone. A cruel, illiterate man, he used his cane not only to discipline his family, but also to literally break the teeth and noses of subjects in the streets who displeased him. He starved the already weak Prussian universities and the fledgling Royal Academies of Science and Art. His one indulgence and source of cheer were the two thousand tall soldiers he col-

der Öffentlichkeit (Neuwied and Berlin, 1974), 17–27; Norbert Elias, *Die höfische Gesellschaft* (Neuwied, 1975), chap. 4, and Jürgen von Kreudener, *Die Rolle des Hofes im Absolutismus* (Stuttgart, 1973). Since the time research for this book was completed, Elias's major works have been translated into English: *The Court Society*, trans. Edmund Jephcott (New York, 1983), as well as *The Civilizing Process: The History of Manners*, trans. Edmund Jephcott (New York, 1978) and *Power and Civility*, trans. Edmund Jephcott (New York, 1982).

8. For very general discussion of King Frederick I in English see Hajo Holborn, *A History of Modern Germany* (New York, 1971), vol. 2, 189–92, and J. A. R. Marriott and C. G. Robertson, *The Evolution of Prussia* (Oxford, 1937), 100–103.

lected, often paying huge sums to have them kidnapped from the far corners of the world. Rather than inviting learned men to the palace, Frederick William relaxed in the evening by holding a *Tabagie*, a late-night, all-male session of drinking, smoking, and noisy camaraderie with his top aides and generals. But Frederick William's ruthless efforts to stamp out the nobility's affection for things urban, sociable, and French were less than completely successful. In 1733 Frederick William agreed to appoint an "Entrepreneur of Receptions," who was responsible for arranging twice-weekly assemblies at the palace during the winter. The court offered its hospitality in response to a request from twenty-four noble families who sought the court's help because they lacked appropriate facilities in their homes for lavish entertainments.[9]

Frederick William's son Frederick the Great (Frederick II) loved the French culture so despised by his father and revived the institutions for its propagation upon becoming king in 1740. The Royal Academy of Science was reorganized, prominent French scholars were imported to provide it with glamorous leadership, and architects and artists were employed in an ambitious building program, including a set of French-style palaces at Potsdam and the opera house on Unter den Linden. Frederick engaged musicians to entertain the French, Scottish, and German intellectuals who were his frequent table companions, some of whom enjoyed Frederick's hospitality at court for months and even years. Frederick even spent a small fortune to bring to Berlin Barberina, a wildly popular Italian ballet dancer.[10] These expenditures notwithstanding, Frederick the Great's reign was not altogether positive for the pursuit of refined leisure in Berlin. Frederick failed to nurture a lively noble sociability either at Potsdam or in the family's city palaces—mainly because he despised women, who were indispensable in organizing high society. Then, too, he abhorred excessive luxury and deliberately rejected a large court household as a useless expense. His parsimonious attitude stifled courtly society and the imitative consumption courts fostered. Frederick preferred his male table companions, camp bed, and beloved dogs at the Sans Souci palace in Potsdam to receptions and parties in the city.[11]

9. On King Frederick William II see Marriott and Robertson, *The Evolution of Prussia,* 107–14, and Nancy Mitford, *Frederick the Great* (London, 1970), 16–19. On the "Entrepreneur of Assemblies" see Ostwald, *Kultur- und Sittengeschichte Berlin,* 64.

10. On Frederick's lifestyle at court see G. P. Gooch, *Frederick the Great* (New York, 1947); Peter Paret, ed., *Frederick the Great: A Profile* (New York, 1972); Mitford, *Frederick;* N. William Wraxall, *Memoirs of the Courts of Berlin, Dresden, Warsaw and Vienna* (London, 1806), 111–44.

11. For his own version of things see Honorée Gabriel de Mirabeau, *Memoirs of the Courts of Berlin and Saint Petersburg* (New York, 1910); on Mirabeau in Berlin see also

In 1786, just before Frederick's death, Mr. Wraxall, an English visitor to Berlin, predicted that once the king was dead, all the court households would again be located in Berlin, and the city would therefore "resume its gaiety."[12] That was precisely what Frederick had feared, for he was most distressed about the temperament of his nephew, who succeeded him as Frederick William II. His reign was brief, from 1786 to 1797, the decade of the French Revolution and the heyday of the salons. Frederick William was a genial man, but neither a very beloved nor a very success-ful king. Just as his meticulous uncle feared, the nephew turned out to be more interested in sleeping late, dabbling in obscure mystical cults, visiting bordellos, and courting a succession of mistresses than in mas-tering the fine-tuning of his uncle's political system. Frederick's phenom-enal success in expanding Prussia's territory, productivity, and fiscal well-being had depended on his own supervision of the smallest detail. Fred-erick William II squandered his uncle's accomplishments, and historians have actually blamed him for the defeat of 1806. The same sexual and moral decadence which contributed to political revolution in France led to national defeat in Prussia.[13] Indeed, the tone of Frederick William II's Berlin court did resemble the Frenchified ambiance of Versailles in an earlier epoch, or, closer to home, the court of Frederick I. A galaxy of am-bitious and scheming mistresses and courtiers vied for the king's favor. Funds were spent on entertaining nobles with dances at the palace. The weak-willed Frederick William II came under the influence of a politi-cally conservative, mystical sect of the Freemasons called the Rosicru-cians, who militantly opposed the deistic rationalism of the Berlin En-lightenment in word and practice and maneuvered the passage of an edict in 1798 censoring the writing of enlightened intellectuals and even the sermons of enlightened preachers. During "Big Willy's" reign, sexual lasciviousness was thus accompanied not by intellectual freedom but re-ligious fanaticism.[14]

Although Prussia's reputation as the home of religious tolerance, ra-tionalized statecraft, and a new German science and scholarship suffered setbacks, not all past accomplishments were endangered by the lazy nephew. Modest improvements were made in a number of areas. The maze of restrictions regulating Jewish life in the city were weakened con-

Gooch, *Frederick*, 188, and John Mander, *Berlin: The Eagle and the Bear* (Westport, Conn., 1959), 39–40.

12. Wraxall, *Memoirs*, 248.

13. For a thoroughgoing comparison between the societies in this era see G. P. Gooch, *Germany and the French Revolution* (London, 1920).

14. On Frederick William II's policies see Geiger, *Berlin*, vol. 1, 23; on the 1789 edict see Brunschwig, *Enlightenment and Romanticism*, 167.

siderably in practice, progressive bureaucrats persuaded the king that the strict mercantilism of his predecessor was stifling production and trade, and the Prussian law code was finally completed in 1794. Despite its failure to challenge the fundamental inequalities inherent in the estate structure, the new code streamlined the judicial process and showed enlightened generosity to divorcing wives and peasants on the royal family's estates. The king finally allowed the Royal Academy of Science to reflect the rising intellectual reputation of the domestic intelligentsia. Royal Academy lectures and publications were now in German, and the number of German academicians was substantially increased.[15]

The last king of Prussia during the salon years was Frederick William III, who ascended to the throne in 1797. This dashing young ruler was married to his cousin, the vivacious Louise of Mecklenburg, and the young couple altered the style of the Prussian court yet again—but not as a return to Frederick II's lonely asceticism. To be sure, Frederick William III did cooperate with the campaign to punish his predecessors' mistresses by taking away their titles, palatial homes, and ample sinecures. But unlike Frederick the Great's style, the new royal couple's ethos was moral, domestic, and child-centered. The couple lived simply and quietly in the palace in Berlin, and the king devoted himself virtuously, if rather ineptly, to the delicate task of negotiating Prussian alliances so as to avoid defeat at the hands of Napoleon. Both king and queen took an interest in social and cultural life outside the palace walls. Queen Louise was involved in the literary scene and a devoted friend of several noble salon women and salonières, especially Duchess Dorothea von Courland, whose salon she visited on occasion. Henry Reeve, another English visitor in Berlin, summarized the new royal couple's attitude, reporting that during the winter months they went to the opera every evening as "private persons."[16]

In other words, the relation between city and court had reversed itself in the seventy-five years since Frederick William I had been persuaded to hire the "Entrepreneur of Receptions." Whereas the urban nobles had previously needed to borrow the palace to entertain in appropriate style, now the court was no longer the only location where courtly society, including the royal family itself, enjoyed themselves. Prussia had finally arrived at the stage France and England had each entered at least a century before, in that social space for the titled and the elegant could now be found in select urban homes. Mr. Reeve described this development

15. Adolf Harnack, *Geschichte der königlich preussischen Akademie der Wissenschaft in Berlin* (Berlin, 1900), 496–500.

16. Henry Reeve, *Journal of a Residence at Vienna and Berlin in the Eventful Winter 1805–6* (London, 1877), 152.

King Frederick William III and Queen Louise

in the vocabulary of the time. During his stay in Berlin during the winter of 1806, Reeve was asked by a Mr. Mansfield, another Englishman living in the city, if he (Reeve) "intended to be presented at court." If yes, then Mansfield offered to invite Reeve to his house, which "was as much as" presenting him at court, since "a *Societé* is held (there) every evening, . . . where one meets the best company in town."[17]

Commercial Leisure

The royal couple could find suitably distinguished events in the city where they could enjoy themselves as "private persons" because new, more commercial, more open public institutions evolved out of and

17. Ibid., 151.

alongside the old, closed courtly institutions. Like their counterparts who traded coins, jewelry, silk, linen, or wool, cultural entrepreneurs were forced to obtain protection, monopolies, or subsidies from the crown. They were free agents only within the mercantilist constraints adhered to by all four eighteenth-century Prussian kings. Monarchs and their court administrations controlled what kind of commercial leisure enterprises came into being. Take, for example, the theater. At the beginning of Frederick the Great's reign, there was neither a courtly nor a commercial theater in Berlin. Berliners had become bored with the acrobatics, shadow-plays, miming, and farce offered by J. C. "von" Eckenberg's traveling troupe. A more serious fare was offered by Herr Schönemann's troupe, which received the king's permission to perform at an improvised stage in the town hall. But Herr Schönemann failed to obtain the crown's permission to build a permanent repertory theater in Berlin. King Frederick preferred French comedy to the serious German plays now being written. The only theater he built was a small one in the Berlin palace where foreign companies performed for an exclusively courtly audience. It was an ironic situation. In 1750, Gotthold Lessing, a leading playwright and the founder of a journal of theater criticism, had to suffer the humiliation of being denied entrance to a performance at the palace theater.[18]

But what was the solution? The directors of the traveling theater companies could not attract large enough audiences for the new German plays to support a permanent theater in Berlin. Although the court neither patronized nor founded repertory theaters open to the public, it still provided less intellectual kinds of mass entertainment, which doomed any attempts to found a permanent commercial theater. So reported a member of Herr Schönemann's troupe during the winter of 1743, when their quarters were still temporary: "we have been acting to empty benches, for as there are special festivities at court every day which anyone can see for nothing, we have no hopes of good takings. Yesterday, for Christmas Eve, there was a masked ball. Operas are being produced with lavish splendour."[19] But as Herr Brumbey asserted, the theatrical scene began to improve toward the end of Frederick the Great's reign despite his disdain for serious drama in the German language. In 1771, a commercial theater was given permission to open in the Behrenstrasse. When Frederick William II ascended the throne in 1786, the commercial troupe from the Behrenstrasse theater was chosen to be the new National

18. A good account of Berlin's theatrical history in this era is W. H. Bruford, *Theatre and Drama in Goethe's Germany* (London, 1950), 90–91, 174–76; on Lessing, 122.

19. Ibid., 93.

Theater's resident company and provided with a stage in the palace. Royal patronage was not adequate, however, to fully support the newly organized theater's entire budget. The remainder of the costs had to be met from the sale of expensive tickets, and attendance was limited mainly to a rather "exclusive public."[20]

The gradual emergence of even this quasi-commercial theater in Berlin had social as well as cultural consequences. Actors, once held to be marginal characters, could settle down in the city and make friends. Actors tended either to be children of actors or those who had strayed from or failed at "the normal course for their caste." As theaters became more permanent, the German plays improved, and courtly society began to take the theater more seriously, the status of acting was enhanced. Putting on amateur plays at home became fashionable among the wealthy, helping to make acting a "nobler" calling. For the first time, a few of the prominent actors in the city came to be accepted in society—not in the highest society, but in society nevertheless—through their connection to the Jewish salonières. Jewish women, hungry for cultivation that could be had by purchasing a ticket, were a large and enthusiastic sector of the play-going audience, and some became friends with the stars of the theater, who often visited their Jewish friends after the play, for refreshments and conversation.[21]

In the same years that commercial theaters were founded, news about how and where to buy other relaxing experiences could be learned for the price of a newspaper. Two competing newspapers had royal permission to publish three times weekly during the last three-quarters of the century. The better of the two, the *Vössische Zeitung,* could be bought on Tuesdays, Thursdays, and Saturdays, either at the Vosses' bookstore or at any royal post office. Newspaper writers and readers in Prussia were lucky, because at least until the edict of 1798, censorship was comparatively weak. Still, because of slow transportation, foreign news tended to be stale. Intellectuals complained that space for book and theater reviews in these four-page newspapers was inadequate and the honorarium paid to journalists likewise insufficient.[22] Whatever the overall weakness of the

20. Rudolf Weil, *Das Berliner Theaterpublikum unter A. W. Ifflands Direktion 1796–1814* (Berlin, 1932), 62.

21. See ibid., 126; on the general changes in actors' status see Eduard Devrient, *Geschichte der deutschen Schauspielkunst* (Berlin, 1929). One view of the motives Jews had for attending the theater is that "Jews who aspired to social acceptance but had difficulty entering Gentile circles may have found sitting in a mixed audience in the concert hall and theatre a convenient way of demonstrating their membership in society at large." See Jacob Katz, "German Culture and the Jews," in Jehuda Reinharz and Walter Schatzberg, eds. *The Jewish Response to German Culture* (Hanover, N.H., 1985), 85–99, at 90.

22. See Margo Lindemann, *Deutsche Presse bis 1815* (Berlin, 1969), and Dieter Paul Bau-

newspapers, classified advertisements publicized a variety of commercial leisure events. Lecture series offered by leading intellectuals were announced there, as were the services of tutors, governesses, and directors of boarding schools for adolescent girls. Here one could also learn of the first "private" art gallery in the city. On January 12, 1788, Jean Marc Pascal let it be known that he displayed his "Art Repository" daily (excepting Sundays) at his house. Artists could offer their work there for sale at a price they set themselves, while he took 10 percent for his services. Herr Pascal added that "all kinds of persons visit, not only from the royal house, but also traveling princes." The new interest of royalty and nobles in the culture being offered for sale to private persons had itself become a status commodity from which Herr Pascal could make a profit. A September 1789 ad called the reader's attention to a lending library operated by the Morino bookstore, where a yearly membership cost three taler. Concerts at the Corsikan Concert Hall were also announced in the newspaper. Sometimes the events proposed in these advertisements sound appropriate indeed for men seeking not only self-improvement but also cultivated companionship. On October 3, 1789, one "Andre, English Teacher," announced (in English) that "he was erecting an English Club, where Gentlemen will meet at my lodgings twice a week during the Winter, and speak nothing but English."[23]

Not all commercial leisure experiences provided as much mental stimulation as the plays, lectures, concerts, or English Clubs. By the end of the century, there were also new places to purchase less demanding leisure experiences, including 658 beer houses, 53 cafes, and 140 inns, as well as the beloved dance halls with their attached bordellos. Public eating, drinking, and conversing often took place in more intimate and selective, but commercial settings nevertheless. The resort spas at nearby springs, for instance, offered a total and elegant leisure. These resorts had the decided advantage of removing the guests from their routine social circles. The popularity of the spas was enhanced because the generation which reached adulthood in the 1790s was mad for all kinds of cures for their migraines, nervous disorders, and other assorted illnesses. Selective yet commercial settings for eating and relaxing could be found in the city as well. At two o'clock every afternoon, Mr. Reeve reported, "good company" met to dine at the Hotel Ville de Paris. The Berlin casino, a suite of rooms where "gentlemen" met to spend an evening "in society," was another such opportunity. By paying the annual subscription price, the

mert, *Die Entstehung des deutschen Journalismus: Eine sozialgeschichtliche Studie* (Munich and Leipzig, 1928).

23. All of these advertisements appeared on the dates noted in the text in the *Vössische Zeitung*.

casino's members could gather to read the newspaper, dine, play cards and billiards, and of course, chat with their friends.[24]

The commercialization of public leisure in Berlin opened a new world of experiences to many who had no hope of entering courtly society. Jews and commoners of both sexes now had public places where they could mix socially with each other and even with nobles, often in pursuit of mutual cultivation. Because the royal family and prominent nobles now took an interest in high culture, their glamour was bestowed on the humbler participants. The commercialization of leisure was, by definition, a partial democratization of leisure, insofar as most of these experiences could be purchased for the price of a ticket. But precisely because commercial leisure involved ticket-buyers as passive consumers, they did not offer much of a chance for forming friendships across estate, occupational, or gender boundaries. Nor were the commercial leisure institutions an adequate setting for those who craved serious intellectual dialogue. Discourse between equals was not a service or a performance that could be bought and sold. Nor could such discussions take place when attendance was open to anyone who could afford a ticket.

Intellectual Clubs

Those who sought an even more selective, intimate, and serious way to socialize while pursuing enlightenment therefore joined or hoped to join an intellectual club. Berliners referred to these gatherings as associations of "private persons," since the "public persons" who represented the state played no role in their founding. Present-day sociologists would call the clubs "voluntary associations," because they were largely autonomous of any educational, court, or commercial institutions. These intellectual clubs were an unprecedented, exciting development allowing noble and commoner gentile men to deepen their personal and intellectual ties. Sometimes a club admitted Jews or women as well. The fact that the clubs were closed insured that the delicate mixing which took place there would be highly controlled. The representatives of the diverse estates and occupations were selected by their colleagues because they possessed the

24. Statistics on the beer houses, cafes, and inns can be found in Brunschwig, *Enlightenment and Romanticism*, 115; on the casino see Reeve, *Journal*, 163, and Victor Hugo Paltsits, "Berlin and the Prussian Court in 1798," *Bulletin of the New York Public Library* 19 (1915), 805. The classic work on all of these kinds of commercial leisure for England in this period, useful for comparative purposes, is J. H. Plumb, *The Commercialization of Leisure in Eighteenth-Century England* (University of Reading, 1973). Reinhold Kuhnert's *Urbanität auf dem Lande: Badereisen nach Pyrmont im 18. Jahrhundert* (Göttingen, 1982) came to my attention too late to be used here.

required intellectual skills and/or political opinions. The resulting ideological homogeneity put any social and religious differences into the background.[25] All clubs had titles, rules, and set procedures for admitting new members, but otherwise a huge diversity of purposes prevailed. In some the presentation and discussion of scholarly papers was the central focus, while others combined less vigorous intellectual entertainments with common meals, conversation, or even dancing. Some clubs met in homes, others in restaurants or rented rooms. The intellectual clubs performed a huge range of functions later met by a variety of institutions, including university seminars, professional associations of scholars, political parties, libraries, and bookstores.

Insofar as an intellectual club took itself seriously, it belonged to a special realm of the *Gelehrtenrepublik,* or the republic of scholars. The scholars' republic was of course not a location in space but a concept formulated by eighteenth-century German intellectuals to describe how they saw their own little world in contrast to the authoritarian inequality of the larger states in which they lived. The world of enlightened scholarship, in contrast to autocratic states, was—or was supposed to become—a democratic, self-governing, international network of thinkers. It was fitting for an intelligentsia so dense in arrivistes and would-be arrivistes to define its utopian vision in egalitarian terms.

The discussion societies were the purest expression of the intelligentsia's intent to organize the distribution of its members' work without reliance on kings or publishers. The most prestigious of the discussion societies was the Royal Academy of Science, which was really both a courtly institution and an intellectual club. Since the academicians helped choose new members themselves, and since a few earned their living at the Royal Academy, some academicians belonged to the free and voluntary world of the scholar's republic. The four sections of the Royal Academy—philosophy, mathematics, natural science, and philology—each met monthly around the horseshoe-shaped table with the inset inkwells in the Royal Academy rooms above the royal stables. Each member could bring one guest to the meetings, often a prominent foreign scholar visiting Berlin. On the king's birthday and other special days, Academy presentations were attended by the royal family and also open to anyone else who wished to attend.[26] But the Royal Academy's treatment of

25. The major study of voluntary associations in Germany in this era is Thomas Nipperdey, "Verein als soziale Struktur in Deutschland im späten 18. und frühen 19. Jahrhundert," published in Nipperdey's collected essays, *Gesellschaft, Kultur, Theorie* (Göttingen, 1976). Magnus Friedrich von Bassewitz did label a group of intellectual clubs "private societies." See his *Die Kurmark Brandenburg* (Leipzig, 1847), 501.

26. Ludwig Geiger (in *Berlin,* vol. 1, 514) quotes a contemporary joke about the balance

Moses Mendelssohn in 1771, when the king refused to confirm him as a member despite the unanimous vote in support of his nomination, shows the limits of the academicians' autonomy. The prestige and facilities which the monarchy bestowed on the academicians had a price. The Royal Academy may have been democratic and meritocratic within, but it existed at the pleasure of the head of a very autocratic structure. The king, not the scholars, made the final decision on who might join their exalted circle.

Some discussion societies more autonomous than the Academy had a fairly specialized focus. The members of the Friends of Natural Science, founded in 1773, met weekly in each other's homes to discuss ongoing research and to inspect each other's natural history collections; they also published their proceedings annually. Sometimes they put their ideas into practice and fought for reason and the scientific method in public campaigns against the "specter" of returning irrationalism among the city population. In 1797, they appointed a commission "to investigate a ghost which has been haunting the house of the Master of Water and Forests at Tegel." Three professors and the minister of education, all members, "set a watch on the spot. They discover[ed] the cord used by the imposter to strike a metal plate, thus making the noise which had terrified the neighborhood." Berlin also had a Medical Society for local doctors and dentists, and a Pharmaceutical Society as well.[27]

Other discussion societies were more intellectually eclectic. The Philomatic Society, founded in 1801, invited select "artists and scholars of all fields" to all its weekly meetings, which included both short lectures and conversation. The Society of Friends of the Humanities was interested in all of the "human sciences." The oldest discussion society in the city, the Monday Club, was founded in 1749, and its twenty-four members and their guests met over a meal in a local inn. A visitor in 1788 reported that members of the Monday Club were mainly "scholars by profession," and complained that "they were a bit pedantic." It was difficult to become a member of the Monday Club—one vote against the candidate sufficed to doom the application. Still, the club was apparently rather accessible

---

between decorative and serious persons at Royal Academy functions: "an Academy of Science is an institute which accepts prominent persons of quality and men of affairs, and now and then also admits a few scholars."

27. On the "Friends of Natural Sciences" see Davidssohn, *Briefe über Berlin* (Berlin, 1798), 22; see also vol. 7 of the *Archiv der "Brandenburgia" Gesellschaft für Heimatkunde der Province Brandenburg zu Berlin* (Berlin, 1902), which was devoted to *Aus den Tagebüchern des alten* [Ernst Ludwig] *Heims*, 62; Bassewitz, *Die Kurmark Brandenburg*, 501; Friedrich Nicolai, *Beschreibung der königlichen Residenzstädte Berlin und Königsberg* (Berlin, 1786; rpt. 1980), 723. On the 1797 commission see Brunschwig, *Enlightenment and Romanticism*, 189.

to the right outsiders who came as guests of the members. In the quarter century after 1787, a total of 2,239 visitors were invited guests of the Monday Club; in 1805 a visitor found a hundred men at the club's "evening table."[28]

The Wednesday Society, on the other hand, was exclusive to the point of secrecy. Founded in 1783, this was a cadre of twenty-four eminent state officials who held to their deism and dedication to rationalism against the tide of religious fanatacism, mysticism, and romanticism that began to compete for ideological favor in Berlin during the late 1780s and the 1790s. Men born noble were not allowed to join the Wednesday Society, although ennobled men were eligible. The society regularly evaluated essays answering the question: "What is Enlightenment?" Before each meeting an essay by one of the members circulated in a locked tube; only members had keys. The discussion at the meeting was recorded, and when it was circulated after the meeting, members wrote further comments for circulation, identifying themselves only by their code numbers. The final products were often published in the *Berlinische Monatschrift*, the leading enlightened journal in the city. The eventual fate of the well-organized Wednesday Society is a clear example of just how precarious voluntary intellectual associations could be, given their dependence on powers far outside the scholar's republic. The 1798 edict to "prevent and punish" secret societies abruptly put an end to this embodiment of the scholar's republic in Berlin.[29]

A second Wednesday Society, which allowed women to join, offered a less rigorous fare. Intellectual "presentations," readings of plays and poetry, and musical performances preceded a "modest supper." Neither card-playing nor tobacco was allowed, and a visitor in 1788 therefore concluded that the second Wednesday Society offered "enjoyment," but definitely not "rough sensuality." Another less rigorous discussion society was the group which met regularly on Tuesday evenings at *Hofrat* Bauer's apartment in the Berlin palace. Prominent officials and professors and their wives met to discuss poetry, science, and recent plays, to participate in social games, private conversations, and to share a meal.[30]

28. The Monday Club's total number of visitors between 1787 and 1809 was provided in Heine Humpel's "Die Entstehung des Vereinwesens in Berlin," State Examination Thesis, Dept. of History, Free University of Berlin, 1970, 144; the 1805 visitor was Ernst Ludwig Heim, whose visit was noted in his diaries published in *Archiv der "Brandenburgia*," 61.

29. On the Wednesday Society see Ludwig Keller, "Die Berliner Mittwochs-Gesellschaft," *Monatshefts der Comenius Gesellschaft* 5 (1896), 67–94; and A. Stölzel, "Die Berliner Mittwochsgesellschaft über Aufhebung oder Reform der Universitäten," *Forschungen zur brandenburgischen und preussischen Geschichte* 2 (1889).

30. On the second Wednesday Society see Davidssohn, *Briefe*, 18; on the Bauer society see Humpel, "Die Entstehung," 166.

Another set, mainly officers and their wives, gathered monthly at the *Verein* (club) founded by General von Scholten, where they heard lectures by two of the club's members and then retired to an evening of dancing or a concert.[31]

Another kind of intellectual club was the reading society, which concentrated more on providing a practical alternative to the high cost of books and journals than on providing dialogue and social events for the well-to-do. Public libraries were not yet open to a large sector of the public, and the royal library, which moved into its own new building in 1784, contained mainly scholarly books. Only high officials could take home the books. There were a few commercial lending libraries which loaned popular novels.[32] Still, the popular demand for novels, almanacs, travel reports, plays, poetry, and literary criticism vastly outstripped the ability of the publishers and booksellers to distribute adequate numbers of books at a price the swelling number of readers could afford. Reading societies were the central way out of the imbalance between the supply and the demand for the written word. Reading societies met either at home or at rooms rented either by the society itself or by a publisher. Members shared the costs of subscriptions to newspapers and journals and of books purchased. Reading societies served a larger and less prestigious constituency than the discussion societies; admission depended more on friendship and the willingness to pay for reading material than it did on scholarly accomplishment. Discussions at the reading societies did not consist so much of learned exchanges between the city's intellectual stars as it did of more casual conversation among the humbler, poorer readers of their books and articles.

The less rigorous and intellectually prestigious the intellectual club, the more likely it was to allow women to join. Not surprisingly, women tended to belong to clubs that met at homes. But even at the clubs where women were admitted, not everyone approved of their presence. Wolf Davidssohn complained that women's right to vote on the membership decisions of the second Wednesday Society kept out "worthy men" who were not approved by the women. In his view, women were "possessed by a higher level of vanity," and "loved to stir up intrigues and conspira-

31. On the club which met at von Scholten's see Adalbert von Hanstein, *Die Frauen in der Geschichte des 18. and 19. Jahrhunderts* (Leipzig, 1900) vol. I, 518.

32. My main sources for information on the reading societies were Marlies Prüsener, "Lesegesellschaften im 18. Jahruhundert," *Börsenblatt für den deutschen Buchhandel* 28 (1972), 188–301, and Barney M. Milstein, *Eight Eighteenth-Century Reading Societies* (Bern and Frankfurt a.M., 1972). Otto Dann, ed., *Lesegesellschaften und bürgerliche Emanzipation* (Munich, 1981), came to my attention too late to be used for this section.

cies."[33] Nor was it just women whose presence was frowned upon at the most prestigious intellectual clubs. Young intellectual men employed in humiliating positions as tutors, teachers, preachers, or clerks also seem to have had difficulty gaining entrée. But providing extensive evidence for this claim using the collective biography is difficult, because membership lists for only a few clubs have survived. The wide variety and large number of clubs makes it plausible to assume that most of the 386 male intellectuals in Berlin were affiliated with at least one intellectual club. The problem is that we do not know which intellectuals belonged to which club. Lacking membership lists, it has been necessary to work in the other direction, compiling a list of club-affiliated intellectuals from the biographical dictionaries. Thus, the list of sixty-nine intellectuals affiliated with one or another intellectual club is a small and not at all random sample. But it is the only source which indicates how those in some of the more well-known clubs differed from the average intellectual in the city. Those in the intellectual clubs tended to be somewhat older than the average intellectual. There were twice as many professors in the clubs as compared to the intelligentsia at large. Teachers, tutors, preachers, and clerks were in turn underrepresented in the clubs. Officials and freelance writers were as well represented in the clubs as they were among the intelligentsia at large. Only the first Wednesday Society explicitly excluded nobles. But at only 6 percent of this sample of club members, nobles were definitely underrepresented in the clubs, since 15 percent of Berlin's intelligentsia was noble.

These numbers suggest that the intellectual clubs mainly served the needs of older, well-established commoner intellectuals employed in the intellectual institutions. But were the men who created these associations really fighters for a republic of scholars, ready to reward talent and ignore caste? Specifically, were these intellectuals as ready to accept Jews as they were to shun nobles? Did the intellectual clubs constitute a new "open society" which would transform Jewish history by providing acculturated but marginal Jewish intellectuals with an alternative network of equally marginal gentiles ready to accept them?[34] At first glance, these numbers do suggest that the answer should be yes. Sixteen percent of

33. Davidssohn, *Briefe,* 18.

34. This is the central question posed by Jacob Katz in his work on this era: see Katz's works cited in chap. 3, note 12. According to H. I. Bach, the intellectual clubs could in principle integrate Jews because they were a new phenomenon: "the acceptance of Mendelssohn and his fellow Jews as members of learned societies . . . was quite unobtrusive because the very composition of these societies lacked any precedent." See Bach's *The German Jew: A Synthesis of Judaism and Western Civilization, 1730–1930* (Oxford, 1983), 59.

the sixty-nine club members in this sample were Jewish, making Jewish men four times as numerous in the clubs as they were in the intelligentsia as a whole. Yet this statistic is misleading, insofar as it is an artifact of the absence of a full list of all members of all clubs to use as the denominator. It is more likely that in reality the Jewish men were only slightly if at all overrepresented among the true total of club members.

But even if Jewish men as a group were not overrepresented among the club members, individual cases dramatically illustrate the success a few Jewish men had in penetrating the club network. Moses Mendelssohn was chosen for membership in the Monday Club and the Wednesday Society as well as by the Royal Academy. He declined to join the Monday Club because his observance of Jewish dietary laws interfered with the shared meal at the inn. He remained an honorary member of the Wednesday Society because of his ill health and the limited time he had for intellectual activities, given his full-time employment in the silk industry.[35] Lazarus Bendavid, a Kantian philosopher who was respected in gentile intellectual circles, was the secretary of the Philomatic Society. Markus Herz and his beautiful young wife Henriette both belonged to the Bauer reading society, and both Herzes and their friend David Friedländer belonged to the second Wednesday Society as well. Henriette Herz, who was very much at the center of things, also hosted a tiny reading society in her own home on Tuesday evenings during the 1780s. Many of its members formed a secret club called the Tugendbund ("League of Virtue") in 1787, whose symbol was the astronomical sign for the sun. The members pledged to call each other by the informal "du," there was "much embracing and kissing, and above all solemn promises were exchanged to seek together 'moral perfection.'" Among the "brothers and sisters" were Henriette Herz herself; Wilhelm von Humboldt, who had a crush on Madame Herz; his future wife, Caroline von Dacheröden; Mendelssohn's daughter Dorothea Veit; and Karl Laroche, the "dazzlingly beautiful" son of the novelist Sophie Laroche.[36]

The presence of a few token Jewish men and women in predominantly gentile clubs, as well as the appearance of mixed clubs where no minority was a token presence, were real accomplishments, with few, if any, precedents in the German-Jewish past. But there were still many "clean-shaven" acculturated Jewish men who were not prominent enough to be asked to join either a mainly gentile or a mixed club, but who were dis-

35. See Alexander Altmann, *Moses Mendelssohn: A Biographical Study* (University, Ala., 1973), 655. A recent additional contribution by Altmann is his "Moses Mendelssohn as the Archtypical German Jew," in Reinharz and Schatzberg, *The Jewish Response*, 17–31.

36. On the League of Virtue see Paul Sweet, *Wilhelm von Humboldt: A Biography* (Columbus, Oh.), vol. 1, 35–36.

satisfied with established institutions of the Jewish community. Their rebellion from status-quo options is illustrated by the founding of several separate Jewish intellectual clubs. (The inclusion of the members of these all-Jewish clubs among the sixteen Jewish intellectuals in clubs is a second reason why the degree of Jewish integration in the clubs is statistically overstated in the sample discussed above.) One small, exclusively Jewish club formed in 1780 was the Lecture Society which met at the home of Dorothea Veit and her first husband, Simon Veit. Dorothea's father was a member too, as were the Herzes and David Friedländer.[37] A far larger group of Jewish men founded the Society of Friends in 1791. The founders were "free-thinkers" who joined together to struggle against such Orthodox religious practices as the much-criticized early burial. They also pledged to help each other when sick, read new writings together, and converse on topics of mutual interest. Women were not allowed to join. The one hundred members met four times yearly for a general meeting and rented rooms in the city during the winter and a garden during the summer, where the Lecture Society's members, who were "denied access to every Christian *Resource*" (association) and who complained that they were "treated with repulsion at public places," could meet on Wednesday afternoons between three and eight for tea, coffee, tobacco, and conversation.[38]

The story of the Freemasons in Berlin shows the same pattern. A few token Jewish men succeeded in entering the official group, whose ideology was quite enlightened. The remaining "clean-shaven" Jewish men were forced to establish their own parallel association, which was neither a part of mainstream secular life nor of the traditional Jewish community. The Freemasons were a secret, international network of local lodges whose members were pledged to an anti-absolutist, socially egalitarian creed. They also shared a passion for alchemy and for the masonic rituals passed down from the medieval builder's guilds. Freemasonry arrived in Germany in the 1770s, almost a half-century after the association was founded in England. Although neither English nor French lodges explicitly excluded Jews, it was rare for Jewish men to be accepted into the official lodges—but at least a tension between principle and practice existed. In German lodges, Jews were excluded in principle. Many accul-

37. On the Veit Lecture Society see Humpel, "Die Entstehung," 166, and Margareta Hiemenz, *Dorothea v. Schlegel* (Freiburg, 1911), 9.

38. On the Society of Friends see Ludwig Lesser, *Chronik der Gesellschaft der Freunde in Berlin* (Berlin, 1842); "Die Gesellschaft der Freunde in Berlin," *Der Orient: Berichte, Studien und Kritiken für jüdische Geschichte und Literatur* 2 (1884), 13–16; Hermann Baschwitz, *Rückblick auf die hundertjährige Geschichte der Gesellschaft der Freunde zu Berlin* (Berlin, 1892).

turated Jewish men in Berlin "looked longingly" at clubs like the Free-masons but had less likelihood of satisfying their longing than they would have had in London and Paris. For in the German Freemasons' efforts to avoid harassment by powerful kings and by the traditional churches, members of the German lodges emphasized their Christian character by explicitly excluding Jews.[39]

For some would-be Jewish Freemasons, the Order of the Asiatic Brethren was the solution to this quandary. Founded in Vienna in 1780 by two disaffected noblemen, the order was more mystical in its ideology than were the official masonic lodges and allowed Jewish men to join, but only under the condition that they symbolically defy their religion of birth by eating pork and drinking milk at solemn ritual celebrations. "Asiatic" lodges were founded in Prague, Innsbruck, Frankfurt am Main, and Hamburg as well as in Berlin,[40] but despite its success, the order was beset by antisemitic and other attacks, never gained recognition as an official Freemason lodge, and disappeared altogether by the end of the century.

Since the two official Freemason lodges in Berlin refused to accept Jews, the "clean-shaven" Jewish men in Berlin could become Freemasons only by joining yet another unofficial lodge. The Tolerance Lodge, founded by two gentile Berliners in 1790, required as the price of admit-tance not symbolic betrayal of Judaism but acceptance of the leadership of gentiles who had a decidedly superior attitude to Judaism and Jews. Among the lodge's goals were to make Jews "more human" and "raise them to higher levels of culture" recruiting Jews whose "open adherence to Christianity was obstructed only by family circumstances." Markus Herz and the bankers Isaac Daniel Itzig and his son-in-law Solomon Levy were mentioned as worthy candidates for membership. Itzig, King Frederick William II's private banker, obtained royal approval from the king for the Tolerance Lodge, which had to suffice in lieu of official recognition by the Freemasons.[41]

From the Monday Club to the Freemasons, the intellectual clubs pro-vided Berlin's intellectuals a crucial opportunity to deepen their relation-ship with those born into different estates and employed in different oc-cupations. The excitement of cooperative intellectual activity and the opportunity to gather outside of and sometimes in opposition to tradi-tional estate-exclusive communities attracted heterogeneous groupings.

39. See Margaret Jacob, *The Radical Enlightenment: Pantheists, Freemasons and Republi-cans* (London, 1981).

40. I have relied here on Jacob Katz, *Jews and Freemasons in Europe, 1723–1939* (Cam-bridge, England, 1970), chap. 3.

41. Ibid., 54.

But the social emancipation realized in the intellectual clubs was severely limited. Those who benefited from participation in the clubs were already among the more privileged intellectuals, mainly older gentile professors. Access to the clubs was difficult for nobles at the summit of the social hierarchy, for young gentile intellectuals employed as teachers, clerks, or preachers, for the city's Jewish intellectuals, and for women of every estate and both religions.

The Emergence of Salons

Not all leisure enjoyed by Berliners was as structured as that offered by courts, commercial institutions, and intellectual clubs. There was time in the schedules of most moderately wealthy persons to spend the afternoon or the evening at the home of a friend or acquaintance, time for a purely social event, an event needing no payment, rules, or official membership lists. Indeed, the smaller and the more informal the gathering, the deeper the connections would be between the participants. This was all very clear to the "clean-shaven" Jews who "looked longingly" at gentile high society. But could "clean-shaven" Jewish men and Jewish women with curls and silk dresses really enter high society? Or, for that matter, could Berlin's commoner intellectuals hope to meet with princes and nobles over dinner or at tea?

Before 1760, there was really no high society in Berlin to which Jews or commoner intellectuals might gain an entrée. For during the first half of the eighteenth century, Berlin did not have the kind of heterogeneous social life in which Jews or intellectuals might have participated. Urban nobles still needed the court's help to socialize in the right style. Socializing at the court itself was limited to the small *hoffähig* (courtly) circle. Commoners with high official appointments rarely took the time or money to consume conspicuously. Even if they had, nobles did not deign to visit commoners at their homes even if they worked with them during the day. Rich Jewish and other foreign financiers relaxed mainly with their own kind. Male scholars relaxed at the homes of other scholars or in taverns. Even very prominent and successful Berlin intellectuals were absolutely morose about their social isolation. Friedrich Nicolai, the author, publisher, and bookseller, complained that in Germany, unlike in France or England, the "estate of writers relates only to itself, or to the learned estate."[42] Socializing, in other words, was limited to estate- and

42. For example, on the male scholars' gatherings which met at the home of Ezechiel von Spannheim see Dorwart, *The Prussian Welfare State*, 221, and Bleich, *Der Hof des König Friedrich Wilhelm III*, 35. Nicolai's lament is cited in Horst Möller, *Aufklärung in Preussen: Der Verleger, Publizist und Geschichtsschreiber Friedrich Nicolai* (Berlin, 1974), 186.

occupation-specific groupings. The style, too, was traditional. Only those with invitations arrived at the right door. Women, if they were present at all, did not dominate the event. Except for the scholars' gatherings, conversation was not especially erudite. Neither in personnel nor in structure could the socializing before 1760 ever challenge the status quo, undermine the social structure, or allow for dangerous mixing between young persons of heterogeneous birth.

But as we have seen, as rising land prices and the allure of city living polarized the nobility, as the Seven Years' War enriched the Jewish mercantile elite, and as the educational system allowed young commoner intellectuals to ascend the social ladder, this narrow style of socializing began to loosen. The courtly, commercial, and club leisure activities allowed for some limited social contact across the dissolving social boundaries. But if contacts made at a court-sponsored ball, at a box in the theater, or at an intellectual club were to be deepened, and if those excluded from these three leisure events were ever to meet each other, a new setting was needed. That new setting was the salon.

The coalescence of a lively salon society in Berlin was a gradual process. Two decades before Henriette and Markus Herz opened Berlin's first salon, a few families began to invite guests from different estates to their homes for dinner. The home of Alexander and Wilhelm von Humboldt's parents, for instance, was considered a *gastfreies* or "hospitable" house. Major von Humboldt was the "gentleman of the bedchamber" in the household of the future Frederick William II, and his wife was from a prominent Huguenot family. The Humboldts entertained local French and Jewish friends at their country estate outside of Berlin, and eminent foreign writers called on them too.[43] Friedrich Nicolai, the writer and bookseller, regularly invited scholars traveling through Berlin as well as his own local friends to his home on Sunday evenings. Those passing through town who did not know him well, but who wanted to see or meet him, left their cards at his bookshop. Nicolai's idea of a lively evening was to invite a few scholars each week representing the major fields of scholarship. From the accumulated calling cards left by those who wished to visit him, Nicolai put together a list that included a few intellectual stars with mutually complementary specialties; they were sent invitations for that week. Moses Mendelssohn, Nicolai's close friend, was invited often, as was Eliza von der Recke, a published author and half-sister of the salonière Duchess Dorothea von Courland. Young Daniel Parthey was the tutor in the Nicolai household. His son Gustav re-

43. See Sweet, *Wilhelm von Humboldt*, vol. 1, chap. 1, and Bleich, *Der Hof des König Friedrich Wilhelm III*, 42.

counted in his memoirs the story of Frau Nicolai's initial opposition to Frau von der Recke's first visit on the grounds that she would be "too aristocratic." Frau von der Recke remonstrated to Herr Nicolai that she was "no aristocratic rabble" and eventually became a dear friend of everyone in the Nicolai household.[44]

Mendelssohn himself regularly entertained eminent gentile visitors. Professor Christian Gottfried Schütz, who taught rhetoric at the University of Halle, gave a report on his 1769 visit to the Mendelssohn household in a letter to a friend. He first visited Mendelssohn in his office at the Bernhard silk firm, and received an invitation to call on Herr Mendelssohn at home the next day. Professor Schütz arrived at three, and soon Friedrich Nicolai, Karl Lessing, and a preacher named Eberhard arrived. From 3 until 7 P.M., there was "no slackening of the discussion. . . . At 7 P.M. we dined with Moses, and that was the period of *galanterie*," with the extended Mendelssohn family and with several daughters of the large Itzig family. Gatherings at the Mendelssohn home were thought to be "unique" at the time, since the guests from "all walks of life" conversed there "in a peaceful atmosphere of animated interests." Extravagant provisions were not an attraction: Frau Mendelssohn counted out the necessary number of almonds and hazelnuts before she served them.[45] The Mendelssohn home was not the only Jewish household where gentile guests were received in the 1760s and 1770s. One of the daughters of Daniel Itzig, Blümchen, married Mendelssohn's friend David Friedländer, a wealthy Königsberg merchant who had settled in Berlin and was a prominent reformer within the Jewish community. The Friedländer "palace" was reported to have been a "center of sociability" for enlightened Jews and gentiles. The wealthy Meyer family's "palace" was also described as a "center of sociability." Markus Levin, known to posterity chiefly as the father of the salonière Rahel Levin, also entertained actors and spendthrift young nobles who visited him to arrange for private loans.[46]

The marked change between the socializing styles of the 1760s and 1770s and those of the 1780s is summarized in the memoirs of Berlin's first salonière, Henriette Herz.[47] Describing a sharp break in her social

44. Gustav Parthey, *Jugenderinnerungen* (Berlin, 1871), 36–37.

45. Altmann, *Moses Mendelssohn*, 159. For another description of social events at the Mendelssohn home see Bach, *The German Jew*, 62.

46. On these families, whose homes Hans Karl Krüger identifies as "centers of sociability," see his *Berliner Romantik and Berliner Judentum* (Bonn, 1939), chap. 1.

47. On the transition between the socializing at the Mendelssohn and Friedländer homes and that of the subsequent generation of "nouveaux-riche" Jews (whose socializing was called salons) see Brunschwig, *Enlightenment and Romanticism*, 262–65.

life, Herz isolated the practice of holding an "open house," which she defined explicitly as the home of a scholar at which "uninvited" friends and those "being introduced" could count on a "hospitable reception," as what was distinctive during the era after 1780. Looking back on the two decades before 1780, she observed that Mendelssohn's had indeed been an open house, while Nicolai's had not, and the difference lay not in the means (the Mendelssohn household was comparatively poor) but in that friends of the entire Mendelssohn household came "uninvited."[48]

Unfortunately for us, Herz had other tales whose telling was more pressing, and she devoted no more space in her memoir to informing posterity about whose home was or was not truly "open" in the quarter century between 1780 and 1806. Her silence is all the more lamentable, since, as her own brief discussion illustrates, the word *salon* was infrequently used by participants to designate the new sort of social event which sprung up in Berlin in the 1780s. Nor was any other single term used regularly. In Hamburg, salon-like events were called *Abendgesellschaften*.[49] The letters and memoirs of salon participants are richer in verbal phrases than in nouns illustrating the particular qualities of salon socializing. Herz's good friend Friedrich Schleiermacher, for instance, once referred to the reasons why particular persons "let themselves be introduced" at specific Jewish homes.[50] Instead of "opening a salon," the phrase used was that someone had "opened" their home to "social intercourse."[51] The term *Hausfreund*, "a friend of the household," was sometimes used to describe specific salon guests.[52] Thus, even though contemporaries did not use the word *salon*, their vocabulary does reveal a distinctive style of social life. The phrase "to let oneself be introduced" suggests that the guests themselves chose to visit a particular salon. The same phrase also suggests how important introductions were in the guests' abilities to transform their desire to attend a salon into their actual appearance there. "To open one's home to social intercourse" makes clear that those who wanted to receive frequent and informal visits from friends and from the right strangers could make this desire known without issuing individual invitations to each person on each occasion.

48. See Julius Furst, ed., *Henriette Herz: Ihr Leben und ihre Erinnerungen* (Berlin, 1858), 124–27.

49. See Wolfgang Nahrstedt, *Die Entstehung der Freizeit* (Göttingen, 1972), 179–83.

50. Friedrich Schleiermacher is quoted in Wilhelm Erman, *Paul Erman: Ein Berliner Gelehrtenleben 1764–1851* (Berlin, 1927), 96.

51. See Margaretha Hiemenz, *Dorothea von Schlegel* (Freiburg im Breisgau, 1911), 9.

52. One of the many examples of the use of this term, which was still used in the early twentieth century to describe events in the eighteenth century, can be found in Hiemenz, *Dorothea v. Schlegel*, 188. The reference is to Friedrich Schlegel's relationship to various Jewish homes in Berlin.

The story of Herz's career as salonière shows that the "making" of an open house could depend as much on the qualities and circumstances of the entire family as it did on the woman's own training and talents. When they married in 1779, Markus Herz was thirty-two and Henriette de Lemos was fifteen. Born the son of a poor Torah scribe in Berlin, Markus Herz had attended medical school in Königsberg, where he also studied philosophy with Immanuel Kant. When he returned to Berlin to practice medicine, he became a close friend and colleague of Mendelssohn's. His work at the Jewish community hospital brought him into contact with his future wife's father, Dr. Benjamin Lemos, the hospital's director. Dr. Lemos's wealthy Portuguese family had come to Berlin via Amsterdam in the previous century. Even before her precocious marriage to Markus Herz, Henriette demonstrated personal qualities which would later prove crucial in her success as a salonière. She was widely known as a spirited child. The children of wealthy Jewish families at the time were allowed to perform secular plays at the small private theaters erected in a few Jewish homes. The Jewish elders, however, frowned on this frivolous habit and planned to forbid it. Twelve-year-old Henriette, in costume, was delegated to plead with the assembled elders and won their permission for the play to go forward. On another occasion, her parents decided to withdraw her from a private girls' day school because her startling beauty attracted so much attention from young men in the streets. But her father continued his daughter's education and taught her French, English, Latin and Hebrew. Later, her husband Markus and her friend Friedrich Schleiermacher continued to guide her reading and language training. Eventually the list of languages she had mastered came to include French, Italian, Portuguese, and Danish, and she also had some competence in Turkish, Malayan, and Sanskrit.[53]

Henriette Herz's classic beauty, intellectual abilities, passion for the newest literary trends, and talent for friendship all contributed to her social successes. Yet Markus's income, professional contacts, and above all, his popular lecture series on natural science held in their home were indispensable in the coalescence of their double salon. As she herself later recalled, it all began as her husband came to have some "very respectable families" as clients in his medical practice. This brought the young couple into "real social relationships" with these unnamed, probably gentile families. Because his lectures took place at home, listeners and

53. On Herz see Furst, ed., *Henriette Herz;* see also (Mrs.) Vaughn Jennings, *Rahel: Her Life and Letters* (London, 1876), 21–38 and 195–99 and M. Kayserling, *Die jüdischen Frauen in der Geschichte, Literatur und Kunst* (Leipzig, 1879), 199–207. Several of Herz's unpublished letters (few are extant) can be found in the Archive of the Leo Baeck Institute in New York City (V3/1).

clients could gradually and gracefully become friends. The lectures attracted a varied and prestigious audience. Members of the royal family attended as did the French Count Mirabeau and the young von Humboldt brothers, brought there by their tutor, Gottlob Kunth. Kunth had first become acquainted with Markus Herz one day when he sought Markus's advice for a lightning rod the Humboldt family was planning to install. The Herzes began inviting the most interesting persons from the natural history lecture audience to dinner beforehand. In this way their double salon evolved, a salon which was double in ideological style as well as in leadership. Henriette discussed poetry and novels with the young romantics in one room while her husband lectured on reason, science, and enlightenment in the other.[54]

The double salon came to an abrupt end when Markus died suddenly in 1803; because the couple had been spending most of his income on the cost of entertaining, Henriette was far too poor to continue entertaining. Her reluctance to convert to Christianity limited the ways she could support herself. She turned down Count von Dohna's marriage proposal as well as Duchess Dorothea von Courland's invitation for her to join the von Courland household as a governess, because both required a change of religion—a step she refused to take while her mother was still alive. Instead, she boarded students and young country girls who had moved into Berlin to seek employment as domestic servants. She converted after her mother died in 1817, but never remarried. And although many of her friends from the salon days remained loyal, her social life never regained the splendor it had while her husband was alive.

A decade after the Herzes first opened their salon, Henriette's childhood friend Rahel Levin opened the city's second and ultimately most famous salon. Levin's story shows that although a rich and intellectually prominent husband played an important role in Henriette Herz's salon, the absence of such a man need not doom a career as salonière if she had the requisite funds, personal qualities, and friends. Levin's father's French, noble, and theatrical guests exposed her at an early age to an elegant, graceful world. Still, although she sat in on the dinners with this glittering crowd, she felt far distant from it. As she put it herself at the time, she felt like a schlemiehl, a "nobody," around these elegant noble guests.[55] When she was still in her early twenties, Levin was explicit that

54. Furst, ed., *Henriette Herz*, 96. In Herz's own words: "through his intellect and as a famous doctor [Markus] Herz attracted people, and I attracted them through my beauty and through the understanding I had for all kinds of scholarship." This is a quote from Hans Landsberg, *Henriette Herz: Ihr Leben und Ihre Zeit* (Weimar, 1913), 50.

55. Levin's feelings on this matter, and her use of the term, can be found in Hannah Arendt, *Rahel Varnhagen: The Life of a Jewish Woman* (New York and London, 1957), 6.

her Jewishness was to blame for her low status. She complained to her friend David Veit, a medical student at Göttingen, that "it is as if some supramundane being, just as I was thrust into this world, plunged these words with a dagger into my heart: yes, have sensibility, see the world as few see it, be great and noble. . . . But I add one thing more: be a Jewess! And now my life is a slow bleeding to death."[56] She and Veit both concluded that the best way to avoid being treated like a Jew was to avoid cities and situations populated with other Jews.[57] Levin's marginality vis-à-vis the established Jewish community was thus largely her own doing. She prided herself with flaunting its customs, such as breaking the Sabbath by openly riding in a carriage through the streets of Berlin with her friend the actress Marchetti.[58] By refusing to marry the suitable Jewish businessmen proposed by her family, she risked the loneliness which was the consequence of daring to move away from the Jewish world while still suffering rejections by the noble one.

Yet slowly, during the early 1790s, Levin tentatively began to enter the elegant noble circles she had worshipped from afar as an adolescent. During summer trips to the spa at Teplitz she met Josephine von Pachta, a nonconformist noblewoman, and Gustav von Brinkmann, a Swedish diplomat and amateur poet stationed in Berlin. Brinkmann was entranced by the intellectual originality of the "little Levi," as he called her, and introduced her to many of his noble friends; it was he who persuaded his prominent noble friends to visit Levin's salon. Although her mother was convinced that these new friends were ruining her daughter's mental and physical health, for Levin they were a significant accomplishment.[59] She spent the mornings writing long and introspective letters, which also helped to improve her German. In the afternoons, she made up for her lack of formal training by studying English, French, and mathematics with tutors. And in the evenings, she was frequently to be found at the opera or the theater. Afterward, her wide circle of gentile friends had their carriages deliver them at her mother's house in the Jägerstrasse, where they climbed the stairs to her attic apartment. There they gossiped and discussed Iffland's new play, Goethe's novels, and the course of the French Revolution. Levin remained single until she was forty-two, in

---

56. Translation from ibid., 4.

57. These mutual admonitions can be found on both sides of the Levin-Veit correspondence. See Rahel (Levin) Varnhagen von Ense, *Briefwechsel zwischen Rahel und David Veit* (Leipzig, 1861).

58. Arendt, *Rahel Varnhagen.*

59. Levin's mother's upset was reported in a letter by Gustav von Brinkmann to Julie von Voss, of May 30, 1802, now in packet 2, Berg-Voss Collection, Goethe-Schiller Archive (GSA), Weimar.

Gustav von Brinkmann

1814. After a lonely existence during the French invasion of the city and the War of Liberation, she converted and married a younger gentile admirer, the diplomat and writer Karl August Varnhagen von Ense. Together, they hosted a second salon in Berlin during the second decade of the nineteenth century, but this was a smaller, more formal salon than the gatherings in the Jägerstrasse had been before 1806.

Not all the Jewish salonières were as physically glamorous as Henriette Herz or as socially rebellious as Rahel Levin. Sara Levy was one of nine daughters born to Daniel and Marianne Itzig; her father was the head of the most powerful and most privileged Jewish family in Berlin at the time.[60] Sara's sisters Fanny and Cäcelie both married wealthy Jewish financiers from Vienna, where each hosted a salon.[61] Sara Itzig, too, mar-

60. See the article on the Itzig family in the *Encyclopedia Judaica* (Jerusalem, 1971), vol. 9, 1150–51. See also Wilhelm Erman, *Paul Erman: Ein Berliner Gelehrtenleben 1764–1851* (Berlin, 1927), and Karoline Cauer, *Oberhofbankier und Hofbaurat* (Frankfurt a.M., 1965).

61. The standard work useful for Cäcelie as well is Hilde Spiel, *Fanny von Arnstein, oder die Emanzipation* (Frankfurt a.M., 1962).

ried within the faith, and neither she nor her husband, a banker named Solomon Levy, ever converted. The Levys' grand home in the center of town across from the stock exchange, with its large adjoining gardens, was an extended family household. Two of Sara Levy's sisters lived there after 1795: her blind sister Recha and her widowed sister Rebekka. The poet Achim von Arnim rented an apartment in the Levy home in 1804, and the daughter of the military preacher Johann Uhden lived there until her death.[62] This heterogeneous household had heterogeneous *Hausfreunde*. Every Thursday a group of ten to fourteen guests were invited for a noon dinner, and on Sunday afternoons, the Levys held an open house for tea. The guests at these occasions included prominent local nobles as well as French diplomats who were visiting Berlin. Frau Levy was praised for her linguistic and musical abilities, if not for her social vivacity or her looks. She apparently spoke French like a native and played the piano for both Hayden and Mozart, two of her most famous visitors. Yet Rahel Levin's husband Karl August Varnhagen found her a bit of a philistine, and Clemens Brentano complained that her salon gatherings were "boring," while others criticized her for namedropping.[63] But neither her aesthetic, social, and mental limitations nor her professed loyalty to Judaism interfered with Frau Levy's role in high society. She continued to receive regular Sunday visits from the prominent until her death in 1854. For all her purported rigidity in conversation, that year, at the age of ninety-three, she impressed a young nephew by emerging from her carriage and dancing in the street![64]

A glamorous but short-lived salon was hosted by Philippine Cohen, who was born Pessel Zülz in 1776. Her father, who changed his name from Zülz to Bernhard, inherited a silk manufactory that once employed Moses Mendelssohn. His daughter Pessel received a generous dowry of 100,000 taler, and the lucky groom she married was Ephraim Cohen, who moved to Berlin from Amsterdam. Berliners called him the "English Cohen" because he introduced English spinning machines to the city.[65] Husband, wife, and two children all converted together in 1800, and Pessel changed her name to Philippine. The Cohen family lived in an

---

62. On von Arnim's stay at the Levy household see Helene Riley, *Ludwig Achim von Arnims Jugend- und Reisejahre* (Bonn, 1978), 108; on Uhden's daughter's sojourn there see Felix Eberty, *Jugenderinnerungen* (Berlin, 1925), 215.

63. On Varnhagen's and Brentano's critiques of Sara Levy see Wilhelm Erman, *Paul Erman*, 96; on Sara Levy's tendency to name-drop see Eberty, *Jugenderinnerungen*, 215.

64. See Eberty, *Jugenderinnerungen*, 251.

65. On Mendelssohn's business relationship with Philippine Cohen's father see Jacob Jacobson, *Jüdische Trauungen in Berlin, 1759–1813* (Berlin, 1968), 150 and 362.

opulent home adjoining Herr Cohen's wool factory, which was jointly owned by the state and Herr Cohen and employed hundreds of workers. Theirs was a large and varied household. Philippine's mother Madame Bernhard had a house in the country but often stayed with her daughter's family in the city. Philippine's sister, Frau von Boye, who had divorced her Jewish husband and proceeded to marry two different noblemen in succession, was a frequent visitor. Two young aspiring novelists, Wilhelm Neumann and Karl August Varnhagen, were live-in employees, Neumann a clerk in the firm and Varnhagen a tutor for the children. Almost daily, a wider society joined the members of the Cohen household for lunch, gossip, piano-playing, and the reading of novels and personal diaries aloud. Karl August Varnhagen later remembered how he would retire to his room to compose character sketches of the guests and return to the group to read them aloud so that the guests could guess at who was being described. Philippine's sister Frau von Boye was friendly with several prominent intellectuals, including Johann Fichte, Jean Paul (Richter), and Friedrich Schlegel. She occasionally played the patron role and once introduced Neumann and Varnhagen to her famous literary friends by inviting them all to join her at her box at the theater.[66] The Cohen salon dispersed just a year after the Herz salon broke up, in the summer of 1804, when Herr Cohen's years of paying more attention to the charms of salon life than to his factory caught up with him. Mismanagement resulted in the collapse of his business; the court took over the factory and issued a warrant for his arrest. His wife, sister-in-law, and mother-in-law lost their entire fortunes, and Herr Cohen escaped to Holland. Unfortunately, Varnhagen, the main source for the Cohen story, left Berlin soon after he lost his job as tutor, and thus the eventual fate of Frau Cohen's salon remains a mystery.

In 1798, after the Herz, Levin, Levy, and Cohen salons were all well established, Friederich Schleiermacher, a promising young preacher who had moved to the city two years before, wrote to his sister explaining why Berlin's most interesting society gathered at Jewish homes. According to Schleiermacher, it was not just that the richest men in Berlin were Jewish, but also that the Jewish financiers' wives and daughters were cultivated and their style of entertaining informal and lively.[67] Noble

66. Frau von Boye's marital career will be evaluated in detail in chapter 7. The major source for the discussion here of the Cohen salon is Karl August Varnhagen von Ense, *Denkwürdigkeiten des eigenen Lebens*, Karl Leutner, ed. (East Berlin, 1954), 81–89. These passages can also be found in vol. 1 of the original, full-length edition of Karl August Varnhagen's memoirs (Leipzig, 1843).

67. Schleiermacher's often-cited letter to his sister about the salons was that of October 22, 1797, in Georg Reimer, ed., *Aus Schleiermachers Leben in Briefen* (Berlin, 1858–63), vol.

complaints about the stiff ceremony of social life at court and the rigidity of noble socializing styles echoed Schleiermacher's emphasis on the distinctiveness of the Jewish elite's lifestyle. Yet the story of a fifth salon, led by the Duchess Dorothea von Courland, shows that entertaining in style was by no means simply a function of one's estate. Indeed, von Courland's story illustrates that if a noblewoman had both enough money and the right attitudes, the problems in the city's social life caused by the rigidity of courtly social styles could in principle have been solved by nobles as well as by Jews.

Von Courland was a member of a prominent noble family from the Baltic provinces. She and her younger half-sister Eliza received a thorough education at home from Dorothea's stepmother, who took learning seriously and enjoyed entertaining intellectual guests and even hired a tutor for the two girls. The young man she chose was Daniel Parthey, who was later employed as a tutor by the Nicolai family and who thus came to introduce Dorothea's half-sister Eliza to the Nicolai family. At eighteen, the beautiful Dorothea was married off to the Duke of Courland. Although much older and quite crochety, the duke encouraged his wife's intellectual interests. They visited cultural shrines in Italy, Immanuel Kant in Königsberg, Frederick the Great in Potsdam, and Moses Mendelssohn in Berlin. But by 1795, when she was thirty-four, the duke had lost his little state of Courland to Russia, in the third division of Poland. He had become increasingly cranky, and Dorothea separated from him. After his death in 1800 she bought a landed estate near Berlin for the summers and a former royal palace on Unter den Linden in Berlin for the winters, where she opened her salon. Von Courland's forthright position as a progressive noble won her admiration from some and disdain from others. She had always been philanthropic and generous, annually spending a quarter of her "pin money" (four thousand taler a year!) on charity. She once canceled a shopping trip to Leipzig in order to loan money to a friend in need. At her estate she raised the wages paid to the peasants and improved the local school; she befriended and provided regular financial support for various impoverished authors. Jean Paul (Richter) and Ludwig Tieck stayed for long periods at her country estate. Dorothea von Courland's noble friends, who included Queen Luise and other women in the royal family, shared her passion for literature, but were frankly shocked at how her egalitarian ideology was expressed in the style of her salon. For von Courland delighted in seating her Jewish and commoner guests next to prominent nobles at the tiny

---

I, 160–64. The letter is cited in Jerry F. Dawson, *Friedrich Schleiermacher: The Evolution of a Nationalist* (Austin, 1966), 23.

tables she preferred over the usual long ones. This was the duchess' highly self-conscious way of easing the estate barriers that divided wealthy Berliners.[68]

A sixth woman identified by historians as having led a salon was Dorothea Veit. Closer inspection allows us to construct a more nuanced portrait of Veit's role as salonière. Indeed, Veit's ultimate failure to gather a regular salon circle around her shows how delicate the whole endeavor was. Dorothea, the oldest child of Moses Mendelssohn, received a more rigorous education than any other Jewish girl in Berlin at the time. Her father allowed her to join the morning lessons he offered at the Mendelssohn home to a select group of young students, a group which included her younger brothers Joseph and Abraham and the two von Humboldt brothers.[69] But as in the case of Henriette Herz, Moses Mendelssohn's progressive views about his daughter's education did not extend to his daughter's marriage, and Dorothea was wed in late adolescence to a man of her father's choosing—Simon Veit, a kindly but decidedly unintellectual businessman. Dorothea's (or Brendel, as she was still called at the time) efforts to host a salon during her fifteen years as Veit's wife, between 1783 and 1798, culminated in the tiny, all-Jewish Lecture Society that met at the Veits on Thursday evenings. But this intellectual club never developed into a true salon, in part because Simon lacked interest in avant-garde literature, in part because Dorothea was a serious person not altogether at ease in society.

But Veit's failure to succeed as a salonière was the least of her problems in these three years. Almost immediately after her marriage in 1783, she had begun complaining bitterly to her friends about her unhappiness with her husband. Nevertheless, she resisted her friend Henriette Herz's

68. Sources used here on von Courland's life were Baxa, *Friedrich von Gentz*, 156; Jennings, *Rahel*, 38; Christoph August Tiedge, *Anna Charlotte Dorothea, letzte Herzogin von Kurland* (Leipzig, 1823); and Hans Schönfeld, "Die letzte Herzogin von Kurland an brandenbürgischen Höfen," *Sonntags-Verlage der Vitung-Zeitung*, no. 595 (September, 1920). A useful unpublished volume, including original pictures and clippings, was collated by Wolf von Tümpling, *Die Herzogin von Curland und Theodor Körner und die Seinigen: Löbichau 1795–1907* (Thalstein, 1917). The volume is now located in the von Courland collection in the rare manuscript library at the Friedrich Schiller University in Jena, in the German Democratic Republic.

69. On Dorothea Veit see Jennings, *Rahel*, 147–49; Heimenz, *Dorothea v. Schlegel*; M. Kayserling, *Die jüdischen Frauen*, 183–97; and Josef Körner, "Mendelssohns Töchter," *Preussische Jahrbücher* 214 (November, 1928), 167–82. On Mendelssohn's morning lessons see Altmann, *Moses Mendelssohn*. Ludwig Geiger's view on Veit and salons was that Veit really did not want to be a "prominent" woman, but rather to be at home with her loved ones. See Geiger's *Dichtung und Frauen* (Berlin, 1896), 149. Kurt Fervers's view was, on the contrary, that Veit was "jealous" of her friends' salons, in his *Berliner Salons: Die Geschichte einer grossen Verschwörung* (Munich, 1940), 76.

entreaties to leave him and kept the sad news from her father, who died in 1786 believing his daughter to be happily married. For another four-teen years Dorothea stayed with Simon and their two sons, until another man came into her life—Friedrich Schlegel, who had moved to Berlin in 1798. They met at the Herz salon when he was twenty-six and she thirty-four. Veit was by no means a beauty, but she had other qualities more valued by Schlegel: intellectual skills and seriousness, the embodiment of his own pronouncements about the qualities a new generation of women should possess. Moreover, Veit was willing to devote her considerable mental powers to Schlegel's intellectual work. Her sacrifices in this arena were consistent both with Schlegel's view that the new emancipated woman should work alongside her mate and with his less theoretical, more opportunistic need for copyist, translator, admirer, and muse.

And so Dorothea moved to a small apartment in an obscure corner of the city, leaving their two sons with Simon Veit. Although she in fact lived alone, it was rumored that she was living with Friedrich Schlegel. Deserted by her siblings for her open defiance of traditional Jewish val-ues, her isolation was compounded by the snubs of her sophisticated gentile friends. Emancipated though they may have been in principle about the sufferings caused by arranged marriages, many still distanced themselves from the scandal of Dorothea Veit's rebellion. Then, too, Schlegel had made many enemies in various literary feuds. Racked with physical illness as well, Veit's only friends were Schlegel, Friedrich Schleiermacher, and Henriette Herz, who defied her husband's order that she not visit Veit. The publication of Schlegel's erotic novel *Lucinde* in 1799, thought to be a description of the couple's new life together, only deepened her ostracism.[70]

The circumstances of Dorothea Veit's life after she left Berlin in 1801 hardly provided her with the material comfort, geographical stability, or minimum social respectability so useful to salon sponsorship. In Jena, the couple's first home after leaving Berlin, Schlegel was embroiled in bitter literary disputes, and Veit was disliked by Friedrich's powerful sis-ter, Caroline Schlegel. The couple was so poor that Veit set herself to work writing a novel in order to keep food on the table. Her conversion to Protestantism in 1804 and the couple's subsequent marriage provided a minimum of social respectability. But in none of the cities where the couple lived after Jena was Veit ever rich or well connected enough to sponsor a salon.

Not all the salonières were strong, intellectually accomplished person-

---

70. On Schlegel's *Lucinde*, see Hans Eichner, *Friedrich Schlegel* (New York, 1970), chap. 4.

alities. Sara and Marianne Meyer were born into an Orthodox and wealthy family, and their parents provided them with a decorative, fashionable education. Like the household of Rahel Levin, even before 1780 the girls' parents' home was later remembered as a "center of sociability." It was there that the young daughters first met and earned the admiration of a string of esteemed gentile intellectuals. Sara, the oldest, was praised by Lessing, Harder, and Goethe for her lively personality and her talent for languages. At an "early" age, Sara Meyer married Jacob Wulff, but after a decade of marriage, she divorced Wulff and converted to Protestantism—although for unknown reasons, she later converted back to Judaism. But she eventually converted back to Protestantism for a second time, in order to marry again to a nobleman, Baron von Grotthuss. The salon she led as his wife declined in the years after 1806, when Berlin was under foreign rule, because the baron lost his fortune. The elegant Sara von Grotthuss thus ended her days in Oranienburg, where her impoverished husband had found a modest position as a postmaster.

Sara's younger sister Marianne was said to be prettier but less goodhearted than Sara. Her love life was certainly more troubled. First, early in the 1780s, she was courted by Christian von Bernstorff, son of the Danish ambassador in Berlin, but his father forbade the misalliance.[71] Next, Count Gessler, the Saxon ambassador to the Prussian court, publicly announced that he would marry her, but he too humiliated her by failing to uphold his promise. Finally, Marianne Meyer married the Austrian ambassador in Berlin, Prince von Reuss. Her salon must have been open in the years before his death in 1799, while she still enjoyed the material and status comforts of being Princess von Reuss. These perquisites could be enjoyed without having to worry about getting along with her husband, since they had separate households. Despite this physical independence, the rules of his world impinged on the glory of being wedded to a prince. For although she had his title, Marianne was still not considered *hoffähig*, and so was forbidden to visit court circles with her husband.[72] When he died in 1799, she moved to Vienna. But whatever advantages she might have expected to enjoy as his widow were denied to her, as his relatives refused to let her continue using his name and title. Finally, she successfully petitioned the Austrian Emperor Francis II to give her permission to use the noble name "Frau von Eyben-

71. On the von Bernstorff rejection see Lawrence J. Baack, *Christian Bernstorff and Prussia* (New Brunswick, 1980), 6–8. On both Meyer sisters see Jennings, *Rahel*, 148–50; and Kayserling, *Die jüdischen Frauen*, 218–20.

72. See Jennings, *Rahel*, 148. In addition to the sources noted above see also Varnhagen's views on the two women, in vol. 4 of his *Denkwürdigkeiten*, 635–42.

berg." Her power as a salonière in Vienna during these years must have been limited indeed, in spite of her friendship with prominent noble families. For in addition to robbing her of her rightful title of "princess," von Reuss's family's rejection of their Jewish daughter-in-law extended to financial deprivation as well, leaving her virtually in poverty.[73]

The ninth woman labeled as a salonière, Rebecca Friedländer, was born Rebecca Solomon, into the same privileged milieu as were the other Jewish salonières, and she shared many of the same social aspirations. Her father was a jewel merchant for the court who changed the family name from Solomon to Saaling. At eighteen, Rebecca married Moses Friedländer, the son of David Friedländer, a wealthy silk entrepreneur active in the reform wing of the Jewish community. But the marriage did not last; she separated from him in 1804, while still only twenty-three. Friedländer lived alone in Berlin, spending her time corresponding with her best friend Rahel Levin, writing a string of poorly received novels, and hosting "aesthetic teas." She eventually converted and changed her name to Regina Frohberg, hoping this step would enhance her literary career and encourage one of her many noble suitors to ask for her hand in marriage. But none of them did, and Friedländer never remarried.[74]

In the first years after her separation from Moses Friedländer, Rebecca Friedländer's apartment was inside the home of a tenth salonière, Amalie Beer. The heyday of Beer's salon was after the Napoleonic era, but its beginnings can be traced to the pre-1806 years. A descendant of the Liebman family, Berlin's premier court Jewish family early in the eighteenth century, Amalie was married at sixteen to Jakob Herz Beer, who owned sugar factories in Berlin as well as in Italy. Their son, Jacob Meyerbeer, later became a renowned composer. Amalie Beer herself was praised for being "a grand lady from her *Scheitel* [a wig worn by religious Jewish women] to her *Schole* [soles of her shoes], cultivated, clever, charming." Her trips to Italy, both for her husband's business and for her sons' education, only increased her sophistication. She received guests from all circles "majestically, with the most perfect skill" and detested solitude; on her birthdays she welcomed hundreds of guests, who arrived in early morning and remained until late at night. The Beer home was later to become a center for the religiously progressive as well as for the social

---

73. Kayserling, *Die jüdischen Frauen*, 220.

74. On Friedländer see Jacobson, *Jüdische Trauungen*, 440; Arendt, *Rahel Varnhagen*, 107; and the memoirs of her nephew: Paul Heyse, *Jugenderinnerungen und Bekenntnisse* (Berlin, 1901), 6. In 1988 my edited edition (with an introduction) of Rahel Levin's letters to Friedländer will be published by Kiepenheuer and Witsch, Cologne, entitled *Briefe an eine Freundin: Rahel Varnhagen an Rebecca Friedländer*.

"The Abrahamson Salon"

elite. Isaac Jacobson organized an early, private, "reform" synagogue there in the 1820s, after the Jewish salons had declined.[75]

Another two women have been labeled as salon hosts, but even less is known about their entertaining style than about the women met thus far. An often reproduced sketch of the sculptor Gottfried Schadow, his converted wife Marianne Devidel, and the engravers Jacob Abrahamson and his son gathered around a table at the Abrahamson home has been used as evidence that the Abrahamsons hosted a salon.[76] But other than the picture, no other details about the Abrahamsons' socializing can be

75. On the Liebmann (or Liepmann) family see Selma Stern, The *Court Jew*, trans. Ralph Weiman (Philadelphia, 1950), 49ff. One of the rare sources on Amalie Beer is the typescript of an article by Kurt Richter, "Amalie Beer und ihre Söhne," which appeared in the *Centralverein Zeitung* (no. 11, Beilage 3, n.d.). (All quotations are from page one of the typescript.) The typescript is in the Beer Meyerbeer Collection (AR 3194) in the archives of the Leo Baeck Institute, New York City. On Beer's son Michael see the (Nazi-oriented) Wilhelm Grau, *Wilhelm von Humboldt und das Problem des Juden* (Hamburg, 1935), 34, and L. Kahn, "Michael Beer," *LBIYB* 12 (1967), 149–60. On Beer's marriage see Jacobson, *Jüdische Trauungen*, 317. On Isaac Jacobson's synagogue in the Beer home see Bach, *The German Jew*, 82–83.

76. The assumption that the depicted gathering at the Abrahamsons was a salon can be found in Bildarchiv Preussischer Kulturbesitz, ed., *Juden in Preussen: Ein Kapitel deutscher*

found. Another home noted by at least one historian as having been a salon is that of J. H. and Helene Unger.[77] He was a prominent editor and publisher, she a prolific author of fiction and non-fiction. Not only is there no primary-source record of the Ungers hosting salon-like gatherings; much about Frau Unger's own ideology suggests that she was hostile to the entire enterprise. For Helene Unger made it quite clear in her writings that she had nothing but contempt for the negative effects that imitation of a decadent aristocratic lifestyle had on status-hungry commoners. Her enormously popular novel *Julchen Grünthal* told the story of a robust young girl from the countryside who was corrupted by French governesses and dissolute noble officers when she came to the city to attend a girls' boarding school. And in her *Briefe über Berlin* ("Letters on Berlin") Unger openly condemned the Jewish salonières for their intellectual pretensions. Another source suggests that this ideological attack was motivated by Unger's jealousy of Dorothea Veit. It seems that in the months in 1798 just before Friederich Schlegel met Veit at the Herzes, he was romantically involved with Helene Unger.[78]

The last two salons on the roster were both led by men. The bookstore owner Andreas Reimer was noted for hosting regular gatherings of the city's intelligentsia, but no details can be unearthed.[79] The banker and entrepreneur Benjamin Veitel Ephraim, a colorful character, is also reported to have hosted a salon. His father, Veitel Heine Ephraim, worked with Daniel Itzig minting coins during the Seven Years' War; both were accused of helping Frederick the Great finance that war by minting and circulating debased and thus inflationary coinage. As a reward for their loyal service, Ephraim was given permission to build a grand palace on the Mühlendamn in the center of town, where his youngest son Benjamin lived an elegant lifestyle, indulging in luxuries like a white carpet, unheard of in Berlin at the time. Unfortunately for him, the consequences of his political activities made it difficult for Benjamin to continue this opulent and sociable life. In 1787 and again in 1790 he was sent

---

Geschichte (Dortmund, 1981), 150. On the Abrahamsons see the brief article in *The Jewish Encyclopedia* (New York and London, 1901), vol. I, 123. Kurt Fervers calls the gatherings at the Abrahamson home a salon in his *Berliner Salons*, 96.

77. This claim was made by Brunschwig, *Enlightenment and Romanticism*, 281–82.

78. On the Unger couple see Flodoard F. von Biedermann, *Johann Friedrich Unger im Verkehr mit Goethe und Schiller* (Berlin, 1927). Helene Unger's *Briefe über Berlin* has been reprinted: (Berlin, 1935). The interpretation that her remarks on Jewish women reflected her personal experience with Schlegel can be found on the flyleaf of Karl August Varnhagen von Ense's copy (in his handwriting) of Unger's *Julchen Grünthal* (Berlin, 1787), now in the Staatsbibliothek in West Berlin.

79. On Reimer see Varnhagen von Ense, *Denkwürdigkeiten* (Leutner edition), 96.

by King Frederick William II on secret political missions, first to Brussels and then to Paris, to negotiate on Prussia's behalf with the French. But after Prussia changed to an anti-French course in 1805, Ephraim was entirely discredited, and in 1806 he was arrested by Prussian authorities for his pro-French sympathies. By the time he died in 1811, he was isolated and impoverished.[80]

Herr Ephraim is the last of the fourteen individuals labeled by historians as having hosted salons in Berlin between 1780 and 1806. This wide spectrum makes it clear that holding a salon is best understood as a matter of degree, not an either-or affair—which does not make definitions useless, for a definition sets the parameters. Existing definitions define salons as gatherings hosted by a woman, with intellectual dialogue as the chief entertainment. Two other items noted in existing definitions are that salon guests had diverse social backgrounds and occupations, and that formal invitations were not issued.[81] But a too rigid use of definitions can close us off to the rich diversity of past life. Even if primary-source descriptions of salon life were more abundant, it would be wrong to limit the salon roster to gatherings that strictly met this four-part definition. Even the most well-documented suggest that the borders between the salon, traditional socializing, and the intellectual clubs were hazy. For instance, Rahel Levin, whose gatherings truly fit the hardest, fourth item of existing definitions—hosting without invitations—also entertained the same friends in more formal ways.[82] Salon hosting is thus

80. A short biography of Ephraim can be found in the *Encyclopedia Judaica* (Jerusalem, 1971), vol. 6, 811. See also [Saul Ascher], *Kabinet berlinischer Charaktere* (Berlin, 1808); Eberty (Benjamin Ephraim's son), *Jugenderinnerungen,* 38; Ingnatz Aurelius Fessler, *Rückblicke auf seine siebzigjährige Pilgerschaft* (Leipzig, 1851), 153; and Joachim Kühn, *B. V. Ephraims Geheimsendung nach Paris 1790/91,* Ph.D. diss., University of Giessen, 1916. On a dinner party at the Ephraims in 1801 see *Aus den Tagebüchern des alten Heim* in *Archiv der "Brandenburgia" Gesellschaft,* 166. Finally, see Dorf Michaelis, "The Ephraim Family and Their Descendents (II)," *LBIYB* 24 (1979), 225–46.

81. In addition to the definitions of the salon found in note 27, Chap. 1, see Habermas, *Strukturwandel der Öffentlichkeit.* For a useful summary of Habermas's argument in English see Peter Hohendahl, "Introduction to Habermas," and Habermas, "The Public Sphere," both in *New German Critique* 3 (1974), 45–48 and 49–55. I am grateful to Joan Landes of Hampshire College for sharing a chapter, "Eighteenth-Century Sources of the Feminist Public Sphere," of her book-in-progress, *Women and the Public Sphere,* which helped me understand Habermas on this point. For another definition of the salon see Narhrstedt, *Die Entstehung der Freizeit;* see also Karl Haase, "Rahel Varnhagens Brieftheorie," M.A. thesis, Munich, Ludwig Maximilian University, 1977, 14 and 33.

82. For instance, on September 3, 1801, Gustav von Brinkmann wrote to Countess Julie von Voss, describing a *soupé* (dinner) he and "Humboldt" had at Rahel's Levin's. The letter is no. 109 in packet 10 of the Brinkmann-Voss Collection at the GSA.

best understood as a tendency, or an ideal type, that was more pronounced among some gatherings than among others.

Not only are salons elusive of definition retrospectively; they were fragile institutions at the time. The quirks of personality and one's familial circumstances were obviously important in the making of a successful salon. This is best illustrated both by the abrupt end of Henriette Herz's salon in 1803 and by the delicate sort of barriers that made it so difficult for Dorothea Veit to open a real salon. Yet the same twists and turns of individual fate that seem to account for which women became salonières at which moment in their lives actually do little to explain the larger pattern of salon society in Berlin. Personality and family circumstances may have determined which individuals succeeded as salonières at what period of their lives, but the larger scale social needs of members of particular estates and occupations, as well as Prussia's political fate, set the larger scene within which individual salons appeared and disappeared. This is dramatically illustrated by the demise of Rahel Levin's salon, once the most popular salon in the city. Unlike the case of Henriette Herz in 1803, in 1806 Levin's financial situation, and thus her ability to entertain, did not alter dramatically. Yet, as we shall see in chapter 8, beginning in that year the material and ideological conditions in which salons flourished disappeared, and so even the charismatic Levin could not hold her circle together.

The fragility of the ties which bound salon participants to each other is understandable, given the extraordinary heterogeneity of that society. (Because it has not been possible to reconstruct the personnel of each and every salon, the term *salon society* refers to the roughly one hundred persons noted in the sources as having attended at least one salon during this quarter century.) As figure 8 shows, a third of the one hundred were female. The female presence in public leisure events was not entirely new. In the decades before 1780 women had come to participate in court life, in the city's new commercial leisure activities, and even in a few intellectual clubs. Still, although in strictly numerical terms salons were only open to a tiny number of women, the emergence of salons represented a dramatic change for wealthy women. On the stage of symbolic and real cultural power, salons were a far greater opportunity for their lucky female participants than commercial or club leisure. The reason was that salons were almost always formed around specific women. Common admiration of her intellectual and personal qualities was one of the bonds which united the guests. And because salons were informal gatherings which met in homes, participation was not an issue about which male committees could legislate.

Figure 8. Estate and Gender of Salon Participants

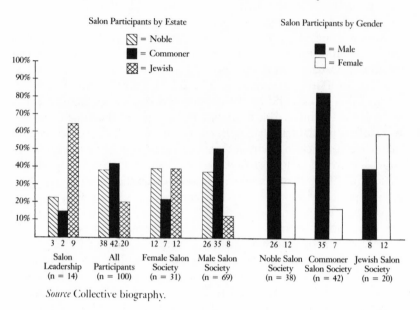

Source Collective biography.

Yet considering that eleven of the thirty-one women in salon society were themselves salonières, the comparative size of the public stage salons provided for women shrinks somewhat. Aside from the salonière herself, specific salons did not by any means always include enough non-salonière women to constitute a female literary network or subculture. Rahel Levin's salon included very few women: an 1805 visitor found only one woman there besides Levin herself.[83] Dorothea Veit complained in a 1798 letter that she hated spending the evenings at her friend Henriette Herz's because women were "not allowed to speak," since they would "profane" the philosophical dialogue.[84] Dorothea von Courland, to be sure, did have an unusually large number of female guests. But this was attributed to her high social rank, which allowed her to flout convention by filling her reception room with women.[85]

If the presence of women at the symbolic center of salon life was a sign

83. The guest's (one "Grafen S.") narrative describing an evening of Levin's salon is reprinted in C. May, *Rahel: Ein Berliner Frauenleben im 19. Jahrhundert* (Berlin, n.d.), 6–16.

84. See Franz Deibel, *Dorothea Schlegel als Schriftstellerin im Zusammenhang mit der romantischen Schule*, in *Palaestra* 60 (Berlin, 1905), 158.

85. See Ostwald, *Kultur- und Sittengeschichte Berlins*, 134.

of emancipation, at first glance it would not seem that salon society was also emancipated by also being dense with Jews. For when the size of the Jewish representation in salons is contrasted with the size of the female representation, it becomes clear that Jews in general did not profit much from salon attendance. Fifteen Jews participated in salon society, and at 15 percent, they were certainly overrepresented in comparison to their proportion of the city at large. But it was mainly Jewish women, not Jewish men, who were overrepresented in salons: the eight Jewish men in salons were a mere 4 percent of the men in salon society, whereas the eleven Jewish women were almost two-fifths of the women in salon society. Jewish women were even more dramatically overrepresented among the salonières, since nine of the twelve women who led salons were Jewish. The noble presence in salons shows a similar pattern. A minority estate was overrepresented among the thirty-one women, but not among the sixty-nine men in salons. A third of all salon participants were noble. Outside of court society, salons had the greatest noble participation of any of the city's leisure activities. Only 6 percent of the members of the intellectual clubs, after all, were noble. But the nobles in salons, like the Jews, were not equally divided among the men and the women. As shown in figure 8, under a third of the sixty-nine men in salons were noble, whereas over two-fifths of the thirty-one women in salons were noble.

The presence of so many nobles was only one of the aristocratic features of salon life. The custom of having strangers congregating inside large and complex households had long been a part of the noble way of life, in city and in country. Veneration of the salonière resembled the admiration (or literally, the "court") noble courtiers paid to medieval and Renaissance queens. In the Berlin salons of the eighteenth century, as in these earlier courts, homage was paid to the cultivated female with reading of original writing and literary discourse. The leading Jewish salonières founded their salons in conscious imitation of the French noble salon tradition in order to synthesize the best of gallic intellectual form and German intellectual content.[86] Even though not all the Jewish salonières' imitation of an ancient role was so self-conscious, hosting a salon surely did "dust" them with a noble "aura." And acting nobly in this way surely helped to legitimize the Jewish salonières as friends, lovers, and would-be spouses for their noble guests.[87]

It follows from the preponderance of nobles and Jews in female salon

86. See Spiel, *Fanny von Arnstein*, 94.
87. My formulation here is very much indebted to that suggested by Carolyn Lougee in her *Le Paradis des Femmes: Women, Salons, and Social Stratification in Seventeenth-Century France* (Princeton, 1976).

Caffée clatché: A contemporary satire mocks the competitive atmosphere of salon socializing

society that most of the commoners in salons were men. As shown in figure 8, a quarter of the salon women but over two-thirds of the salon men were commoners. The occupational profile of salon men was not dissimilar to that of the sampled men from the intellectual clubs. As shown in figure 9, professors were overrepresented in salons, albeit less so than in the intellectual clubs. Both clubs and salons had about as many officials as did the male intelligentsia at large. But both preachers and clerks had as much difficulty arriving in salons as they did in being invited to join an intellectual club. Accordingly, most of the male salon participants were employed in four upper-income occupations: landowners, officials, merchants, and professors. The strong showing of landowners was a consequence of the strong noble representation; many nobles still lived from agricultural profits. Both nobles and well-educated commoners contributed to the number of officials in salons. The few Jewish men in salons were almost exclusively merchants, and the professors, many of whom were arrivistes, had reached the pinacle of the intellectual institutions.

It is obvious from their comparative youth that the salon men employed in these four occupations had not achieved their positions after long struggles up the social ladder. As shown in figure 10, in 1800 a fifth of all of Berlin's intellectuals, only a tenth of the men in clubs, but almost two-fifths of the men in salon society were under thirty-five. As we shall see, the youth of the salon men had much to do with salon society's distinctive heterogeneity. But this and much else is still mysterious about just how these diverse men came together.

Chapter Two identified the social needs of the two estates whose members were crucial in catalyzing salons. Chapter Three reconstructed Ber-

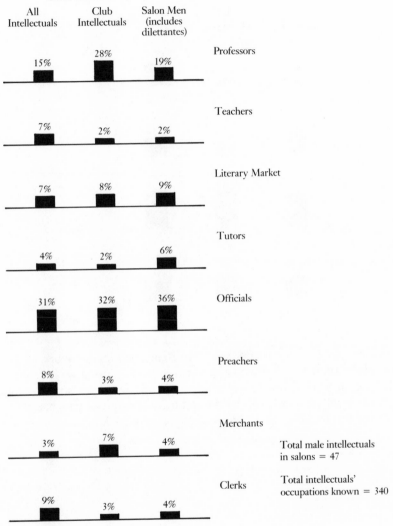

Figure 9. Occupations of Berlin Intellectuals, Club Intellectuals, and Salon Men

All Intellectuals	Club Intellectuals	Salon Men (includes dilettantes)	
15%	28%	19%	Professors
7%	2%	2%	Teachers
7%	8%	9%	Literary Market
4%	2%	6%	Tutors
31%	32%	36%	Officials
8%	3%	4%	Preachers
3%	7%	4%	Merchants
9%	3%	4%	Clerks

Total male intellectuals in salons = 47

Total intellectuals' occupations known = 340

Source: Collective biography.

lin's intelligentsia, who lived for their intellectual passions and would thus seek entrance to salons. This chapter has drawn the map of public institutions in which salons had their place.

To unravel the mysteries that remain, we must move directly to the

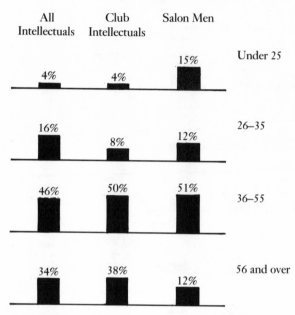

Figure 10. Age of Berlin Intellectuals, Club Intellectuals, and Salon Men

	All Intellectuals	Club Intellectuals	Salon Men	
Under 25	4%	4%	15%	
26–35	16%	8%	12%	
36–55	46%	50%	51%	
56 and over	34%	38%	12%	

Source: Collective biography.

inside of salons, to the friendships, love affairs, and literary work which bound the salon men and women to each other. For just as we have seen the long-range structural causes of salons, so too, we must also focus our gaze upon the individuals alive then and there, individuals who had their own reasons for arriving at the door of a particular salon.

FIVE | *Salon Men*

Princes and Scholars

When the French author and salonière Germaine de Staël visited Germany in the spring of 1804, she despaired about how hard it was to get princes to mix gracefully with scholars. In Germany, Madame de Staël lamented, "the nobles have too few ideas, the men of letters too little practice in business." But despite Germany's defects, the famous visitor found social life in Berlin far superior to that of other German cities: "no spectacle in all Germany was equal to that which Berlin presented. . . . sciences and letters are cultivated there; and, at dinners, both ministerial and private, where the men meet together, the separation of ranks, so prejudicial to Germany, is not rigidly enforced, but people of talent of all classes are collected."[1] The socializing between men of talent from several "classes" so appreciated by de Staël had evolved gradually in the quarter century since the Herzes opened their double salon in 1780, and the salon crowd became ever more heterogeneous as the years passed. By the end of the era, just before Napoleon's troops invaded Berlin in October 1806, the range of "classes" represented in salons was wide indeed.

The wealthy and cultivated Jewish hostesses were, of course, a crucial magnet in drawing together this heterogeneous society, but the salonières were obviously not alone sufficient for the emergence of salon society. Away from the Jewish hostesses' drawing rooms, friendships across the barriers of estate, religion, and occupation bound the sixty-nine men

---

1. Anne Louise Germaine (Necker) Staël-Holstein, *Germany*, 3 vols. (London, 1814), vol. 1, 21 and 166.

who composed the majority of salon society. Without these outside ties among male participants, salons could never have coalesced.

In the beginning, salon society was composed mainly of older, well-established male intellectuals whose dominant ideology (and that of most intellectuals outside salon society) was enlightened rationalism. French culture was admired, often slavishly, an enthusiasm that was not yet seen to clash with an intensifying Prussian nationalism. Thus, when the Herzes opened their double salon, Berlin intellectuals happily combined loyalty to Prussia and enlightened rationalism, synthesizing the two creeds in a passionate conviction that despotism would be more enlightened in Prussia than it had been in France. This belief inspired the loyalty of young intellectuals outside of Prussia as well. The young Christian Wilhelm Dohm, who later settled in Berlin and became famous for his treatise on the "civic betterment" of the Jews, applied repeatedly for a post in the progressive Prussian bureaucracy while at the university at Göttingen.[2] Gustav von Brinkmann, the Swedish diplomat who brought so many nobles to Rahel Levin's salon, summed up what the word *Prussia* meant for this generation. One evening a friend of Rahel Levin's, the Countess von Schlabrendorf, announced that "Jews and commoners" deserved to be ranked "under the class of Negroes." Von Brinkmann was indignant, for with these prejudiced words the countess "entirely condemned Prussia"—her antisemitism was objectionable because it was unenlightened and therefore unpatriotic.[3]

The male guests at the Herz salon in 1780 shared von Brinkmann's passion for the practical work of enlightenment. The first men to come to the Herzes for dinner were gentile commoners, publishing intellectuals Markus Herz had met in the few intellectual clubs he was allowed to join. These were older, famous men, who had their hair powdered and curled every morning and wore dark-colored breeches. Their wives, who did not usually accompany them to the Herzes, wore bonnets and high collars. Johann Biester edited the *Berlinische Monatschrift,* the city's most important Enlightenment journal. Karl Philipp Moritz, a novelist, journalist, and professor at the Royal Academy of Science, was the son of a hat maker and notorious for his astonishing mobility. Friedrich Nicolai, one of Germany's most renowned publishers and booksellers, was the loyal friend of Markus Herz's own mentor, Moses Mendelssohn. Johann Reichardt was an influential conductor. One of the few Jewish men

---

2. Ilsegret Dambacher, *Christian Wilhelm von Dohm* (Frankfurt, a.M., 1974), 11–15.

3. Letter from Gustav von Brinkmann to Julie von Voss, June 10, 1802, Brinkmann-Voss Collection, packet 11, GSA, Weimar.

David Friedländer

to visit the Herz salon was David Friedländer, a textile entrepreneur, a private banker, Jewish community leader, and published author. And it was probably at the Herz salon that David Friedländer met the preacher Wilhelm Teller. In 1799 Friedländer excited a great controversy with his appeal to Teller that Jews should be accepted into the Protestant church by a "dry baptism," without having to affirm the irrational claims of Christianity.[4]

Noblemen were as scarce in the Herz salon as Jews, even if the most prestigious nobles in the state—members of the royal family itself—did

4. In addition to the men named in the text, other guests at the early Herz salon included Christian Wilhelm Dohm, Johann Engel, Karl Wilhelm Ramler, and Johann Spalding. On Biester see the article in the *NDB* (Berlin, 1968), vol. 2, 234; on Moritz see the article in the *ADB* (Leipzig, 1880), vol. 22, 308–11; on Nicolai see Horst Möller, *Aufklärung in Preussen: Der Verleger, Publizist und Geschichtsschreiber Friedrich Nicolai* (Berlin, 1974). On David Friedländer, whose "dry baptism" proposal is discussed in chap. 7, see Immanuel Heinrich Ritter, *Geschichte der jüdischen Reformation*, part 2: *David Friedländer, sein Leben und sein Wirken* (Berlin, 1861).

Markus Herz

grace Markus Herz's science lectures. But their presence was within the classic terms of the intellectual club: an event with set times and a shared intellectual goal. In 1780, it was still considered too déclassé for princes to dine at a Jewish home or visit unannounced. One exception was Count Honoré de Mirabeau, who was sent to Berlin in 1786 on a secret mission by the French government to assess the impact of the expected death of King Frederick.[5] But Mirabeau was a foreign noble, and as such idiosyncratic in the Herz salon, where the guests were typically officials, professors, or preachers by profession, publishing authors, most in their

5. For Mirabeau's views of Prussian life just before Frederick the Great's death in 1786 see Count de Mirabeau, *Memoirs of the Courts of Berlin and Saint Petersburg* (New York, 1910).

forties or fifties.[6] Many were members of the Monday Club, the Wednesday Society, or the Royal Academy of Science; several belonged to more than one prestigious intellectual club. These enlightened, rather established intellectuals first gravitated to the Herz home because of Markus's lectures on natural science and Kantian philosophy, although Henriette's physical and intellectual charms and the couples' willingness to spend on lavish entertainments no doubt also contributed to their ability to attract prominent members of the notable intellectual clubs to their home. Thus at first, the Herz salon—and therefore salon society altogether—was essentially a domestic, more private extension of the intellectual clubs, both in personnel and in ideology.

The guests became more varied in the 1790s, as Henriette acquired her own set of younger friends, some of whom had been on the fringes of the Herz salon in the 1780s while still in their teens. Wilhelm and Alexander von Humboldt were first brought there in 1786 by their tutor, Gottlob Kunth; Wilhelm soon became a frequent visitor and an intimate friend of Henriette's. She tutored him in Hebrew, and he wrote her secret letters from his estate in Tegel using Hebrew characters, complaining about missing Berlin and dejectedly referring to his Tegel estate as the "Castle of Boredom."[7] The Tugendbund ("League of Virtue"), which Henriette and Wilhelm founded in 1787, with its private symbols and chain of letter-writing intimates, brought more young gentile intellectuals into Henriette's orbit. It was through the League that Herz came to know Karl Laroche, the handsome son of the famous novelist Sophie Laroche, and Caroline von Dacheröden, who later married Wilhelm von Humboldt.

Rahel Levin, a childhood friend of Henriette and one of the younger persons on the sidelines in the first years of the Herz salon, later went on to lead her own salon in the mid-1790s, one that brought together an even more diverse and prestigious collection of guests. Levin was put off by the sentimentality of the League of Virtue's rituals, perhaps because she did not need an intellectual club to meet elegant gentiles. Beginning in the mid-1790s, the rebellious noble women she met during her summer visits to Bohemian spas became her friends, and through them she gradually attracted a larger circle of gentile admirers. The diplomat and amateur poet Gustav von Brinkmann was the crucial figure in this process. Von Brinkmann was an enthusiastic *Gesellschaftler,* or always "good

6. Biester and Dohm were officials; Moritz, Engel, and Ramler were professors at a gymnasium or a knightly academy; Spalding and Teller were prominent preachers. The average age in 1785 of the eight men listed here or in note 4 above was forty-six.

7. See Paul Sweet, *Wilhelm von Humboldt, A Biography* (Columbus, Oh., 1978), vol. 1, 18–19; on the League of Virtue see vol. 1, 35–36.

Friedrich Schleiermacher

company," who delighted in making introductions and in maneuvering socially innovative relationships. It was von Brinkmann who introduced the von Humboldt brothers and their friend, Friedrich Gentz, to Levin.[8] Gentz in turn brought along his theologian friend from university days at Halle, Friedrich Schleiermacher. Schleiermacher was no stranger to Jewish society; ever since he moved to Berlin in 1794, Schleiermacher had been a loyal *Hausfreund* of the Herz salon. He was originally introduced to the Herzes by Count von Dohna, whose children he tutored. When Friedrich Schlegel moved to Berlin in 1797, von Brinkmann introduced Schlegel to Schleiermacher, as well as to the Herzes and to Rahel Levin. Wilhelm von Burgsdorff, who was close to the Humboldt brothers, brought along to Levin's attic gatherings his friend, the up-and-coming novelist Ludwig Tieck. By 1800, when Jean Paul (Richter), an-

8. On von Brinkmann see Albert Leitzmann's introduction to the volume he edited: *Wilhelm von Humboldts Briefe an Karl Gustav von Brinkmann* (Leipzig, 1939), vii–xiii.

other much feted, once-impoverished novelist, arrived in Berlin, visits to Levin's salon had become one of the city's chief attractions. When Johann Fichte, Germany's new star philosopher, fled Jena in 1799 because of a public battle with the university over his atheism, he too found an intellectual and social home in Levin's salon.[9]

The kind of men who visited the Herzes in the early 1780s differed strikingly from those who were dropping by at Rahel Levin's after the theater in the late 1790s: they were younger and less established in their careers, disdained wigs and powder, and some wore bright yellow breeches. Their wives and sisters abandoned bonnets and curled their hair more simply.[10] Although there were too few women in any of Berlin's fourteen salons to constitute a literary subculture, the female sensibility was more important to the younger men of the later salons than women or thoughts about women's nature had been to the older men of the earlier salons. The intellectuals in the later salons wrote poetry and novels more often than the treatises on natural science or popular education favored by the earlier group. Whether or not they actually wrote more letters, or spent more time engaged in face-to-face discourse, the men of the later salons took letters and conversation more seriously as literary forms than their predecessors had. Led by Friedrich and A. W. Schlegel and by Friedrich Schleiermacher, the men who visited the salons of the 1790s fought against what they depicted as the extreme rationalism of the mature Enlightenment, whose bastion had been Berlin just fifteen years before. The younger men of the later salons rallied around Goethe, whose novels were decried by Nicolai, the most eminent of Berlin's enlightened intellectuals. The acrimony between defenders of the late Enlightenment and the early romantics came to a head over politics as the revolution in France progressed, for many romantic intellectuals in Berlin eventually turned against the revolution. It was Friedrich Gentz who translated and disseminated Edmund Burke's attack on the course the revolution had taken, agreeing with Burke in his defense of history, custom, and social hierarchy against rational, egalitarian change.[11]

Women, emotion, and belle-lettres were thus more important to the

9. On Fichte's dismissal from his professorship at the University of Jena because of his radical atheism and his 1799 arrival in Berlin see Immanuel Hermann Fichte, *Johann Gottlieb Fichtes Leben und literarischer Briefwechsel* (Leipzig, 1862), 290–310.

10. On changes in Berlin's fashions in this era see Felix Eberty, *Jugenderinnerungen eines alten Berliners* (Berlin, 1925), 31, 46 and 47.

11. On the literary developments of the period, see Karl S. Guthke, *Literarisches Leben im achtzehnten Jahrundert in Deutschland und in der Schweiz* (Bern and Munich, 1975); on the connection between literature and politics in the era see Klaus Epstein, *The Genesis of German Conservatism* (Princeton, 1966); on Gentz see the most recent German biography: Jacob Baxa, *Friedrich von Gentz* (Vienna, 1965).

younger men of the later salons than they had been for the older men of the early salons. The younger guests at the later salons were also increasingly likely to be noble. Rahel Levin was regularly visited by Prince Louis Ferdinand, King Frederick's glamorous nephew. Several of Levin's other intimates belonged to old and powerful Prussian noble families, including the von Finckensteins, the von Schlabrendorfs, the von Pachtas, the von Radziwills, and the von Dohnas. Some of Levin's foreign noble friends were exiled aristocrats in flight from revolutionary France; they included Prince de Ligne, Count Alexander von Tilly, and Madame de Genlis. Nor was Levin the only Jewish salonière with high noble friends. Sara and Marianne Meyer both married men with high titles and were close to the von Ligny, von Clary, and von Courland families. Sara Levy's connections to local and foreign nobles were in part a family heritage; her father, Isaac Daniel Itzig, had been the first Jew in Prussia to receive the rights of a Prussian citizen, the first Jew to buy a landed estate near Berlin, and the private banker for King Frederick William II. Her sisters, Fanny von Arnstein and Cäcelie von Eskeles, also hosted salons in Vienna that attracted prominent nobles.[12]

Noble and Jewish mixing in public was of course not without immediate precedent. The new public institutions that appeared in the late 1700s provided opportunities for nobles and Jews to join together at musical, theatrical, and intellectual events, at least as passive consumers. But contemporaries were intensely aware that it was a large step for members of powerful or even royal noble families to spend their leisure hours in Jewish homes. A Jewish home was anything but neutral territory. No matter how rich, how lavish their spending, or how cultivated their daughters, Jews remained low on the estate hierarchy; extensive taxes and humiliating regulation of the Jewish community persisted until 1812, and the populace remained openly antisemitic. Even so celebrated a figure as Moses Mendelssohn could be assaulted by a drunken antisemite on the streets of Berlin and be taunted by Immanuel Kant's philosophy students when he visited Kant's Königsberg classroom in 1777.[13]

---

12. On Isaac Daniel Itzig see Karoline Cauer, *Oberhofbankier und Hofbaurat: Aus der Berliner Bankgeschichte des XVIII Jh.* (Frankfurt a.M., 1968), 17–35; on the two Itzig daughters in Vienna (who both married ennobled Jews) see Hilde Spiel, *Fanny von Arnstein, oder Die Emanzipation* (Frankfurt a.M., 1962).

13. Hilde Spiel describes precisely this transition—from concerts to salons—in the life of Fanny von Arnstein in Vienna: "a relaxed, mixed meeting, which hitherto only took place in public concerts and at musical *soirées*, was transplanted into private chambers" (see *Fanny von Arnstein*, 151). Mendelssohn's experience with the drunken antisemite is recounted in a 1829 quotation from David Friedländer, Mendelssohn's friend. The quote is cited in Alexander Altmann, *Moses Mendelssohn: A Biographical Study* (University, Ala., 1973), 351.

Visiting a rich Jewish home was by no means the ultimate honor a noble could pay a Jew; an even greater honor would have been for a prince or noble to invite a Jew to his or her own home, where all the other guests would be noble. But even the more modest act of visiting a Jewish home bestowed a huge amount of status on the Jewish host. Before the salons of the 1790s, royalty or high nobles rarely visited Jewish homes or invited Jews to theirs except as a token gesture, such as the attendance of Princess Anna Amalia, King Frederick's sister, at Henriette de Lemos's *Succoth* celebration, or Moses Mendelssohn's invitation to an audience with King Frederick at Potsdam.[14] Noble participation in the later Berlin salons was on a scale and at a level of intimacy that went well beyond the noble-Jewish ties of earlier decades. That noble visits to Jewish homes were preceded by noble-Jewish mixing at promenades, concerts, plays, and lectures or token social calls puts subsequent noble participation in the later salons into context but does not explain it.

Noble visits were all the more remarkable because they did not take place at a time of noble prosperity. The Junkers' position in agriculture and the bureaucracy was inadequate to meet many nobles' financial needs. One consequence of this impoverishment was that many Prussian nobles made special efforts to demarcate, rather than dilute, the boundaries separating them from wealthy members of other estates. And although the monarchy reserved top official and military positions for nobles, at the same time and in contradictory fashion it also continued to ennoble more and more commoners.[15] As the nobility became less powerful economically, many nobles placed increasing importance on their exclusive titles, the right marriages, and closed, stiff, ritualized social events. In short, economic impoverishment did not necessarily make nobles more enlightened. Even in the salons' best years during the 1790s, noble reliance on Jewish bankers seems to have led as easily to antisemitism as it did to willingness to make friends with the Jewish bankers or to marry their daughters. For example, Achim von Arnim, who was a visitor at Sara Levy's salon and met his future wife, Bettina Brentano, at the Levy home, became an outspoken antisemite and eventually founded a club that explicitly excluded Jews and women. It has been suggested that his antisemitism derived in part from his resentment of the Jewish

14. On Princess Anna Amalia's visit see Julius Furst, ed., *Henriette Herz: Ihr Leben und ihre Erinnerungen* (Berlin, 1858), 18. On Mendelssohn's visit to the royal palace at Potsdam see Altmann, *Moses Mendelssohn*, 276; on his visits with nobles see 283 and 716.

15. Frederick William II (1786–97) ennobled five times as many commoners as Frederick II did, and Frederick William III (1797–1840) ennobled over twice as many commoners as Frederick II had. See Fritz Martiny, *Die Adelsfrage in Preussen vor 1806*, Beiheft 35 of the *Vierteljahrsheft für Sozial- und Wirtschaftsgeschichte* (Stuttgart, 1936), 72.

Achim von Arnim

bankers whose loans were needed by his family.[16] In other words, neither shared experiences at cultural events, the endangered condition of the nobility as an estate, nor the economic dependence of individual nobles on individual Jewish bankers can alone explain why so many high nobles visited the later Jewish salons.

To account for this mystery, it is necessary to examine the lives of the sixty-nine men who attended at least one of Berlin's fourteen salons between 1780 and 1806—a far smaller, more competitive circle than the total number of intellectuals affiliated with the intellectual clubs.[17] In part,

16. Helene Riley, *Achim von Arnims Jugend- und Reisejahre* (Bonn, 1978), 5.

17. The total number of Berlin intellectuals who belonged to at least one intellectual club was undoubtedly far higher than the biased sample of sixty-six famous intellectuals from the better-documented clubs which was analyzed in chapter 4. The total number of Berlin intellectuals affiliated with at least one intellectual club could have been as large as

competition among commoner intellectuals to gain entrée to salons was so stiff because a number of places in salon society seem to have been reserved for non-intellectuals. Thirteen, a fifth of the sixty-nine salon men, left behind no words in print. They may have written hundreds of letters and had reputations as brilliant conversationalists. But since they did not publish, their thoughts could not become known to strangers, and they certainly could not earn money from their words. These unpublished salon men are called *dilettantes* here, in the late-eighteenth-century sense of the term, when it was used frequently by cultivated Germans to mean an enthusiast, a lover (*Liebhaber*) of some art.[18] In an era when many academic and artistic disciplines were new and pursued by amateurs whose wealth permitted leisure time, to be called a dilettante conferred prestige.

Precisely because the unpaid pursuit of the arts was a privilege reserved for those with leisure and money, it is not surprising that the men in salons were a privileged subset of the city's intelligentsia. Almost half (26) of the sixty-nine salon men were noble. Over half (35) of the salon men were gentile commoners; only eight of the salon men were Jewish. Male salon society was thus more noble than was the group of men affiliated with the intellectual clubs, of whom only 6 percent were noble. The salon men also included more nobles than the male intelligentsia as a whole, of whom only 15 percent were noble. As figure 11 shows, salon men were more likely to have been officials and considerably less likely to have been professors than was the average intellectual. Tutors and writers were marginally more likely to be in salons than in the clubs, while clerks, preachers, and teachers were as poorly represented in salons as in the clubs. The sampled club men were older, on average, than was the average intellectual. As figure 10 shows, only 12 percent of the club men were thirty-five or under in 1800, as compared to a fifth of the intelligentsia. The salon men were younger by far; almost two-fifths of them were thirty-five or under in 1800.[19]

---

several hundred. Unfortunately, primary sources do not exist to reconstruct this entire group.

18. See Johann Christoph Adelung, *Grammatisch-kritisches Wörterbuch der hochdeutschen Mundart* (Leipzig, 1796), vol. 2, 2062, who defined the "Liebhaber" as: "welcher einer vorzüglichen Grad des Vergnügens an Dinger gewisser Art und deren Besitze findet . . . in den schönen Künsten der Liebhaber, Ital. *Dilettante,* derjenige, welcher eine vorzügliche Neigung zu diesen Künsten und den Kunstwerken träget, ohne selbst ein Künstler zu sein."

19. The reader will note that the salon men have been compared here to two different groups. When there was sufficient data on the club men, as with age, I have contrasted the two subgroups of the intelligentsia (salon men and club men) with the intelligentsia as a whole. When the data on the club men was too biased to be meaningful, as with profession, I have contrasted the salon men to all intellectuals who did not attend salons. (This contrast

At the same time that salons were exclusive and frequented by many nobles, salon men as a group were also more upwardly mobile than were the intellectuals who did not attend salons. An equal proportion—one half—of the intellectuals in and out of salons were born into families in the middle-income strata. But among salon men, a smaller proportion (17 percent as compared to 25 percent) were still employed in middle-income positions in 1800. A second statistic points to the same trend. Not only did proportionally fewer salon men remain at the same income level as their fathers, proportionally more salon men escaped to a higher level than was the norm in the intelligentsia at large. Over a third of the salon men managed to move into the upper-income group, whereas only a quarter of the intellectuals outside salons did so. These numbers suggest that salons were a place where arriviste men could mix with the cream of Berlin society.[20]

Dilettantes and Other Nobles

The thirteen noble dilettantes, half of the twenty-six noblemen in salons, did not arrive at the salonières' door because of their intellectual accomplishments. Their presence in salon society was testimony to the fact that as long as one was an aristocrat, some combination of title, personality,

---

is sharper than comparing salon men to the entire intelligentsia, which includes the salon men.) One additional caveat: strictly speaking, only the fifty published intellectuals among the salon men were a subset of the intelligentsia. The thirteen male dilettantes in salons were technically a subset of some unknown larger group, whose limits are deliberately not defined here.

20. Unfortunately, the mere fact that a higher proportion of arriviste intellectuals were found in salons than in the intelligentsia at large cannot help choose between Norbert Elias's or Kark Mannheim's model of how European salons function to affect their participants' mobility. Norbert Elias described the Parisian salons of the late seventeenth century as literal agents of male upward mobility. Elias's interpretation was wittily summed up in Chauncey Tinker's phrase describing the process of mobility in the English salons of the seventeenth century. These salons, Tinker wrote, transformed "hacks into courtiers." (By "hacks" Tinker meant impoverished writers, not mediocre ones.) Karl Mannheim interpreted central European salons as having played precisely the reverse role. In societies where education and intellectual activity constituted one of the few avenues of upward mobility, Mannheim observed that many more were eager to gain entrée to salon-type circles than could actually be accommodated there. Mannheim saw salons as restricting, rather than facilitating mobility, since in his view only those who were already arrivistes were allowed into select gatherings like salons. See Norbert Elias, *The Civilizing Process: The History of Manners* (New York, 1978), 20. (I have interpreted Elias's use of the term "courtly society" to apply to salon society); Chauncey Tinker, *The Salon and English Letters* (New York, 1915); Karl Mannheim, "The Problem of the Intelligentsia: An Inquiry into Its Past and Present Role," in his *Essays on the Sociology of Culture* (London, 1956), 91–166, at 140.

or friends would suffice to gain admittance. If, on the other hand, one had been born a commoner, possession of a literary reputation was obviously much more important. The titles of the noble dilettantes were impressive indeed: three of the thirteen were princes; another six were counts. The most frequent occupation among the thirteen noble dilettantes was diplomacy; others were military officers or bureaucrats, or lived as cultivated gentlemen on their landed estates. The diplomats were frequently of foreign birth, serving a foreign power while in Berlin: Count Christian von Bernstorff was with the Danish embassy in Berlin during the 1790s; Count Casa-Valencia, and his assistant, the legation secretary Dan Raphael d'Urquijo, both represented Spain; Prince Heinrich von Reuss was the Austrian ambassador to Prussia until his death in 1799. Count Karl von Finckenstein was training to be a diplomat before he left Berlin to represent Prussia in a diplomatic post in Vienna in 1799. Major Peter von Gualtieri, an Italian who had spent years at court in Versailles, eventually served Prussia both militarily and diplomatically.[21]

Foreigners and Prussians who worked abroad had less investment in maintaining customary caste prejudices than did local nobles. The diplomats' distance from the norms of the Prussian Junkers could only be enhanced if they also had high titles and belonged to old and powerful foreign noble families. The personal freedom to flaunt tradition could be vastly aided by a secure position at the summit of the status hierarchy. That some of these foreign dilettantes, like several noble intellectuals, were either French or had lived in France was of huge significance. A French nobleman was much more likely than a local Junker to appreciate the particular charms of a mixed society and to be cultivated enough in the arts and sciences to mix gracefully with serious intellectuals. The presence of French nobles among their friends surely made Henriette Herz's and Rahel Levin's intention to synthesize French and German culture a more realistic goal. To be sure, this was not the first occasion that Frenchmen found their way to Berlin; that tradition went back to the Huguenots' arrival in the seventeenth century. But the upheavals of the French Revolution precipitated a smaller and more elite emigration

21. On von Bernstorff see Lawrence J. Baack, *Christian Bernstorff and Prussia* (New Brunswick, 1980) and Karl August Varnhagen von Ense, *Denkwürdigkeiten des eigenen Lebens,* Karl Leutner, ed. (East Berlin, 1954), 537. (Note: all references to Varnhagen's *Denkwürdigkeiten* without citation of a volume number refer to this abridged 1954 edition.) Casa Valencia is also mentioned briefly by Varnhagen in *Denkwürdigkeiten,* vol. 4, 81; on d'Urquijo see Hannah Arendt, *Rahel Varnhagen: The Life of a Jewess* (London, 1957), 71–76; on von Reuss see Varnhagen, *Denkwürdigkeiten* 535, Baxa, *Gentz,* 38; and Cauer, *Oberhofbankier,* 85; on von Finckenstein see Arendt, *Rahel Varnhagen,* 27; on von Gualtieri, see Karl August Varnhagen von Ense, ed., *Galerie von Bildnissen aus Rahels Umgang und Briefwechsel* (Leipzig, 1836), vol. 1, 159–70.

to Berlin, which in the 1790s was an attractive refuge for nobles fleeing political upheaval. Court life under Frederick William II (1786–97) was opulent and rather decadent, and perhaps more fundamentally, the general law code of 1794 secured the traditional economic and status privileges for the nobility.

Still, nobles in flight from the revolution were by no means always as conservative in their social behavior as the sheer fact of their flight from revolutionary France might suggest. Major Gualtieri delighted in mocking the prominent by befriending the déclassé and made a point of praising Friedrich Gentz to his courtly friends at a time when Gentz was not yet ennobled or at all popular with such people. Von Gualtieri often departed social events at the royal palace in Berlin with the announcement that he intended to "go to Mademoiselle Levin's, where the cleverest people gathered, and even to the queen he explicitly praised this social circle as one for which many others could be abandoned."[22] Emigré noble dilettantes could also influence local noble dilettantes who became their friends. When Prince Louis Ferdinand was nineteen, his parents took him to an elegant nearby spa. The resort was filled with "super-cultivated" French immigrants, who fascinated the young Junker prince with their "alluring and flattering conversations." The young prince took the style and conduct of these French nobles as a model, and when he returned to Berlin later that year his family and friends found him "completely transformed."[23] Like other noble dilettantes, Prince Louis Ferdinand maintained his loyalty to a French lifestyle even as his politics became decidedly anti-French. Thus later, when the prince became an ardent opponent of Napoleon, he retained his friendships with French nobles and his enthusiasm for the sexual mores of the French nobility. He shocked even his ardent admirers with his public, long-standing love affair with Rahel Levin's close friend Pauline Wiesel. He also lived openly and had children with another commoner, Henriette Fromm.[24]

The foreign noble dilettantes in salons tended to be old in years as well as rich in exotic, un-Prussian experiences. The local noble dilettantes in salons, in contrast, were far younger: Wilhelm von Burgsdorff, Count Alexander von Dohna, Prince Louis Ferdinand, Prince Anton Radziwill, and Count von Finckenstein were all in their twenties during the 1790s.[25]

---

22. Varnhagen, *Galerie,* vol. 1, 165.

23. Ibid., vol. 2, 450.

24. Other sources on the prince include Baxa, *Gentz,* 52, and Eduard Schmidt-Weissenfels, *Rahel und ihre Zeit* (Leipzig, 1857), 56.

25. On von Burgsdorff see Varnhagen, *Galerie,* vol. 1, 101–18; on von Dohna, see *NDB,* vol. 4, 53; on von Radziwill see Friedhelm Kemp, ed., *Rahel Varnhagen im Umgang mit ihren Freunden: Briefe 1793–1833* (Munich, 1967), 452.

Many of the local noble dilettantes found their way into salon society by way of a friendship with Rahel Levin. Von Burgsdorff was brought into her circle by his friend, the ubiquitous Gustav von Brinkmann, who introduced von Burgsdorff to Levin at the spa at Bad Teplitz in the summer of 1795.[26] Levin was Prince Louis Ferdinand's trusted confidante; he frequently escaped from the privations of military duty to visit Berlin during the 1790s. The prince prized his time with Mademoiselle Levin. He charmed a crowd of friends in her attic apartment with his piano compositions, and spent long hours talking over his love affairs alone with her in the afternoons. Count Karl von Finckenstein's relationship with Levin was even more intimate. They were engaged, and probably lovers, from 1795 to 1799. The two met at the theater. Tall, blond, and handsome, the count belonged to Prussia's most powerful noble family. Count Alexander von Dohna also came from an old and powerful family. A friend of Alexander von Humboldt's from the universities at Frankfurt an der Oder and Göttingen, Count von Dohna had been introduced at the Herz salon by his children's tutor, the young theologian Friedrich Schleiermacher.[27]

Participation in revitalized educational institutions often transformed the values of the local Prussian noble dilettantes, and the new values motivated many nobles to visit salons. The stories of two of the local noble dilettantes (who were cousins), Wilhelm von Burgsdorff and Count Karl von Finckenstein, illustrate how drastic the transformation of noble values could be. These two men's friendships shed light not only on the new values, but also on the noblemen's usefulness in the upwardly mobile journeys of the less prestigious men whom they befriended. Von Burgsdorff, born in 1772 to an ancient Prussian family, attended the Friedrichswerder Gymnasium in Berlin, where he met Ludwig Tieck, a talented son of a rope-maker one year his junior.[28] The friendship continued after the gymnasium experience, and in 1791 both young men went on to study at Halle University, where they wrestled with the different professional paths chosen by their families. Tieck's father felt that only theology could provide his son with scholarships and eventual employment; von Burgsdorff did his family's bidding by studying law. But von

26. The trip to Bad Teplitz is noted in the article on von Burgsdorff in the *NDB*, vol. 3, 50.

27. On von Dohna (whose full name was Dohna-Schlobitten) see the article on him in the *NDB*, vol. 4, 53; on Schleiermacher's appointment as a tutor in the von Dohna family see Jerry F. Dawson, *Friedrich Schleiermacher: The Evolution of a Nationalist* (Austin, 1966), 23. A selection from Wilhelm Dilthey's biography of Schleiermacher has been translated in H. P. Rickman, ed., *W. Dilthey: Selected Writings* (Cambridge, England, 1976), 35–77.

28. See the article on von Burgsdorff in the *NDB*, vol. 3, 50.

Burgsdorff's financial generosity eventually allowed Tieck to give up the hated theology—fortunately for Tieck, who later became famous for his profligate spending habits when he was badly in debt. At one time when he was "hopelessly in debt over his ears, he served oysters, asparagus, and French champagne."[29] Tieck's friendship with von Burgsdorff proved useful in this regard. In the fall of 1792 he wrote his sister from Halle that she should not concern herself about his poverty: "I am going around a lot with Burgsdorff—he is my best friend here! I can loan as much money as I like from him, when I urgently need it; so don't worry unnecessarily about me."[30]

As for von Burgsdorff, at first, in 1795 and 1796, he continued to fulfill his father's dreams by working as a junior lawyer for the Prussian court in Berlin. But he soon rejected the life of the state official in favor of that of the roving literary dilettante, living for the enjoyment of art and friendship. He stayed with Wilhelm and Caroline von Humboldt in Jena in 1797, where the two men spent the evenings absorbed in discourse with Friedrich Schiller. Tieck spent many seasons living with von Burgsdorff and other mutual friends at von Burgsdorff's rural estate in Ziebingen. In 1796, von Burgsdorff spent the summer with Rahel Levin at the spas at Karlsbad and Teplitz. In addition to going about with impoverished writers and Jewish women, von Burgsdorff also rebelled by refusing to marry his family's choice for his wife. Instead, his romantic attentions were directed to the wives of two of his dearest friends, Tieck and von Humboldt. He was rumored to be the father of a child each wife bore in these years.[31] That everyone remained friends through these episodes is testimony to how authentically emancipated sexual life was for this circle.

Although von Burgsdorff had cash to spare to help support Tieck's champagne, he himself had his own financial worries. In 1807 he was forced to sell his rural estate.[32] His relationship with Tieck shows how

29. See Klaus Günzel, ed., *König der Romantik: Das Leben des Dichters Ludwig Tieck in Briefen, Selbstzeugnissen und Berichten* (Tübingen, 1981), 12.

30. Ibid., 108. Although Tieck was obviously intimate with several progressive nobles, in Achim von Arnim's view he was "not fully accepted" by the "important" nobles in Berlin. See Reinhold Steig, *Achim von Arnim und die ihm nahe standen*, 3 vols. (Stuttgart and Berlin, 1904), vol. 3, 3.

31. On von Burgsdorff's relationship with Tieck's wife see Günzel, *König der Romantik*, 141; on his relationship with Caroline von Humboldt see Paul Sweet, *Wilhelm von Humboldt: A Biography* (Columbus, Oh., 1978), vol. 1, 180. See also Alfons Feder Cohn, ed., *Wilhelm von Burgsdorffs Briefe an Brinkmann, Henriette von Finckenstein, Wilhelm von Humboldt, Rahel, Friedrich Tieck, Ludwig Tieck und Wiesel* (Berlin, 1907).

32. Günzel, *König der Romantik*, 232.

egalitarian literary patronage had become since the days when the patron published and distributed the author's books.[33] Tieck did not need von Burgsdorff's help in getting into print; indeed, he was rather successful at manipulating the capitalist literary market, as shown by his victory in a suit against Friedrich Nicolai's son and successor for tampering with his work.[34] But Tieck obviously did rely on his noble friend for loans, hospitality, and connections. In the case of Tieck and von Burgsdorff, the patron was not a distant figure but a close friend of the client. Von Burgsdorff chose to help Tieck not to gain prestige by playing the patron role, but because he possessed the intellectual skills and interests to judge Tieck's talent for himself. The patron thus lent financial and personal support because he participated directly in literary life, not because he received indirect status through funding the work of a lowly supplicant. That all of this should have come to pass can be traced in part to the fact that von Burgsdorff and Tieck attended the same gymnasium and university. Their friendship is a dramatic example of how educational institutions facilitated the mixing of estates, a mixing which could eventually lead to deep emotional and financial ties across the social hierarchy.

Wilhelm von Burgsdorff's cousin Karl von Finkenstein, another noble dilettante in salons, was also touched by the change in noble values. Yet in von Finkenstein's case, the new values were only sufficient to draw him near to salon society. He could not bring himself to act on these values if the result would be ostracism from his exceedingly privileged family. Indeed, the tale of Karl von Finckenstein's love affair with Rahel Levin shows how serious the challenge of new values was for a noble dilettante. Unlike his cousin von Burgsdorff, who was passionate about literature, or Prince Louis Ferdinand, who could play and even compose for the piano, Count Karl von Finckenstein brought only his title to Levin's salon. He had no talents, no interests, no projects to discuss in salon conversations. Finckenstein could thus only represent his estate in salons, unlike other nobles who had the intellectual skills to express themselves as individual personalities.[35] But the idea that everyone, even the titled, was supposed to bring a personality, a talent, or a literary reputation to the salon was upsetting to Karl von Finckenstein, whose eventual decision not to marry Rahel Levin revealed his unwillingness to

33. For comparative purposes see Karl Julius Holzknecht, *Literary Patronage in the Middle Ages* (New York, 1966).

34. Günzel, *König der Romantik*, 171.

35. The difference between "signifying" and "expressing" oneself in society in this era is outlined in Richard Sennett, *The Fall of Public Man: On the Social Psychology of Capitalism* (New York, 1977), in chaps. 3 and 4.

truly enter a social circle that demanded some defiance of his title.[36] For Levin demanded that von Finckenstein stand up to his family's objections to his engagement to a Jew, that he independently, actively choose her. Unable to do so, he broke with Levin. Yet Karl's cousin Wilhelm von Burgsdorff was clearly in Levin's camp, and it was he who consoled Levin for the suffering that his more status-conscious cousin was causing her.[37]

Individual personality was thus crucial in determining the degree of a noble's openness to accepting friends, lovers, and spouses from the lower orders. But social changes were also at work that transcended the varying strengths of their expression in particular individuals. The same social and cultural forces which moved a Wilhelm von Burgsdorff to form a lasting relationship with a poor commoner also touched those, like Karl von Finckenstein, who ultimately resisted making such relationships permanent. What was remarkable about Karl von Finckenstein's relationship with Rahel Levin was not that in the end he rejected her, but that she was at a box in the theater where she could meet him; that several of his own noble friends, including the dashing Prince Louis, would already be her intimates; that he, a notably "non-serious" dilettante, would find salon society an acceptable, if not an altogether unproblematic place to spend time; that even this weak-willed member of a conservative family would become engaged to a Jew and stay engaged to her for four years.

Although they all shared the sociological similarity of publishing their writing, not all of the thirteen noble intellectuals among the salon men were equally prominent in their mental stature. Published intellectuals, nobles included, could possess rather modest intellectual talents and publish little of lasting significance. This was so for three of the thirteen noble intellectuals—Count Alexander von Tilly, Prince Karl von Ligne, and the crucial Gustav von Brinkmann—who resembled the foreign noble dilettantes in their backgrounds, occupations, ages, and social worlds. Like the foreign noble dilettantes, all were foreigners, and all had either diplomatic or military positionss. All three had a secure entrée to court society but enjoyed going slumming in salons. Although all three published, they were known at the time for their social, not their intellectual skills. Count von Tilly's notoriety, for instance, was altogether unintellectual. He was gossiped about because of his "endless number of adventures," which included the time that the wife of a civil servant he had rejected in love threw herself in the River Spree. The count com-

---

36. For a poignant, empathetic description of this relationship see Arendt, *Rahel Varnhagen*, chap. 2.

37. A few of von Burgsdorff's letters to Levin from this period are published in Varnhagen's *Galerie*, vol. 1, 111–17.

pleted his memoirs in 1816, and shortly thereafter ended his own life by shooting himself in the head.[38] The Prince von Ligne spent years making the rounds of the chic courts of Spain, France, and Russia. To be sure, Prince von Ligne had a somewhat more serious reputation than did Count von Tilly. Von Ligne was known as an "epicurean *philosophe*," and published thirty-four volumes of his collected essays.[39] Von Brinkmann's literary reputation was also quite good; his pseudonomously published poetry was well received, and Goethe himself sought out von Brinkmann's poetic advice on one occasion. Still, von Brinkmann's cherished medium was not the published page but the letter. He once wrote more than a thousand letters to a fictitious friend. Hearing of this, Prince Louis Ferdinand quipped that "Brinkmann is truly divine; lovers write letters because of love, he loves because of letters."[40]

The presence of foreign noble intellectuals in Berlin was a boon for the formation of salon society. These men brought with them into salons a French appreciation for amorous adventure and for light-hearted conversation altogether lacking in Prussia. But it was even more significant for salons that local noble intellectuals made such a decisive break with the world into which they were born, and their change in values was even more dramatic than that made by the local noble dilettantes. It was one thing for a noble dilettante to spent his leisure time reading and discussing literature with commoner intellectuals, or even to discreetly aid them financially. It was another thing entirely for a young noble to avoid or abandon the bureaucratic, military, and diplomatic offices intended to save the nobility from its economic dilemma. The local noble intellectuals in salons were not just making social history when they rebelled against long tradition and against their families to make intellectual creation the center of their lives. With these creations noble salon men often made intellectual history in a grand style. Included among the local noble intellectuals in salons were both von Humboldt brothers, Wilhelm the political philosopher and Alexander the scientist; Heinrich von Kleist, the playwright and novelist; Achim von Arnim, the poet and folklorist; Adelbert von Chamisso, the poet and novelist; Friedrich von Hardenberg (Novalis), the poet, and Baron Friedrich de la Motte Fouqué, who wrote popular historical novels.

Explaining why the men became so committed to serious intellectual work will in turn unravel a good part of the mystery about why nobles came to salons in the first place. Their passion for a rigorous life of the

38. Varnhagen, *Galerie*, vol. 2, 1–5.
39. Ibid., vol. 1, 81–93.
40. Cited in Carl Atzenbeck, *Pauline Wiesel: Die Geliebte des Prinzen Louis Ferdinand* (Leipzig, 1925), 44.

mind increased the likelihood that they would organize their social lives on rational rather than on customary criteria. Since most of the noble intellectuals, like the local noble dilettantes, were quite young when in salons (their average age in 1800 was seventeen), they were in salons at a time in their life when they could act on these rational principles in their choice of career, friends, and lovers. Their passion for intellectual work meant that their friends would also be likely to be other publishing intellectuals, most of whom were commoners. The creative labors of the noble intellectuals transformed patrons into authors, destroying that distinction far more dramatically than the friendships between noble dilettantes and commoner authors had done. When Adelbert von Chamisso collaborated with Karl August Varnhagen and Wilhelm Neumann on a novel, it was von Chamisso who took care of the publication costs and who was thus simultaneously author and patron.[41]

Yet not all of the noble intellectuals could afford to help their colleagues born without a title. For the financial dilemmas of many of the noble intellectuals reflected the contemporary dilemmas of the noble estate at large, mediated by bad luck or by bad management. Heinrich von Kleist's father lost out to his own brothers and inherited neither money nor land, merely the family house in Frankfurt an der Oder. Prince von Ligne squandered his originally considerable wealth by what one friend called his own "admirable carelessness."[42] Adelbert von Chamisso's family, originally from France, lost their wealth in the course of the revolution and of emigration.[43] The financial insecurity of many noble intellectuals made the decision to pursue an intellectual career a painful one. After finishing university at Halle, Achim von Arnim devoted himself full-time to his literary work, in spite of and very much constrained by his family's continuing money problems.[44] When Heinrich von Kleist decided to quit military service to attend university, his family was irate. Kleist reported on his family's anger in a letter to his former tutor: "they broached my limited means; they pointed out the doubtful prospect for bread on my new-chosen path, the promised security of my old one. The destiny that faced me, years of studying some dry discipline, years of

41. The collective work, which included writing by Varnhagen and Wilhelm Neumann, was entitled the *Grünen Musenalmanachen* and was published in 1805. See Werner Feudel, *Adelbert von Chamisso: Leben und Werk* (Leipzig, 1971), 54, and Varnhagen, *Denkwürdigkeiten*, 94.

42. On von Kleist's father's inheritance see Joachim Mass, *Kleist: Die Fackel Preussens* (Vienna, Munich, and Basel, 1957), 10; on von Ligne's trouble see Varnhagen, *Galerie*, vol. I, 81.

43. See Feudel, *Adelbert von Chamisso*, 1–10.

44. See Philip B. Miller, ed., *An Abyss Deep Enough: Letters of Heinrich von Kleist with a Selection of Essays and Anecdotes* (New York, 1982), 23.

torment with the dry drudgery of an unpaid teaching assistantship, in order eventually to earn some meagre bread."[45] When young von Chamisso proposed studying at the University of Halle, his family added status to the list of objections: "they condemned his scholarly ambitions as useless and as not appropriate for their station."[46] The opposition families showed for their sons' pursuit of the life of the mind could be well founded. Not only was the remuneration offered by academic labor relatively meager and its status quite low; pursuing knowledge could nevertheless cost a good deal of money. After Wilhelm and Alexander von Humboldt's father died in 1779, Frau von Humboldt continued to rely on Gottlob Kunth to organize her son's education. In addition to Kunth's wages, this commitment meant paying for the young men's year-round residence in Berlin, subscriptions to the best lecture series in town, and university study. Frau von Humboldt had to mortgage her landed estate to afford the expenses.[47]

The university experience was crucial in forging the noblemen's commitment to intellectual work. As the noble estate came increasingly to rely on employment in the bureaucracy, university attendance became a more accepted stage in the noble way of life. At least six of the noble intellectuals are known to have attended university, where lifelong, cross-estate friendships were begun. Von Brinkmann met Schleiermacher at the University of Halle; Alexander von Humboldt met George Forster at Göttingen.[48] Attendance at lecture courses performed a similar function: alongside the von Humboldt brothers at one of Professor Fischer's lectures on mathematics could be found Joseph Mendelssohn, Moses's son.[49] Ironically, university study proved to be decisive in the rejection of the bureaucratic careers for which it was designed, and in these cases the state's strategy for rescuing the nobility backfired. Baron de la Motte Fouqué, von Kleist, and von Chamisso all quit the military to have more time to study, while Wilhelm von Humboldt worked for only one year as a state official in Berlin before he retired to Tegel with his own young family to read and write in solitude. In this case, newly acquired economic solvency was a prerequisite for becoming a gentleman scholar— von Humboldt's mother had died in 1796, and he inherited a considerable estate.[50]

During the 1790s, the noble intellectuals' rejection of the military and

45. Ibid., 23.
46. See Feudel, *Adelbert von Chamisso*, 38.
47. See Karl Bruhns, *Life of Alexander von Humboldt*, 2 vols. (London, 1873), vol. 1, 9.
48. Ibid., 22.
49. Ibid., 20.
50. Ibid., 30.

the bureaucracy in order to write was in part a reflection of their distaste for King Frederick William II's corrupt and fanatical regime. The brightest young noble intellectuals in the 1790s wanted a new way of life. However great the privileges their estate affiliation, they were willing to move to the edge of aristocracy of birth in order to join the republic of scholars. Alexander von Humboldt summed up the new attitude when he confided to a friend that he and his brother both avoided using their noble predicate "von" whenever possible.[51]

The von Humboldts could afford to disdain the use of their title. Everyone treated them as nobles anyway, and they continued to enjoy the material security and prestige a title bestowed. For aspiring commoner intellectuals, the goal was to obtain a title. They no doubt agreed with Rahel Levin that "as long as one nobleman exists, one must also be ennobled."[52] Of the thirty-nine salon men born into commoner families, seven succeeded in becoming ennobled during their lifetimes. The eventually ennobled salon men were considerably older when they visited salons (their average age was thirty-six in 1800) than the salon men who received their titles at birth. Whatever achievements won them their titles, it was a protracted endeavor. For two of the seven, Christian Wilhelm Dohm and Friedrich Stägemann, both sons of preachers, the route to ennoblement was a traditional one. Both studied law at the university and served the Prussian state loyally as prominent civil servants.[53] To be sure, they were both serious intellectuals, publishing books and articles on the side, but their occupational and social ascent was a reward for their employment as officials.

But the careers of four of the other ennobled salon men show that by now publishing could help one get ahead in life in a way unheard of in previous decades. For these four ennobled intellectuals, successful publication was either crucial to their success at gaining the noble title or their motivation for seeking ennoblement in the first place. Friedrich Schlegel's fame as literary historian, critic, publicist, and lecturer, as well as his conservative views, were useful in obtaining both a position and a title from the Austrian emperor. Friedrich Gentz, too, first became famous as an author and journalist before receiving an income and a title from the Austrian monarchy. Johannes Müller, a roving Swiss intellectual, was ennobled as a reward for his conservative historical writings as

51. Ibid., 7.

52. This quote is cited by Arendt, in *Rahel Varnhagen*, 186.

53. On Dohm see Dambacher, *von Dohm;* on von Stägemann see the article in the *ADB,* vol. 35, 383–86; von Stägemann's memoirs have been included in Franz Rühl, *Aus der Franzosenzeit: Ergänzungen zu den Briefen und Aktenstücken zur Geschichte Preussens unter Friedrich Wilhelm III* (Leipzig, 1904).

well as for his diplomatic missions.[54] Karl August Varnhagen was, unlike these three, not beholden for his own "von Ense" to any king or emperor; "von Ense" was actually an old family title fallen into disuse until Varnhagen discovered it in an antiquated genealogy. The title proved to be useful when, after long and deep-seated confusions about his career, Varnhagen decided to abandon his father's occupation, medicine, in favor of a diplomatic career. His rejection of the life of a "bourgeois patriarch" to seek his "fortune as a roving adventurer" was not unlike a von Burgsdorff or a Wilhelm von Humboldt leaving officialdom.[55] The difference was that without an inherited income, Varnhagen needed a job that would allow him to support Rahel Levin in proper style and still provide him time to devote to literary composition and literary conversation. Diplomacy was the answer, and his new-found title helped him to obtain a post.

The story of Friedrich Gentz's career shows how both literary talent and strategic friendships in and out of salons could aid a salon man in moving into the noble estate. Gentz did not begin his ascent very low on the commoner hierarchy; his father was a prominent state official and his mother was from a leading noble Huguenot family in Berlin. In the late 1780s, Gentz had a modestly paid bureaucratic position in Berlin. But new friendships with older noble dilettantes and with noble intellectuals his own age made possible a social life of much greater glamour than that enjoyed by his bureaucratic colleagues. In the ensuing decade of the 1790s, Gentz deepened his contacts with the prominent. In addition to enjoying the "precarious respectability" of the Jewish salons, Gentz spent long hours with his friend Prince Louis Ferdinand at the Cafe "Stadt Paris," at a variety of local gambling tables, and at the city's elegant brothels—all of which caused him to go deeply into debt, since by 1792 he was married but still earning less than eight hundred taler a year.[56] He had become a prolific author of anti-Napoleonic political essays and eventually was able to parlay his talents as a publicist and his increasingly conservative views into a position (and an accompanying title) with the Austrian monarchy. This delighted Gentz, for he was eager to leave behind his creditors in Berlin, earn a better salary, receive a noble title, and have more time to write and to indulge his costly passions.

Gentz's transition from official to ennobled publicist, from Berlin to

54. On Schlegel see Varnhagen von Ense's article on him in his *Galerie*, 225–38. On Gentz see Baxa, *Gentz*.

55. See Karl Misch, *Varnhagen von Ense in Beruf und Politik* (Gotha, 1925), 16. See also Varnhagen's memoirs, ed. Karl Leutner, *Denkwürdigkeiten des eigenen Lebens* (East Berlin, 1954).

56. See Sweet, *Wilhelm von Humboldt*, vol. 1, 24.

Vienna, from powdered wig to carefully trimmed curls was simultaneously a change in his friends. Although he retained his ties to von Humboldt and to von Brinkmann, he came to disdain both scholars and Jews in favor of the most elegant noble families. By 1803, when Gentz left Berlin for the last time, he had realized that "professors, writers, and members of the lesser bureaucracy were fatally middle class," and that politically "the world was run by counts, princes, and archdukes, and he was determined to make their world his world."[57] His sinking estimation of scholars and Jews, both once quite important to him, was expressed even before he had fully changed his social circle, in an 1801 letter to von Brinkmann. Gentz complained that his friend, who was well connected to court circles, was neglecting him. Gentz confided that his only consolation was that "it is neither *Jews* nor *scholars* who are depriving me of your companionship." He continued the lament, full of despair "that those whom I would like to obtain as friends are precisely those to whom I am inferior."[58]

Moving from the commoner to the noble estate was clearly not a feat open to just any intellectual. Those who maneuvered their way into the aristocracy began their climb fairly high on the commoner ladder, were often successful journalists, and had noble friends and connections from the outset. More importantly, since the crown still controlled access to the noble estate, the parvenu intellectual needed the right politics to be endorsed by the crown. The obliging monarchy was more often Austrian than Prussian, and the ennoblement came well after salons had declined in Berlin. But salon attendance assisted in the slow polishing process. Friedrich Schlegel, Karl August Varnhagen, and Friedrich Gentz all made noble friends in the salons; in Gentz's case, the "precarious respectability" of Jewish salons in Berlin and in Vienna served as an ideal stepping stone for his social rise. As Rahel Levin was to realize with much bitterness, Gentz was all too ready to discard his Jewish friends, who had introduced him to the "truly" respectable, as soon as he was no longer "inferior to those whom he wished to know."

Arriving, or Upward Mobility

Only a few of the arriviste salon men managed to crown their upward mobility with that glorious prize, a noble title. Others had to be content with changing income levels within the commoner estate, or even more modestly, with merely changing occupations at the same income level.

57. Ibid., 51.
58. Gustav von Brinkmann to Julie von Voss, Berg-Voss Collection, GSA, 7 July 1801.

We know for certain that salon attendance was statistically correlated with upward mobility, for at some point in their lives a greater proportion of salon men had moved up into a higher income level than had the proportion of intellectuals who had no entrée into salons. Unfortunately, the sources are not precise enough to capture the salon men's positions both before and after they attended salons, making it impossible to be sure that it was salon attendance which actually facilitated the men's upward mobility. Nevertheless, a comparison of the occupations of the salon men with the occupations of intellectuals outside salon society can give indirect insight into what jobs salon men may have moved out of and which new jobs upwardly mobile salon men may have found. As was shown in figure 9, officials were marginally overrepresented in salons, and professors were overrepresented to an even greater degree. This means that these were two posts which upwardly mobile salon men might have obtained.

Not so for several other occupations, which were poorly represented among the salon men. Merchants made a weak showing both in and out of salons. At the lower end of the income hierarchy, preachers, clerks, and teachers were almost entirely absent from salons. Yet together these three middle-income occupations provided employment for almost a third of Berlin's intellectuals. Since the preachers and teachers found it difficult to enter the salon social world, they rarely had the opportunity to use connections made in salons to move into upper-level positions as officials or as professors. Yet middle-income men employed in other occupations were less excluded from salons than were the unfortunate preachers, clerks, and teachers. Tutors, booksellers, and freelance writers were actually overrepresented in salons as compared to their presence in the intelligentsia at large. To be sure, those who worked in these three intellectual institutions together only made up 15 percent of the sixty-nine salon men. If they did not dominate salon society numerically, still, those tutors, booksellers, and writers who did get the chance to join in salon society might well have used salon contacts to move up in the world. For writers and booksellers these connections were especially important. Unlike tutors, or even clerks, neither writers nor booksellers worked in an institutional context where they could mix with prominent noble colleagues.

Several of the most famous salon men, including Karl Philipp Moritz and Ludwig Tieck, were among those who moved from the middle to the upper income level—or at least its fringes—when they became publishing intellectuals. A closer look at two cases shows both the triumphs and the traumas of the upwardly mobile journey. Johann Fichte's odyssey was largely a triumphal one, in making both social and intellectual history. Fichte was born in 1762 in Rammenau, where his father was a linen weaver.[59] The preacher of his village church took an interest in the precocious child, and when Fichte was eight arranged for him to display his startling gifts to a gathering of local nobles.[60] It was on this occasion that young Fichte found his first patron, Freiherr von Miltitz, who invited Fichte to live with him at his castle, and later paid for Fichte to live with and be educated by yet another preacher. From there Fichte went on to a boarding school. At eighteen Fichte enrolled at the University of Jena, and it was then that he learned how precarious patronage could be. Von Miltitz died, but Fichte's own family could not provide for his upkeep at university. Deeply ashamed of his poverty in the university setting, Fichte supported himself by tutoring. Eight years later, by the time he was twenty-six, Fichte was still earning his keep as a tutor in Zurich, where his writings won him the friendship of the "most intellectual and esteemed" men of the city.[61] When he left Zurich, Fichte hoped that his Zurich friends' connections would help him obtain a position either accompanying a prince to a knightly academy, or perhaps as a teacher at a princely court. But none of these posts materialized, and Fichte's situation deteriorated even further. Herr Rahn, his Zurich patron, lost his fortune and could not come to Fichte's aid. Too proud to approach a prominent stranger in person, Fichte sent Immanuel Kant an essay he had written on Kant's work. In the cover letter, Fichte described the imminent danger of his having to return to his hometown and pawn his belongings. Kant came to the rescue by obtaining Fichte a position as tutor for a count's family in Danzig. Unfortunately, Fichte did not get on well with the family, and he returned to Zurich, proceeded to marry his patron's daughter, and moved in with Herr Rahn.

At age thirty-one, Fichte's material situation was still decidedly insecure. Yet by this time his writings were well regarded enough for his prominent friends to urge that he offer an extended series of lectures in Zurich. This never came to pass, because in that same year, 1793, Fichte was offered a professorship at Jena. Under the leadership of Goethe and Schiller, Jena was just then coming into its own as one of Germany's most exciting intellectual centers. Now Fichte had finally achieved a professorship. But his monetary distance from the upper strata was still considerable. The yearly salary paid to a junior professor at Jena in 1793 (excluding publishing income and lecture fees, which the students paid directly to the professor) was a mere two hundred taler.[62] But although

59. See Immanuel Fichte, *Fichtes Leben*, 16–18.
60. Ibid., 16.
61. Ibid., 34.
62. Ibid., 193.

his lectures were popular with the students, and his support for the French Revolution and his critique of Kant well received by his colleagues, Fichte did not last out the decade at Jena. A fight with the administration over his refusal to recant after declaring his atheism publicly cost Fichte his hard-earned professorship. With the aid of Christian Wilhelm Dohm, who took pride in befriending Fichte, he fled to a more cosmopolitan, more tolerant Berlin in 1799.

Although Fichte's liberalism was mixed with more than a touch of antisemitism, he was happy to attend the Jewish salons.[63] Just as Fichte's lack of enthusiasm for Jewry in general did not hinder him from associating with individual Jews, it did not stop key Jewish members of salon society from admiring him and his work. Rahel Levin and her brother, the playwright Ludwig Robert, were eager listeners at Fichte's lecture series in 1806, which aimed to rouse Berliners against their French occupiers in the name of a new Prussian patriotism.[64] By the time of his death in 1814, Fichte held a professorship in philosophy at the newly established University of Berlin. By then, his total income must have been well over six hundred taler, placing him securely in the upper-income level. In the end he was thus a case of successful upward mobility, father a weaver and son a famous professor. For Fichte, patronage was crucial in his climb. As with so many other salon men, the patron-client relationship became a bond of friendship and even a family tie. Fichte's story is especially interesting, because he was able to succeed at moving upward socially and professionally while still espousing an egalitarian, even an anti-aristocratic social philosophy.

A comparison of Fichte's journey with that of the novelist Jean Paul (Richter) suggests that the traumas of Fichte's odyssey may have been eased by his immersion in the academic world rather than in the freelance literary life. Richter is judged by some to have been the first writer in German history to have supported himself exclusively from his pen, and his life story shows the personal pain he paid for this distinction.[65] Richter suffered because although publishing was increasingly a rationalized, capitalist enterprise, aristocratic patrons and aristocratic fans were both

63. For background on the apparent contradictions of Fichte's ideas and behavior regarding Jews and Judaism see J. Levy, *Fichte und die Juden* (Berlin, 1924), and Edward Schaub, "J. G. Fichte and Antisemitism," *Philosophical Review* 49 (1940), 37–52.

64. Fichte's nationalism should not be equated with the Christian patriotism discussed in chap. 8; on Fichte's mockery of Achim von Arnim's ideology see Levy, *Fichte*, 10. For background see Eugene Anderson, *Nationalism and the Cultural Crisis in Prussia, 1806–1815* (New York, 1939). On Rahel Levin's attitude to Fichte and his lecture series see Arendt, *Rahel Varnhagen* (1974 ed.), 127–31.

65. See Günter de Bruyn, *Das Leben des Jean Paul Friedrich Richter: eine Biographie* (Frankfurt a.M., 1978), 60.

directly involved in the creation of literature in a way that they were not so closely involved in academia. As Ludwig Tieck's story showed, the chance to spend one's time writing novels rather than studying theology was due in part to the writer's ability to forge personal relationships with noble patrons. Like Tieck and Fichte, Richter was born into a family in the lower ranks of the middle income level. His father and his grand-father alike had been impoverished schoolmasters in the village of Hof. Johann Paul, who was only later to adopt the Frenchified pen name Jean Paul, spent much of his life earning his keep in the same way, living in the family home in the village of his birth. At eighteen he went off to Leip-zig to study theology at the university, and before he was twenty he had published a satirical novel, for which he earned an honorarium of 126 taler. But his absolute impoverishment forced him back to Hof. As it was he had to depart Leipzig incognito; it seems that all of his belongings, including the coat on his back, were either pawned or not paid for.[66]

For the next thirteen years, Richter lived at home in Hof and taught school. All his spare hours were devoted to writing his satirical novels, which eventually became widely successful. By 1800, Jean Paul's popular-ity with prestigious noble readers led to an invitation to visit Herder and Goethe in Weimar, which was followed by a visit to Berlin. His reception in these literary capitals was enthusiastic; in Weimar he stayed at Herder's home, in Berlin with his publisher, Herr Matzdorf. Jean Paul's "arrival" in Weimar and Berlin gave him an opportunity to crown his literary success with social success. And, to be sure, he enjoyed socializing with the noble and otherwise cultivated women he had so gently caricatured in his novels. He visited Duchess Dorothea von Courland's estate at Löbichau and became a close enough friend of Henriette Herz that she later sent him parcels of the special beer he loved.[67]

Yet in the end Jean-Paul rejected "le Monde" for the traditional and intensely familiar world of his family and his neighbors in Hof. His friends observed that he wanted to get to know noble women only to describe them better in his books.[68] Richter came to believe that authen-tic friendships between nobles and commoners were impossible, and he feared that by adapting to the loose morals and calculated artificiality of aristocratic society he would lose the best that was in himself. He discov-ered that the freedom he gave to the heroes of his books to marry noble women was not a freedom he himself desired.[69] Thus Jean Paul Richter

66. Ibid., 47.
67. Ibid., 242 and 331.
68. Ibid., 223.
69. Ibid., 355.

not only agreed with Fichte's radical democratic ideology, he also found himself unable and unwilling to complete his professional upward mobility by upgrading his interpersonal universe. His story shows how ambiguous upward mobility could be for intellectuals and how different the same salons looked to different guests. Although for Friedrich Gentz, who started out quite high and was unambivalent about climbing to the very top, the Berlin salons had a merely "precarious" respectability, for Richter, coming from far below and most ambivalent about climbing, the same salons represented the epitome of aristocratic society.

Jewish Salon Men

The stories of the salon men who managed to change their estate or their income level by becoming intellectuals shows how important personal friendships were in the making of their public careers. But friendship presumed at minimum a common language. Because of their exclusion from secular educational institutions and their restriction to money-exchange occupations, most Jewish men in eighteenth-century Germany spoke only Yiddish. Without complete mastery of German and French, graceful, literate conversation and friendship with gentiles were impossible. Yet in spite of these linguistic barriers, some Jewish men in Berlin did possess prerequisites most useful in forging an intellectual career. Many in the community were fantastically wealthy, and their wealth also changed the lives of less fortunate, poorer Jewish men. For the wealthy households offered employment as tutors and merchant's apprentices to poorer boys who were either born in Berlin or wandered there from Poland or from elsewhere in Germany.[70] In addition to wealth and the leisure it made possible, Jewish men belonged to a culture in which learning and scholarship were cherished values. Moreover, in the last decades of the eighteenth century Jewish scholarship in Germany became less and less restricted to traditional Orthodox themes and methods. Berlin became a center for the revival of Hebrew and for a new critical, enlightened Jewish scholarship. The intellectual origins of Reform Judaism go back to debates that racked Berlin's Jewish community in these years.

In spite of the financial and intellectual advantages offered by Jewish life in Berlin, in the late eighteenth century the disadvantages for male Jewish intellectuals were actually more telling. Jewish men were poorly represented among Berlin's intelligentsia, although they did make a marginally better showing in the smaller world of salons than they did in the intelligentsia at large; eight of the sixty-nine salon men were Jewish. Yet

70. See Altman, *Moses Mendelssohn,* 353.

even this modest success was overshadowed by that of the Jewish women, who were far more prominent among the salon women than the Jewish men were among the salon men. That is precisely what is fascinating about these salons—that they provided a public cultural stage for Jewish women at a time when Jewish men had not yet achieved their characteristically high level of participation in German intellectual life.[71]

The Jewish salon men divide neatly into an older and a younger generation. The older cohort included Mendelssohn and his two leading disciples and personal friends, Markus Herz and David Friedländer. Born in mid-century, these men had come to adulthood well before salons flourished in the last two decades of the century. Although all three were published authors, Mendelssohn extensively and prominently so, none of the three earned his income from an intellectual institution. Rather, their posts and their mobility paths were traditional ones for Jewish intellectuals. Mendelssohn arrived in Berlin from Dessau in 1743, when he was a penniless student of fourteen following his local rabbi to Berlin. Beginning as a tutor for Isaac Bernhard's children, Mendelssohn moved on to become a clerk and eventually a manager of Herr Bernhard's silk factory.[72] David Friedländer was born in Königsberg and came to Berlin in 1772, when he was twenty-two, to work in Daniel Itzig's firm. Friedländer went on to found his own silk factory. Markus Herz's background was closer to that of the impoverished young Mendelssohn than to that of the well-heeled young Friedländer. His father was a Torah scribe and tutor in Berlin; the family plan was for Herz to become a rabbi. But instead he studied medicine and philosophy at the University of Königsberg, where he became a personal friend of Immanuel Kant. When Herz returned to Berlin with his medical degree in 1770, he joined the staff of the Jewish hospital directed by his future father-in-law, Dr. Benjamin de Lemos.[73]

It was not just the occupations of Mendelssohn, Friedländer, and Herz which were traditionally Jewish. Each married a Jewish woman, and two

71. See Paul Mendes-Flohr, "The Study of the Jewish Intellectual: Some Methodological Proposals," in *Essays in Modern Jewish History*, F. Malino and P. C. Albert, eds. (East Brunswick, N.J., 1982), 142–72. See also Michael Meyer, "Reform Jewish Thinkers and Their German Intellectual Context," in *The Jewish Response to German Culture*, J. Reinharz and W. Schatzberg, eds. (Hanover, N.H., 1985), 64–84.

72. See Altmann, *Moses Mendelssohn*.

73. See the entry on Markus Herz in Abbé Denina, *La Prusse Littéraire sous Fréderick II* (Berlin, 1790); see also Wilhelm Grau, *Wilhelm von Humboldt und das Problem des Juden* (Hamburg, 1935), 34, who notes that Herz was von Humboldt's medical doctor. There is also a biographical sketch of Herz in *Büsten berlinischer Gelehrten mit Devisen*, J. Krüppeln, C. Nentke, C. Paalzow, eds., (Leipzig, 1787). Herz's title (*Hofrat*), given for his lectures, is noted by Otto Berdrow, *Rahel Varnhagen: Ein Lebens- und Zeitbild* (Stuttgart, 1902).

of the three wives were chosen with the aid of her father.[74] None of the three converted. To be sure, all three men did enjoy professional contacts with gentile men, but these relationships had their origins in goal-oriented endeavors, and the friendships rarely included the men's sisters or wives. Mendelssohn's friends Gotthold Lessing and Friedrich Nicolai engineered Mendelssohn's entrance onto the German intellectual stage by publishing an essay he had written without asking Mendelssohn's permission. The friendship between these three developed through shared intellectual work. David Friedländer's tie to Wilhelm von Humboldt, on the other hand, was primarily an economic one: Friedländer was von Humboldt's personal banker. This banker-client relationship did gradually become a friendship, albeit a somewhat distant one.[75] Markus Herz met his gentile friends through his medical practice, at the few intellectual clubs he was admitted to, or at his lectures. What was significant was that Mendelssohn, Herz, and Friedländer were active publishing authors and prominent public figures in the liberal wing of the Jewish community. Their gentile friends were dedicated to making enlightened gestures at a time—in the 1780s—when Jewish equality was much discussed. If neither Jewish accomplishment nor gentile good will existed, it is unlikely that these ties across estate barriers would have been forged. Thus although the three men's ties to gentiles were extensive in the context of eighteenth-century Europe, the style of their friendships was not. Contacts grew out of goal-oriented endeavors, and these three Jewish men were essentially tokens in the secular intellectual world.

The five younger Jewish salon men, whose average age in 1800 was twenty-two, were far more assimilated in every regard. To begin with, the economic achievements of their fathers provided them with the time and the money to pursue their intellectual interests. The social space of clubs and salons, as well as the expansion of the literary market, allowed them to achieve a level of integration into gentile society that went well beyond that of the older generation of Jewish salon men. Four of the younger set, Julius (Itzig) Hitzig, Israel Stieglitz, Hermann (Ephraim) Eberty, and Ludwig (Levin) Robert all had wealthy merchant fathers; David Koreff's father was a rich doctor.[76] Three of the five (Stieglitz,

74. On Mendelssohn's marriage see David Biale, "Love, Marriage, and the Modernization of the Jews," in *Approaches to Modern Judaism* (Chico, Calif., 1983), 7.

75. See Sweet, *Wilhelm von Humboldt*, vol. 1.

76. On Hitzig, see *Gelehrtes Berlin im Jahre 1825*, J. E. Hitzig and K. Büchner, eds. (Berlin, 1826); Krüger, *Berliner Romantik und Berliner Judentum* (Bonn, 1939), 13–23, 56, and 76; the Leutner edition of Varnhagen's *Denkwürdigkeiten*, 93–97; and Frida Nussbaum, *Julius Edward Hitzig als Biograph seiner Freunde* (Vienna, 1933). On Eberty see Dorf Michaelis, "The Ephraim Family and their Descendents (II)," *LBIYB*, 24 (1979), 225–46, and Eberty,

Eberty, and Koreff) continued in the traditionally Jewish occupations of their fathers; Hitzig and Robert both found positions in the literary market, Hitzig as a publisher and Robert as a freelance writer. Three of the five changed their names, and four of the five converted. Hitzig's name change was later mocked by Heinrich Heine:

> . . . Thereupon I took
> A carriage and I went
> Over to the *Kriminalrat* Hitzig's,
> Who was once called Itzig—
>
> When he was still an Itzig
> He dreamt that he saw his name
> Written in the sky
> And in front of it the letter "H."
>
> "What does this 'H' mean?"
> He asked himself—"Herr Hitzig
> Or *Heil'ger* (Saint) Itzig? Saint
> Is a nicer title—but
>
> In Berlin it would never do."—Finally
> Tired of brooding he called himself Hitzig.
> And only the faithful know
> In the Hitzig is hidden a saint.[77]

In contrast to the friendships of the older Jewish salon men, this group made close friendships with gentile men when they were still too young to have made significant intellectual contributions. Eberty, Hitzig, and Robert were prominent members of the Polarsternbund ("Northern Star Association"), the literary club to which Karl August Varnhagen, Adelbert von Chamisso, and Wilhelm Neuman also belonged. Israel Stieglitz was one of Wilhelm von Humboldt's closest friends during his university years, so close that one shocked historian later declared the "atmosphere" of their friendship (if not the friendship itself) to have been a homosexual one.[78] Thus there were lasting bonds outside of salon society between Jewish and gentile intellectuals. But salons were a crucial meeting place. Ludwig Robert, Rahel Levin's favorite brother, was one of the few Jew-

---

Jugenderinnerungen eines alten Berliners. For a substantive summary of Koreff's life see Karl August Varnhagen von Ense, *Biographische Portraits* (Leipzig, 1871), 1–45; see also Grau, *Wilhelm von Humboldt*, 34, and Krüger, *Berliner Romantik*, 16.

77. This is my translation; the German version can be found in Spiel, *Fanny von Arnstein*, 361.

78. See Grau, *Wilhelm von Humboldt*, 26.

ish men "allowed" at her salon; he was also the only Jewish man in salon society to marry a gentile woman.[79] The younger Jewish intellectuals often met their gentile friends through their mutual relationship to a Jewish salonière. The Jewish and the gentile members of the Polarstern-bund first joined literary forces during their visits to Philippine Cohen's salon. Neuman was a clerk and Varnhagen was a tutor at the Cohen household.[80] Ludwig Robert's friendships with gentiles, too, were often cemented at his sister's salon, and his presence there was rumored to have been due to his accident of birth rather than to his literary achievements.[81]

But for Jewish men born far outside of these charmed circles, salons could appear alien, glittering, and altogether inaccessible. That harsh truth was dramatically illustrated by the story of Salomon Maimon. Born in Poland in 1754, by the age of fourteen he was already a learned rabbi with a growing reputation and married with several children.[82] Avid to master secular languages and culture, Maimon left his hometown and family and traveled by boat and by foot to Germany. But his attempt to gain entrance to Berlin, the city famous among Jews for the access they had there to secular learning, failed miserably, and he was forced to spend the night in the Jewish beggars' dormitory outside the gate to the city. The next morning, the elder from the community assigned to interview Maimon was decidedly unimpressed with Maimon's ragged clothes, broken German, and secular philosophical ambitions. As a consequence, he was not allowed to enter Berlin. After several years spent elsewhere in Germany, Maimon had made himself somewhat more presentable. And so on his second try he managed to gain entrance to the city. Mendelssohn, Markus Herz, and Solomon Levy (the husband of the salonière Sara Levy) all aided Maimon in one way or another. Yet in spite of Maimon's impressive intellectual gifts and his growing success as a published

79. On Robert, see Krüger, *Berliner Romantik*, 15, 23, and 56; Margarete Cohen, "Ludwig Robert: Leben und Werke," Ph.D. diss., Göttingen, 1923; the entry on Robert in the catalogue *Preussische Bildnisse des 19. Jahrhunderts: Zeichnungen von Wilhelm Hensel* (Nationalgalerie Berlin, 1981), 88; Lothar Kahn, "Ludwig Robert, Rahel's Brother," *LBIYB*, 18 (1973), 185–200, and Miriam Sambursky, "Ludwig Roberts Lebensgang," *Bulletin des Leo Baeck Institutes*, 15, N.F. no. 52 (1976), 1–48. See also Varnhagen von Ense's article on Robert in his *Vermischte Schriften* (Leipzig, 1843), part 2, 54ff.

80. See the abridged edition of Varnhagen's memoirs: *Denkwürdigkeiten des eigenen Lebens*, 81.

81. This is the judgment made by Cohen, "Ludwig Robert," 24.

82. The best source on Maimon is Jakob Fromer, *Salomon Maimons Lebensgeschichte* (Munich, 1911). Maimon's own extremely interesting autobiography has been translated: *Salomon Maimon: An Autobiography*, Moses Hadas, ed. (New York, 1967). See also Altman, *Moses Mendelssohn*, 360ff.

David Koreff

Julius Hitzig

Ludwig Robert

Salomon Maimon

scholar, he never managed to fit into Berlin society, gentile or Jewish. He refused to flatter people; for instance, he was opposed to calling people by their titles.[83] Once at a dinner party, "the conversation came around to the topic of courtesy. Maimon managed to say directly to the face of the woman of the house that it was a mistake, which originates from the French, to believe that women deserve respect; rather, that they much more deserve our pity."[84] On another occasion Maimon was walking late at night on the streets of Berlin when his accompanying friend used the word "Harmonie." Maimon called out in "pure Yiddish loud into the night: 'Harmonie, Harmonie! What is Harmonie?' Out of the background the voice of the nightwatchman resounded: 'Harmonie, Harmonie! Will the Jew please, in the devil's name, keep his mouth shut in the deep of the night?'"[85] Eventually even his wealthy Jewish patrons withdrew their support, and Maimon left Berlin for a second time. He spent his last years living on the rural estate of a noble patron, and died lonely and isolated from both the gentile and Jewish communities. He was buried as a heretic outside the walls of the Jewish cemetery.[86]

The story of Maimon's tactlessness and his resulting exclusion from salon society is yet another example of how the intellectual world of eighteenth-century Berlin was still small enough for friendships to matter a great deal in intellectual success. The private world of shared lodgings and meals and the exchange of letters was intricately intertwined with the public world of university attendance, tutoring positions, professorships, publications, and salon attendance. Because of long-term structural changes in the economy and in the educational system, Berlin's intelligentsia was much more heterogeneous in its estate and income composition than it had been in previous decades. Small, face-to-face intellectual institutions amplified the trend toward a more open and diverse intelligentsia. The men in salons were an even more heterogeneous society than was the intelligentsia at large or any of the intellectual clubs. Salon men were more likely to be noble, to have achieved upward mobility, and to be Jewish than was the average intellectual. Personal, cross-estate friendships brought these diverse men together, and salons provided them with the chance to further extend their circle of useful friendships, which in turn aided them in their professional and intellectual lives.

Men formed the majority of salon participants, and the bonds between

83. Fromer, *Salomon Maimons*, 29.
84. Ibid., 30.
85. Ibid., 29.
86. See Herbert Friedenthal, *The Everlasting Nay: The Death of Salomon Maimon* (London, 1944).

many of them were forged before salons came onto the scene in Berlin, or outside salons after they appeared. In this way the sixty-nine salon men and their ties of friendship may be understood to have been one cause which brought the salons to life, while at the same time the salons functioned to meet these men's intellectual and social needs. But it was women who hosted the salons, and were thus at salon society's center, both literally and symbolically. It is to their lives that we now turn.

SIX | *Salon Women*

Publication and the Public Woman

Although Madame de Staël cast a disdainful eye on the social life of much of Germany on her 1804 visit, Berlin glittered as the significant exception. There, she rejoiced at the wide diversity of men who gathered in the salons. But in her view Berlin's women did not enjoy the exceptional status she granted to the city's men. "This happy mixture is not yet extended to the society of the women: there are among them some whose talents and accomplishments attract every thing that is distinguished to their circles, but, generally speaking, at Berlin, as well as throughout the rest of Germany, female society is not well amalgamated with that of the men."[1] Elsewhere de Staël took issue with another defect in the German women, complaining that they were "affected" and "sentimental." But in spite of these faults, she concluded that the German women "were superior to the men" and summed up her ultimately positive assessment in the telling metaphor that "there is nothing more clumsy, more smoke-filled in the moral as in the physical sense, than German men."[2]

1. Anne Louise Germaine (Necker) Staël-Holstein, *Germany,* 3 vols. (London, 1914), vol. 1, 166. The quote cited here is based on my translation of the original French, rather than the English version. The English version reads "female society is not as well amalgamated *as* that of the men," whereas the French reads "la société des femmes n'est pas bien amalgamée *avec* celle des hommes." See de Staël's *De L'Allemagne,* Chronologie et Introduction par Simone Balayé (Paris, 1968), 134.

2. These more positive reactions to women in Germany are quoted in J. Christopher Herold, *Mistress to an Age: A Life of Madame de Staël* (London, 1959), 254. Herold does not cite his primary source except to note that "these quotations are taken from letters written in November and December 1803."

Madame de Staël's specific criticisms of society women in Berlin can hardly be attributed to her unfamiliarity with the city's leading salonières. Gustav von Brinkmann was her guide to Berlin society, and it was he, salon society's ubiquitous "introducer," who brought de Staël to dinner at Dorothea von Courland's and arranged for her to enjoy a long discussion with Rahel Levin that April of 1804.[3] The profound differences in the public power of wealthy, educated Frenchwomen as compared to their German counterparts must be remembered when pondering de Staël's disappointment in Berlin's society women. Contemporaries understood that even by the first years of the nineteenth century, Germany still possessed only a pale version of the social climate that had nourished generations of powerful female intellectuals in France. To be sure, the sheer number of women publishing in Germany had increased toward the end of the century. But becoming a productive intellectual was only one dimension of the larger endeavor. German women still found it difficult to use the printed word to become national public figures who played any role at all in male intellectual circles. The sheer absence of a counterpart to de Staël in Germany was in itself ample demonstration of this national difference.[4] Thus de Staël's very special Frenchwoman's eyes may have made it difficult for her to assess the place of the Berlin salon women in their own national context.

In any case, de Staël's observations were not entirely negative. After all, she admitted that some Berlin women had "talents and accomplishments" that attracted "everything which is distinguished" to their circles. In this chapter we finally meet the salon women and recount these talents and these accomplishments. Only then can we enter the past directly and assess for ourselves whether de Staël's criticisms of the Berlin salon

3. For discussion of the trip see Alfred Götze, *Ein Fremder Gast: Frau von Staël in Deutschland 1803/04* (Jena, 1928), 121. A recent biography of de Staël, which came to my attention too late to be used here, is Renee Winegarten, *Mme De Staël* (Leamington Spa, England), 1985.

4. The comparative paucity of female intellectuals in Germany in this era can be seen from surveying three recent books: J. R. Brink, ed., *Female Scholars: A Tradition of Learned Women before 1800* (Montreal, 1980); Patricia H. Labalme, ed., *Beyond Their Sex: Learned Women of the European Past* (New York and London, 1980); and Paul Fritz and Richard Morton, *Women in the Eighteenth Century and Other Essays* (Toronto and Sarasota, 1976). Two primary sources useful in reconstructing German women writers in the era are George Christoph Lehms, *Biographies Teutchlands galanten Poetinnen* (Frankfurt a.M., 1715), and Carl von Schindel, *Die deutschen Schriftstellerinnen des 19 Jh.*, 3 vols. (Leipzig, 1823–25, rpt. New York, 1978). See also Natalie Halperin, "Die deutsche Schriftstellerin in der zweiten Hälfte des 18 Jh.: Versuch einer soziologischen Analyse," Ph.D. diss., Frankfurt a.M., 1935. On the absence of a de Staël in Germany see Günter Jäckel and Manfred Schlösser, eds., *Das Volk braucht Licht: Frauen zur Zeit des Aufbruchs 1790–1848 in ihren Briefen* (Darmstadt and Zurich, 1970), 29.

women were justified. And only the discovery of the salon women's "talents and accomplishments" can explain how these women attracted a "happy mixture" of men to their salons, even if de Staël was correct that they themselves were poorly "amalgamated" with their male guests. Precisely because their social achievements were so notable in their own national setting, de Staël's disappointment in the Berlin salon women presents a bit of a puzzle. Should posterity, too, find the *salonières* wanting?

Insofar as there were two men for every woman in salons, the numbers match de Staël's observation that the salon women were not very "amalgamated" into masculine high society. Female salon society, after all, was only half as large as male salon society. The proportion of guests who were women was even smaller. A third of the thirty-one salon women led their own salons, leaving only twenty-one women as guests at other women's salons. A contemporary report noted that few women could be found at Rahel Levin's salon, and Dorothea Veit lamented that women were not encouraged to join the discussion at Henriette Herz's salon. Dorothea von Courland was reportedly free to invite so many women to her salon only because she was a duchess. These contemporary observations match the objective record left by the numbers. Not only were the salon women too few to dominate the salon men, there were too few women per salon for them to create a separate intellectual circle apart from men.

But what about another of de Staël's complaints, that among themselves the salon women were not as much a "happy mixture" of classes as the men were? In reality, de Staël's impression that the salon women were not a very heterogeneous circle was surely justified regarding the proportion of gentile commoners among the salon women. But her comments were not at all correct about the proportion of nobles or Jews among salon women. Her pronouncement that Berlin's salon men were more socially diverse than the women may well have been sparked by the significant contrast in the amount of upward mobility among the commoner salon men as compared to the women. Over half of the men in salon society were born without a title. To be sure, only seven of the commoner men in salons managed to change estates by becoming nobles. But the proportion who moved up in a less dramatic fashion— from the middle-income strata to the upper strata—was significant. A third of the salon men achieved this move, mainly by becoming officials or professors.

The group of commoner women in salon society for whom this intra-commoner mobility was even possible was, in contrast, very small indeed. Only six (a mere 18 percent of the thirty-one salon women) were commoners. Noble women were a far greater proportion of the women than noble men were of the men; a full half of the salon women were born into the nobility. And Jewish women constituted the majority of the salonières and a third of all salon women. De Staël's declaration that the women constituted less of a "happy mixture" of classes was therefore correct in the technical sense, if one distinguishes between "classes" and "estates." For it was those born into the noble and Jewish estates, not those commoners who were clambering to climb into a higher income group, who were well represented among the salon women. But although she was thus technically correct, this narrow interpretation of de Staël's claim surely misses the point. The point is that de Staël's derision of the salon women for being less of a "happy mixture of classes" than the salon men was quite wrong, given the truly dramatic mixture of estates among the salon women. The noble-Jewish mixture was every bit as unusual in the context of eighteenth-century Germany, perhaps even more unusual, than was the mixing of income groups among the commoner men. Although the absolute number of individuals involved was tiny, this noble-Jewish mixing had volatile symbolic implications for contemporary Berlin society. Perhaps de Staël's failure to note the "happy mixture" of estates among the salon women was because of her own French experience. She was accustomed to noble women orchestrating high society, whereas this event was a novelty in Germany, especially in Prussia. Then, too, she may well have considered the leading role of Jewish women in Berlin society odious rather than happy.

As we learned in the last chapter, a fifth of the salon men were dilettantes, that is, they won their place in salons not by their published literary achievements but by some combination of their social standing, occupation, personal charm, friendships, and unpublished writing. Given the institutional and ideological barriers to female authorship in the eighteenth century, it was to be expected that the proportion of unpublished dilettantes among the salon women would be far larger than among the men. And so it was. Twenty-one of the thirty-one salon women left behind no published record of their intellectual life. Yet it is noteworthy that unlike the male dilettantes in salons, who were universally nobles, the social composition of the female dilettantes closely mirrored that of the salon women as a whole. Noble women were no better represented among the dilettantes than among the authors. This means that compared to the men, the proportion of noble women who published was quite high. And conversely, a greater proportion of unpublished non-noble women than men made their way into salon society.

Both the subjective experience and the objective consequences of authorship were obviously different for the salon women than they were for the men in salons.

Of the eleven authors among the salon women, five were born into noble families. That noble women became authors in this setting represented a double achievement. Like the noble male authors, these women had to overcome the Prussian Junkers' historic disdain for an urban, intellectual, cultivated way of life. But their achievement was not just a victory over the traditional values of the estate into which they were born; it was also a triumph against a tradition across the social hierarchy which had kept the number of German women authors small during the seventeenth and early eighteenth centuries.[5] The life story of Eliza von der Recke illustrates how hard a would-be noble author had to fight against family and tradition to secure a place in the literary world. The privileges of Eliza von der Recke's material circumstances insured that she had the leisure to read, to travel, and write. Yet her need to fight against her family in order to develop herself intellectually shows that the way of life she chose was still controversial in noble circles.

Although she had visited Berlin regularly since she was teenager, von der Recke herself was not in the city enough to be a dominant figure in salon society. Her main tie to the salon society in Berlin was through her half-sister Dorothea von Courland. Eliza had an apartment in von Courland's palace on Unter den Linden and spent various winters there over the years; both her brothers were top civil service officials in the city. Her family ties insured that she was very much *hoffähig* at the Berlin and Potsdam courts. Yet from the time that they were quite young, Eliza and Dorothea von Medem had discovered a world beyond their rural estate and beyond courtly society. While the two sisters were growing up in the 1770s at home on the von Medem estate in Courland, their tutor had been Daniel Parthey, who eventually became a prominent publisher and bookseller in Berlin. When they later visited Berlin as teenagers, Parthey, who was by then a tutor for Friedrich Nicolai's children, introduced the von Medem sisters to the leading authors of the city. Thanks to their extutor's connections, both young women were introduced to Moses Mendelssohn, Johann Biester, and Johann Spalding.[6]

5. In addition to the sources cited in note 5 above see the extensive bibliography in Elisabeth Friedrichs, *Die deutschsprachigen Schriftstellerinnen des 18. und 19. Jahrhunderts: Ein Lexikon* (Stuttgart, 1981).

6. The most recent and comprehensive source on von der Recke is Christine Träger, ed., *Elisa von der Recke: Tagebücher und Selbstzeugnisse* (Leipzig, 1984). See also Schindel's biography of her in his *Die deutsche Schriftstellerin*, vol. 2, 138ff. For a detailed account, see Gustav Parthey, *Jugenderinnerungen* (Berlin, 1871).

Dorothea von Courland

The rational and egalitarian values Eliza developed through these friendships met resistance at the von Medem home in Courland. Seven years older than Dorothea, Eliza grew up under the care of her father's second wife. Unlike his third wife, Dorothea's mother, Eliza's mother provided her daughter with no intellectual training whatsoever. At sixteen, Eliza was married off to Herr von der Recke against her will, after a fierce struggle with her father. Her wealthy and well-placed husband did everything possible to squelch his wife's interests in intellectual matters. After five years they separated, and that same year their three-year-old daughter died.

Eliza then began many years of travel throughout Europe, staying for months at a time in Hamburg, Dresden, or St. Petersburg. In later years, when her health deteriorated, she followed her doctor's orders by moving to Italy. As she developed herself intellectually, von der Recke sought out friends who nurtured enlightened values. These friends were badly needed, since the von Medem clan was antagonistic to what they saw as Eliza's bluestocking tendencies. Her family in Courland had been alienated by her intellectual interests all along. Von der Recke's grandmother was outraged one day when she was informed that her granddaughter, who was then in her thirties, was reading a book written by a Jew, Moses Mendelssohn! Von der Recke's book denouncing Count Alessandro Cagliostro, whom she had first met at the family home in Courland, proved to be the decisive break with her family. Her attack on Cagliostro, a charismatic Italian mystic who became a popular "guru" to many Prussian Junker families in the 1780s, summarized and publicized von der Recke's rationalist values.[7]

Von der Recke's publications—she wrote eight books and a score of articles—all emerged directly from her own experiences; her tract against Cagliostro even incorporated selections from her diary. Another book consisted of descriptions of her travels with the author Sophie Becker; a later critic declared that with this volume von der Recke elevated travel criticism "into an art."[8] No record survives of how pressing her material motives were for publishing or how much she profited from publication, but it is clear that von der Recke could not always support herself in the appropriate style. Because von der Recke could not afford her own home in the city, her half-sister Dorothea provided Eliza with quarters in her Berlin palace. In the end, whatever she gained monetarily from publishing, hers was clearly a life where devotion to enlightened values and to

---

7. Von der Recke's grandmother's outrage is reported in Schindel, *Die deutschen Schriftstellerinnen*, vol. 2, 140. For her views on Cagliostro see Träger, *von der Recke*, 276–78.

8. This judgment is made by Johannes Scherr, *Geschichte der deutschen Frauenwelt* (Leipzig, 1911), vol. 2, 212.

the literary life were not only of dubious practical benefit, but perhaps more painfully, brought von der Recke into significant conflict with the world into which she was born.

In both her ideology and in her social life, Helene Unger was more distant from both courtly and salon society than Eliza von der Recke. Yet Unger is classified here as a salonière because she organized her own informal lecture society, labeled by at least one historian as having been a salon. We know that she was definitely not a frequent guest at the Jewish salons, for she wrote openly of her disdain for the Jewish salonières. But as her life story shows, integration into Jewish salon circles was obviously not a prerequisite for literary productivity in late eighteenth-century Berlin. As an author, editor, translator, and co-worker in her husband's publishing firm, Helene Unger created a secure place for herself on the Berlin literary scene. Her passage from the family of her birth into the city's intellectual community could not have been as difficult as the journey traveled by Eliza von der Recke. To be sure, she too was born with a noble title; her father was a general in the Prussian army. But since hers was an urban family, her cultivated values were unlikely to have stimulated the familial opposition that von der Recke's bluestocking lifestyle aroused in her provincial noble family. Unger distanced herself even further from noble prejudices against the literary life when she married down on the estate hierarchy, to the commoner J. H. Unger, a leading publisher and bookseller in the city. Helene took an active role in running her husband's publishing firm while he was alive and directed it alone after he died in 1804.[9]

By the 1790s, Helene Unger had become one of Berlin's most active novelists. Her literary fame did not come early in life. She kept up a steady, productive pace but chose to have her work appear anonymously until she was forty-six. Unger translated Rousseau, wrote children's books and a cookbook, and published her letters to her brother under the title *Briefe über Berlin*. Her most popular book, *Julchen Grünthal*, appeared when she was fifty-three and hit the German public "like a

---

9. On Unger see Flodoard von Biedermann, *Johann Friedrich Unger im Verkehr mit Goethe und Schiller* (Berlin, 1927), xiv–xxxvii; Christine Touaillon, *Der deutsche Frauenroman des 18. Jahrhunderts* (Vienna and Leipzig, 1919), 244ff; Elise Oelsner, *Die Leistungen der deutschen Frau in den letzten vierhundert Jahren auf wissenschaftlichem Gebiet* (Breslau, 1894), 225ff. Lily Braun praised Unger for her "rare, sharp views" about contemporary women's education in her "Der Kampf um Arbeit in der bürgerlichen Frauenwelt," *Archiv für soziale Gesetzgebung und Statistik* 16 (Berlin, 1901), 45. Unger's lecture society is mentioned in Klaus Günzel, ed., *König der Romantik: Das Leben des Dichters Ludwig Tieck in Briefen, Selbstzeugnissen und Berichten* (Tübingen, 1981), 507. Touaillon, *Frauenroman*, 244, refers to her social events as a "salon," as does Henri Brunschwig, *Enlightenment and Romanticism in Eighteenth-Century Prussia* (Chicago, 1974), 281–82.

bomb."[10] The novel told the story of a virtuous young girl from the countryside whose parents sent her to a girls' boarding school in the city, where she was taught embroidery, French, and piano; her fellow students encouraged her to spend hours each day on her "Toilette" and clothing and to emulate noble behavior. She eventually ran off with a prominent but irresponsible suitor and found herself involved in a series of unfortunate and unhappy adventures. In the second volume of the book, Julchen Grünthal returned to her rural family, utterly contrite about how the boarding school had ruined her life.[11]

The message of *Julchen Grünthal* was clear: a dissolute, declining nobility was corrupting the morals of honorable commoners through upwardly mobile romances and marriages. Unger opposed every aspect of this social exchange and exhorted mothers to stop this movement up the estate hierarchy by educating their daughters at home. Ironically, despite her own active role in her husband's firm, her publications, and her lecture society, Unger argued against women taking an active role in public life. She also crusaded against what she obviously saw as a related development, the romantics' encouragement of "free morals." There was thus a direct connection between Unger's anti-salon ideology and her private antipathy to the Jewish salonières, whose lives were dramatic illustrations of how free morals and public roles contributed to upwardly mobile marriages.

Unger's opposition to the values and behavior at the center of salon culture placed her decidedly out of step with Berlin literary society in the 1780s and 1790s. In the early years of the Enlightenment—notably the Leipzig circle around Johann Gottsched in the 1740s—Unger's model of an essentially private and virtuous female intellectuality prevailed. This model returned to favor with the later romantics, who came to oppose sensuality, divorce, and female cultural power as the salons declined in the second decade of the nineteenth century.[12] In the intervening early romantic epoch, the Jewish salons were a striking embodiment of everything Unger opposed. The salons showed that intellectual cultivation could indeed become socially dangerous. Love affairs between men and

10. This phrase was used by Adalbert von Hanstein, *Die Frauen in der Geschichte des deutschen Geisteslebens des 18. und 19. Jahrhunderts*, 2 vols. (Leipzig, 1899–1900), vol. 2, 306.

11. For extended summary and analysis see Helga Meise, *Die Unschuld und die Schrift: Deutsche Frauenromane im 18. Jahrhundert* (Berlin/Marburg, 1983), chap. 3.

12. On the early romantics' rejection of the "learned woman" model developed by Gottsched and his circle see Silvia Bovenschen, *Die imaginierte Weiblichkeit: Exemplarische Untersuchungen zu kulturgeschichtlichen und literarischen Präsentationsformen des Weiblichen* (Frankfurt, a.M., 1979).

women of different estates and income groups were one consequence of shared literary activity in a setting that was notably permissive in the context of the sober Prussian past. As we shall see later, these love affairs, if they became marriages, strongly challenged the social hierarchy.

Like Helene Unger, Caroline de la Motte Fouqué was also on the margin of salon society; her main tie to the salon world was through her second husband, a close literary associate of Karl August Varnhagen and Adalbert von Chamisso.[13] Caroline herself was friendly with Rahel Levin. The de la Motte Fouqués lived for most of the year on their rural estate outside Berlin but came into the city regularly to meet with their literary friends. Like Helene Unger, de la Mott Fouqué opposed women taking on public roles. Her antagonism to women's public power alienated de la Motte Fouqué from prominent salon women, just as Unger's parallel views isolated her from the key salonières. Contemporaries thus interpreted the hostility Dorothea Veit felt for de la Motte Fouqué as anger at de la Motte Fouqué's position against public roles for women. Ironically enough, Caroline de la Motte Fouqué was a prolific, productive author. As with Helene Unger, her ideological opposition to women assuming a certain public style did not prevent de la Motte Fouqué from making herself known to strangers through her intellectual labors. Both women obviously distinguished the private, domestic act of writing from face-to-face prominence in salon society. Their tendency to publish their first books anonymously is, however, a hint of the deeper conflicts Unger and de la Motte Fouqué may have felt about how public even the quiet act of publishing was.

Caroline de la Motte Fouqué was tall and graceful, with an air deemed "regal" by her friends. She had been raised in a rural but cultivated noble family, and prominent Berlin intellectuals often came to visit her family home while she was growing up. Her first husband, a young officer known for his addiction to gambling, eventually killed himself with a rifle shot. The young widow then returned to her parents' estate, and eventually married a second time to Friedrich de la Motte Fouqué, a local noble writer who had abandoned studying law at the university in Halle in order to pursue a military career. Friedrich later abandoned the military life as well, pleading ill health, and proceeded to join his new wife at her family's estate and devote his full energies to writing immensely popular romantic historical novels. But in spite of his wife's productiv-

13. On de la Motte Fouqué see (Mrs.) Vaughn Jennings, *Rahel: Her Life and Letters* (London, 1876), 99–116; Schindel, *Die deutschen Schriftstellerinnen*, vol. 1, 130–32; Vera Prill, *Caroline de la Motte Fouqué*, Heft 137 of *Germanische Studien* (Berlin, 1933), and the article in vol. 7 of the *ADB*, 198ff.

ity—she published thirteen novels and three collections of short stories between 1806 and 1831—Caroline's works were "quietly ignored"; she was accused of imitating his style. Nevertheless, Karl August Varnhagen and her husband encouraged her to persevere; it was a female friend, Rahel Levin, who disapproved of one of de la Motte Fouqué's first novels when Levin read a draft of the manuscript in 1810. In the end, although her publication record requires that she be classified here as an author and not a dilettante, de la Motte Fouqué came to be known in literary Berlin more for her letters and for her role as inspirational "muse" than for her published works.[14]

For all their published productivity, Eliza von der Recke, Helen Unger, and Caroline de la Motte Fouqué did not put their literary energy to work within the salon context. Von der Recke and de la Motte Fouqué each had one close tie with a salonière, but neither developed a dense net of friendships among salon women. Personal distance from key salon personalities or lack of an ongoing residence in Berlin limited the intensity of these three women's involvement in the major salons. In contrast, a fourth noble salon woman, Madame Félicité de Genlis, actively intervened in the lives of several younger salon women—by teaching them French, befriending them, and even taking one back to Paris with her. De Genlis arrived in Berlin at age fifty-four, ripe in personal, pedagogic, and literary experience. Unlike the local salon men, who could meet and fall under the spell of a variety of exotic French men, it was far rarer for local salon women to enjoy sustained social exposure to a prominent Frenchwoman.

De Genlis was born in 1746 into a respectable noble family named Ducrest. Her early education was eccentric at best: she was dressed either as a boy or in medieval armour when a child; later she learned to read music even though she had not yet mastered the alphabet. At sixteen, she was married off to Count de Genlis, a colonel in the army whom her father had met while imprisoned abroad by the English.[15] The count's wealth was a boon to the Ducrest family, since Félicité's father died shortly after the wedding, leaving his widow and children without an inheritance. But the marriage, which had begun badly, did not go well; the count's parents objected to their son's choice of a wife, and the union

14. This is the judgment made by Prill, *Caroline de la Motte Fouqué*, 12. The quote above about her work being "quietly ignored" is the judgment of Schindel, *Die deutschen Schriftstellerinnen*, vol. 1, 131.

15. A useful summary of de Genlis's life can be found in the *Nouvelle Biographie Générale* (henceforth *NGB*) (Paris, 1858), vol. 19, 901–10; see also the discussion of de Genlis in Eva Reitz, "Helmina von Chézy," Ph.D. diss., Frankfurt a.M., 1923, 32–34.

was kept secret from his parents. The couple quarreled, and soon husband and wife began living separately. It was then that Madame de Genlis began to earn her keep as a governess in the king's household, teaching the children of Louis XIV's brother, who was later to become the Duke of Orléans. She was able to obtain this post because although she spent a good deal of time when first married in active pursuit of luxury and pleasure, she had also managed to give herself a thorough education. But it was not until she had acquired pedagogic experience as a governess that Madame de Genlis put her education to work in published form. Her first book, published in 1782, when she was thirty-six, was a treatise outlining the pedagogic program appropriate for princes. For the next decade de Genlis enjoyed considerable success as an author—her second book was on religion—and as a public figure, but by the early 1790s her life in France had become problematic in a number of respects. Mutual political distrust and suspicion eroded her relationship with the duke's family. While living with his family in Switzerland in 1793, she learned that her estranged husband had been guillotined, and she inherited nothing of his large estate. She herself was placed on the list of those whose lives were in danger if they did not leave France.

And so in 1794 she arrived in Berlin, ready for a new life. The authorities, unfortunately, did not cooperate. For if Madame de Genlis was not liberal enough to stay in France, King Frederick William II was convinced that she was too liberal to stay in Prussia. He proceeded to brutally expel her, leaving Madame de Genlis to roam about outside the Prussian border. But when Frederick William III ascended the throne in 1797, he allowed her to return to Berlin. And so began a feverishly productive time for de Genlis. She wrote three novels during her three years in Berlin, supporting herself by teaching French to a circle of younger women. Among her students were Dorothea Veit and Veit's friend Esther Gad. Her special friend was Helmina von Chézy, who would soon follow de Genlis back to Paris. Madame de Genlis prospered after she departed Berlin in 1800. Napoleon provided her with a handsome apartment and pension, and commissioned regular political and social commentaries from her. In her later years she was judged to be "bizarre, morose, and irascible," but she continued writing until her last days. All in all, de Genlis must have been a powerful role model for the younger salon women.[16]

Helmina von Chézy profited most concretely from Madame de Genlis's influence and patronage. Von Chézy was the third generation of a

16. See the article in the *NBG*, vol. 19, 909.

matriarchal literary family which was quite idiosyncratic in eighteenth-century Berlin.[17] Although von Chézy was technically noble by birth, she, like her mother and grandmother before her, was anything but privileged. All three faced numerous material obstacles in their literary careers. These three women's lives show that impoverished but precocious women could use informal patronage to realize their talents in much the same way as poor young men like Ludwig Tieck or Johann Fichte. But their journeys toward a productive literary career were consistently thwarted by marriages arranged by their own mothers. Since writing was an essentially domestic activity, a husband chosen for his wealth or his title and without consideration for his genuine interest in his wife's intellectual projects could greatly damage a young wife's literary future. In this way the mother's social ambitions for herself and her daughter—even if the mother herself was a writer—could easily backfire on the daughter's own intellectual development.[18]

Helmina von Chézy's grandmother was Anna Louise Karsch, a poet born in Poland and married to a textile artisan. Karsch was brought to Berlin in 1761 at the age of thirty-nine by a Baron von Kottwitz, who wished to rescue the poet from her unhappy marriage, obscurity, and poverty. The baron accomplished the first two tasks, but not the third. Once she was settled in Berlin, Anna Karsch remained poor, largely because Baron von Kottwitz died shortly after she arrived. Luckily, she quickly made friends with several of Berlin's most prominent enlightened intellectuals, who tended to her welfare in matters practical and intellectual. Actually, Anna Karsch's unusual background was more crucial to her fame in Berlin than were her literary achievements in themselves. Her friends Johann Sulzer and Johann Gleim helped her organize subscriptions series to sell her published poetry and to obtain invitations to write poems celebrating national celebrations. They eventually convinced Frederick William II to stabilize her economic situation by purchasing Karsch a house near the end of her life.

Anna Louise Karsch brought her six-year-old daughter Caroline with her to Berlin when she arrived from Poland. Three years later, a friend of Karsh's arranged for nine-year-old Caroline to attend a local girls'

17. On von Chézy's mother and on her grandmother (Anna Karsch) the two main sources are Elisabeth Hausmann, *Die Karschin, Friedrich des Grossens Volksdichterin* (Frankfurt a.M., 1933) and Schindel, *Die deutschen Schriftstellerinnen*, vol. 1, 245–55. See also Heinrich Spiero, *Geschichte der deutschen Frauendichtung seit 1800* (Leipzig, 1913), 3–4.

18. Another example of a literarily accomplished woman who arranged her daughter's marriage to a man many found inappropriate was Sophie von La Roche. See Ludmilla Assing, *Sophie von La Roche, die Freundin Wielands* (Berlin, 1859).

boarding school, where her main training was in religion and the "domestic arts." At fourteen, Caroline returned home to live with her mother, and at sixteen, Anna Karsch arranged for Caroline to marry a simple young man by the name of Hempel, whom Karsch had adopted at a young age and whose request to marry her daughter she felt unable to refuse. Karsch later had reason to regret this generosity to Hempel, for the marriage was a complete disaster. Hempel was totally lacking in intellectual sophistication, and Caroline's only consolation was her son, born when she was only sixteen. Caroline spent most of her days on embroidery and household tasks and wrote only in her spare evening hours, while her husband and son slept. Princess Amalia, King Frederick the Great's unhappy sister who lived in a palace in the city, took on the project of cultivating Caroline's intellectual talents. The public fruits of this patronage were an ode, published without Caroline's knowledge when she was twenty, and a play that enjoyed wide popularity when it was produced in Berlin.

After ten years of unhappiness in her marriage, Caroline finally overcame her religious scruples and submitted to her friends' exhortations to divorce Hempel. She and her son moved back with her mother, and her life continued on peacefully until her mother came up with another groom—Herr von Klencke—the son of a noble widow who had befriended Karsch. He fell violently in love with the recently divorced Caroline Hempel, but unfortunately for her, his inheritance was small, and he had no prospects for bureaucratic office. His mother was opposed to a marriage to the lowly daughter of Anna Karsch, but the union eventually took place in 1782, when Caroline was twenty-eight. The couple had a daughter, Helmina. But Frau Wittwe-Major Klencke still conspired to break up her son's marriage, and ultimately she was successful. Caroline, the survivor of two arranged marriages gone awry, spent the rest of her days living in her mother's home, impoverished, despairing, spending most of her time embroidering, and writing only a little.

Helmina von Chézy, the third generation in the Karsch trio, was more successful than her mother or grandmother in the sheer volume of writing she published. But like her mother's life before her, Helmina's was scarred by an early and disastrous marriage arranged by her own mother. Growing up in a household with a mother and a grandmother who were writers, Helmine von Klencke developed into an intense young girl who used to become ill from studying too hard. At fourteen, she completed the manuscript of a satirical novel modeled in the style of Jean Paul (Richter); she sent it to Richter for his evaluation, but he never responded. But when she was sixteen, her impoverished mother, Caro-

line—who would die three years later—began to fear that Helmina
would be destitute after her own death. The man Caroline von Klencke
chose to save her daugher from poverty was Carl Freiherr von Hastfer.
Von Hastfer may have been both noble and solvent, but the marriage
did not succeed, and a year later the couple was divorced. The next year,
in 1801, a penniless eighteen-year-old Helmina went off to Paris to join
her friend and teacher, Madame de Genlis. Friends blamed Helmina's
association with de Genlis for making Helmina "vain and worldly;"
latter-day commentators put the blame on Caroline von Klencke for "let-
ting" her daughter follow Madame de Genlis.[19]

The young Helmina von Hastfer was able to survive in Paris only because her friends from salon circles in Berlin came to her aid. She moved
in with Dorothea Veit and Friedrich Schlegel, who had moved to Paris
from Jena in 1801. A Berlin bookseller and editor commissioned Helmina
to write regular articles on Paris for German readers. This in turn helped
Helmina obtain a regular editing post with one of Johann Friedrich Cotta's journals. David Koreff, the Jewish doctor from Berlin so popular
with several prominent salon guests, had also migrated to Paris, and Koreff wrote to Julius Hitzig back in Berlin about obtaining translating
assignments for the desperate Helmina von Hastfer. Koreff reminded his
friend Hitzig that "all of us young men" try to help her obtain work to
support herself. Madame de Genlis tried to get Helmina a governess
position with a prominent French family, but she was rejected for being
too young.[20]

Helmina von Hastfer remarried soon after she arrived in Paris, to Anton von Chézy, a professor of Oriental languages whom she met at the
Veit-Schlegel household, but eventually this marriage too faltered, and
Helmina's need to support herself resumed. She and her two sons left
France in 1810, and she spent the next years traveling about Germany
pursuing courtly support for hospital nursing, a patriotic cause she espoused and a possible career for herself. Through it all, Helmina von
Chézy continued to write and publish. She translated works by Madame
de Genlis, wrote a biography of her mother Caroline von Klencke, "the

19. On the novel the young Helmina von Klencke sent to Richter see Immanuel Hermann Fichte, *Johann Gottlieb Fichtes Leben und literarischer Briefwechsel* (Leipzig, 1862), 217.
The accusation that she was "vain and worldly" is cited in Reitz, "Helmina von Chézy." 36.
Schindel has a separate article on von Chézy; see his *Die deutschen Schriftstellerinnen,* vol. 1,
89–99; he discusses her departure to Paris on 90.

20. Koreff's 1810 letter is cited in Karl August Varnhagen von Ense's *Biographische Portraits* (Leipzig, 1871), in his chapter on Koreff. De Genlis's attempt to obtain Helmina a
governess position is noted in Schindel, *Die deutschen Schriftstellerinnen,* vol. 1, 92.

daughter of Karsch," and published her travel reports, as well as her poetry, with the subtitle "by the granddaughter of Karschin."[21]

From Eliza von der Recke to Helmina von Chézy, neither the five salon authors born noble nor the two salon authors born commoners had an easy time achieving literary productivity. Except for de Genlis, salon women rarely provided each other with practical aid or even intellectual inspiration either in or out of the salon setting. The men they met in salons were actually a more frequent source of patronage for the five gentile salon authors. But even this male aid could not solve the central dilemmas of their lives and their work, which were in the private world. Some salon authors were born into families without financial worries, but even so, a daughter bent on an intellectual life usually had to fight against her family to obtain an education. A few lucky salon authors were born into families where female intellectual work was encouraged, but often the poverty of these families made it difficult for them to let their daughters marry for love. In truth, the problem of inappropriate marriages interfering with women's intellectual work cut across the social hierarchy. Upwardly mobile arranged matches with men indifferent—if not hostile—to their wives' intellectual projects disrupted the lives of almost all of the gentile authors among the salon women. Helene Unger's apparently companionate marriage was the exception. Even though the Jewish authors we turn to now were raised in a culture that valued intellectual achievement and had fathers and husbands who were usually wealthy, they too had problems reconciling authorship and marriage. For Jewish salon authors shared with their gentile counterparts the dilemma of exiting from an arranged marriage and deciding what to do next.

As with so many of the gentile authors, for three of the four Jewish salon authors breaking away from early arranged marriages was a major life event. Sometimes the consequences of their divorces made possible a life richer in intellectual and emotional experiences. Yet like most of their gentile counterparts, for most of the Jewish salon authors life after divorce held new kinds of pain, pain which did not necessarily enhance their literary productivity. But if troubled first marriages were a fate common to salon authors of both faiths, in other ways the Jewish authors' circumstances were distinctive. For their families of birth provided them with a combination of material and intellectual nurturance that few of the gentile authors enjoyed in conjunction.

In terms of the sheer magnitude of her father's intellectual stature, Dorothea Veit was the luckiest of the four Jewish authors among the

21. Ibid., 93.

salon women. Her second husband, Friedrich Schlegel, also ranked among the intellectual stars of the generation after Mendelssohn. Yet in spite of her relationship to these two famous men, the sum of Dorothea Veit's own literary achievements hardly constituted a glamorous career. Her early training ranked among the most thorough of any young girl who came of age in eighteenth-century Germany.[22] Mendelssohn included her in the morning lessons he gave to her brother Joseph and to the two von Humboldt brothers. Young Brendel (as Dorothea was still called when a teenager) also joined her friend Henriette Herz in organizing amateur theatrical productions in local Jewish homes. The rigor of Mendelssohn's daughter's intellectual background is captured in the contemporary evaluation that she was "trained to a masculine independence of thought and character."[23]

Yet in her married years, until she was thirty, her unusual training did not result in any published literary work. At first glance, Dorothea Veit's 1798 break with her financially successful and kindly, but unintellectual husband Simon might be viewed as the chance to fulfill herself intellectually. It certainly seemed that way at the time, both to Friedrich Schlegel and to Veit herself. Not only was Schlegel impressed with Veit's mental powers; he was also on record in print in support of education for women.[24] But Dorothea Veit's intellectual life after her divorce turned out to be an ironic one indeed. She wrote and published, motivated mainly by Friedrich Schlegel's chronic inability to earn enough from lecturing and publishing to support his wife and the two sons she eventually brought into their household. But the sheer volume of her productivity was hidden behind Schlegel's name. Not one of her articles, translations, or even her novel *Florentin* was published with her own name on the first page.

Moreover, Schlegel's personal style damaged rather than enhanced Veit's overall quality of life. To begin with, her ostracism by family and friends alike after she left Simon Veit was only partially caused by their consternation that Friedrich Schlegel frequently stayed with Veit in her new apartment on the edge of town. Another reason for attacks on the notorious couple was because of the literary feuds in which Schlegel was already entangled. His erotic novel *Lucinde,* which was widely thought to be based on his relationship with Dorothea Veit, further exacerbated

22. This is a claim made by M. Kayserling, *Die jüdischen Frauen in der Geschichte, Literatur und Kunst* (Leipzig, 1879), 183.

23. Jennings, *Rahel,* 147.

24. For an overview of Schlegel's views on women—including women's education—see chapters 5 and 6 of Sara Friedrichsmeyer, *The Adrogyne in Early German Romanticism,* Stanford German Studies vol. 18 (Bern, Frankfurt a.M., New York, 1983).

Friedrich Schlegel

the couple's isolation even within the supposedly emancipated circles of salon society.[25] Dorothea's social loneliness was hardly ameliorated by the couple's escape to Jena in 1799, where Friedrich's brother August did his best to integrate the couple into the local avant-garde coterie. But Friedrich's frequent pronouncements denouncing powerul writers made him and his companion Dorothea "unpopular" in Jena.[26]

Thus a literary life with Schlegel was by no means an easy one. Yet

25. On her ostracism by family and friends see Kayserling, *Die jüdischen Frauen,* 185–88. For discussion of how the couple's personal relationship effected the novel see Peter Firchow's introduction to his translation of *Friedrich Schlegel's Lucinde and the Fragments* (Minneapolis, 1971), 20–22.

26. See Franz Deibl, *Dorothea Schlegel als Schriftstellerin im Zusammenhang mit der romantischen Schule,* vol. 40 of *Palaestra* (Berlin, 1905), 3.

insofar as the poverty of the Veit-Schlegel household motivated Veit to write and publish, an argument could be made that Veit's alliance with Schlegel stimulated her productivity. Her most important publication was the novel *Florentin*, which she wrote while the couple lived in Jena. The novel's characters were based on Veit's noble friends in Berlin, including a woman who dressed as a man and one who had an abortion. Although some critics subsequently judged Veit to have been a better novelist than Schlegel, *Florentin* was not well received at the time, and she never produced the promised second volume.[27] In spite of the absence of her name on the covers of her publications and thus her absence from the public stage of authorship, Veit enjoyed the esteem of several prominent male authors. Clemens Brentano sent along several manuscripts for her comments. She kept up a correspondence about literary matters with Ludwig Tieck. Several salon men pledged themselves to help her find freelance writing assignments; in 1799 and again in 1801, she wrote to Gustav von Brinkmann about a translation project, pridefully reminding him to keep her need for this work a secret.[28]

As the years passed and the Veit-Schlegel household became less impoverished, Veit, now Dorothea von Schlegel, wrote less and less for publication. All along, Veit's time to write and publish even under Schlegel's name had been restricted by the huge amount of practical work she performed at home. She was the copyist for all of Friedrich's manuscripts and also worked on many essays published in journals he edited. During the many years that the couple had little money for servant help, Veit also did a good deal more cooking, cleaning, and shopping than the typical salon woman.[29]

Through it all, Dorothea Veit was enthusiastic about the joy she found in life as Friedrich Schlegel's "journeyman." Some latter-day observers had been dismayed by her subordination to her husband's intellectual career. Her two conversions—to Protestantism in 1804 and, with Schlegel, to Catholicism in 1808—intensified her critics' conclusion that Dorothea Veit lacked integrity.[30] That would seem a harsh and unhistorical

27. For a summary of the novel see Ludwig Geiger, *Dichter und Frauen: Vorträge und Abhandlungen* (Berlin, 1896), 133–40; on its reception see Margaretha Hiemenz, *Dorothea von Schlegel* (Freiburg im Breisgau, 1911), 28.

28. On her literary relationships with Brentano and Tieck see Hiemenz, *Dorothea von Schlegel*, 45. Veit's 1799 request to von Brinkmann is discussed by Deibl, *Dorothea Schlegel*, 8.

29. For details see Hiemenz, *Dorothea von Schlegel*, 54 and 83, and Kayserling, *Die jüdischen Frauen*, 192 and 194.

30. The "journeyman" self-description is cited by Hiemenz, *Dorothea von Schlegel*, 28. Criticism of Dorothea was voiced both by contemporaries and historians. Achim von Arnim refered to her as the "worshipper of the Dalai Lama Friedrich Schlegel." He is quoted

judgment. Dorothea Veit risked a great deal when she left Simon Veit in 1798. She defended her decision to leave him as the emancipatory act of a frustrated woman of intellect and principle.[31] Her extreme loyalty to Schlegel may well have been a necessary counterforce to draw her away from the intense orbit of family and friends. The punishing response to her decision to leave her family, both by Jewish family members and by supposedly enlightened gentile salon friends, no doubt exacerbated Veit's intense dependence on Schlegel. However repulsive it may seem today, Veit's publications, even under her husband's name, were an accomplishment in the terms of the eighteenth century. That she was able to write a novel, translate and complete scores of essays and reviews is a testimony, however ironic, to the eduation she received from her father and to her own talent and tenacity.

The barriers to truly successful authorship faced by Henriette Herz seem to have been more straightforwardly internal than the barriers Dorothea Veit came up against. Herz never suffered a sharp break with the Jewish community, although she enjoyed a triumphant success in charming gentile courtiers and intellectuals. She never had to negotiate the consolations and demands of a Schlegel who offered release from a traditional community at the price of serving his practical and career needs. Then, too, Herz did not lose an intellectual mentor when she left her family home to wed Markus Herz. Her physician husband took over her training when they married, concentrating on her great strength, the acquisition of languages. Markus Herz aided Henriette's intellectual development in other ways too. His income, connections and natural science lectures were useful, perhaps even indispensable aids as she created her own role as salonière. The couple remained childless, so absorption in domestic joys and sorrows did not pose any conflicts with authorship.

In addition to her husband's support for her intellectual endeavors, Henriette Herz's close friend Friedrich Schleiermacher nurtured her writing, constantly encouraging her to devote herself more ardently to writing books and essays. Schleiermacher certainly held Herz's intellectual judgments in high esteem; he asked her to read his manuscripts and solicited her suggestions during the day the two spent together walking and talking every week while Schleiermacher lived in Berlin in 1794 and

---

in Paul Kluckhohn, *Die Auffassung der Liebe in der Literatur des 18. Jahrhundert und in der deutschen Romantik* (Halle, 1931), 381. Even Friedrich himself was later condemned for the marriage; Ricarda Huch declared that relationship as altogether unworthy of Schlegel's earlier ideals. See her "Die romantische Ehe," in *Das Ehe-Buch,* ed. Hermann Keyserling (Celle, 1925), 157. See also Hannah Arendt's criticism of Dorothea in her *Rahel Varnhagen, The Life of a Jewish Woman* (London, 1957), 25.

31. The letter to von Brinkmann is discussed in Deibl, *Dorothea Schlegel,* 24.

again beginning in 1799. With Schleiermacher's practical assistance, Herz completed two translations of English novels, and she finished her memoir toward the end of her life.[32] But however disciplined Herz was when it came to acquiring new languages and to completing translations, she did not turn to writing original prose to earn the money she badly needed after Markus died in 1803. In the lean years of her early widowhood, Herz sought out governess positions and hosted boarders in her home rather than attempting to live on income earned by publication.

Esther Gad was born into a far more obscure family than either Veit or Herz, and she never achieved the fame the other two women enjoyed, either inside of or beyond salon circles. Yet in her own modest way Gad's conflicts and crises paralleled those experienced by Dorothea Veit and other Jewish salon women. Born and raised in Breslau, in her early years she showed little interest in intellectual matters. But by the time she was ten she often stayed up all night engrossed in a book. Her brother agreed to teach her what he had learned in school on a daily basis. When he went off to Dresden for a time, she taught herself French to surprise her beloved brother on his return. She subsequently taught herself Italian and then English.[33] In 1791, when she was twenty-one, Gad achieved her first publicity with a poem she wrote for a Jewish school which opened that year in Breslau. In that same year, Gad married Samuel Bernhard, a rich businessman from Frankfurt an der Oder. The couple moved to Berlin, where Esther, now Frau Bernhard, made friends with Madame de Genlis and Dorothea Veit. Gad began publishing poetry and articles in prominent journals. A 1798 piece devoted to the fitness of women to be authors earned Gad a reputation as a "second Wollstonecraft."[34] Gad had not been in Berlin long before she made decisive changes in her personal life. In 1796, she was divorced, and in 1800, she converted. Two years later, when she was thirty-five, Gad married again, this time to a court physician then living in England. Gad may well have had more in common with her second husband than she had with her first. Her second husband, Dr. Wilhelm Domeier, was a member of several learned societies and a frequent contributor to medical journals. Throughout her second marriage—the couple eventually settled in Portugal—Gad con-

---

32. Herz's memoir was published with an introduction by Julius Fürst, ed., *Henriette Herz: Ihr Leben und ihre Erinnerungen* (Berlin, 1858); the standard biography is by Hans Landsberg, *Henriette Herz, ihr Leben und ihre Zeit* (Weimar, 1913). See also Kayserling, *Die jüdischen Frauen*, 198–208. On Schleiermacher's help with Herz's translations see Oelsner, *Die Leistungen*, 217.

33. For a brief notation on Gad see Friedrichs, *Schriftstellerinnen*, 23. The only extensive narrative source on Gad's life is Schindel, *Die deutschen Schriftstellerinnen*, vol. I, 102–06.

34. Ibid., 104.

tinued to write and publish. She translated two books by her friend de Genlis and worked with "zeal" on a novel. Although Jean Paul (Richter), to whom she sent an early draft, liked the book very much, it was unfinished when Esther Gad died in 1823.[35]

Rebecca Friedländer, the last and youngest of the four Jewish authors among the salon women, was certainly the most prolific, at least in terms of the sheer volume of novels she published—an eventual total of sixteen volumes. Her first novel appeared in 1808, when Friedländer was twenty-five. In her early novels Friedländer's literary style was the roman à clef about salon society, a choice which eventually alienated her from Rahel Levin, her closest friend in those years. *Schmerz der Liebe* ("The Pain of Love"), Friedländer's 1810 novel, was a story of competition for love, worry about misalliance, rebellion against arranged marriage, and enjoyment of luxury. The narrative unfolds by the reader's overhearing the conversations at the salons of a Gräfin von Aarberg and reading the letters exchanged by the characters. The novel, like Friedländer's writing in general, received a fairly devastating reception. Her publisher, to be sure, advertised that her "lively situations" and her "character descriptions" were the work of a "feminine sensibility," and that her new book could count on the approval of the "elegant reading world." But her nephew Paul Heyse portrayed her as lacking any talent, and considered it a "riddle" how her "wretched products could have found a publisher at all." In 1811, Karl August Varnhagen (using a pseudonym) published an utterly damning review of three of Friedländer's recent novels. He began by blaming the rush of mediocre women's writing on their participation in intellectual interchanges, which led some of the women to believe that they themselves were intellectuals. In Varnhagen's opinion, their tales of private life and of love should not have been allowed to emerge from "the secrets of hidden hours." Varnhagen had nothing good to say about Friedländer's books: the characters were thin, the plots simple-minded, the dialogue stilted. He concluded by wishing that the author would enjoy "in other circles all of the happy success which is denied to her in this one."[36]

35. Ibid., 104. An additional publication seems to have appeared in both English and German. The German citation is: Esther Lucie Bernhard-Domeier, *Kritische Auseinandersetzungen mehrerer Stellen in dem Buch der Frau von Staël über Deutschland* (Hanover, 1814).

36. Karl August Varnhagen von Ense's review was published under the pseudonym "August Becker." He reviewed *Louise, Schmerz der Liebe* and *Erzählungen*, in *Die Musen* (Berlin, 1811). The review was found among Rahel Levin's 1805–10 letters to Rebecca Friedländer, now at the Jagiellonian Library in Cracow, Poland. The copy of the review found among the letters to Friedländer has the name "Varnhagen" written under the name "Becker" in Karl August Varnhagen von Ense's handwriting.

Published biographical material on Friedländer (born Rebecca Salomon) is sparse. See

It is not clear how much money Friedländer earned from her novels, or how much money she needed. Moses Friedländer was, after all, the son of a rich banker and entrepreneur, and divorcing him had not left Rebecca in poverty. For although her own father had not possessed an "oversized" fortune, it was divided evenly among all of the six siblings, and each inherited enough to "live without cares."[37] A description of Friedländer's lifestyle does not suggest abject poverty. Her nephew Paul Heyse described Friedländer's visit to the Heyse home in Berlin when he was a child: she sat in a darkened room "at her dressing table with white kid gloves the whole day long, while her fat, pockmarked maid made tea for her."[38]

Rebecca Friedländer's novels may not have been well received by the critics, and perhaps her earnings did not pay for her kid gloves and her maid. But even if publishing brought her neither praise nor wealth, entrance onto the literary stage brought Friedländer into contact with marriageable noble dilettantes. During 1805 and 1806 her chief literary adviser was Count von Egloffstein, and Friedländer hoped to turn their relationship into a romance and a marriage. Her dream was not realized, and she next fell in with a French officer stationed in Berlin, Count Frederic d'Houdetôt, an avid reader of avant-garde literature.[39] But Count d'Houdetôt also declined to marry Friedländer. Her loyal confidant though these doomed affairs was Rahel Levin, who was all too experienced with such endeavors. But the friendship later went sour, when Levin became convinced that Friedländer's portrait of the salonière in her 1810 novel, *Schmerz der Liebe,* was based on herself, and was angry that the portrait was negative. Thus in this instance Friedländer's literary achievement damaged rather than enhanced Friedländer's interpersonal life. In subsequent years Friedländer converted to Christianity—she had already been publishing and traveling under the gentile-sounding name Regina Frohberg—but she never remarried.[40]

Jacobson, *Jüdische Trauungen, in Berlin, 1723–1859* (Berlin, 1968), 440, as well as Ludwig Geiger, "Marie oder die Folgen des ersten Fehltritts, ein unbekannter Roman," *Zeitschrift für Bücherfreunde* n.s. 9 (1917), 58–62. See also Arendt, *Rahel Varnhagen,* 107.

37. Little is known about Moses Friedländer. See Jacobson, *Trauungen,* 440, and on his attempt to be exempted from the Jewish marriage tax because his mother belonged to the Itzig family see Karoline Cauer, *Oberhofbankier und Hofbaurat* (Frankfurt a.M., 1965), 36. On the division of the inheritance of the Salomon family see Paul Heyse (her nephew), *Jugenderinnerungen und Bekenntnisse* (Berlin, 1901), 6.

38. Heyse, *Jugenderinnerungen,* 9.

39. See the article on von Egloffstein in the *ADB,* vol. 5 (Leipzig, 1877), 680–82. On d'Houdetôt see the entry on him in the *NBG,* vol. 25 (Paris, 1865), 25.

40. For discussion on Friedländer's literary relationship with Levin see my "Inside Assimilation: Rebecca Friedländer's Rahel Varnhagen," in *German Women in the Eighteenth*

Each of the eleven authors among the salon women utilized a different constellation of life circumstances to make her way onto the printed page. A few, mainly the Jewish women, were lucky enough to receive a solid education at home. Salon participation did help some salon authors get their words into print, although the help came more frequently from salon men than from other salon women. However it was that they managed to become public figures by publishing, these eleven women were making history when they did so. For even if their intellectual labors were not nurtured by an exclusively female literary community, they did belong to one of Germany's first cohorts of female authors. The unpublished salon women, in contrast, left no accessible, polished record of their thoughts, visions, or aesthetic sensibilities. Yet they too made history with their letters, with the character sketches they passed around to their friends, and their literary conversations.

Indeed, there was actually a closer connection between the dilettantes and the existence of salons than there was between the authors and salons. At the most elemental level, in terms of numbers, dilettantes made up two-thirds of female salon society, and were thus obviously crucial in the delicate emergence of the institution. At a more symbolic level, the dilettantes' witty yet well-informed conversations were consciously viewed by salon participants as an activity which would improve the style and even the content of German literature. Moreover, much of the romantic literature of the era, with its confessional, emotional tone, bore a closer resemblance to salon conversations and letters than did the literature of previous and subsequent eras.[41] To be a dilettante in the German context was to bring a noble and a French tone to a national intellectual life whose ambience had long been provincial and professorial.

The salon dilettante lived in what was perhaps the most glorious epoch for a letter-writing culture, at a time when the content and style of letters was less bound to formula than ever before. Simultaneously, letters played a central role in intellectual life, a role that would diminish as intellectual institutions became more formalized in the subsequent century. As we learned in chapter 4, newspapers were still infrequent and

---

and Nineteenth Centuries, R.-E. Joeres and M. J. Maynes, eds. (Bloomington, 1986), 280–81.

41. Two good introductions to the literary profession in eighteenth-century Germany are H. Kiesel and P. Münch, *Gesellschaft und Literatur in 18. Jh: Voraussetzungen und Entstehung des literarischen Markts in Deutschland* (Munich, 1977), and Georg Steinhausen, *Geschichte des deutschen Briefs* (Berlin, 1889). See also Klaus Haase, "Rahel Varnhagens Brieftheorie. Eine Untersuchung zum literarischen Charakter des Privatbriefs in der Romantik," M.A. thesis, Munich, Ludwig Maximilian University, 1977.

censored in late-eighteenth-century Germany, making letters a crucial source of news. New intellectual disciplines and new kinds of literature were born in these years from letters. Travelers' letters were polished to become books of travel reportage and eventually anthropology; the epistolatory novel grew into the psychological novel; scholars' correspondences came to be published in fledgling scholarly journals. As private communications found new outlets as public, published commodities which could be sold for a profit, the culture of "private" letter-writing became more public. Rolf Engelsing aptly called writing letters in the eighteenth century a "half-public" activity.[42] Letters were often read aloud; they were sometimes sent on to a third person; their style and contents could become known to important strangers; all of this, even if the letters were never published. Here, as in so many other aspects of salon culture, the distinction between private and public was not as fixed as it would subsequently become. In their half-public quality letters were much like salons. Both letters and salons offered intellectual women a stage which they lacked in later decades, when intellectual life was more intricately organized. Letters and salons both allowed women to participate in the literary scene, even though they were still excluded from most formal educational and employment opportunities. Letters could play a particularly key role in literary culture since it was only now, in the late eighteenth-century, that belle-lettres was emerging from private letters to become an intellectual discipline in its own right. In Germany belle-lettres was still a discipline that could be practiced at home and for which there was as yet neither a set formal training nor an organized profession. In both the quiet hours at the desk and the noisier ones when guests came to visit, the homes of wealthy literary women were still public places. Because of this subtle yet decisive publicness of activities that would later become more private, letter-writing and salon participation were two ways that talented women could become famous without leaving home and without publishing their words.

Noble dilettantes were crucial members of female salon society literally as well as symbolically. Although they shared the crucial *von*, the ten noble dilettantes actually belonged to three distinct social worlds. The courtly dilettantes tended to keep a physical distance from the Jewish

---

42. Rolf Engelsing, *Der Bürger als Leser: Lesergeschichte in Deutschland 1500–1800* (Stuttgart, 1974), 296. See also Reinhard Nickisch, "Die Frau als Briefschreiberin im Zeitalter der deutschen Aufklärung," *Wolfenbüttler Studien zur Aufklärung* 3 (Wolfenbüttel, 1976), 29–66. See also Birgit Panke, "Bürgerliches Frauenbild und Geschlechtsrollenzuweisungen in der literarischen und brieflichen Produktion des 18. Jahrhunderts," *Beiträge zur feministischen Theorie und Praxis* 5 (Munich, 1981), 6–10.

salons, even if they made it their business to be well informed about goings-on there. Dilettantes married to officials often had closer friendships than the court women did with Jewish salonières, although this very closeness later backfired when many of these official dilettantes turned antisemitic. It was a third group, the rebels among the noble dilettantes, those who had entrée to courtly and official circles but who behaved in ways that alienated their more proper noble friends, who catalyzed the formation of salon society.

The leading noble dilettante at court in the years after 1797 was Queen Luise herself, the wife of King Frederick William II. A central element in the queen's popularity with the intelligentsia was the seriousness with which she took literary matters: she wrote poems to her female friends on ornate cards; she was a dedicated visitor to the opera and the ballet; she received (and presumably sometimes responded to) appeals for her patronage of the literary projects of her humbler friends.[43] Another important noble dilettante at court was Frau von Berg, a powerful lady-in-waiting who organized social events at court. The "spirited" Frau von Berg was friends with several important salon men, including Prince von Ligne, Friedrich Gentz, Jean Paul (Richter), and Gustav von Brinkmann. Von Brinkmann's long gossipy letters to von Berg's daughter, Julie von Voss, suggest that mother and daughter alike wanted to be kept abreast of gossip about déclassé salon society while overtly disdaining its participants.[44]

Of the two noble dilettantes married to officials, the experiences of Caroline von Humboldt were the most telling for the ultimate unraveling of Jewish salon society. (The other official's wife, Elizabeth von Stägemann, had been on the fringes of Jewish salon society in the 1790s; she and her husband opened their own rather antisemitic salon in 1808.)[45] Before her marriage in 1791, when the eventual wife of Wilhelm von

43. On Queen Luise see the article in the *ADB*, vol. 19, 815–25. Two books which came to my attention too late to be used here are Friedrich Adami, *Luise Königin von Preussen* (Gütersloh, 1906), and Paul Bailleu, *Königin Luise, Ein Lebensbild* (Berlin and Leipzig, 1908). Queen Luise should not be confused with her cousin by marriage, Princess Luise von Radziwill (née von Hohenzollern), who was a close friend of Dorothea von Courland.

44. On Frau von Berg see Günter de Bruyn, *Das Leben des Jean Paul Friedrich Richter: eine Biographie* (Frankfurt a.M., 1978), 228; Baxa, *Friedrich von Gentz* (Vienna, 1965), 115–17, and Reinhold Steig, *Achim von Arnim und die ihn nahe standen*, 3 vols. (Stuttgart and Berlin, 1904) vol. 3, 14. Von Brinkmann's letters to von Voss are in the Berg-Voss Collection in the *GSA*, Weimar.

45. On the von Stägemann couple see the article in the *ADB*, vol. 35, 383–86. See also Steig, *Achim von Arnim*, vol. 3, 13. There is an entry for von Stägemann in *Gelehrtes Berlin im Jahre 1825*, J. E. Hitzig and K. B. Büchner, eds. (Berlin, 1826), 274.

Humboldt was still Caroline von Dacheröden, she became close friends with several Jewish salonières. She was a member of the Tugendbund along with Henriette Herz and Dorothea Veit, and also became friendly with Rahel Levin. In this period von Dacheröden ardently admired the erudition of her Jewish women friends, confiding to her fiancé that her admiration was tinged with just a bit of jealousy of their intellectual skills.[46] After their marriage Caroline and Wilhelm left Berlin, although the two might well have quit Jewish salon society even if they had remained in the city. For Caroline became increasingly antisemitic during the first decade of the nineteenth century. Beginning in 1803, she cut off her friendship with Levin, and when Caroline von Humboldt met her by chance in 1811 she wounded Levin deeply by addressing her as "Sie" and not the former intimate "du."[47]

In different ways, then, the dilettantes among the salon women affiliated with either courtly or official circles kept their distance from Jewish salon society. Some among them may have attended Dorothea von Courland's salon and even may have had on-and-off friendships with Jewish salonières. But although these courtly and official dilettantes can justifiably be labeled as salon participants, they were not central in the complicated coalesence of the Jewish salons. To be sure, their very ambivalence toward the Jewish salonières was itself a significant historical development. That women as prominent as Caroline von Berg or Caroline von Humboldt should have even been involved enough with the Jewish women to demand gossip about them or to later draw away from intimacy with them was a testimony to the Jewish women's social power in the city in the 1780s and 1790s.

It was the four rebellious noble dilettantes, however, who were really a crucial force in bringing the Jewish salons to life. These women had intimate ties to Jewish salon women, to key progressive noble men in salons, and to the avant-garde intellectual stars among the commoner salon men. Reconstructing their social worlds brings us to the catalytic center of salon society. Here was a very small, intimate inside circle which was heterogeneous in its religious, social, and gender composition. Here, among the rebellious noble dilettantes, the commoner actresses, and the Jewish dilettantes was the dense social community lacking among the salon authors. The ties binding the rebellious noble dilettantes to the actresses and to the Jewish dilettantes obviously did not nourish the discipline and ambition needed to publish. Of course, these dilettantes

46. See Arendt, *Rahel Varnhagen* (1957 edition), 17; see also Wilhelm Grau, *Wilhelm von Humboldt und das Problem des Juden* (Hamburg, 1935), 57 ff., and 81.
47. See Arendt, *Rahel Varnhagen* (1974 edition), 210.

seem to have talked a great deal about the literary creations of others. They used their own literate skills to communicate with each other, to write regularly in their diaries, to compose unpublished sketches and poems, and to participate as active, opinionated readers of their salon friends' manuscripts and published books. Nevertheless, for the history of the Berlin salons it was not the dilettantes' literary accomplishments per se that are central, but instead how their shared literary interests and rebellious values contributed to the wide diversity of their closest friends.

As we learned in chapter 4, Dorothea von Courland's rebellion was more a matter of public than personal style; she defiantly mixed guests at her salon and sought to insure that they got to know each other as individuals.[48] The second rebel noble dilettante, Countess Caroline von Schlabrendorf, expressed her deviance in more personal ways. Her closest friends in salons were Rahel Levin and Gustav von Brinkmann. What information survives about von Schlabrendorf's life story is more the stuff of dramatic legend than precise detail. She was born into an unusually progressive family; her uncle Count Gustav von Schlabrendorf was a prolific essayist who lived in Paris during the French Revolution and sent back enthusiastic reports to the German press.[49] Caroline's husband, who seems to have been a distant relation allied with the mystical courtiers surrounding King Frederick William II, died early, leaving her without formal duties to courtly society. She turned instead to friends chosen for their personal qualities. She was known for traveling alone in men's clothing, a step she took to increase her independence and "so as not to be reminded every moment that she was merely a woman."[50] It was Caroline von Schlabrendorf who accompanied Rahel Levin to Paris in the summer of 1801, when Levin was recovering from her failed love affair with Karl von Finckenstein, and it was rumored that von Schlabrendorf had an abortion while abroad with Levin. She was known for her willful, argumentative style, "defending the French Revolution in Prussia and the rights of the emigrants and the court in Paris."[51]

But far more than Duchess Dorothea von Courland or Countess Caroline von Schlabrendorf, it was the more obscure Josephine von Pachta who helped bring together the tight mixed group at the center of salon society. Her entrance into the circle of salon friendships came in the summer of 1795, when the Prince von Ligne introduced von Pachta to Rahel

48. See chap. 4, note 68.

49. See Varnhagen von Ense's article on Gustav von Schlabrendorf in his *Denkwürdigkeiten und Vermischte Schriften*, vol. 4 (Leipzig, 1843), 422–76.

50. See Varnhagen von Ense's article on Caroline von Schlabrendorf in his *Galerie von Bildnissen aus Rahels Umgang und Briefwechsel*, 207–21.

51. Ibid., 208.

Levin at a spa in Töplitz.[52] Von Pachta was Catholic, from Bohemia; she was blond, statuesque, and known for her decisive, rationalist style. She read Kant, defended democracy, and argued against the injustices of the hereditary nobility. Through Levin—with whose immediate family von Pachta became friendly as well—she gained the acquaintance of other Jewish salon women, including the two Meyer sisters, Frederike Liman, and Dorothea Veit. Although von Pachta never lived permanently in Berlin, she visited the city frequently from various homes in Austria and Bohemia and mixed with salon personalities when many of them moved to spas for the summer. Von Pachta's closest noble male friends tended to be the Jewish women's lovers and patrons: Karl von Finckenstein, Wilhelm von Burgsdorff, Prince von Reuss, Friedrich Schleiermacher, and Friedrich Schlegel. Josephine von Pachta was thus in a perfect position to intervene when two of her friends from different estates had a complicated falling-out. And intervene she did, especially in the late 1790s when Rahel Levin and Karl von Finckenstein were finding it so difficult to balance out the competing claims of love and status.[53] Von Pachta herself was not a stranger to the conflict between private passion and social propriety. In spite of the acrimony such conflicts could cause, von Pachta carried out her rebellion in a remarkably decorous style. This was thanks in part to her progressive father, in part to the social permissiveness of Prague and Vienna, the cities where she lived on and off for most of her life, and perhaps most importantly, thanks to her own defiant spirit. From the outset of her marriage Josephine and her husband had not gotten along, but divorce was impossible in the Catholic context. The animosity between the two led von Pachta to worry that she would lose the considerable inherited property she had brought into the marriage. But her father's gracious intervention with her husband saved her inheritance, while she continued to live apart from her husband.

Von Pachta's difficulty with her husband was exacerbated by the fact that she had been living for several years with her son's tutor, a professor named Joseph Meinert.[54] Meinert had first been hired by von Pachta after she dismissed her son's previous tutor, a man of fifty-seven years. This first tutor had fallen so painfully in love with Josephine that he threatened suicide if she did not reciprocate, and he eventually had to be sent off for medical treatment. Von Pachta became a patron for Meinert as well as his lifelong companion; she used her influence to get him a

52. See Varnhagen von Ense's article on von Pachta in his *Biographische Portraits*, 170ff., as well as his article on her in his *Galerie von Bildnissen aus Rahels Umgang und Briefwechsel*, 171ff.

53. Varnhagen, *Biographische Portraits*, 188.

54. Ibid., 186.

professorship at the university in Prague. The couple lived in a comfortable, unpretentious style, which earned them the respect of those who might have otherwise disapproved of the couple's unmarried state.

Like Josephine von Pachta, Pauline Wiesel's rebellion was enacted more in the private world than in the public one. She was born into a noble family which mixed in courtly circles, but she married down on the estate hierarchy, to a French official.[55] While she was still in Berlin, until 1808, Wiesel did not live with her husband, living instead with her mother in a local *Gasthaus*. Her oldest salonière friend was Rahel Levin, who ardently admired Wiesel for her thoroughly emancipated sensual style.[56] For passion was, indeed, Wiesel's chosen arena for iconoclastic behavior. Her most famous lover was Prince Louis Ferdinand, whom she met at a ball given by Sara (Meyer) von Grotthuss.[57] But there were many other men in her life, including several prominent salon men. Major Gualtieri was in love with her at one time, as was Gustav von Brinkmann. Wilhelm von Humboldt once expressed his gratitude to Wiesel for giving him "some of the happiest hours of his life."[58]

In structural terms, these eight female noble dilettantes were the direct counterparts to the noble dilettantes among the salon men. By participating in the salons, noble dilettantes of both genders brought status, literary interests, and sometimes also informal literary patronage to their less prestigious friends. But the four commoner dilettantes among the salon women, in contrast, had no counterparts among the men. Three of the four were actresses: Frederike Unzelman, Christel Eigensatz, and one called simply Marchetti. (Classifying them as dilettantes underscores that the category includes all who did not publish, rather than including only those about whom we know that they wrote "literarily significant" letters and other unpublished writing.) The friendships of a few of the actresses with prominent noble salon men and women shows how dramatically the standing of actors had improved in Germany. The actresses' bonds with salon men were usually romantic ones; the most notorious at the time was Christel Eigensatz's relationship with Friedrich Gentz.[59]

55. See Carl Atzenbeck, *Pauline Wiesel: Die Geliebte des Prinzen Louis Ferdinand von Preussen* (Leipzig, 1925), 28.

56. See Arendt, *Rahel Varnhagen* (1974 edition), 206–07.

57. See Atzenbeck, *Pauline Wiesel*, 33.

58. See von Humboldt's letter to Gustav von Brinkmann of February 4, 1804, published in *Wilhelm von Humboldts Briefe an Karl Gustav von Brinkmann*, Albert Leitzmann, ed., (Leipzig, 1939), 160–61.

59. On Unzelman see Rahel Levin's mention of her in her *Briefwechsel zwischen Rahel und David Veit* (Leipzig, 1861), 103; she is identified by A. F. Cohn, ed., *Wilhelm von Burgsdorff Briefe*, in *Deutsche Literaturdenkmale* 139, Dritte Folge, no. 19 (Berlin, 1907), 203. On Eigensatz and her relationship with Friedrich Gentz see Baxa, *Friedrich von Gentz*, 20.

The actresses' presence in salons helps explain why salon society had a reputation, no doubt undeserved, as a literal hotbed of dangerous sexuality. But the commoner dilettantes' presence in salons is yet another reminder that salons facilitated a pattern of female mobility that was quite different from that experienced by the salon men.

The remaining six dilettantes among the salon women were Jewish. Here was the sector of salon society where the majority of Berlin's salonières were clustered; every one of the six led her own salon. The intellectual level of the Jewish dilettantes was often very high, much higher, in fact, than that of several Jewish authors. The individual who exemplified this paradox was of course Rahel Levin. Her conversations, letters, and aesthetic judgments earned her the admiration of a string of important men. Although a few of her letters were published late in her life, she never wrote with publication in mind. The two Meyer sisters, Sara and Marianne, used their mastery of French, their character sketches, and their letters to good advantage in attracting prominent noble guests to their salons.[60] Amalie Beer, Philippine Cohen, and Sara Levy did not achieve the Meyer sisters' level of dilettantish sophistication or Rahel Levin's more serious encounter with high culture. Nevertheless, all three enjoyed a reputation for literate conversation that could not have been irrelevant in their success as salonières. But this dabbling in literature could ultimately effect deeper, more private changes in a Jewish woman's life than smoothing her entrée into high society, important as that entrée was. We now turn to a closer inspection of the early lives of the six Jewish dilettantes and of the four Jewish authors in salons. Three of the dilettantes eventually married out of their faith and up the social scale, as did three of the Jewish authors in female salon society. The eventual intermarriages of these six Jewish salon women represented the penultimate stage in the intricate, laborious process of using literature to move up the social ladder.

The victory over the past, over discrimination, and over Jewishness won in these intermarriages was experienced by these women as a personal victory. And even though these six intermarriages directly affected a mere handful of individuals, they were, from the perspective of social history, the culmination of that complex net of social exchanges which bound all the salon participants to each other. To discover how these intermarriages came to pass, we must magnify the detail of that moment

Marchetti is mentioned in the abridged edition of Varnhagen von Ense's *Denkwürdigkeiten des eigenen Lebens,* 81.

60. On the Meyer sisters see chap. 4, notes 71 and 72.

in the Jewish women's lives when they first tasted the delights of secular culture yet still remained within mainly Jewish circles. At the time, when the salon women were adolescents and just-marrieds, observers may have judged that they managed a successful balance between innovation and tradition. Yet, by examining the latent contradictions of these years we will later be able to grasp why this apparent balance eventually unraveled into divorce, conversion, and intermarriage.

Socialization and Early Marriage

For some historians, the Jewish salon women's eventual readiness to abandon Jews and Judaism originated in the kind of primary education they did—and did not—receive: too little traditional Jewish education and too much decorative secular education.[61] Indeed, for several centuries before the salon era, Jewish girls in Germany did not enjoy the same religious education as their brothers; they were not regularly trained either in Hebrew or in the Talmud (the written discussion of Jewish law), nor did Jewish law require their regular attendance at the synagogue. A mid-eighteenth-century source records that girls were not even allowed to remain in the same house where tutors were training the community's boys in these subjects.[62] The most popular way for girls and women to absorb traditional learning was through study of the *Tzenah Urenah,* a simplified Yiddish Bible which included moral exhortations and parables. The classic interpretation thus holds that the salon women would not have drifted from faith and community if they had received a more rigorous Jewish education which bound them intellectually to their tradition.

The women's alienation from their faith was only increased when they gained a merely decorative level of secular learning. The very superficiality of their exposure to a new intellectual universe is thought to have intoxicated them without really grounding them in an alternative mental

61. A good example of this view can be found in Max Brod, *Heinrich Heine* (Berlin, 1935), 70; see also Solomon Liptzin, *Germany's Stepchildren* (New York, 1944), 26, for a most condemnatory analysis of what the salon women did with their secular education.

62. On Jewish girls' education in mid-eighteenth-century Germany see J. Eschelbacher, "Die Anfänge allgemeiner Bildung unter den deutschen Juden vor Mendelssohn," in *Beiträge zur Geschichte der deutschen Juden,* Festschrift for Martin Philippson, (Frankfurt a.M., 1916), 168–77, and M. Güdemann, *Geschichte des Erziehungswesens und der Kulter der Abendländischen Juden* (Vienna, 1884), vol. 1. See also Robert S. Rosen, introduction to *The Memoirs of Glückel of Hameln* (New York, 1977), xiv; Elizabeth Koltun, ed., *The Jewish Woman: New Perspectives* (New York, 1976); and the first two chapters in Charlotte Baum, Hyman, and Sonya Michel, *The Jewish Woman in America* (New York, 1975).

discipline. Tutors were hired for them to learn proper German, French, and English, and to teach the harpsicord; they were allowed to subscribe to lending libraries to keep up with the flood of novels published in Germany in these years. Funds were found for the pens, paper, postage, and leather-bound diaries the women used to appropriate the new secular culture in their own words and share this new world with their Jewish and sometimes with their new gentile friends. Their brothers and husbands, so goes this view, had less incentive as adolescents to perfect their German or to master French, since their eventual occupational choices were restricted narrowly to commerce and finance, where they worked mainly with other Jewish men. The parents' willingness to pay for all this training in the language and habits of a sophisticated new world presumably originated in the fathers' historic indifference to their daughters' religious education. Since fathers did not take their daughters' intellectual development seriously, they allowed them to follow their own desires. Practical matters also played a role in this parental financing of the salon girls' dabbling in high culture. Unlike the daughters of most Jewish families in western and in eastern Europe at the time, the extraordinary wealth of the women's families meant that their labor was not needed in the home, in the shop, or in the family's commercial endeavors. Thus the variety of practical skills a Glückel of Hameln had mastered earlier in the century were not necessary to help support the family businesses of Berlin's fantastically wealthy Jewish elite.[63]

But a closer look casts doubt on whether it was either religious or secular education in the primary and adolescent years that really explains why women's and men's assimilation patterns as adults were so different. It is obviously true that the women did not receive a serious Jewish education. But there is reason to doubt that the majority of their male counterparts enjoyed such training either, or that in wealthy families the boys' exposure to secular learning was less than that enjoyed by the girls. A much-lamented problem with the boys' religious education was that their teachers were young tutors from Poland who relied on a rote, traditional pedagogy. In 1772, one such teacher wrote a treatise proposing that King Frederick the Great forbid the import of Polish-born tutors. The local teacher, who felt superior to the Polish tutors because he had

63. See *The Memoirs of Glückel of Hameln* for an example of the important role wives could play in the family's commercial enterprises at the beginning of the century. Julius Carlebach's description of the Jewish women's role in the era seems wrong for this particular group of elite women: see his "Family Structure and the Position of Jewish Women," in W. E. Mosse, A. Paucker, and R. Rürup, eds., *Revolution and Evolution: 1848 in German-Jewish History* (Tübingen, 1981), 170.

been born in Germany, complained about the "fanatical" and "barbaric" ideas distributed by the impoverished "eastern" *Schulmeistern*.[64] Inadequate traditional education motivated the young men to turn their attention to secular studies. Indeed, throughout the eighteenth century, several young Jewish men in Berlin managed to acquire a first-class secular training. For instance, as early as the third decade of the century, Aaron Gumpertz learned German, French, and mathematics from tutors and from a local rabbi; he participated in courses offered by the city's top gymnasia and from the Royal Academy of Science. In the 1760s, Lazarus Bendavid was taught German by his mother, French by a tutor, and Latin by a gymnasium professor. By the 1790s, when Rahel Levin's brother Ludwig Robert came of age, he was allowed to attend the full course of studies at the French gymnasium in the city. And as support grew in the community for Moses Mendlessohn's credo that opening Jewish minds to secular intellectual skills was the central path to the renewal of Judaism, the opportunities once open to a few to acquire worldly learning became more widely available. The Jewish "Free School" founded by David Friedländer offered a religious as well as secular education to the city's younger and poorer boys.[65]

Nor is it so clear that the secular skills acquired by wealthy Jewish girls deserved to be denigrated as totally frivolous. Both Henriette Herz and Dorothea Veit received a rigorous secular education from their fathers. It is difficult to determine just how learned some of these women were because their own pronouncements on the subject are ambiguous. Rahel Levin complained that she grew up like a "wild savage," without the skills to properly participate in the intellectual life of her times. Yet she learned a passable French from tutors, and, beginning at age eighteen, she used her correspondence with David Veit, a young Jewish medical student, to improve her German. She studied mathematics with a tutor; she read Voltaire, Rousseau, Kant and Fichte; for a time in the 1790s she was Goethe's leading advocate in Berlin. To be sure, her German was gram-

64. The treatise is discussed in Moritz Stern, *Beiträge zur Geschichte der jüdischen Gemeinde zu Berlin* (Berlin, 1926).

65. See the full account of Aaron Gumpertz's life in David Kaufmann and Max Freudenthal, *Die Familie Gomperz* (Frankfurt a.M., 1907), 167–200. See Bendavid's autobiographical sketch in S. M. Lowe, ed., *Bildnisse jetztlebender Berliner Gelehrten mit ihren Selbstbiographien* (Berlin, 1806). On Ludwig Robert see "Ludwig Robert, Leben und Werke," Ph.D. diss., Göttingen, 1923; Lothar Kahn, "Ludwig Robert, Rahel's Brother," in *LBIYB* 28 (1973), 185–200; and Miriam Sambursky, "Ludwig Roberts Lebensgang," in *Bulletin des Leo Baeck Instituts* n.s. 15 (1976), 1–48. On the Jewish Free School see Michael Meyer, *The Origins of the Modern Jew: Jewish Identity and European Culture in Germany, 1749–1824* (Detroit, 1967), 58.

matically flawed and her handwriting was often illegible.[66] But her anger at her lack of a thoroughgoing secular education was possibly more a reflection of the high goals she set for herself than a reflection of a particularly deficient training, given the fixed limitations on female learning imposed in almost every estate, class, and region of eighteenth-century Europe.

Considering the boys' problems in getting a good Jewish education, the success of many of them in acquiring a good secular education, as well as the quite rigorous secular training available to a few Jewish girls, the argument that a gender-specific early education determined later differences in the men's and women's experiences becomes problematic. Perhaps Jewish historians' own attempts in the late nineteenth century to improve the religious education of Jewish girls accounts for their emphasis on the deficiences of the salon women's training in the previous century. The problems in using early education to explain adult assimilation are underscored by remembering the distinctiveness of the Berlin social scene. For although some early mastery of the rudiments of high culture may have been necessary for subsequent acts of assimilation, such mastery was by no means always followed by social integration. Wealthy young Jewish women in Hamburg, Vienna, and Frankfurt had an early education whose strengths and weaknesses resembled that enjoyed by the Berlin salon women. But the girls raised in these other cities rarely grew up to enjoy the social acceptance experienced by their counterparts in Berlin.[67]

A closer inspection suggests that it was the women's social opportunities when they were already in their early twenties which provided them with the motives and the opportunities to polish their secular intellectual skills. For the contrast in the men's and women's experiences was not as strong in their early years as it was later, when they had radically different experiences in penetrating Berlin's new public leisure institutions. As recounted in chapter 4, Berlin's acculturated Jewish men had great difficulties in joining the city's intellectual clubs, and eventually most had to make do by forming their own all-Jewish clubs. There were,

66. On Herz's education see Julius Furst, ed., *Henriette Herz,* 19; on Dorothea Mendelssohn's training see Hiemenz, *Dorothea von Schlegel,* 6, and M. Kayserling, *Die jüdischen Frauen,* 183. On Rahel Levin's intellectual training see the most detailed biography of her: Otto Berdrow, *Rahel Varnhagen: Ein Lebens- und Zeitbild* (Stuttgart, 1902).

67. Rich comparative information on the Jewish women in these other cities can be found in M. Kayserling, *Die jüdischen Frauen;* on the overall situation of the Jewish communities in these cities in this period, see Helga Krohn, *Die Juden in Hamburg 1800–1850* (Hamburg, 1967); I. Kracauer, *Geschichte der Juden in Frankfurt a.M. 1150–1825* (Frankfurt a.M., 1927); Hans Tietze, *Die Juden Wiens* (Leipzig, 1933) and Hans Jäger-Sustenau, "Die geadelten Judenfamilien im vormärzlichen Wien," Ph.D. diss., Vienna, 1950.

of course, some important exceptions to this trend in the generation who came into adulthood in mid-century, notably David Friedländer, Markus Herz, and Mendelssohn himself. In the next generation the number of Jewish men who succeeded in joining gentile clubs and in making gentile friends increased even more when Julius Hitzig, Ludwig Robert, Benjamin Ephraim, Israel Steiglitz, and David Koreff came of age. Some of these Jewish men who succeeded in joining the clubs also succeeded in entering salons. As shown in figure 10, eight of the sixty-nine men who attended one or more salons were Jewish. Since Jews were only 2 percent of the city's population and a mere 3 percent of the city's intelligentsia, in proportional terms they were well represented in salons. But Jewish women were far more overrepresented among the thirty-one salon women than the Jewish men were among the salon men. For the twelve Jewish women in salons were 37 percent of all women there.

The women's success in the salons was actually a more direct link to their eventual intermarriages than was their early education. It was not simply that salon friends and salon performances stimulated the women to increased mastery of secular skills. More importantly, in salons they could meet glamorous potential marriage partners. That so many of these potential partners should have actually married the Jewish women they met in salons was shocking to their contemporaries. Few acts would change the Jewish women's lives more dramatically than this, for marriage was the central social act for a woman in the eighteenth century. Whether she married, whom she married, and when she married affected a woman's standard of living, social status, and ability to host a salon. To be sure, in the eighteenth century marriage also shaped men's lives in a decisive way. But for men, marriage was only one of several institutions which affected their eventual social position.

But before we can recount the steps that led up to these women's marriages, it is imperative to become more precise about exactly who it is whose marital tales are being reconstructed here. As summarized in figure 11, nine Jewish salonières hosted some kind of social circle in Berlin between 1780 and 1806, ranging from famous, regular crowded gatherings to more irregular, modest entertaining. Three additional Jewish women definitely attended salons. To expand the number of women beyond twelve, eight friends or sisters of the "official" twelve Jewish salon women have been added to the collective biography. Although we lack positive proof that all eight attended salons, all were intimately connected with those who did, and all twenty are called "salon women" in this and the next chapter. Born between 1761 and 1787, these women came into adulthood in the years when salons flourished in Berlin. By definition, they were not at all representative of the Jewish community at large.

Figure 11. Jewish Salon Women in Berlin

Name at Birth	Date of Birth	Age at First Marriage	Estate of First Husband (Age)	Divorced/ Widowed	Converted	Estate of Later Husbands
†Rahel Levin	1771	41	Ennobled/Varnhagen von Ense (29)		Yes 1814	Noble/Prince von Reuss
†Henriette de Lemos	1764	15	Jewish/Markus Herz (32)	Widowed 1803	Yes 1817	
†Sarah Itzig	1761	22	Jewish/Solomon Levy (23)		No	
†Marianne Meyer	1763	15	Jewish/UK	Divorced	Yes	Noble/Prince von Reuss
†Sara Meyer	UK	"early" (1778)	Jewish/Jacob Wulff (20)	Divorced 1788	Yes (twice)	Noble/Baron von Grotthuss
†Brendel (Dorothea) Mendelssohn	1764	19	Jewish/Simon Veit (19)	Divorced 1799	Yes 1802	Ennobled/F. von Schlegel
†Malka (Amalie) Lipmann	1772	16	Jewish/Jacob Herz Beer (19)		No	
†Pessel (Philippine) Zülz	1776	18	Jewish/Ephraim Cohen (26)		Yes 1800	
†Rebecca Solomon (Saaling)	1782	19	Jewish/Moses Freidländer (26)	Divorced	Yes (Regina Frohberg)	
Rebecca Itzig	1763	21	Jewish/David Ephraim		Yes	

Figure 11. (continued)

Name at Birth	Date of Birth	Age at First Marriage	Estate of First Husband (Age)	Divorced/Widowed	Converted	Estate of Later Husbands
Julie Solomon (Saaling)	1787	40	Commoner/Karl Heyse		Yes	
Marianne Solomon (Saaling)	1786	Single for life		Yes		
Blümchen Moses	UK	(1773)	Jewish/Joseph Arnstein	Divorced 1777	Yes	Noble/Kriegsrat von Bose
Rebecca Moses	UK	UK			Yes	Noble/von Runkle
Marianne Devidel	UK		Commoner/G. Schadow		Yes	
Esther Gad	1770	21	Jewish/Samuel Bernard	Divorced 1796	Yes 1800	Commoner/Dr. W. Domeier
Rösel Spanier	UK	(1783)	Jewish/David Fränkel (32)			
Hitzel Zülz	UK	(1791)	Jewish/Isaac Fliess (21)	Divorced	Yes	Noble/Major von Boye
Fradchen Marcuse	UK	(1786)	Jewish/Abraham Liebman (19)		Yes 1809	
Jente Ephraim	UK	(1792)	Jewish/Dr. I. Stieglitz (25)		UK (husband converted 1800)	

† = salonière

Not only did almost all of their fathers belong to the Jewish economic elite; by virtue of their affiliation with salon society, these women had access to a presgitious and heterogenous social universe. Since the number of adult Jewish women in Berlin at the time numbered somewhere near seven hundred, the social exposure enjoyed by this tiny salon group was atypical indeed.[68]

It followed from the great wealth of most of the Jewish salon women's fathers, and the caste-like character of the Jewish plutocracy that marriage was a central event in preserving and extending familial wealth and power. Moreover, arranged and early marriages were crucial if the alliance was to be made with the right family. If the daughter was young, her virtue was sure to be intact. The coincidence of affluence and legal insecurity in the Jewish community made carefully chosen marriages particularly crucial. Rich Jewish fathers were eager to add wealthy and well-connected sons- and daughters-in-law to their families. Both sets of parents usually belonged to small, closed group of merchants in a monopolistic economic system. But since permission to live legally in the city was itself a substantial prize, money and connections were not the only relevant considerations in choosing a mate for one's child. Controlling the size and wealth of the Jewish community was accomplished by strict regulation of the right to settle children in Berlin. Daughters could inherit their father's *Schutzbrief* ("letter of protection") only under special conditions, and sons did not have it much easier. Even the more privileged families could pass their Schutzbrief only on to their oldest son; younger sons were often forced to marry women from outside the city and settle there. In order to maintain the maximum intergenerational residential cohesion under these restrictive conditions, all efforts were made to marry the daughters off to local men who already had or would inherit their father's Schutzbrief. The marriage itself was an expensive event. Beyond the dowry, wedding, and cost of setting up a new household, a special tax also had to be paid, pegged to the size of the dowry.[69]

In spite of the delicate negotiations surrounding arranged Jewish marriages, to the outside world the system seemed to work well, at least at the outset of the salon era. In 1781, Christian Wilhelm Dohm observed

68. See chap. 2, note 38 for the methods and sources used to make this calculation. (I assume that the number of adult women was the same as the number of adult men, lacking information to the contrary.)

69. See Jacob Jacobson's introduction to the volume he edited: *Die Judenbürgerbücher der Stadt Berlin 1800–1851* (Berlin, 1962), for details of the inheritance regulations of the *Schutzbrief*. See also Josef Meisl, *Protokollbuch der jüdischen Gemeinde Berlin, 1723–1854* (in Hebrew) (Jerusalem, 1962).

that Jewish family life was "purer," and more free from "unnatural vices" than the family life of gentile families in Prussia at the time.[70] Dohm's judgment deserves to be taken seriously, since he had no reason to gloss over special Jewish problems. Indeed, Dohm's aim in his book proposing the "civic betterment" of Prussian Jewry was to acknowledge the purported faults in Jewish behavior by explaining them as the result of historic oppression rather than of unchanging national character. There was little about the early years of most of the twenty women's first marriages to contradict Dohm's evaluation. All but two of the women married, the majority, fifteen of the twenty, to Jewish men. Only for the most famous brides is the process of choosing the groom known. Henriette was twelve when her father, the director of the Jewish hospital in Berlin, announced that he had selected two men who were appropriate for her to marry. She had only to choose between a rabbi and a physician. Having selected the latter, she promptly found herself engaged to Dr. Markus Herz, although she had only met him once. By the age of fifteen she found herself married to this genial but ugly man who was more than twice her age. Moses Mendelssohn's daughter Dorothea also had no choice in her marriage at nineteen to Simon Veit.

Even without more individual stories illustrating the process by which marriages were arranged, other evidence suggests that arranged marriage was the rule among Berlin's Jewish elite. It cannot have been sheer chance that both bride and groom often came from the premier families in Berlin or elsewhere. Pessel Zülz, whose father owned a large silk manufactory, married Ephraim Cohen. The groom hailed from Holland; once in Berlin, he opened an enormous wool manufactory in the center of town employing hundreds of workers. Rebecca Itzig, one of the nine daughters born to Daniel and Miriam Itzig, married David Ephraim, son of Veitel Heine Ephraim, the third partner in Daniel Itzig's and Moses Isaac's coin-minting manufacture that flourished during the Seven Year's War. The young couple's "poetry album" signed by visitors to their home between 1784 and 1796 shows a tight network of intimate siblings and other relatives.[71] Rebecca Solomon, whose father was a court jeweler to

70. Christian Wilhelm Dohm, *Uber die bürgerliche Verbesserung der Juden* (Berlin, 1781), 9. The translation is entitled *Concerning the Amelioration of the Jews* (Cincinnati, 1957). Regarding antisemites' views of Jewish "sexual passions in this era" see George Mosse, "Jewish Emancipation: Between Bildung and Respectability," in J. Reinharz and W. Schatzberg, eds., *The Jewish Response to German Culture* (Hanover, N.H. and London, 1985), 1–16, at 4. Mosse points out that Dohm's emphasis on the "purity" of Jewish family life was an explicit response to antisemitic attacks on "impure" Jewish sexual passions.

71. The only extensive account of the Cohen household is that by Karl August Varnhagen von Ense, in *Denkwürdigkeiten des eigenen Lebens*, 77–85. The Itzig poetry album is

Rebecca Itzig Ephraim

King Frederick the Great, married Moses Friedländer, whose father David was himself a wealthy silk entrepreneur. David Friedländer's own wife belonged to the Itzig family. The small number of eligible families from which appropriate spouses might be chosen was thus yet another constraint on marriage choice, and as a result the city's Jewish elite was an extremely inbred one.

The same combination of circumstances which led to arranged matches also led to a quite early age of marriage for the brides. It was best to insure the proper alliance as soon as possible, even if that made for a rather long engagement. The age at which Jewish women married in different times and places has varied enormously, depending on the economic and legal constraints on mate choice. To marry at eighteen, the average age at which the Jewish salon women married, was in fact early

now with the Itzig family papers in the archive of the Leo Baeck Institute in New York City.

compared to the typical Jewish woman who married in the same years in the same city. A compilation of brides' ages of marriage from the complete list of 170 Jewish weddings in Berlin between 1780 and 1790 shows that the norm was to marry at twenty-four, six years later than the average salon bride. A recent claim that Henriette Herz's early age of marriage was typical for Jewish women in Berlin at this time is thus quite wrong.[72] The salon brides were therefore atypically young in contrast to their local Jewish contemporaries. On the other hand, to marry at eighteen was considerably later than seems to have been the norm for Jewish brides in eastern Europe, where in the eighteenth and well into the nineteenth century, brides as young as thirteen were reportedly a frequent occurrence.[73]

There has been considerable complaint over the decades about the negative consequences of the practice of arranged and young marriages among the Jewish elite in Berlin. Harry Abt, for instance, was convinced that Mendelssohn doomed the future of his own reform program to failure by holding fast to the tradition of marrying off young daughters to grooms chosen by their fathers.[74] In Abt's view, Mendelssohn's rationalistic reform of Judaism may have been adequate to his own individual situation while he lived. But unless the loyalty of the young women of the next generation could be preserved, and thus a vigorous Jewish family life insured, the Mendelssohnian program could not be passed on intact to the nineteenth century. Arranged marriages as well as a deficient religious training were blamed then and later for driving young women away from the faith. The critics of arranged marriages concluded that by stimulating converstion and thereby contributing to the difficulties faced by religious reformers, such marriages had negative consequences beyond the era for the eventual fate of Judaism in modern Germany.

72. These data have been compiled from the complete roster of Jewish marriages published by Jacobson, *Jüdische Trauungen in Berlin*. For background in customs of Jewish marriages in Germany in this era see Herman Pollack, *Jewish Folkways in Germanic Lands (1648–1806): Studies in Aspects of Daily Life* (Cambridge and London, 1971), 29–39. See also Emil Friedberg, *Das Recht der Eheschliessung in seiner geschichtlichen Entwicklung* (Leipzig, 1865), 702–04, regarding state regulations on Jewish marriage during the early nineteenth century. The erroneous claim about Herz was made by Ingeborg Weber-Kellerman, *Die deutsche Familie* (Frankfurt a.M., 1974), 4.

73. For data on nineteenth-century Bavarian Jews' ages at marriage, and a critique of earlier claims on the matter, see Steven Lowenstein, "Voluntary and Involuntary Limitation of Fertility in Nineteenth Century Bavarian Jewry," in Paul Ritterband, ed., *Modern Jewish Fertility* (Leiden, 1981), 97. On early ages of Jewish brides see David Biale, "Love, Marriage, and the Modernization of the Jews," in Marc Lee Raphael, ed., *Approaches to Modern Judaism* (Chico, Calif., 1983), 7.

74. Harry Abt, "Dorothea Schlegel bis zu ihrer Vereinigung mit der Romantik," Ph.D. diss., Frankfurt a.M., 1925.

But none of these grand, long-term issues seem to have troubled the women at the time. At the outset of their marital careers it was by no means clear that the young brides themselves were all opposed to arranged and early marriages. Henriette Herz, for instance, attributed her own enthusiasm to marry young to the privations of being a dependent daughter, as compared to the privileges of being a wife. She later remembered that she was content to marry an older, unknown man if it meant being able to buy new bonnets and have her own hairdresser. At the time married women were generally considered to lead freer lives than single women.[75] With their husband's social and financial backing, they were surely freer to entertain in style. With the exception of Rahel Levin, all the successful salonières were married to wealthy Jewish men in the years when they hosted their salons.

Other contemporary reports suggest that even if the bride did oppose a marriage arranged by her parents, her friends could note how the compensations of the arrangement might enhance her own personal development. When Ignatius Fessler, a militant Freemason who traveled around a good deal, visited the Benjamin Ephraim family in 1791, he took a special interest in the fate of one of Ephraim's daughters, probably Adele. Fessler sympathized with her unhappiness at having no role in choosing her spouse, but reminded her that she would be able to "take consolation in art."[76] Both Herz's admission that marriage was the ticket to certain personal and social pleasures and Fessler's admonition that art would pull her through a life with an ill-chosen husband suggest that the salon women's distinctive intellectual and social growth continued after marriage.

Companionship in Arranged Marriages

But was Abt correct that the Jewish elite's practice of arranged marriage so greatly doomed the Mendelssohnian program? Or, translated into the language of family history, were the eventual break-ups of many of the salon women's arranged marriages due to the absence of companionate marriages among Jews in Germany at this time? In its family-history version, this question has recently engaged considerable debate. Some historians hold that the practice of arranged marriages among German Jews had begun to decline several decades before the salon women came onto the marriage market in the last two decades of the century. Other

75. On Herz's view see Kurt Fervers, *Berliner Salons: Die Geschichte einer grossen Verschwörung* (Munich, 1940), 53.

76. See Ignatz Aurelius Fessler, *Rückblicke auf seine siebzigjähre Pilgerschaft* (Leipzig, 1851), 154.

historians are less convinced that there was any precocious modernity in the marriage practices of the seventeenth- and early-eighteenth-century Jewish community in Germany. They argue that Jewish couples' freedom to choose each other, if need be in defiance of their parents' concern to maximize familial wealth and status, only became possible late in the eighteenth century. A third, compromise position has evolved, emphasizing that arranged and companionate marriages should be seen as two points on a spectrum rather than as two mutually exclusive kinds of behavior. This argument stresses that couples "found each other," albeit within a limited, parentally controlled social network. And even when they did not initiate the marriage, this did not mean that they did not grow to value and love each other over time.[77]

One large problem in using past lives to choose between these three interpretations is the difficulty of finding adequate primary evidence to determine the experiental quality of particular relationships. When the challenge is to determine how companionate a particular set of marriages was, such evidence is of course crucial. Emotional claims asserted even by the actors themselves in memoirs and letters require delicate interpretation, insofar as such claims may well have reflected contemporary expectations and ideals rather than real experience. Still, the salon women left behind both objective and subjective evidence that can be used to gain insight into how companionate their first marriages were. One oblique, but nevertheless useful bit of objective evidence is the comparative ages of the brides and the grooms. Even if the spouses had little or no choice in the match, and even if the bride was still in her teens, surely the chances that the couple would be companions would be enhanced if the two were closer rather than further apart in age. We know the age of six of the grooms who married the eight Jewish salon women whose age of marriage is known. The gap between Henriette and Markus Herz's

77. See Biale, "Love, Marriage, and the Modernization of the Jews," 2; Biale summarizes here the work of Azriel Schochat, *I'm Hilufei Tekufot* (in Hebrew) (Jerusalem, 1960), 162–73, and the article by Jacob Katz, "Marriage and Marital Relations at the End of the Middle Ages," (in Hebrew), *Zion* 10 (1945–46). Schochat argues that arranged marriages declined early in the century; Katz counters that they remained prevalent throughout the eighteenth century. The irony—from the perspective of this chapter—is that Katz's example of a non-arranged marriage is that of Mendelssohn himself, who insisted that his own children marry the mates of his choice.

Biale himself articulates this third position, in contradistinction to both Schochat and Katz. This more flexible notion of how love could play a role in arranged and "semi-arranged" marriages in the nineteenth century is also used by Marion Kaplan, "For Love or Money: The Marriage Strategies of Jews in Imperial Germany," *LBIYB* 28 (1983), 263–300. For general background on companionate marriages in this period in Germany see Heidi Rosenbaum, *Formen der Familie* (Frankfurt a.M., 1982), 285–87.

ages—he 32 and she 15—was decidedly unusual among this tiny group. When they married, Sara Itzig was 22 and Solomon Levy was 23; Dorothea Mendelssohn, 19 and Simon Veit, 19; Amalie Liepman, 16 and Jacob Herz Beer, 19; Pessel Zülz, 22 and Ephraim Cohen, 26; Rebecca Solomon, 19 and Moses Friedländer, 27. This makes an average age gap of only 3.2 years, small indeed when compared to the 17 years separating Henriette and Markus Herz.

Using subjective memoirs to document the feelings the spouses had toward each other places us on even shakier ground in trying to determine how companionate the first Jewish marriages were. In only a few cases is there anything in print, either by one of the mates or even about them. Again, Henriette Herz's life is one of the rare ones which is well documented. A nineteenth-century chronicler of the Herzes' lives portrayed a rather distant relationship, reporting that Markus called Henriette "das Kind" ("the child"), and their bond was less that of a "happy marriage" than that of a "happy relationship."[78] In this view, it was that passionlessness as well as Henriette's childlessness that led her to look to "friends, literature, and art" for her happiness. Dorothea Veit's lack of delight in her husband Simon is also well documented. It is not clear how much of the problem lay in his physical appearance; he was reported as having been "plain" and "not good-looking." From their wedding day forward, Dorothea became "taciturn" and "withdrawn." Friends noted that the two had little in common in their preferred languages and intellectual interests; he spoke mainly Yiddish and was involved in his business affairs, while she spoke French and German and kept up with the latest literary developments. Her father, who came to worry about his children's fates in his last years, actually thought that his daughter Dorothea was happily married. Indeed, she badly wanted him to think this, so much so that before her father died in 1786, she refused to give in to her friend Henriette Herz's pleas that she separate from Simon Veit. After her father's death, the birth of the Veit couple's two sons probably contributed to reasons why she remained with her husband. But their eleven years together cannot have been without some contentment. Otherwise, it is difficult to explain Simon Veit's many kindnesses to Dorothea after their separation. His loyalty is a testimony to the survival of some strong bond with between the two, even if it was not passion.[79]

Sometimes the opportunities provided by a couple's extraordinary wealth made the question of companionship or its lack less pressing. Karl August Varnhagen's description of the Cohen household, where he tu-

78. See Kayserling, *Die jüdischen Frauen,* 199.
79. On Dorothea Veit's relationship with Simon Veit see ibid., 183.

tored the children, suggests that the fantastic wealth of some of the salon couples made possible an emancipated style of social relationships where intimate companionship was not required for family harmony. It had long been common for noble husbands and wives to live at some physical and emotional distance from each other, especially in France but also in Prussia. When the Jewish elite achieved fantastic wealth and sophisticated acculturation, some couples imitated this practice. The Cohen household, for instance, was a large and varied one, including the numerous workers in Herr Cohen's adjoining wool factory, a clerk, and a tutor. Frequent visitors included Frau Cohen's mother and married sisters and a string of local musical and literary personalities. At one point during Varnhagen's employment in the household, Herr Cohen was devoting his attentions to one Mademoiselle Seiler, a singer, and Varnhagen himself seems to have been carrying on a flirtation with Frau Cohen.[80]

The apparent absence of a happy companionship between the Herzes, the Veits, and the Cohens can be seen as the consequence of arranged matches uniting mates of different ages and different degrees of involvement in secular culture. But even as these three cases show, a misguided arranged match did not necessarily result in a divorce. Wealth itself and an absorption in friendships and the life of the mind seem to have compensated less than happy wives. Henriette Herz stayed with Markus until his death in 1803; Philippine Cohen appears to have remained with her husband even after he fled Berlin because of bankruptcy in 1804; the Veits stayed together for eleven years before Dorothea departed for a new life with Friedrich Schlegel. For the other twelve of the salon women who married Jewish men, we are completely uninformed about the quality of their emotional lives. Yet five of the other twelve marriages endured until one of the spouses died. Sara Levy, Amalie Beer, Rebecca Ephraim, Fradchen Liebman, and Jente Stieglitz all remained married to their Jewish spouses. The lives of the Levys and the Beers are excellent evidence that it was possible to play a leading role in the city's social life, remain Jewish, and remain married to one's original Jewish spouse. Both Sara Levy and Amalie Beer spoke foreign languages, had the respect of important gentile friends, and hosted enduringly popular salons. Such a life was thus not incompatible with an endogamous, probably arranged marriage. Nor was the extensive acculturation associated with salon leadership always incompatible with lasting marriage. Sometimes one or both

80. One noble salon woman who lived apart from her husband was Dorothea von Courland; see Christoph August Tiedge, *Anna Charlotte Dorothea, letzte Herzogin von Kurland* (Leipzig, 1823). On life in the Cohen houschould see Varnhagen von Ense, *Denkwürdigkeiten*, 81.

partners in a stable Jewish marriage converted and changed their names without causing the demise of the marriage. The Cohens converted together with their children in 1800; Rebecca Ephraim's husband David converted sometime before 1811 and became Andreas Johannes Schmidt; Fradchen and Abraham Liebman converted together in 1809, she becoming Frederike Liman and he becoming August Liman; Jente Stieglitz's husband Israel, a physician who was a close friend of Wilhelm von Humboldt, converted in 1800.[81]

The lives of the salon women who lived for a time without husbands are vivid illustrations of the hardships which the comfortably married probably sought to avoid. The classic case was Rahel Levin, who did not marry until she was forty-one. It is not clear why she never married a Jewish man at the age her friends Herz and Veit did. It was surely not because her family was too poor to provide her with a dowry, as has been claimed. She had an inheritance of 18,000 taler, albeit meager when compared to Philippine Cohen's 100,000 taler or Moses Isaac's daughters' 80,000 each. But if it was not lack of money for a dowry, why did Rahel Levin not marry a Jewish man when at the typical age for a daughter of the merchant elite? Levin's failure to marry traditionally was probably caused more by her own rebellion against Judaism and her special success in high society than by Jewish suitors' rejection of her. She was engaged twice to noblemen, once between 1795 and 1799, and once again, in 1801, when twenty-nine. By the time both affairs had ended badly, the financial disruption caused by the Napoleonic War and troubles with her mother and brothers had reduced her income to eight hundred taler a year.[82] This was not a bad income for a single person. But Levin had been accustomed to a rather expensive lifestyle, going to the theater regularly, renting carriages, living on the top floor of the large family home in the center of the city. But since she and her mother were not getting on well, Levin moved out in 1809. Then, because she was a woman living alone, a good deal of her income had to be devoted to hiring a male servant. And because she was often ill, her funds also had to go for expensive

81. On Sara Levy see Wilhelm Erman, *Paul Erman: Ein Berliner Gelehrtenleben 1764–1851* (Berlin, 1927), 94–96, and Eberty, *Jugenderinnerungen,* the chapter on "Madame Löwy." Published material on Beer is rare: see Jacobson, *Jüdische Trauungen,* 317, and the Beer-Meyerbeer Collection (AR 3194) in the archives of the Leo Baeck Institute, New York City. On the Cohens' conversions see Jacobson, *Jüdische Trauungen,* 362–63; on David Ephraim's conversion see 292; on the Limans' conversions, see 304; on the Stieglitzs' conversions see 349–50.

82. See Arendt, *Rahel Varnhagen,* 3. For a fuller account of her financial situation see Berdrow, *Rahel Varnhagen,* 144–45. One scholar who claimed that Levin was "poor" is Kay Goodman, in her stimulating "Poesis and Praxis in Rahel Varnhagen's Letters," *New German Critique* 27 (1982), 123–40.

medical care. Levin's social loneliness after her salon circle dispersed in 1806 made the absence of a husband and a family all the more difficult to bear emotionally.

Henriette Herz also suffered socially and economially from being single after Markus died in 1803. As a widow, she found her standard of living vastly and rapidly reduced. The problem was that too little had been saved; much of Herz's income had been devoted to their lavish salon entertaining. Henriette had her mother and a blind single sister living at home to support, and she refused to accept governess positions that would have required her to change her name and convert. Instead, she rented rooms to young female boarders from the countryside and helped them obtain positions as servants in the city. But this income kept her standard of living spartan indeed, in part because the city's widows' fund reduced its payments so radically in the years of the Napoleonic War. Eventually she obtained the necessary financial help from her old friend Wilhelm von Humboldt, who intervened in 1845 to secure Herz a yearly pension from the crown.

In spite of all of the social and economic advantages a lasting marriage provided, nine, almost half the twenty salon women, eventually divorced their Jewish husbands. To understand why the rate of divorce and subsequent intermarriage was so high among the salon women, several mysteries remain to be explored. Therefore, we need to examine the external attributes of the intermarrying couples and the emotional tone of their relationships, both of which help to account for each side's motives for marrying across a wide divide on the estate hierarchy. Beyond the mutually advantageous exchanges behind the intermarriages, changing opinions about religion, as well as the sexual freedom legitimized by a variety of Berlin's distinctive institutions, also played a role in the making of these unusual matches. By reconstructing the meaning and the extent of conversion in Berlin in these years, we discover how the women managed the formal change of religion, which was a necessary step between divorce and intermarriage.

Before they embarked upon the radical disjunctures of divorce, conversion, and intermarriage, the Jewish salon women had committed only part of their lives to a glittering gentile world. When they went on to catapult themselves almost completely out of the Jewish world, they gained tremendous personal freedom. But with this freedom came loneliness and condescension from those same friends they depended on to build this new life. Why, we may well wonder, should they have had the historic chance to venture beyond a balanced acculturation into a heady, if risky integration?

SEVEN | *Seductive Conversion and Romantic Intermarriage*

Divorce and Conversion

In 1776, Moses Isaacs died in Berlin. Along with Isaac Daniel Itzig and Veitel Heine Ephraim, Isaacs had made a fortune during the Seven Years' War minting coins and supplying the army. Isaacs left behind an estate of three-quarters of a million taler in gold, most of which was organized into a family trust extending to the life of his grandchildren. The only stipulation Isaacs placed on his will was that should any of his five sur-viving children convert to Christianity, they would forgo their share of the inheritance. The first of his children to convert were his two daughters, Rebecca and Blümchen, who both proceded to marry noblemen. In 1789, their two unconverted brothers appealed to King Frederick the Great to uphold their father's will and exclude the two defecting sisters from the inheritance. King Frederick ruled in agreement with the broth-ers more out of loyalty to the deceased Isaacs than out of an aversion to Jewish conversion to Christianity. Whatever the king's motives, the sis-ters felt they had been treated unfairly. In 1786 they sued in the civil courts to have the anti-conversion clause of the will declared invalid. The first court's decision was in their favor, ruling that the anti-conversion clause was inappropriate in a Christian state, insofar as it interfered with the inheritance rights of Christian subjects, in this case the two newly Protestant Isaacs daughters. But later that year a higher court reversed this decision, judging from the viewpoint of the dead Jewish parents rather than that of the newly Christian daughters. This second court ruled that Jewish as well as Christian parents had the right to determine who could inherit their property. Later that same year, this second decision was itself overturned by a third court. In the end, the anti-conversion clause was declared invalid, which meant that the daughters had won their inheritance after all. But in an absolutist age, the king, not the judiciary, had the last word. When Frederick William II ascended the throne later in 1786, he followed his uncle's example and again confirmed Isaacs's controversial will, depriving the rebellious daughters of their inheritance.[1]

Thus it seemed that the converted sisters, who by this time had both married noblemen and bore the names von Runkle and von Bose, would each lose the 80,000 taler she was to inherit had she not converted. This was a considerable loss, since a top bureaucrat in Berlin at the time earned 2,500 taler a year, and a well-paid professor elsewhere in Germany rarely earned more than 800 taler a year.[2] The converted sisters' complaint against the final ruling on the will attracted considerable public attention. To make peace, the unconverted brothers agreed to privately settle with their sisters, to the tune of 75,000 each. The tale gradually became more and more ironic. Since one of the brothers eventually converted, his children were denied an inheritance from the estate. Finally, by the middle of the nineteenth century, the only beneficiary of the trust was the converted son of the only one of Isaacs's five children who had remained Jewish.

The story of the Moses Isaacs family trust poignantly captures how wealthy Jewish families in Berlin were divided by disagreements over conversion and intermarriage in the last two decades of the eighteenth century. As this tale depicts, it was the daughters rather than the sons born into the Jewish elite who tended to enjoy the social opportunities which made these kinds of rebellion possible in the first place. To be sure, Jewish women were hardly the only rebels in salons. Many of the dilemmas faced by the Jewish salon women were shared by other salon friends. As we have seen, salon women of all faiths and from all estates tended to divorce husbands who had been chosen for them by parents but impeded their intellectual development. These divorces were one rather drastic solution to the conflict between arranged marriages and public roles on the literary scene. But the intensity of the Jewish salon women's experience of this universal conflict was distinctive. Their remarriages, usually

1. For a summary of the case see Warren I. Cohn, "The Moses Isaacs Family Trust—Its History and Significance," *LBIYB* 18 (1973), 267–80. The trust is also discussed briefly in Jacob Jacobson, *Jüdische Trauungen in Berlin 1723–1859* (Berlin, 1968), 214–15.

2. For these and other wage rates for specific occupations in Berlin in this period see Johann Goldfriedrich, *Geschichte des Deutschen Buchhandels*, vol. 3 (Leipzig. 1909; rpt., Aalen, 1970), 94; W. H. Bruford, *Germany in the Eighteenth Century* (Cambridge, 1971), 331; and Hans Gerth, *Bürgerliche Intelligenz um 1800: Zur Soziologie des deutschen Frühliberalismus* (rpt., Göttingen, 1976), 29 and 45.

out of the faith and usually to noblemen, brought together representatives of two radically diverse estates, albeit estates which had come to possess mutually complementary resources and needs. In this chapter we explore the steps taken by the Jewish salon women on the road to these intermarriages. First, they had to extricate themselves from their Jewish husbands and meet a suitable replacement, and then change their religion so as to allow a new match.

Just as it was difficult to use surviving sources to directly enter the private experience of the salon women's arranged marriages, so too it is the rare case where it is possible to be exact about the interpersonal causes of the nine divorces among the twenty women. In several cases—that of Dorothea Veit, the two Meyer sisters, Rebecca Friedländer, Esther Gad, and Pessel Zülz—we do know that the salon women were highly acculturated. Dorothea was absorbed in a serious reading program and participated in several intellectual clubs. Sara and Marianne Meyer's linguistic and literary skills were admired by intellectuals as prominent as Goethe and Herder. Friedländer held "Aesthetic Teas" and published a score of novels; Gad published articles. Pessel Zülz, the sister of Philippine Cohen, appeared in a later incarnation as the Baroness von Boye and was a friend of Johann Fichte's and Ludwig Tieck's. Less is known about their husbands, most of whom were bankers and entrepreneurs. Just how uninterested the husbands were in secular high culture, and how such lack of interest might have contributed to the decision to divorce is rarely known. Simon Veit is the only husband who we know caused his wife sorrow over his intellectual and linguistic parochialism. Not only is case-by-case information scanty; it would also be wrong to presume that there were no acculturated Jewish men in the city whom these women might have married in a less complicated Jewish marriage market. There were men in Berlin who had mastered the tools and tasted the enjoyments of secular culture. But the Jewish elite's practice of arranged early marriage, grounded as it was in highly practical constraints, did not allow for a priority on cultural compatibility when it came to the project of creating new families.

Of the nine divorcees, we know for certain that seven eventually remarried, all to gentiles. One of those who never remarried was Rebecca Friedländer, who divorced Moses Friedländer when she was twenty-three, converted, and changed her name to Regina Frohberg. But none of her gentile admirers, mostly noble military officials interested in literature, were willing to marry her. Her salon friends who also divorced their Jewish husbands, usually also when still in their twenties, had better luck than Friedländer in transforming noble admirers into husbands. Indeed, five of the seven married a nobleman the second time, and the

second husband of a sixth, Dorothea Veit, Friedrich Schlegel, was ennobled after their marriage. Marianne Meyer was divorced from her first
Jewish husband when still young. Two noble suitors backed away at the
last moment, and it was then that she married Prince von Reuss.
Blümchen Moses married Joseph Arnstein in 1773 and was divorced four
years later; eventually she married Kriegrsrat von Bose. Esther Gad married Samuel Bernard when she was twenty-one, divorced him when
twenty-six, and eventually married the physician of an English duke.
Philippine Cohen's sister Pessel Zülz married Isaac Beer Fliess in 1791;
after their divorce she married Major von Boye, and after a second divorce, Pessel married a second nobleman, a Swedish officer named von
Starre. Gentile husbands were not only found by those entering a second
marriage. Three of the salon women married gentile men the first time
around. Rahel Levin's eventual husband, the writer and diplomat Karl
August Varnhagen von Ense, found his noble predicate in an ancient
family genealogy; Marianne Devidel, the daughter of a wealthy Viennese
court jeweler, eloped to marry Gottfried Schadow, the Berlin sculptor;
Rebecca Friedländer's sister Julie Saaling married Karl Heyse, later a
classics professor at the University of Berlin.[3]

Jewish historians of the nineteenth century, especially Heinrich
Graetz, saw a direct connection between salon participation and intermarriage. For Graetz, salons were decadent, sinful gatherings where
women literally lost their virtue. The few surviving primary-source nar-
ratives describing salons lend no support whatsoever to this notion. To
be sure, most salon gatherings may have lasted until late into the evening, but the main activity was intellectual dialogue. But might there
have been another sort of connection between salon participation and
intermarriage, insofar as salons functioned as a courtship arena for misalliances? Dorothea Veit did meet Friedrich Schlegel at Henriette and
Markus Herz's salon, and Rahel Levin first met Karl August Varnhagen
at Philippine Cohen's when he was employed there as a tutor. For other
misalliances the role of the salon as a marketplace for meeting exotic
partners is less well documented. Julie Saaling first met Karl Heyse when
he was a tutor to young Felix Mendelssohn-Bartholdy, but the Mendels-

3. On Friedländer see Paul Heyse, *Jugenderinnerungen und Bekenntnisse* (Berlin, 1901),
6; Jacobson, *Jüdische Trauungen,* 440; Hannah Arendt, *Rahel Varnhagen: The Life of a Jewess*
(London, 1957; rpt., New York, 1974). 107; and Ludwig Geiger, "Marie oder die folgen des
ersten Fehltritts, ein unbekannter Roman," *Zeitschrift für Bücherfreunde,* n.s. 9, no. 1 (1917):
58–62. On Esther Gad (married, Bernard and later Domeier) see Elisabeth Friedrichs, *Die
deutschsprachigen Schriftstellerinnen des 18. und 19. Jahrhunderts* (Stuttgart, 1981), 23. On Devidel see Karl Blechen, *Daniel Chodowiecki, Johann Gottfried Schadow* (Berlin, 1960), 33; on
Paul Heyse's tutoring post see his own *Jugenderinnerungen,* 10.

sohn-Bartholdys did not host a salon in the strict sense of the term. For several couples (or would-be couples) like Marianne Meyer and Prince von Reuss, or Rebecca Friedländer and Karl von Egloffstein, we do know that both partners attended salons. But there is no direct evidence that the initial meeting took place at a specific salon.[4]

Yet it would be wrong to conclude that salon relationships played no role in encouraging these controversial misalliances. For the climate of opinion about intermarriage had shifted even among respectable Jews by the time salons came onto the scene. An older generation of acculturated Jews had done what they could to nip potential intermarriages in the bud. For instance, when Adele Ephraim was being courted by Franz von Leuchsenring, von Leuchsenring's friend Moses Mendelssohn threatened to cut off relations with him if he did not abandon his relationship with the young Ephraim woman. In contrast, the salon women's contemporaries, Jewish and gentile alike, often encouraged intimacies between women and men born into different estates. Not only did Henriette Herz suggest to Dorothea Veit that Veit leave her husband at the very outset of their marriage; after Veit left her family Herz continued to see her in defiance of Markus Herz's order that she boycott Veit. One noble salon man who enjoyed stirring up cross-estate romances and intrigue was the ubiquitous "introducer" for Rahel Levin's salon, Gustav von Brinkmann. Von Brinkmann wrote long letters analyzing in which ways various women friends looked and sounded Jewish and how this affected their chances at intermarriage. In 1790 von Brinkmann's friend Wilhelm von Humboldt took von Brinkmann to task for telling the father of Rösel Fränkel, one of the salon women, about his daughter's "domestic situation." Von Humboldt did not remark on the details, but he did make clear that Frau Fränkel's father was "most agitated" by von Brinkmann's news.[5]

But if the suitors met in salons or elsewhere were to become husbands, conversion was necessary. There was no civil marriage in Prussia until 1846, so to marry a Christian one had to become a Christian. (Thus

4. See Heinrich Graetz, *Geschichte der Juden* (Leipzig, 1900), vol. 16, 160. A contemporary description of Rahel Levin's salon by "Graf S." which shows that intellectual dialogue was central in salons can be found in C. May, *Rahel: Ein Berliner Frauenleben im 19 Jahrhundert* (Berlin, n.d.), 7–16. On the Mendelssohn-Bartholdy household see Heinrich Jacob, *Felix Mendelssohn und seine Zeit* (Frankfurt a.M., 1959).

5. On the von Leuchsenring episode see Karl August Varnhagen von Ense, *Denkwürdigkeiten und vermischte Schriften*, vol. 4 (Leipzig, 1843), 494 and Leitzmann, *Wilhelm von Humboldts Briefe an Karl Gustav von Brinkmann* (Leipzig, 1939), 169. On the Veit-Herz episode see Furst, *Henriette Herz*, 11. On the von Brinkmann-Ephraim episode see Leitzmann, *Wilhelm von Humbolts Briefe, 11*.

because by the time they married, both partners were Christians, these marriages were technically and legally not intermarriages. But because a converted Jew remained a Jew in the eyes of most contemporaries, these marriages are called intermarriages here.) From what we can reconstruct, deciding to convert was a painful step for many of the salon women. Just as some of their gentile salon friends tried to supervise their marital choices, so too gentile salon friends sought to guide the women's religious choices. Friedrich Schleiermacher, for instance, long tried to convince his friends Henriette Herz and Rahel Levin to desert their faith. In 1799 Schleiermacher had already decided that "Judaism is long since dead," and he mocked those who "yet wear its livery but sit lamenting beside the imperishable mummy, bewailing its departure and its sad legacy."[6] The growing strength of romanticism provided new intellectual incentives to convert, alongside the deistic reasons enlightened intellectuals had put forward just a few years before. Deists had argued that because Judaism and Christianity shared a core of universal truths, the two religions would ultimately merge, and so Jews might as well become Christians in the short run. In the last years of the old century and the first years of the new one, the romantic younger salon men offered the Jewish salon women additional reasons to convert, by advocating a more positive, more mystical, more pantheistic version of Protestantism.[7]

The enthusiasms of the salon women's friends, both for cross-estate entanglements and for the intrinsic virtues of Christianity, surely contributed to the decision many of the women made to change their faith. But surely the willingness of prestigious suitors to become husbands provided an incentive of a more immediate, more personal kind. More than half of the salon women's conversions were connected with marriages to gentiles. The seven divorced salon women who remarried converted, as did three women whose first marriages were intermarriages. An additional six women converted but never intermarried, either because admirers declined to become husbands or because Jewish husbands converted with their wives. The one single woman who seems to have converted because she was motivated by authentic conviction, with no would-be gentile husband waiting in the wings, was the widowed Henriette Herz. This leaves at most three of the twenty salon women who died in the religion into which they had been born. (In one of these three

---

6. This quote appears in Schleiermacher's *On Religion: Speeches to Its Cultured Despisers,* trans. John Oman (New York, 1958), 238; it was cited by Michael Meyer in his "Reform Jewish Thinkers and Their German Intellectual Context," in J. Reinharz and W. Schatzberg, eds., *The Jewish Response to German Culture* (Hanover, N.H., 1985).

7. See Meyer, "Reform Jewish Thinkers," 70.

cases conversion was likely, but lack of documentation makes it impossible to be sure.)[8]

The strong association between conversion and intermarriage, especially intermarriage to noble men, suggests the women changed religions at least in part because they were socially opportunistic and craved the higher positions possessed by Christians in a radically unequal society. Indeed, for many intermarriages there is evidence of this motive. Yet whatever status-hungry desires propelled them into a new, Christian world, many of the women retained strong ties to friends and relatives who remained Jewish. Although the salon women had access to a glamorous social world mainly closed to their parents, brothers, and husbands, many also showed a loyalty to their still-Jewish families, especially their mothers, if not to their first Jewish husbands. Often this loyalty resulted in poverty and loneliness at a vulnerable time. Not all was immediately abandoned for social advancement. Herz lost governess positions because she would not convert while her mother was alive; Dorothea Veit also would not convert and marry Friedrich Schlegel while her mother lived. After divorcing her Jewish husband, Sara Meyer converted to Protestantism, but parental pressure influenced her to return to Judaism. Eventually she converted a second time to Protestantism in order to marry Baron von Grotthuss.[9]

It was not only family loyalty that bound a minority of the salon women to their faith. Sara Levy, Amalie Beer, and Fanny von Arnstein (Levy's salonière sister who lived in Vienna) all had a principled position against conversion, and all argued against it to friends and relatives considering conversion.[10] All three, it should be noted, had lasting marriages to Jewish men. But Sara Levy and Amalie Beer were in the minority. As for those who did eventually convert, they may have retained ties to an earlier generation even after conversion, and they may have felt remorse about the non-religious motives for their actions. Yet at best such constraints affected the timing of their departure from Judaism. The pros-

8. One of the three who probably converted was Jente Stieglitz, whose father, Benjamin Ephraim, and husband, Dr. Israel Stieglitz, both converted. See Jacobson, *Jüdische Trauungen*, 349. The two Jewish salon women we know did not convert were Sara Levy and Amalie Beer.

9. On Sara Meyer's return conversion to Judaism see Kayserling, *Die jüdischen Frauen*, 217.

10. On Sara Levy's position on conversion see Nahida Ruth Lazarus, *Das jüdische Weib* (Berlin, 1922), 153; on Fanny von Arnstein's position see Hilde Spiel, *Fanny von Arnstein, Oder die Emanzipation* (Frankfurt a.M., 1962), 83. Very little has been published about Beer; the typescript of Kurt Richter's short article "Amalie Beer und Ihre Söhne" is in the Beer-Meyerbeer Collection (AR 3194) in the archives of the Leo Baeck Institute in New York City.

pect of intermarriage, especially to a noble, was, after all, a heady incentive for a Jewish woman in the eighteenth century; marriage was virtually a woman's only route to upward mobility. To be born Jewish and to marry noble was really a double jump up the ladder of corporate estates at a time when economic classes cutting across the estate hierarchy were only beginning to form. However fabulously wealthy members of the Jewish elite were, the Jewish community was far below most commoners and below all nobles in terms of civic rights and privileges. And in the Prussian context, before the modest reforms of 1806–14, there was little hope that the nobility's privileges and prestige would be attacked by either the masses, the state bureaucracy, or the crown.

Marrying Up

Even this tiny cluster of six Jewish-noble and four Jewish-commoner marriages was somewhat of a milestone in the context of Jewish life in Germany. That not merely gentile, but noble gentile families would accept Jewish women as daughters- and sisters-in-law was a new and serious turn of events in Jewish-German history. Why so new? There had been contact between Jews and gentiles which sometimes culminated in conversion as far back as the late seventeenth century in Berlin. But previous social contacts had been mainly between men, with the limited purpose of scholarly or commercial exchange. The wives and daughters of Berlin's court Jews in an earlier epoch did not have extensive social contact with the families of the princes whom their husbands and fathers served financially.[11]

Given that seven of the ten intermarriages were second marriages, often following on the heels of arranged, non-companionate matches, it might be surmised that the intermarriages were love matches. After all, several courtships leading up to these intermarriages were carried on in salon society, a circle whose members frequently rebelled in print and in practice against arranged marriages and their role in maintaining the established social structure. Indeed, several of the more famous intermarriages were clearly companionate matches. Dorothea Veit and Friedrich Schlegel were both, at least initially, delighted to have found each other

11. Useful data on conversions throughout Germany in this era can be found in Jacob Katz, *Out of the Ghetto: The Social Background of Jewish Emancipations, 1770–1870* (New York, 1978), chap. 3. For a more detailed account see B. Z. Kedar, "Continuity and Change in Jewish Conversion to Christianity in Eighteenth-Century Germany," (in Hebrew), *Studies in the History of Jewish Society* (in Hebrew), E. Etkes and Y. Salmon, eds. (Jerusalem, 1980). I am grateful to Todd Endelman and to David Biale for bringing the Kedar article to my attention.

spiritually and intellectually. Although his ardor cooled as the years passed, she remained his devoted companion through years of hardship and sacrifice. Rahel Levin's marriage to Varnhagen was not a marriage of sensual passion, but it decidedly was one of literary cooperation and personal devotion. Julie Saaling seems to have lived in happy companionship with Karl Heyse; she as a fairly serious student of poetry, and he as professor at the new University of Berlin. Both were devoted to their son Paul, who became the first novelist in Germany to win a Nobel prize. On the other hand, some intermarriages were definitely not companionate matches. Marianne Meyer, for example, never even lived with her Count von Reuss; the two maintained separate residences and obviously conducted separate social lives—which was necessary since she was never admitted at court. Unfortunately, information is far too sparse on the remaining couples to determine which trend was the rule.[12]

But even if companionate relationships were the dominant trend, it would be wrong to conclude that mates chose each other only because of their mutual emotional resonance, that looks, status, and wealth played no role. Even though the existence of these intermarriages shows that the choice of mates was now formally much freer in these circles than it ever had been for Jewish women in Germany, the direction the women moved when they chose their own mates does not seem to have been a random one. For when we examine the personal qualities and social attributes of the intermarried spouses, the total sum of many partner's ledgers of status, wealth, looks, and/or intellectual skills seem to have been roughly equal in their sum, although not at all similar in their parts. The noble husbands were rich in status but often poor in property or personal qualities. The converted brides tended to be rich in money, and many were also rich in beauty or cultivation.

For neither the noble nor the commoner gentile grooms who married the salon brides tended to be the most eligible. Having been rejected by two noble suitors, Rahel Levin had to abandon her hope of the overnight social legitimation that would have come her way as a countess. However sensitive and dedicated to her literary pursuits, Varnhagen was, after all, fourteen years her junior, and without secure career prospects for much of their courtship. Marianne Meyer's Prince von Reuss was much older and "ugly as the night." When he died, his family succeeded

12. It has been difficult to find out the financial details of Jewish-Jewish, as well as of converted-Christian marriages. The few marriage contracts from eighteenth-century Jewish marriages in Germany found in the archive of the Leo Baeck Institute do not contain specific financial details. And contracts from Christian marriages (which might have involved a converted partner) are difficult to find because notarial records have not been systematically preserved in Germany.

Karl August Varnhagen von Ense

in denying her the title that was hers by marriage, and she was forced to petition the Austrian crown to be allowed to call herself Frau von Eyben-berg. Friedrich Schlegel may have been a young literary lion, but he was a decidedly underemployed one. By running off with him Dorothea Veit may have escaped from the leisured boredom of a life with Simon Veit, but it was an escape into the frantic copying, translating, and writing necessary to feed her family. Without her ex-husband's financial gener-osity, things would have been even more difficult.[13] Baron von Grot-thuss, Sara Meyer's second husband, lost his fortune during the Napo-

13. On Veit's inheritance see Margaretha Hiemenz, *Dorothea von Schlegel* (Freiburg im Breisgau, 1911), 18.

leonic era, and the couple lived modestly in Oranienburg, where the baron was employed as postmaster.

Regardless of how poor or unattractive a noble groom might have been, his title was valuable to a would-be Jewish bride. Her Jewish origins, even if formally covered over with a new religion, would undoubtedly be a source of embarrassment to the groom and his family. In an era when the status of a new in-law would typically affect the parents and siblings of both mates, taking on a once-Jewish relative was a major decision. It would certainly ease the pain if she had compensatory qualities. Perhaps the most obvious of these was financial. The eventual resolution of the Moses Isaacs episode shows that divorced and converted Jewish salon women could indeed still bring their inheritance with them when they intermarried, albeit in this case after a complex legal battle. At times the bride's inheritance was far smaller than that of Moses Isaacs's daughters, yet this money was a crucial means of support in periods when the intermarried couple experienced financial difficulties. Thus Dorothea Veit's modest inheritance aided her and Friedrich when he had problems piecing together an income from lectures and publishing. Sometimes it was not the wife's own inheritance but her parents' financial resources which were of help. Marianne Devidel's father, a rich jewel merchant in Vienna, supported Johann Schadow, his daughter's new husband, when he traveled to Italy to study art.[14]

Thus at the most basic level, the Jewish-noble marriages represented an exchange of status for wealth, an exchange that originated in the economic fate of the larger social groups to which the brides and the grooms belonged. For as we have seen, this tiny group of Jewish-noble marriages was the culmination of the mutually complementary, long-term structural strengths and weaknesses of the noble and the Jewish estates. Many noble families in Prussia suffered from a capital shortage in the last decades of the eighteenth century, because without primogeniture landed estates were frequent subdivided in an era of boom land prices. Because of the restrictions imposed as a condition for their presence in Prussia, many members of the Jewish estate had the excess capital unavailable to so many Prussian Junkers. These funds in turn financed the time and resources for Jewish women to acquire the cultural polish which so many Junkers lacked. Thus these marriages had an underlying structural logic.

The economic developments of the 1760s and 1770s exacerbated the nobles' need of Jewish wealth and, simultaneously, made many Jewish merchants even richer. Discrete private loans to those who could afford the high interest rates was one way that the Jewish bankers increased the

14. Blechen, *Daniel Chodowiecki, Johann Gottfried Schadow*, 33.

wealth they acquired in the Seven Year's War. Private loans were crucial at a time when the public banking system was still extremely primitive in Prussia. We know the details about only a few exchanges of this kind involving the families of salon women and men. Rahel Levin's father made loans to nobles and to actors; Friedrich Gentz and Achim von Arnim (two salon men who did not, in fact, intermarry) were both in and out of debt to Jewish bankers. In other cases, we simply know that a gentile salon man used a Jewish banker to manage his finances, without knowing whether private loans were actually transacted. Wilhelm von Humboldt's banker was David Friedländer; Sara Levy's husband Solomon served as the banker for several gentile salon men.[15] Indeed, several accounts of the origin of the Jewish salons attribute the initial contact between Jewish women and noblemen to the noblemens' visits to the women's fathers to arrange for private loans. Hannah Arendt went so far as to suggest that the intermarriages between Jewish salon women and noble men were a continuation of the creditor-debtor exchanges of the earlier years.[16]

The coincidence of noble poverty, Jewish wealth, and the absence of a public banking system by which money could be loaned anonymously all help explain the inner social logic of the Jewish-noble intermarriages, yet these economic factors alone are by no means a sufficient explanation. First, noble economic dependence on Jewish creditors seems to have led to antisemitism as easily as it might predispose nobles to a willingness to socialize with and marry Jews. Second, too little is known about the finances of specific couples to be sure that every intermarrying spouse's finances reflected that of the estate. And even when this was the case, it is hard to show that economic or status gain was in fact the main motive for the intermarriage. Finally, even when there seems to have been an economic motive, it was still a giant step for nobles to move beyond borrowing from rich Jewish fathers and socializing with their daughters to actually marrying these daughters. The status-wealth exchange could easily have led to the loans and to the salons, without culminating in intermarriage.

Moreover, money and financial connections were not the only coun-

---

15. On the connection between von Arnim's financial problems and his anti-Semitism see Helene Riley, *Ludwig Archim von Arnims Jugend- und Reisejahre* (Bonn, 1978), 5; on Gentz's financial ties to Jews see Paul Sweet, *Wilhelm von Humboldt: A Biography*, vol. 1 (Columbus, Oh., 1978), 210. The von Humbolt-Friedländer financial connection is mentioned in Albert Leitzmann, ed., *Wilhelm von Humbolts Briefe*, 166; the best sources on Sara and Solomon Levy are Wilhelm Erman, *Paul Erman*, and Felix Eberty, *Jugenderinnerungen*, in the chapter on "Madame Löwy."

16. Arendt, *Rahel Varnhagen*, 146.

terbalancing possession that status-poor Jewish brides offered their status-rich gentile grooms. Many salon women were of exceptional beauty (although, to be sure, it was not always those whose lovely images have survived who intermarried), and the romantics' enthusiasm for the Oriental, the exotic, and the sensual enhanced the Jewish women's desirability.[17] Perhaps more salient than their wealth or looks were many of the women's intellectual skills and interests. To be sure, the romantic view of life did not call for women to become authentically learned or professional scholars; rather, the ideal female companion was supposed to be well educated, well read, and intellectually inspiring. The Jewish salon women were frequently heralded by their male friends for their impressive intellectual performances, and the romantics' celebration of these qualities only increased the women's fame and symbolic cultural power. Of course, the Jewish women's performances appeared infrequently on the published page, and Jewish women were not overrepresented among the authors in salons. But that was precisely why romantic ideology was so useful to them, for even without publishing Jewish salon women had intellectual glamour. To cite the paradigm case, Gustav von Brinkmann was totally taken with the "little Levi's" (Rahel Levin's) intelligence and brought all his friends to meet her. For it was Levin who possessed the most intellectual glamour of any of her circle, and this intellectual glamour was crucial in Varnhagen's attraction to her. Soon after they became so attached to each other in the summer of 1808, he went around to mutual friends collecting her letters; later he sent some of them to Goethe and arranged for selections of her correspondence to be published.[18]

To note that the gentile grooms often had financial or personal defects which diminished their status and that the converted Jewish brides often had financial or personal strengths which compensated for their lack of status is still an external view. Pointing out that many of the couples possessed complementary estate labels, wealth, or cultural skills does not necessarily mean that the search for mutually enhancing titles, property, or cultural style was anyone's conscious motive for choosing a particular

17. See chap. 4 of Charlene A. Lea, *Emancipation, Assimilation and Stereotype: The Image of the Jew in German and Austrian Drama, 1800–1850* (Bonn, 1978). I am grateful to Marion Kaplan for bringing this book to my attention.

18. See Konrad Feilchenfeldt, *Varnhagen von Ense als Historiker* (Amsterdam, 1970), as well as Susan L. Cocalis, "Der Vormund will Vormund Sein: Zur Problematik der weiblichen Unmündigkeit in 18. Jahrhundert," in Marianne Burkhard, ed., *Gestaltet und Gestaltend: Frauen in der deutschen Kultur,* in *Amsterdamer Beiträge zur neueren Germanistik,* vol. 10 (Amsterdam, 1980); for an older work on the theme see the collection of biographical essays by Margarete Susman, *Frauen der Romantik* (Jena, 1929).

mate. These were complex adults with intricate emotional and intellectual lives. Existing subjective records revealing their motives for marrying show that decisions were made on emotional rather than on opportunistic grounds. Of course, there may have been a complex interaction between a desire for material or social self-improvement and feelings of affection,[19] but to ignore the role of love in the intermarriages would be especially inappropriate, considering that at least overtly, these were freely chosen mates. After all, the novelty of these marriages in their historic context rested on the fact that they were not arranged. When marriages were arranged by families of the Jewish elite, then the mates would, by definition, tend to have homogeneously equal external ledgers. What was notable about the intermarriages was the heterogeneity of each partner's ledger—even though this heterogeneity does not seem to have been haphazard.

But recounting how a mutually useful exchange of status for wealth, beauty, and intellect was fulfilled in these intermarriages still does not provide a sufficient explanation of why they occurred. To move closer to a full explanation we must turn to institutions and ideologies that helped set the particular tone of life in late-eighteenth-century Berlin. It is useful to remember that the institutional setting of the salon, where many couples met and courted, helped to legitimize the Jewish women as brides for noble men because opening one's house on a regular but informal basis to friends and acquaintances was a practice that had long been restricted exclusively to nobles. The wealth that made it possible for the Jewish elite in Berlin to live in large households, create a cultivated, luxurious environment, and entertain in style had often been possessed only by nobles in the European past. Similarly, the freedom to defy sex-role stereotypes denying women any role in the creation or dissemination of culture had long been a freedom enjoyed only by noble women. Thus when Jewish women adopted once-noble behavior, they "dusted" themselves with a noble "aura" which helped to legitimize them as wives for noble husbands. The noble legacy of salons, to be sure, did not apply directly in Prussia, where the Junkers had traditionally been rural, poor, tight-fisted, and uncultured. Yet for centuries, elsewhere in Germany, in France, in Italy, and in England, noble women, in and out of courts, had sponsored salon-like gatherings. Precisely at the historic moment when economic pressures were forcing young and educated nobles into the city, the association of local, Jewish-led salons with an ancient (even if somewhat foreign) noble institution cannot have been unimportant.

19. I am grateful to Martin Bunzl for stressing this point in conversation.

Insofar as the Jewish salon women imitated a noble tradition which required enormous wealth, and did so within the confines of the home, their behavior may be regarded as backward-looking. Their privileges and their social success were beyond the reach of the vast majority of women at the time. Nor could this model of emancipation realistically be emulated in the Prussia of the next century, when imitating nobles became a more problematic route to status for wealthy and educated non-nobles. Although the Jewish women's imitation of noble behavior was backward-looking in this sense, their success at the ancient art of salon-hosting proved useful for a decidedly forward-looking endeavor, namely for the social mobility they achieved via intermarriage.

Outside the salon, too, a particular cluster of values and institutions helped to facilitate these intermarriages. Berlin in the late eighteenth century was a city known for its sexual freedoms, and the wait for a second marriage did not require postponement of erotic satisfactions. Contemporary writers constantly complained that morals in Berlin had reached a low ebb by the last decades of the eighteenth century. Nineteenth-century historians tended to agree and were generally relieved that this hedonistic era had been short-lived.[20] Several groups and institutions were blamed for making the city so rife with sexual activity, beginning with the court at the top of the social hierarchy, whose masked balls offered opportunities for quasi-anonymous intrigues between persons from different places on the social hierarchy. A character in a contemporary play lamented that if a "sugar-sweet lad in uniform," or "a little baron" should take a "wife of an artisan" or a "daughter of a civilian" to "such places, then one can bet ten to one that he will not bring her back home as he got her."[21]

As more noble families came to spend winters or the entire year in the city, opportunities were found within households for sexual activity across class lines. Domestic servants fresh from the countryside were prey to the lusts of their socially prominent male employers. As a contemporary complained, not only did "the wanton attitude of their superiors spoil the girls' innocence, . . .[but] city food and drink and even city

20. Good summaries of these complaints can be found in Alfred Schier, *Die Liebe in der Frühromantik* (Marburg, 1913); Genevieve Bianquis, *Love in Germany* (London, 1964); Curt Gebauer, "Studien zur Geschichte der Bürgerlichen Sittenreform des 18. Jahrhundert," *Archiv für Kulturgeschichte* 15 (1923), 97–116; Karl Adolf Menzel, *Zwanzig Jahre Preussischer Geschichte, 1786 bis 1806* (Berlin, 1849); and Hans Ostwald, *Kultur- und Sittengeschichte Berlins* (Berlin, 1924), 114–16.

21. As cited in Oscar Helmuth Werner, *The Unmarried Mother in German Literature: With Special Reference to the Period 1770–1800* (New York, 1917), 42.

work intensified the sexual instinct of country girls."[22] Sometimes the center of these domestic entanglements was the lady of the house; it was not uncommon for a lower-class tutor to fall in love with his students' mother or sister. The state's marriage restrictions for military personnel also contributed to the prevalence of extramarital sexual activity: officers could marry only upon reaching a high rank and receiving permission from the crown; common soldiers also had difficulty obtaining permission to wed. Since Berlin was the central garrison town for Prussia's large army, these restrictions resulted in a large number of prostitutes in the city. According to one estimate, as many as one out of every seventeen women in Berlin made her living by selling her body.[23]

Outside the military, too, the crown imposed strict barriers intended to prevent marriage outside of caste lines. Nobles needed explicit permission to marry commoners. The institution of morganatic or "left-handed" marriage essentially legalized mistress-keeping while protecting the property and lineage of the powerful. Nobles who were allowed this privilege could literally take a second wife. But neither such wives, who were usually from the lower classes, nor the progeny from such marriages could inherit the property or the title of the husband.[24] The severe restrictions on marriage within the city's Jewish community also reflected the principle that the cohesion of estates could be maintained only by preventing exogamous marriages. Yet ironically, because of the many social and legal constraints on marriage choice, many wished to leave marriages they had been forced to enter. Here the comparative permissiveness of the Prussian and the Jewish divorce laws made cross-estate second marriages possible, which was crucial if salon love affairs involving married persons were to result in remarriages. Prominent scholars and bureaucrats had long argued that Prussia's population must increase if the kingdom was to prosper. Liberal divorce laws facilitated remarriage and thus increased reproduction. In 1794, a new law code issued in Prussia included the most advanced divorce provisions in Europe, giving the divorcing woman considerably more rights than did the subsequent Ger-

22. Ibid., 42.
23. One good example of a tutor-mother match was that between an important bureaucrat under Frederick William II, Johann Christoph Wöllner, and the only daughter of the von Itzenplitz family, Wöllner's employers. See Epstein, *The Genesis of German Conservatism* (Princeton, 1966), 356–57. On Berlin prostitutes see Bianquis, *Love in Germany*, 20; see also Hans Ostwald, *Das Berliner Dinentum* (Leipzig, n.d.).
24. See Reinhard Mestwerdt, "Das Sozialbild der Ehe im Spiegel von Gesetzgebung und Rechtsprechung der letzten 150 Jahre," Ph.D. diss., Göttingen, 1961, 55; of related interest is Rene König, "Zur Geschichte der Monogamie," in Ruprecht Kurzrock, ed., *Die Institution der Ehe* (Berlin, 1979), 9–16.

man law code of 1901. Jewish divorce law was also traditionally lenient, unless the husband's whereabouts were unknown, in which case the wife could not receive a divorce.[25]

Kings, nobles, servants, tutors, soldiers, prostitutes, and lenient divorce laws were not the sole targets of blame for Berlin's moral decay. The intelligentsia who participated in Berlin's literary circles, like their counterparts elsewhere in Germany, especially in Jena, were noted for their frequent extramarital affairs, abortions, illegitimate children, divorces, and remarriages. Many salon participants' free-spirited sexual style became notorious because they themselves celebrated this behavior in print. Romantic writers like Friedrich Schlegel, Friedrich Schleiermacher, Ludwig Tieck and Jean Paul (Richter) wrote novels, criticism, and essays praising feelings, individualism, sensuality, friendship, and cultivated women; life was to become a work of art. In the view of the romantic intellectuals, arranged marriages and the traditional stigma attached to divorce prevented the full development of the personality. These romantic intellectuals often belonged to salon society and often lived out their own theories in their private lives. Salons populated with nobles and intellectuals provided a perfect setting for the formation of a bohemian sexual style, in which intellectuals imitated the emancipated behavior of the urban nobility.[26] The romantic intellectuals' writings, their fame, and their own behavior helped create a climate where intermarriage was fashionably exotic.

The romantic intellectuals advocated sexual emancipation, women's role as cultivated muse, and they also had a predilection for dark-haired, exotic women, a cluster of valves that may have contributed to some salon men's willingness to marry converted Jewish salon women. But paradoxically, other aspects of the romantics' thinking worked in the opposite direction. Because they emphasized nationalism over universalism and emotion over reason, romantic intellectuals came to be less enthu-

---

25. See S. B. Kitchen, *A History of Divorce* (London, 1912), 162–64; Marianne Weber, *Ehefrau und Mutter in der Rechtsentwicklung* (Tübingen, 1907; rpt. Aalen, 1971); Hugo Hauser, "Die geistigen Grundlagen des Eherechts an der Wende des 18. zum 19. Jahrhundert," Ph.D. diss., Heidelberg, 1940; Heinrich Dörner, *Industrialisierung und Familienrecht* (Berlin, 1974); and Dieter Schwab, *Grundlagen und Gestalt der Staatlichen Ehegesetzgebung in der Neuzeit* (Bielefeld, 1967), 172–92. See Paula Hyman, "The Other Half: Women in the Jewish Tradition," in Elizabeth Koltum, ed., *The Jewish Woman* (New York, 1976), 105–13.

26. See Barbara Beuys, *Familienleben in Deutschland* (Hamburg, 1980), 343; Wilhelm Novack, *Liebe und Ehe im deutschen Roman zu Rousseaus Zeiten, 1747–1774* (Bern, 1906); Karl Guthke, *Literarisches Leben im achtzehnten Jahrhundert in Deutschland und in der Schweiz* (Bern and Munich, 1975); and Roy Pascal, *The German Sturm and Drang* (Manchester, England, 1953).

siastic than their enlightened predecessors about friendship with and civic rights for Jews. Although the antisemitic dimension of romanticism did not fully emerge until a later period in the movement's history, it did appear toward the close of the quarter century during which salons flourished in Berlin and was present even within the supposedly utopian salon circle itself. Even salon men generally considered progressive, such as Wilhelm von Humboldt and Gustav von Brinkmann, were not above sharing antisemitic jokes about their Jewish friends.[27] Thus although romanticism may have enhanced the attraction of the Jewish women to romantic intellectuals as women, the same ideology diminished the women's attractiveness as Jews.[28] In this way the changing ideological mood in Berlin first contributed to the popularity of the Jewish salons but later helped to destroy them.

In sum, mutually advantageous exchanges of status and wealth, the status-enhancing context of the salon, the sexual freedoms of late-eighteenth-century Berlin, and some dimensions of romantic ideology all played a role in motivating the salon women's intermarriages. No one of these four causes alone can explain the intermarriages, but together all four causes do make them historically plausible, if not necessarily inevitable. Of course, ten intermarriages do not make a pattern, but they were the culmination of the wider success that rich Jewish women in Berlin had in the pursuit of highly polished acculturation and swift social integration. These successes were noteworthy at the time, and initial work suggests that they were also anomalous in comparison to the experiences of Jewish women in nineteenth-century Germany. Interpreting the meaning of the intermarriages is thus as important as assessing their causes.

Prussia has long been viewed as a land where upward mobility was blocked by a rigid social structure, which in turn retarded the lively contact between elites so useful elsewhere in the development of political democracy. The assimilationist successes enjoyed by this handful of wealthy Jewish women suggests that one important kind of mobility may have been overlooked by historians because it was experienced by women rather than men. Insofar as marriage was one of the few ways for

27. See the Leitzmann edition of von Humboldt's letters to von Brinkmann, cited above.

28. See Julius Carlebach, "The Forgotten Connection—Women and Jews in the Conflict Between Enlightenment and Romanticism," *LBIYB* 24 (1979), 107–38, as well as Carlebach's "Family Structure and the Position of Jewish Women," in W. E. Mosse, A. Paucker, and R. Rürup, eds., *Revolution and Evolution: 1848 in German-Jewish History* (Tübingen, 1981), 170.

families to exchange status for wealth without challenging the set hierarchy of male occupations, women sometimes had more opportunities for upward mobility via marriage than men did via education and employment. One reason is that when status was exchanged for wealth, it was usually the woman who brought the wealth and the man who brought the status. This was so for several reasons. First, if status was embodied in a title, only a man could bring it into a new generation; a noble woman marrying a commoner lost her title when she married him. Inheritance customs also contributed to the "female up" pattern, since wealth could be carried intact into the new generation by the woman in her dowry. And a third reason was that it was considered more graceful for the woman to be below the man on the status hierarchy.

The chance to radically change one's place in society by marrying up surely made life emotionally confusing for the women involved. Their behavior has been judged as the socially opportunistic betrayal of their religion and people, yet much other evidence suggests that this was not how the women saw their own acts. Instead, they seem to have viewed their salon circles, conversions, and intermarriages as the achievements of an often painful fight for personal freedom. In the eighteenth-century setting, at the summit of Berlin's social hierarchy, this fight for emancipation could not, by definition, be a fight to free oneself from the constraints of established society. Nor could it be a fight for the legitimation of one's religious or gender group. No, the Jewish salon women defined their emancipation in the same way as the upwardly mobile male intellectuals of the era: as social integration into high society and high culture, which was seen as the model of civilized humanity.[29]

If we step outside the charmed salon circles to examine the conversions and intermarriages of the less fortunate (and possibly less tormented) Jews in Berlin, we discover that the salon women's departures from Judaism were not as idiosyncratic as they appear at first inspection. For these "mass" converts the social exchanges may not have been with the creme de la creme, and the institutional setting may not have been as glamorous as the salon. The gentile men these converts mixed with and married may not have had such nuanced intellectual positions about religion or female emancipation. Yet the parallels between the much-discussed behavior of the famous few and that of the anonymous and obscure are striking.

29. Phyllis Mack of Rutgers University stressed this point in her comment on an earlier version of the chapter presented at the Columbia University Seminar on Women and Society in April 1984.

Even though there is much social and historic logic to explain the salon women's conversions, in other ways their change of faith was an ironic stage on their journey toward individual emancipation. The intellectual and social successes achieved by leading Jews in Berlin tempted them to deepen their ties to gentiles by breaking their ties with other Jews, and the closer the Jewish salon women came to being accepted by the cream of Berlin society, the more urgent it became to convert to Protestantism. But it was precisely their Jewish qualities that attracted gentiles to the salon women in the first place. Their fathers' wealth, their cultivation in secular high culture, and their darkly "exotic" looks could all be identified as "Jewish" attributes, and were all particularly captivating for the early romantic generation of Berlin intellectuals. Yet this very Jewishness had to be formally eliminated if courtships were to end in marriages.

Jewish historians were often distressed by the irony that successful social integration seemed to culminate in conversion and intermarriage. To be sure, they tended to be impressed by the salon women's mastery of secular culture and by the heterogeneity of the guests they attracted to their homes. But these historians have also usually been dismayed that so many of these same women abandoned their faith. They have admitted that their salons were historically significant, since, in Jacob Katz's words, the salons were "the first time an entire Jewish sector forged real bonds with German society." Indeed, in one rather dramatic, if somewhat exaggerated formulation, salons "brought Jew and Christian closer" than in any other European setting during the eighteenth century. But few Jewish historians have been able to weigh the totality of salon women's social success dispassionately. The mixing between Jews and gentiles in salons was judged to have been "decadent," of an "unwholesome quality."[30] Heinrich Graetz disapproved so strongly of the salon women's behavior that he claimed they did Judaism a service by converting.[31] These women were blamed not only for their own departure from the fold, but for the conversion of Berlin Jews not affiliated with salon society. Historians have cited contemporary observers who

---

30. The claim about closeness of Jews and Christians in salons was made by Adolf Leschnitzer, *The Magic Background of Modern Anti-Semitism: An Analysis of the German-Jewish Relationship* (New York, 1956), 14. The "decadent" critique was made by Raphael Mahler, *A History of Modern Jewry, 1770–1815* (London, 1971), xxi; the "unwholesome" quote is from H. G. Adler, *The Jews in Germany from the Enlightenment to National Socialism* (Notre Dame, 1969), 53.

31. H. Graetz's condemnation can be found in his *History of the Jews* (Philadelphia, 1894), vol. 4, 425.

claimed that by 1800 only a small proportion of Berlin's Jewish families had been untouched by the conversion "epidemic." And they have labeled the incidence of conversion in Berlin in the last decades of the eighteenth century a "wave," a "mania," and a "flood" that left Berlin Jewry "bordering on dissolution."[32] Were previous historians correct to describe the incidence of conversion in eighteenth-century Berlin as a "wave"?

In the past, historians have had little statistical evidence with which to substantiate their assertions, because statistical surveys of Jewish conversion compiled by churches, missionary societies, and state agencies do not extend back into the eighteenth and early nineteenth centuries. A few twentieth-century historians have attempted to remedy this situation by piecing together fragmentary statistics on conversion during the so-called epidemic era. Abraham Menes attempted this in 1929, because he doubted that Heinrich Graetz could have been correct in claiming that half of the Berlin Jewish community converted in this era. Menes believed that conversion statistics for all of Prussia, based upon parish reports to the government, were available only from 1816; the only source he located for the earlier years was a Jewish petition from 1811 listing the names of forty Berlin families who had lost at least one member to Christianity in the preceding "five to eight" years.[33] Since 405 Jewish families reportedly lived in Berlin in the last decades of the eighteenth century, Menes concluded that a tenth, not a half of the community, had left Judaism in these years.

Since Menes's work, two Israeli historians have labored to document the extent of conversion and analyze the motives of converts in Germany

32. See S. M. Dubnow, *Die neueste Geschichte des jüdischen Volkes* (Berlin, 1920), vol. 1, 197 and 202; Mahler, *A History of Modern Jewry*, 150; Heinz Mosche Graupe, *Die Entstehung des modernen Judentums: Geistesgeschichte der deutschen Juden 1650–1942* (Hamburg, 1969), 155; Arthur Ruppin, *The Jews in the Modern World* (London, 1934; rpt. New York, 1973), 328; N. Samter, *Judentaufen im neunzehnten Jahrhundert* (Berlin, 1906), 4; Adler, *The Jews in Germany*, 24.

33. Abraham Menes, "The Conversion Movement in Prussia during the First Half of the Nineteenth Century," *YVO Annual of Jewish Social Science* 6 (1951), 187. Another scholar skeptical about Graetz's claim that "half" of the Berlin community converted was Eugen Wolbe, *Geschichte der Juden in Berlin und in der Mark Brandenburg*, (Berlin, 1937), 231. Even recent scholars seem to have accepted a version of Graetz's extreme estimate. The author of the "Apostasy" article in the 1972 *Encyclopedia Judaica* article states that in late-eighteenth-century Berlin, "more than half of the descendents of old patrician Jewish families converted" (vol. 3 [Jerusalem, 1971], 206). A copy of the petitions, including the names of the families, can be found in Ismar Freund, *Die Emanzipation der Juden in Preussen*, vol. 2 (Berlin, 1912); discussion of it by Freund can be found in his first volume, 214–19. See also Jacob Toury, *Soziale und politische Geschichte der Juden in Deutschland* (Düsseldorf, 1977), notes 2, 3, and 10 and pages 52 and 54.

in the preindustrial era. Ezriel Schochat's main primary source was a missionary institute in Halle established in 1728, whose reports and other missionary sources he used to estimate that over three hundred Jews converted in Germany between 1700 and 1750. On the basis of this and other evidence, Schochat concluded that in early eighteenth-century Germany conversion was "a country-wide plague." Schochat's radical conclusion has recently been challenged; Benjamin Kedar has criticized Schochat's use of the missionary records and stressed that the extent of conversion in the early eighteenth century can be judged only when a complete series of church records going back to the seventeenth century has been located. In the meantime, Kedar has used a more accessible source, secondary reports of Nazi genealogical research, to reconstruct a set of conversion statistics covering 1640 to 1799. Although these statistics are neither geographically nor chronologically complete, Kedar used them to question Schochat's plague thesis. Kedar also analyzed anecdotal reports of individual conversions, and concluded that there was a definite broadening of converts' motives toward the end of the eighteenth century. This postwar Israeli research represents a large step forward in the historiography, even though neither Schochat nor Kedar was able to use a complete series record for any one city (let alone for several cities) extensive enough to allow for precise measurement of either the extent of conversion or of the changing motives for conversion.[34]

Without the precision provided by a truly complete series record, it has been difficult to judge the accuracy of claims about the social composition of Berlin's eighteenth-century converts gleaned from anecdotal accounts. Even without such evidence, several scholars were sure that there was a change in the social origins of the typical convert in the last decades of the eighteenth century in Germany. It has thus been suggested that converts in the seventeenth and early eighteenth centuries were typically born into the "lower" or the "socially dejected" classes, whereas by the close of the century "rich" and "learned" Jews began to convert as well.[35] Thus the existing historiography suggests that the rising social position of the converts and a presumed increase in the rate of conver-

---

34. See Kedar, "Continuity and Change."
35. Gerhard Kessler, *Judentaufen und judenchristliche Familien in Ostpreussen,* in *Familiengeschichtliche Blatter/Deutsche Herold,* Jahrgang 36 (Leipzig, 1938), 51; Barrie M. Ratcliffe, "Crisis and Identity: Gustave d'Eichthal and Judaism in the Emancipation Period," *Jewish Social Studies* 37 (1975), 122; Katz, *Out of the Ghetto,* 105. Friedrich Schleiermacher's 1799 statement that hitherto converts had been "ruined individuals" who were "close to desperation" lends credence to those who emphasized the prevalence of non-elite converts as late as the last decades of the century. The quotation appears in Alfred D. Low, *Jews in the Eyes of the Germans* (Philadelphia, 1979), 179.

sion both contributed to contemporary alarm about an "ominous" rise in the rate of conversion.

The sex of the converts has also been at issue. The few historians who speculated about the converts' gender concurred that it was in fact mainly women who left the fold in late-eighteenth-century Berlin. But a mainly female cohort of converts in the eighteenth century would contrast sharply with patterns of conversion in the nineteenth and twentieth centuries, when male converts consistently outnumbered female converts.[36] Nor would a largely female cohort of converts fit the motives historians have assigned to converts during the era of emancipation: the desire for political equality or better employment.[37] Neither motive could have led a Jewish woman to turn Christian, since Christian women had neither political rights nor prestigious occupations.

To use the term "wave" to describe the conversions of this era is to imply that the incidence—or at least the proportion—of conversions in Berlin dropped in the subsequent period. But here also evidence has been lacking. Jacob Katz, for instance, claimed that the number of converts decreased after the Prussian edict of emancipation in 1812. Katz reasoned that the motives for conversion weakened once Jews who could meet the property qualifications were able to receive local (Berlin) citizenship and to take advantage of educational and occupational opportunities previously closed to them.[38] Hannah Arendt reached the opposite conclusion;

36. Those historians who pointed to the predominance of female converts include Katz, *Out of the Ghetto*, 122; Ernest-Ludwig Ehrlich, "Emanzipation und christlicher Staat," in Wolf-Dieter Marsch and Karl Thieme, eds., *Christen und Juden: Ihr Gegenüber von Apostelkonzil bis heute* (Mainz, 1961), 147–81, at 155; Max L. Margolis and Alexander Marx, *A History of the Jewish People* (Philadelphia, 1927), 622; N. Samter, *Judentaufen*, 78; Dubnow, *Die neueste Geschichte*, 193; Wolbe, *Geschichte der Juden*, 231. For general discussion of the tendency of Jewish men to marry out more than Jewish women and for the specific rates at which they did so see Uriah Zevi Engelman, "Intermarriage Among Jews in Germany, U.S.S.R., and Switzerland," *Jewish Social Studies* 2 (1940), 165; Leonard J. Fein, "Some Consequences of Jewish Intermarriage," *Jewish Social Studies* 33 (1971), 44–58, at 45; Bernard Lazewitz, "Intermarriage and Conversion: A Guide for Future Research," *Jewish Journal of Sociology* 13 (1971), 41–64, at 42; W. Hanauer, "Die jüdisch-christlichen Mischehen," *Allgemeines Statistisches Archiv* 17 (1928), 519; Marion A. Kaplan, "Tradition and Transition: The Acculturation, Assimilation and Integration of Jews in Imperial Germany: A Gender Analysis," *LBIYB* 27 (1981), 263–300.

37. For example, see Dubnow, *Die neueste Geschichte*, 204, or Ludwig Geiger, "Vor hundert Jahren: Mitteilungen aus der Geschichte der Juden Berlins," *Zeitschrift für die Geschichte der Juden in Deutschland* 3 (1899), 185–233, at 233. One exception to this generalization is Ernest-Ludwig Ehrlich, who was alone in finding a majority of female converts and a female-specific aim for conversion: intermarriage. See Ehrlich's "Emanzipation und christlicher Staat," 154.

38. For a highly unscientific approach see Solomon Liptzin, *Germany's Stepchildren* (New York, 1944), 26. Wolbe, *Geschichte der Juden*, 231, claimed that a high rate of conver-

she suggested that the number of converts in Berlin actually increased after 1812. Arendt thought that the number of conversions in the city before 1806 had in fact been low. The reason, in her view, was that before 1806 Prussia included numerous poor Polish Jews who had become Prussian subjects in the Polish annexations of 1772, 1793, and 1795, and who provided a backdrop against which the Berlin Jews were seen as exotic, exceptional tokens. Wealthy Jews in Berlin could be socially accepted in these years without converting because gentiles saw them as pleasing exceptions when compared to these more primitive eastern Jews. According to Arendt's logic, the Berlin Jews lost this token status when Prussia lost her Polish territories in 1806. The result, in Arendt's entirely speculative prediction, was that in the early nineteenth century Berlin Jews had to convert to gain social acceptance, and more did so after 1812 than in the last decades of the eighteenth century.[39]

The longevity and extent of the discussion about Jewish conversion in Berlin in the late eighteenth and early nineteenth centuries shows how important the problem has become to scholars. But without new sources, the subject of Jewish conversion in Berlin was destined to be one of those tantalizing problems that can never be put to rest.

But the possibility of compiling a rich and complete series record of Jewish conversions does exist after all. Its origin, ironically enough, was in a sinister project undertaken by a regime that sought to remove Judaism and Jewry from the earth. After February 1933, the adoption of the "Aryan clause" by private, public, and Nazi party agencies forced millions of Germans to prove their "Aryan" ancestry at least as far back as their grandparents. The Reichstelle für Sippenforschung ("Agency for Genealogical Research") therefore encouraged and sometimes paid churches in large cities to photograph decrepit parish registers and produce an alphabetical card register for baptisms in order to satisfy the enormous number of requests for genealogical documents.[40] Jewish, Turkish, Gypsy, and "Moorish" converts to Protestantism who were

---

sion continued up until the third decade of the nineteenth century. For Katz's analysis see his *Out of the Ghetto*, 122.

39. Hannah Arendt, *The Origins of Totalitarianism* (New York, 1958), 59.

40. The Reichstelle für Sippenforschung (R.S.F.) was a state office under the administration of the ministry of the interior; it was later called the Reichssippenamt. As was typical in the Third Reich, a party office existed with functions overlapping those of the state office. The party's office for genealogy bureaucracy was called the Amt für Sippenforschung. See Fhr. von Ulmenstein, *Der Abstammungsnachweis* (Berlin, 1938), 12ff. For a useful summary in English of the adoption of the Aryan clause and the "professional" genealogists who profited from the clause's implementation see Karl A. Schleunes, *The Twisted Road to Auschwitz: Nazi Policy toward German Jews, 1933–39* (Urbana, Chicago, and London, 1970), 130.

originally entered into the parish registers alongside "normal" Christian child baptisms were catalogued in a separate file called the "Judenkartei," presumably because the vast majority of converts (or baptized adults) had been Jewish. Since Nazi doctrine defined Jews racially and not religiously, converts out of Judaism needed to be identified as such. The contents of such files could eventually determine life or death. By the terms of the Nuremberg Laws of 1935, not only the number of grandparents born Jewish but the age at which any one of them may have converted out of Judaism dictated whether the grandchild was classified as Aryan or non-Aryan.[41]

In order to locate converts whose descendants lived in Berlin but who themselves had not converted in Berlin, the church officials decided to compile a second card index for mixed marriages. More correctly stated, this was a file of marriages between converted Jews and Christians, since before 1846 there was no civil marriage in Prussia. While the conversion series covers almost three centuries, from 1645 through 1933, the intermarriage series runs only from 1800 to 1846.[42] The information contained on each of the approximately 10,000 cards (in both the conversion and the intermarriage series) is extensive, including the name, age, sex, and father's occupation of each convert. Moreover, it seems reasonable to conclude that distortion in the data is small, and more importantly, random. Since the clerks who labored at the project had to prove their political loyalty, there is little reason to believe that removal of cards to protect descendants of converts could have resulted in underrepresentation of the real number of converts.[43]

According to statistics derived from analysis of the "Judenkartei," contemporaries who believed there was a rapid rise in the number of converts in the last decades of the eighteenth century were correct. Between

41. The tendency for a local church to produce a "Judenkartei" seems to have varied with the size of the city and the consequent difficulties which ensued when trying to locate genealogical information which was classified by parish and not in alphabetical order. For a discussion of how the data of a grandparent's conversion could affect the racial status of the grandchild see von Ulmenstein, *Der Abstammungsnachweis,* 33.

42. The conversion and intermarriage cards are in the Evangelisches Zentralarchiv (Protestant Church Archive) in West Berlin.

43. Officials directing this genealogy bureaucracy seem to have been extremely concerned with the removal of cards to protect the descendents of converts. An advertisement for the files used stressed how the cards are "zuverlässig aufbewahrt" ("dependably deposited") in this particular file: the advertisement is in file 577 of the Reichssippenamt files (R39) in the Bundesarchiv in Koblenz, West Germany. Dr. Kurt Mayer, director of the R.S.F., described his firing of a Herr Fahrenhorst for falsifying records in his "Begründung" document of March 18, 1935, file 2, R39, Bundesarchiv. A case of "mass" falsification by a "band" in Hungary in 1938 is summarized in a clipping of July 2, 1938 from *Angriff am Abend,* file 567, R39, Bundesarchiv.

1700 and 1767, a total of 153 Jews left Judaism in Berlin. As figure 12 shows, during the first two-thirds of the century the number of Jewish baptisms was steady and small. On the average, only three Jews converted each year. Beginning in 1768, however, the number of baptisms began to climb. In the last third of the century the average number converting each year jumped to eight. Between 1770 and 1779 the number of conversions was 18 percent larger that it had been between 1760 and 1769. The group that converted in the 1780s was, in turn, almost twice as large (by 93 percent) as the cohort of the 1770s. And in the last decade of the century, the number of converts grew by another 56 percent.

This series of rather sharp increases in the number of conversions during the last three decades of the eighteenth century was not followed, however, by a drop sharp enough to justify applying the term "wave" to the eighteenth-century conversions. Figure 12 shows that the rate of conversion during the first third of the nineteenth century continued upward, despite sporadic declines. Whether or not the reasons for her prediction were correct or not, Arendt was right and Katz was wrong about the increase in conversions in the early nineteenth century. The late-eighteenth-century curve looks more like the foothills than the peak of a mountain. The steady increase in conversion in the early nineteenth century is still evident even after examining the relative rather than the absolute growth in the proportion of Jews who converted. Figure 13 factors

Figure 12. Conversions in Berlin, 1700–1850

Source: "Judenkartei" (EZA, West Berlin).

Figure 13. Jewish Converts in Berlin per 3,000 Jewish Residents of Berlin, 1750–1850

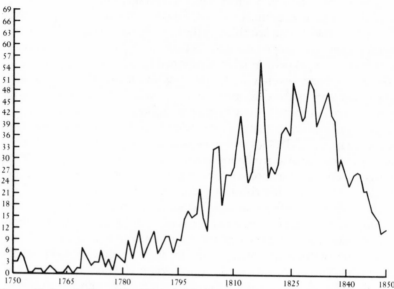

Sources: Herbert Seeliger, "The Origin and Growth of the Berlin Jewish Community, *LBIYB* 3 (1958), 159–68 (Jewish population of Berlin); "Judenkartei" (EZA, West Berlin).

out the effect of the changing Jewish population of Berlin by showing the number of converts per 3,000 Jews living in Berlin. (The Jewish population in Berlin was quite stable between 1770 and 1817, hovering around 3,300.)[44] Thus the curve displayed in figure 13 only begins to slope downward in the third and fourth decades of the nineteenth century, when the Jewish population of the city increased sharply.

But there is reason to doubt that the Jewish population of Berlin alone is in fact the correct denominator to use when calculating the changing proportion of Jews who chose baptism. Authors of contemporary novels and autobiographies as well as historians have stressed that Jews from smaller German towns sometimes came to Berlin in order to be baptized.[45] Unfortunately, it is not known whether such immigrant converts

44. My source for the changing Jewish population of Berlin is Herbert Seelinger, "Origin and Growth of the Berlin Jewish Community," *LBIYB* 3 (1958), 159–69.

45. See anon., *Charlotte Sampson oder Geschichte eines jüdischen Hausvaters, der mit seiner Familie dem Glauben Seiner Väter entsagte,* (Berlin, 1800), the story of a young Jewish woman who leaves Berlin to convert and intermarry, but runs into difficulties at the village church. Another, real-life tale of this sort can be found in *Salomon Maimon: An Autobiog-*

tended to become Berlin residents before or after their baptism. The geographical designation that appears on some cards is no help at all with this problem, since it is not clear whether the noted location was the convert's place of birth or his or her current residence. Still, in spite of the lack of direct evidence, there are good reasons to believe that before 1812 the number of converts who came to Berlin in order to convert could not have been very large. Before Prussian Jewry was granted freedom of residency in 1812, the government's high wealth requirement for settlement in Berlin made it difficult for any except extremely wealthy Jews to obtain permission to live in Berlin. One might argue that the wealth requirement may not have applied to Jews who entered Berlin solely to convert, and who left the city immediately. But such an arrangement would necessitate that such would-be converts would have to confess their real intentions to the Jewish elders who aided in monitoring entrance to the city. Thus the conjecture that the wealth requirement would not apply to temporary immigrant converts seems ultimately implausible. Moreover, unlike Vienna, the number of Jews living illegally in Berlin in this period was not large.[46] Thus for a variety of reasons it may be assumed that the group of Jews at risk to convert was not significantly greater than the number of Jews registered as living in Berlin. To be sure, a few clever individuals might have succeeded in entering Berlin just in order to change their faith, making the group at risk to convert somewhat larger than the legally permitted Jewish population of Berlin. The consequence would be that by understating the number at risk to convert, using the recorded Jewish population of Berlin as the denominator may result in slightly overestimating the proportion who did convert.

Unfortunately, questions about the adequacy of the denominator of Jews at risk to convert do not end here. For using the annual population figures as the denominator is still not precise enough to ascertain the exact proportion of Berlin Jewry that converted during any particular cluster of years. Even if there were no Berlin converts who maintained a residence outside the city at all, the recorded Jewish population of Berlin is in fact still not the total number of Jews who were at risk to convert during any specific period. In order to learn this far larger number, it is necessary to know how many persons were alive for how long during this period, not merely the number who were there at its beginning and

raphy, ed. Moses Hadas (New York, 1967), chap. 21. Another real-life conversion in a small town succeeded; see Julius Fürst, ed., *Henriette Herz,* 55, 58, and 65.

46. On the proportion of Jews without a *Schutzbrief* ("letter of protection") who managed to live in Vienna in this period see Hans Tietze, *Die Juden Wiens* (Leipzig, 1933), 127, and Hans Jäger-Sunstenau, "Die geadelten Judenfamilien im vormärzlichen Wien," Ph.D. diss., Vienna, 1950, 63.

at its end.[47] To calculate this "person-years" figure, birth, migration, and age-specific death rates for the Jewish community would be required. Unfortunately, none of these numbers are now known, nor can they easily be reconstructed.[48] Since the mean Jewish population of Berlin between 1770 and 1799 was 3,535, all that can safely be concluded for now is that the 249 who converted during these three decades were at maximum 7 percent of those at risk to convert during these years. Since, no doubt, many more than 3,535 Jewish persons were at risk to convert in Berlin during some part of these thirty years, the real denominator was much larger, and thus the real proportion converting was surely far smaller than 7 percent.

There are fewer statistical problems when looking inside the convert population at the age, gender, and social composition of the 249 converts. Almost two-thirds of the converts were children five years old or younger. Most of the rest of the converts were in their twenties. For although converts between twenty and twenty-nine were only a fifth of all 249 converts, this twenties cohort constituted three-quarters of all of the adult converts (fig. 14). As for the gender of the converts, historians who speculated that they were predominately female were indeed correct. Sixty percent of the converts of all ages were women. As figure 15 shows, the preponderance of female converts in these three decades contrasts sharply with the gender ration of the preceding and subsequent decades. During the first two-thirds of the eighteenth century, male and females converted in roughly equal proportions. Yet from 1770 to 1804 more women than men converted in almost every year. A comparison of the aggregate sex ratios of the emancipation era with later periods highlights the uniqueness of the female predominance in the 1770–1804 period. In these three decades women were 60 percent of all Jewish converts, whereas in the next half century the proportion of women converting dropped to 43 percent.

The gender of the adult converts very definitely varied with their age. Child and adolescent converts, on the other hand, were equally divided

47. The tendency to think of the conversion rate solely in reference to the recorded population can be seen in the stimulating unpublished manuscript by Ivar Oxal, "The Jews of Pre-1914 Vienna: Two Working Papers," Dept. of Sociology and Social Anthropology, The University of Hull, England, 95–97. I am grateful to Monika Richarz for bringing this work to my attention, and to the late Allan Sharlin for clarifying the problem of the denominator.

48. The Jewish community's birth records (in German using Hebrew script) are a part of the Jacob Jacobson Collection (AR 7002) in the archive of the Leo Baeck Institute in New York City. It is not yet known whether death and migration information is also contained in these files. Linking families by use of common surnames will be difficult, since the practice of taking on surnames was new then and most irregular.

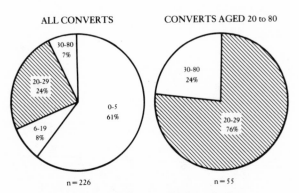

Figure 14. Age of Converts in Berlin, 1770–99

ALL CONVERTS

CONVERTS AGED 20 to 80

30-80
7%

20-29
24%

0-5
61%

6-19
8%

30-80
24%

20-29
76%

n = 226

n = 55

Source: "Judenkartei" (EZA, West Berlin).

between male and female, and this had a certain logic. The younger converts could not have had gender-specific motives for converting, since they probably did not have any motives at all. Their decisions to convert were made for them, most likely by their parents. Although one might speculate that parents might tend to convert boys rather than girls, in order to enhance boys' occupational opportunities, this group of child converts had as many girls as boys. But in contrast to the equal gender ratio among the child converts, adult men and women tended to convert at quite different ages, as shown in figure 16. Almost 80 percent of the converts in their twenties were women. But this proportion was reversed among the older converts. A mere 20 percent of the converts over thirty were women.

Age and gender are exceedingly straightforward variables which are available for almost all 249 converts and require no sophisticated classificatory decisions. This is by no means the case with the converts' social positions. To begin with, only slightly more than half (134) of their fathers' occupations were noted on the cards. And even where the occupation is known, raw occupational titles alone tell little about the social composition of the converts, without a way to classify occupations into social strata. This is not because of a paucity of research about the economic life of Berlin Jewry in this era. But none of these economic histories are detailed enough to provide a classificatory schema which could be used to sort the converts' fathers' occupations and to compare them to the occupations of the unconverted. In lieu of such assistance, I have constructed a three-tiered division of the fathers' occupations. I included large-scale merchants (*Kaufmänner*), entrepreneurs, bankers, and profes-

Figure 15. Male and Female Jewish Converts in Berlin, 1750–1850

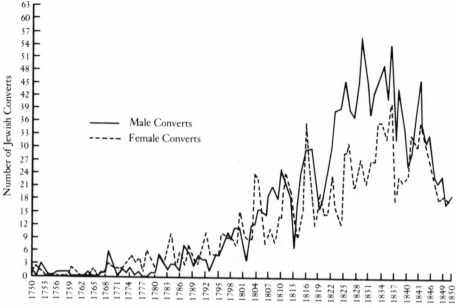

Source: "Judenkartei" (EZA, West Berlin).

sionals in the upper-income group; clerks, small-scale traders (*Handels-männer*), brokers, peddlers, shopkeepers, and master artisans in the middle-income group; and beggars, servants, day laborers, and apprentice artisans in the lower-income group.[49]

Forty percent of the converts' fathers had upper-income occupations, another 40 percent had middle-income positions, and the remaining 20 percent of the fathers were in the lower-income group. The large number of upper-income converts means that the social composition of the convert group was roughly representative of Berlin's Jewish community at large. The term *upper-income group,* to be sure, is imprecise; current

49. The most detailed occupational division of the Jewish community can be found in Stefi Jersch-Wenzel, *Juden und 'Franzosen' in der Wirtschaft des Raumes Berlin/Brandenburg* (Berlin, 1978), table D, 260. Jersch-Wenzel's source for her useful tables is Jacobson's published marriage lists [*Jüdische Trauungen in Berlin 1723–1859* (Berlin, 1968)]. Since marriage was so restricted by the state, use of his work may have led to a distortion in favor of the rich in Jersch-Wenzel's tables. A more severe problem in adapting this profile for my purpose here is that since it clumps persons into *Handel* (trade) and *Gewerbe* (industry), it cannot be easily used to establish a social hierarchy of rich and poor.

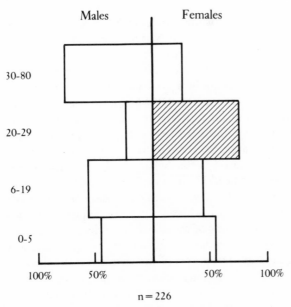

Figure 16. Age by Gender of Converts in Berlin, 1770–99

n = 226

Source: "Judenkartei" (EZA, West Berlin).

knowledge of the community's social structure consists only of aggregate estimates. Estimates of the proportion of the Jewish community that was "rich" or "wealthy" range from a maximum of two-thirds down to a minimum of 40 percent.[50] Either estimate, it should be remembered, means that Berlin Jewry had a vastly greater proportion of wealthy persons than any other Jewish community within Germany or Europe at the time. The similarity between the size of the upper income group among the converted and the unconverted seems to confirm historians' suggestions that the social position of converts was rising over time. Indeed, figure 17 shows that the convert population's social composition had not always matched that of the community at large. Rather, the proportion of converts whose fathers had upper income positions began to equal

50. For some comparative occupational classifications of two other European Jewish communities during the nineteenth century, see Paula Hyman, "Jewish Fertility in Nineteenth-Century France," 78–93, at 87 and 92, and Steven M. Lowenstein, "Voluntary and Involuntary Limitation of Fertility in Nineteenth Century Bavarian Jewry," 94–111, at 104–105, both articles are in Paul Ritterband, ed., *Modern Jewish Fertility*, vol. 1 of *Studies of Judaism in Modern Times*, ed. Jacob Neusner (Leiden, 1981).

that of the community as a whole only beginning in the 1780s, when the proportion of upper-income converts began to increase considerably.

Did the social origin of the converts tend to make much difference in the age at which they converted? Not for upper- or middle-income converts, whose age structure closely resembled that of the converts as a whole. But the lower-income converts were, in contrast, almost all children under five. What about a systematic variation between the social origin and the sex of the converts? At first glance the answer would have to be no. All three income groups among the converts had about two-fifths males and three-fifths females, precisely the same sex ratio as that of the converts at large. Yet there is good reason not to be satisfied with this answer. That reason is that whatever the advantages of the three-income group stratification of occupations used here, this particular schema obscures another useful kind of division among Jewish occupations, namely the distinction between those employed in merchant occupations at various levels of the social hierarchy and those employed in artisan occupations. Divided in this fashion, some differences between the sexes do emerge. Daughters of merchants converted more often (63 percent) than did the daughters of artisans (47 percent). As we shall see shortly, there was a strong correlation between the female rate of conversion and the female rate of intermarriage. Access to the mercantile sector

Figure 17. Social Origin of Converts by Decade

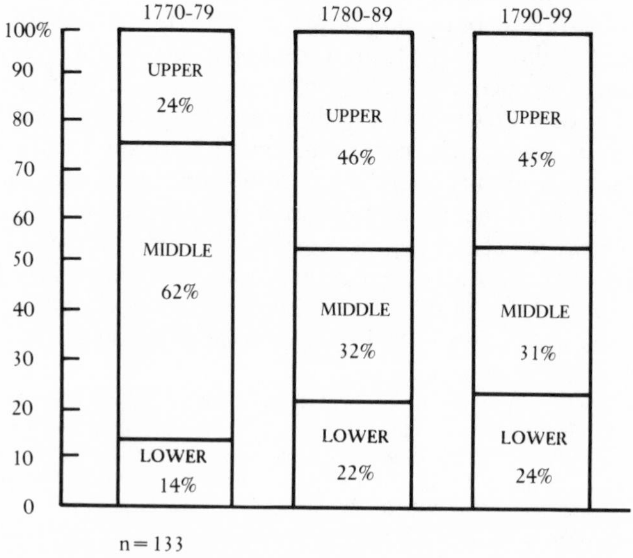

n = 133

Source: "Judenkartei" (EZA, West Berlin).

as well as wealth itself may well have been a motive for gentile grooms marrying converted Jewish brides, and thus daughters of men employed in the merchant sectors may have had special incentives to convert in order to intermarry.

Before moving on to inspect the intermarriage records, it is appropriate to pause and look backward once more at the conversion pattern. Child conversion was consistently high throughout the thirty years. More females than males converted. Adult converts were mostly females in their twenties. Although the total exodus from the community in these years clearly did not exceed 5 percent, the kinds of persons who departed were a significant loss in terms of the community's demographic future and morale. The high numbers of female converts in their twenties undoubtedly made it difficult for Jewish men to find local Jewish wives. Now it might be argued that since wealthy Jewish families often found appropriate spouses for their children from outside Berlin, the conversion of wealthy Berlin women may not have been such a serious loss. On the other hand, it must also be remembered that daughters who would inherit the right of residence (Schutzbrief) were in great demand, since their husbands could then rely on their wives' "protection" to remain in the city. It was highly desirable for local families to marry a son off to a bride with a Schutzbrief, since it was so difficult for even the wealthiest families to obtain residency permits for all of their sons. Thus the claim still seems to hold that the loss of Jewish women was significant for the demographic future of the Berlin community. Moreover, the loss of the daughters was not merely demographic. The home and the family are central to Jewish life, and Jewish women have in many times and places played the chief role in nurturing their religious communities.[51] The wealth of the converts was as salient as their tendency to be females. The conversion of wealthy members of the community, especially of wealthy men, meant a loss of real and potential political leadership. The richest families in the city had long provided the community with its intermediaries with the Prussian state. The departure of the wealthy also suggests that more and more Jews who may not have had pressing material reasons to convert were finding their Jewishness hard to live with psychologically and socially, and thus developed what might be called a "negative Jewish identity." But proving that this partic-

51. For some comparative perspectives see Elizabeth Koltun, ed., *The Jewish Woman: New Perspectives* (New York, 1976), and Charlotte Baum, Paula Hyman, and Sonya Michel, eds., *The Jewish Woman in America* (New York, 1975), chap. 2. Marion Kaplan, in *The Jewish Feminist Movement in Germany* (Westport, Conn., 1979), chap. 1, argues that early-twentieth-century Jewish women in Germany tended to stay more loyal to family and faith than did many Jewish men.

ular cohort of obscure individuals converted because they had such a negative Jewish identity is quite difficult.[52]

Ironically enough, statistics may provide a surer guide to this group of converts' motives than subjective testimonies, which are sparse in any case. Our reconstruction of the gender, age, and social composition of the converts has helped somewhat in pinpointing motives, largely by eliminating motives which could only have been held by a certain kind of person. Thanks to the intermarriage records, it is possible to pursue the critical question of the motives for a conversion a bit further. The great value of the intermarriage records is that they allow us to draw parallels between those who converted and those who went on to marry gentiles. It thereby becomes possible to explore a very major question, namely, whether the upper-income merchant daughters who converted in their twenties did so in order to intermarry.

The conversion records show that the female predominance over male converts which began in the late eighteenth century reversed itself by the third decade of the nineteenth century. As figure 18 demonstrates, the intermarriage records (which only begin in 1800) also show female predominance during the first decade of the nineteenth century. And, as with conversions, the male intermarriage line climbed above the female line during the second decade of the century. Moreover, the extent of the female preponderance among the converts and and those intermarrying was almost identical. Between 1800 and 1809, converted Jewish females were 69 percent of those who intermarried, whereas between 1811 and 1846 they were only 41 percent.

Beyond the basic fact that more women than men married out, a comparison of the social origin of converted Jewish men and women who married gentiles in the first decade of the nineteenth century shows that they were born on different ranks of the social hierarchy and moved in different directions when they married out. Three-quarters of the (converted) Jewish grooms were from upper-income families, but their gentile brides were almost all from middle-income families. In other words, converted Jewish men tended to be born high, but married down socially when they married out religiously. The larger group of (converted) Jewish brides, on the other hand, came twice as frequently from middle-

---

52. There is a useful discussion of this problem in Kedar, "Continuity and Change." Two primary sources used here were J. C. Leberecht, *Authentic Narrative of the Life and Conversion of J. C. Leberecht, A Jew, Who died in the Faith of the Son of God November 13, 1776 at Königsberg in Prussia* (London, 1920), and Johann Felix Schimerle, *Sendschreiben eines Proselyten, Johann Felix* (Oehringen, 1760). For these and for other references I am endebted to Todd Endelman for providing me with a copy of the extensive bibliography he prepared on conversion.

Figure 18. Converted Jewish Outmarriers, 1800–46

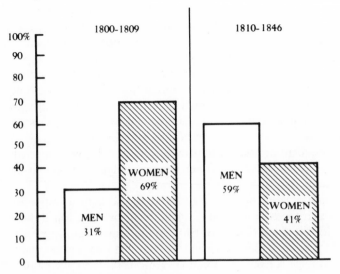

Source: "Judenkartei" (EZA, West Berlin).

income families and far less often from upper-income families. (Lower-income Jews were poorly represented among either the brides or the grooms.) Although the brides were less lucky than the converted grooms in their families of birth, they had better luck on the intermarriage market. Roughly half of the brides married down socially, but the other half made horizontal social matches. The Jewish brides' gentile grooms tended to be closer to them in age as well as in social position than the outmarrying men were to their gentile mates. The brides' own mean age was twenty-eight, and the mean age of their gentile grooms was thirty-one. The Jewish men who married out, in contrast, were, on average, fifteen years older than their gentile brides. Their own mean age was thirty-eight, and their brides' mean age was twenty-seven. Since closeness in age may well have been associated with companionate (rather than socially opportunistic) marriages, this pattern suggests that the converted women's intermarriages tended to be more companionate than those of the converted men.

Comparing the gender, social position, and ages of those who converted and those who intermarried shows that the female proportion of both groups was similar, and that the reversal in this sex ratio occurred in both groups at roughly the same time. Comparison of the converted men and women who married out shows that the women tended to marry up socially when they married out, and that they were closer in age to their gentile grooms than the Jewish men were to their gentile brides. The parallels between the proportion of both groups which was female, the timing of the switch in gender ratios, and the luck that many Jewish women had in marrying gentile men of good social position all suggest that the women's intermarriage prospects were good enough to stimulate what might be called "anticipatory" conversion. Since intermarriage, rather than educational or professional opportunity, was likely to be the way a converted woman made actual the higher status made possible by conversion, preparation for possible intermarriage may have been a frequent motive for female conversion. This was especially telling in an age where there was no civil marriage between unconverted Jews and Christians.

Comparing the intermarriage series to the conversion series in the years when the two series are compatible provides a fourth kind of evidence for the claim that conversion and intermarriage were more closely linked for women than they were for men. Figure 19 shows that for every hundred male converts between 1800 and 1846, there were only thirteen men who married out. The female conversion/outmarriage ratio was three times as high, since for every hundred female converts there were thirty-nine women who married out. In other words, converted men were less likely to intermarry than converted women. Most likely, this was because employment, rather than the possibility of intermarriage, was what prompted men to convert. This does indeed suggest that although evidence is lacking for the eighteenth century, conversion and intermarriage in Berlin were more closely associated for Jewish women than for Jewish men in the first half of the nineteenth century.

Conversion was, of course, no guarantee that this penultimate act of acculturation would lead to authentic social ties with gentiles. After all, converted families in nineteenth-century central Europe often socialized and married into other converted families, having as few contacts with authentic gentiles as did unconverted Jews.[53] Intermarriage was a much more dramatic stage than conversion was in the process of social integration. That is why it is important to measure how high the incidence of intermarriage was in this first major chapter of the assimilation story. Due to the labors of Jacob Jacobson, Berlin Jewry's archivist until 1942, it is possible to answer this question. The Nazi intermarriage records show that fifty-five converted Jews married gentiles in Berlin between 1800 and 1809. Jacobson's published list of Jewish marriages in Berlin

53. See Marsha Rozenblitt, *The Jews of Vienna, 1867–1914: Assimilation and Identity* (Albany, 1983), chap. 6.

Figure 19. Female and Male Conversion and Intermarriage in Berlin, 1800–46

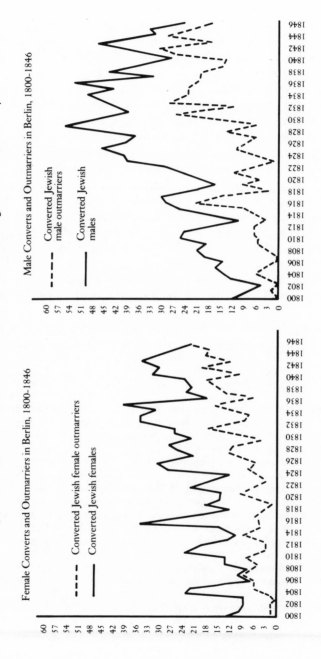

shows that there were 175 marriages between unconverted Jews in Berlin during the same decade.[54] Unfortunately, the mere possession of these two numbers does not provide a simple rate of intermarriage. For there are three rather different ways to calculate the rate of intermarriage, which makes generalization extremely tricky. Using one method, the fifty-five individuals who intermarried were 14 percent of the 405 individual Jews who married at all in this decade. Using a second method, comparing the intermarriages with the 230 marriages in which a Jew was involved, 24 percent of the marriages were intermarriages. Using a third method, the ratio of mixed (55) to endogamous marriages (175) was 31 to 100. Most published intermarriage statistics use the third denominator (Jewish-Jewish marriages), although the second denominator, all marriages involving a Jew, is also used. But the point here is that on either measure, the 1800–09 Berlin rate was phenomenally high. This was a threat to the community of far greater dimensions than the conversion rate. The intermarriage rate was twice the rate of intermarriage in the United States before 1840. It was also twice as high as the intermarriage rate in Germany a full century later, in 1901. The Berlin intermarriage rate for 1800–09 was only 13 percent smaller than the intermarriage rate in Germany in 1933.[55] To be sure, these comparisons are suggestive rather than conclusive. More research is needed to measure the effect of the changing proportion of Berlin Jews who married at all. The state's pre-1812 restrictions on how many and which Jews could marry may well have

54. Jacobson was the director of the Gesamtarchiv der deutschen Juden until 1942. Jacobson's personal and scholarly papers are at the archive of the Leo Baeck Institute (AR 7002), New York City. Reference to reimbursement made to Jacobson by the "Reichssippenamt" for archival work is mentioned in a letter by Dr. Mayer of October 17, 1939, R. 39, file 39, Bundesarchiv. Jacobson's edition of primary marriage records is *Jüdische Trauungen in Berlin, 1723–1859* (Berlin, 1968).

55. For a more detailed description of this problem and a formula for transforming one rate into another rate see Hyman Rodman, "A Technical Note on Two Rates of Mixed Marriage," *American Sociological Review* 30 (1965), 776–78. For further technical discussion of intermarriage computations see C. A. Price and J. Zubrzycki, "The Use of Intermarriage Statistics as an Index of Assimilation," *Population Studies* 16 (1962), 58–69. Statistics using as the denominator the number of endogamous Jewish marriages (for which the Berlin rate in 1800–39 was 31 percent) include Germany, 1933, 44 percent: in I. Gordon, *Intermarriage: Interfaith, Interracial, Interethnic* (Boston, 1964), 179, and Germany, 1901, 16.9 percent: in Uriah Zevi Engelman, "Intermarriage Among Jews in Germany, U.S.S.R., and Switzerland," *Jewish Social Studies* 2 (1940), 157. Statistics using the total number of marriages in which a Jew participated (the Berlin rate being 24 percent) include the United States, mid-eighteenth-century: 10 percent, the United States, pre-1840: 16 percent; see Gordon, 179. No comparative statistics using as the denominator all individual Jews who married have been found. (In all these comparisons I equate converted Jews with Jews, since no civil marriage was possible in Berlin at this time.) Some sources use as the denominator all Jews: see Hanauer, "Die jüdisch-christlichen Mischehen," 518.

made the denominator unusually small and therefore the intermarrying proportion during these years artificially large.[56]

Why Did Women Leave the Faith?

The romances between young men and women of different faiths that ended at the altar in Berlin were notorious at the time. These misalliances agitated the memoir, novel, and pamphlet writers of the day, who were angry, delighted, or merely amused that such things could come to pass. Comparisons with subsequent intermarriage patterns suggest that outside as well as inside of salon society, the rate at which these romances ended in intermarriage was unusually high. Both contemporary alarm and statistical comparisons raise two burning questions. Why was intermarriage so frequent in Berlin in these years? And why did more Jewish women than men convert and marry out?

Before answering these questions, it needs to be clarified whether the female predominance among those leaving Judaism in Berlin in these years was not in truth a mere statistical artifact. The same state regulations on Jewish settlement and marriage that distorted the social and age structure of the community could well have also distorted the community's sex ratio in an age-specific way. If there were more Jewish women than men in Berlin in the age groups at which Jews converted, this alone might explain the high female rates of conversion and intermarriage. The post-1815 drop in the female rates of conversion and intermarriage might then represent nothing more than a return to a normal sex ratio among the age groups from which converts and and those marrying out came. Unfortunately, the data necessary to settle this issue are absent. Although the community's birth records have survived, they have not been reconstructed into family units. More importantly, there are no records of the age and gender of those who were forced to leave Berlin in these years because of residence and marriage restrictions.

Although we may never know how the state's restrictions on which children of which families could settle and marry may have affected the community's underlying sex ratio, it is clear how these restrictions determined the social and age composition of the converts.[57] The difficulty of obtaining permission to settle or marry in Berlin gave to poor Jews

56. Jacob Jacobson observed that the numerous conversions and intermarriages of this era were a result of the state's limitation on Jewish marriages, in his *Die Judenbürgerbücher der Stadt Berlin 1800–1851*, (Berlin, 1962), xxxiii.

57. A useful account of these regulations can be found in Selma Stern, *Der preussische Staat und die Juden: Dritter Teil: Die Zeit Friedrichs des Grossen*, Erste Abteilung (Tübingen, 1971), chap. five.

whose residence in Berlin was either illegal or tenuously legal an incentive to gain exemption from the regulations by ceasing to be Jews. This motive for conversion was especially strong among young female domestic servants who worked for the city's richest families. Sometimes pregnant and often without husbands, they changed their faith to remove obstacles to their continued residence in the city. Their illegitimate children were often given over to orphanages. And if it was indeed mainly servants' children who filled the ranks of the child converts, two mysteries about the converts would be partially clarified. First, the servants' children's conversions would account for the lower-income origins of most of the child converts. Second, the servants' own conversions would account in part for the predominance of females in their twenties among the adult converts. If their seducers were not Jewish, and if they went on to marry their seducers, these female servant converts may well have contributed to the high female intermarriage rate as well.[58]

The servant converts were similar to most converts in the German-Jewish past, insofar as their conversion was caused in some way by their poverty. But the conversion records show that poor women were not the only Jewish women to leave their faith in these years. Why were wealthy young women also so ready to convert, and so lucky on the intermarriage market? To answer this question, it is necessary to shift attention away from the anonymous converts and back to the twenty salon women. Unfortunately, the salon women have an oblique relationship to the women on the conversion and intermarriage cards; none of the salon women who converted or intermarried did so in Berlin in the specific years analyzed here, and so do not show up on the cards. However, in spite of this documentary gulf between the two groups, since we know more about the lives of the salon women than we do about the anonymous converts, returning to the salon women can illuminate the motives of their more obscure contemporaries.

Of the twenty salon women, at least seventeen converted, and ten married gentiles. Why? Although their formal Jewish educations tended to be deficient, so too was the Jewish education of most men from similar families in their generation. And although many salon women managed to master secular languages and disciplines, either with their fathers' help or on their own, so too did many men of their generation. What was distinctive about the salon women's acculturation was not their early

58. This finding is consistent with Jacob Jacobson's claim that the high number of children converted were the "key" to understanding the conversion "movement" of the period: *Die Judenbürgerbücher*, xxxiii. For a summary in English of this volume see Jacobson's "Some Observations on the Jewish Citizens' Books of the City of Berlin," *LBIYB* 1 (1955), 317–31.

education, but rather the social opportunities that became open to them in the 1780s and 1790s. The theater, salons, and reading, discussion, and friendship societies where they made friends with prominent gentile men provided them with a new social universe, a universe which was closed to most Jewish men. It was these social experiences in their years as young adults that gave them both the incentive to master secular skills and the chance to polish them. But their new social universe also provoked conflict and turmoil in the salon women's lives, because by the time they met gentile men, most of them were already married to Jewish businessmen. They had had little choice in the matter; the wealth and small size of the community and the state's marriage regulations all contributed to the practice of arranged marriages at an early age. Thus if the exogamous love affairs that blossomed in salons were to come to pass, first divorce from the Jewish husband and then conversion were necessary. Often the gentile groom was cash-poor, if status-rich. Since the brides were either wealthy themselves or had access to wealth, there was a definite economic logic to these intermarriages.

It is therefore clear how for salon women the prospect of intermarriage encouraged conversion. Because it has not been possible to link individuals from the conversion cards to those on the intermarriage cards, it is difficult to determine whether the same close association between conversion and intermarriage was true for women on both sets of cards. Nor do we know how closely the social lives of the women on the cards resembled those of the salon women. Still, the parallels between the salon women and the anonymous women on the cards are suggestive. Women in both groups tended to convert in their twenties. And women in both groups tended to marry up or across socially when they married out.

But as we already glimpsed earlier, intermarriage was not the only incentive for women to convert. The intellectual climate both inside and outside of acculturated Jewish circles also encouraged conversion. Actually, this same intellectual climate may have influenced the decisions of Jewish men even more strongly than it did the decisions of Jewish women. Berlin's particular intellectual climate in these years thus helps to explain why wealthy men converted, even though they did not seem to have had either material or romantic incentives to do so. Deism was the first ideology which favored conversion. Earlier, in mid-century, enlightened intellectuals in Prussia had been more theistic than deistic. But toward the end of the century the notion that Judaism and Christianity shared a common set of core assumptions gained ground among Prussian thinkers. There were those who went so far as to hope and plan for the day when the two religions would cease to be separate institutional entities. Just how optimistic Jewish intellectuals had become about this common future was dramatically revealed in an anonymous pamphlet published in 1799 in Berlin. It was an open secret around town that the real author was David Friedländer, friend of Moses Mendelssohn, wealthy silk manufacturer, and a prominent leader in the Jewish community. In this pamphlet Friedländer proposed to Wilhelm Teller, a leading liberal Protestant minister in Berlin, that the heads of "leading families" of the Jewish community convert en masse to a rationalized form of Christianity. With "dry baptism," Jewish men, at least, would gain the political rights still denied them as Jews, without hypocritically endorsing the non-rational elements of Christianity. Teller unequivocally rejected Friedländer's proposal, declaring it absurd that Friedländer should think that the less rational dimensions of the Christian faith could be separated from what Friedländer, at least, identified as its deistic core. Teller advised Friedländer to give up hope of using "dry baptism" as a shortcut to political emancipation and urged him to work for religious reform within his own faith.[59]

Teller's rejection of Friedländer's proposal suggests that Jewish intellectuals were more optimistic than Christian intellectuals about how soon Judaism and Christianity would cease to be separate religions. Still, the very fact that Friedländer would publicly—if anonymously—propose "dry baptism" was significant in two ways. First, his proposal shows that a prominent Jew could expect a prominent Christian to find "dry baptism" a plausible notion, if not necessarily a desirable one. Second, Friedländer's proposal shows that in these years a prominent Jewish leader took leaving Judaism more seriously than reforming it. In the ensuing decades the reform tendency within Judaism would gain strength, both intellectually and institutionally. One of reform Judaism's attractions was the failure of attempts like Friedländer's to find a third path between traditional Judaism and traditional Christianity. In this way the absence of a reform alternative within Judaism was an internal incentive to convert, just as the fragile deism of Christian intellectuals was an external incentive to convert.

Insofar as the men were obviously socialized to take intellectual mat-

59. The publication appeared anonymously with the title *Sendschreiben an Hochwürden Herrn Oberconsistorialrat und Probst Teller zu Berlin von einigen Hausvätern jüdischer Religion* (Berlin, 1799). Whether there actually were other authors or not and if so, who they were, has not come to light. Although many knew of Friedländer's authorship at the time, he did not publicly admit it until 1819. For discussion see Ellen Littmann, "David Friedländers Sendschreiben an Probst Teller und sein Echo," *Zeitschrift für die Geschichte der Juden in Deutschland* 6 (1935), 92–112, and Immanuel Heinrich Ritter, *Geschichte der jüdischen Reformation*, Zweiter Teil: *David Friedländer, sein Leben und sein Wirken* (Berlin, 1861).

ters more seriously than the women were, both deism and the absence of a reform alternative were more likely influences on men's decisions to convert than they were on women's decisions. Yet at the same time both of these incentives to convert affected women in a particular way. A contemporary novel, *Charlotte Sampson,* described the impact of Friedländer's proposal within the Jewish community. The story begins with a group of Jewish elders waiting in suspense for the minister's response to the proposal. When the news comes that the proposal has been rejected, one of the elder's daughters promptly runs off to a small village to convert and then proceeds to marry her gentile lover. *Charlotte Sampson* suggests that "dry" baptism was seen not only as a way to make "wet" baptism unnecessary for Jewish men in search of political or occupational advancement, but also as a potentially painless solution for Jewish women on the road to intermarriage.[60]

The external intellectual incentives to convert also affected women in a particular way. By the first years of the nineteenth century, the extreme rationalism and deism of the late Enlightenment came under attack by a new generation of young intellectuals. Indeed, it was in the salons that the early romantics formulated and elaborated their critique of the mature rationalist Enlightenment. Eventually, the romantic movement would turn quite antisemitic, as it became more mystical, nationalistic, and conservative. But in its early years the romantics provided an incentive to convert that was as strong as that provided by the enlightened deism of an older generation. And the incentive to convert provided by the romantics was an especially potent lure for Jewish women. As we have learned, several romantic intellectuals became personal friends of the Jewish salon women. These men, especially Friedrich Schleiermacher, argued that conversion offered Jewish women a way to achieve personal and intellectual emancipation. (Whether the anonymous women on the cards had similar interpersonal experiences must remain a mystery for now.) The romantics' enthusiasm for the exotic and the foreign was also an incentive for Jewish women to convert, insofar as romanticism disposed intellectual men to wax rhapsodic about dark-haired Jewish women. In this way gentile men, who had more control over their choice of mate than gentile women did, may well have been influenced

---

60. Reference to the derisive term "dry baptism" is made by Low, *Jews in the Eyes of the Germans,* 178. For a bibliography of relevant primary articles see the appendix to H. D. Schmidt's "The Terms of Emancipation, 1781–1812," *LBIYB* 1 (1955), 28–51, at 46 and 27, and Littmann, "David Friedländers Sendschreiben," 105–07. For useful background information see Horst Möller, "Judenemanzipation und Staat: Ursprung und Wirkung von Dohms Schrift Über die bürgerliche Verbesserung der Juden," in *Deutsche Aufklärung und Judenemanzipation,* W. Grab, ed. (Tel Aviv, 1980).

by romanticism to find Jewish women acceptable, even fashionably desirable mates.[61] Thus just as deism was fading as an external ideological motive for conversion, early romanticism provided a parallel external ideology that encouraged gentile men to marry Jewish women, in turn causing Jewish women to convert in preparation for intermarriage.

Thus if poor Jewish women had material and legal incentives to convert, wealthy Jewish women had their own set of romantic and ideological incentives to leave their faith. Both poor and rich Jewish women, each in their own way, achieved a kind of emancipation when they converted or married out. For poor Jewish women, the freedom gained was a precondition for survival in the city, a step made necessary by the Prussian state's policies, which kept the Berlin Jewish community small and wealthy. For wealthy Jewish women, conversion and intermarriage were a reaction—even a protest against—the restricted way of life required of wealthy and privileged Jews in Berlin at this time. In many ways the price for the Jewish elite's economic success was paid by their children, who suffered from these families' rigid, parentally controlled marriage practices. To be sure, wealthy Jewish families elsewhere in central and western Europe also controlled their daughters' marriages. But the special difficulties of settling children in Berlin, the degree to which Jewish women in Berlin had mastered secular skills, and the way that romantic intellectuals were enamored of wealthy Jewish women all combined to make rebellion against arranged marriages a realistic project.

The readiness of gentile men to take advantage of the attractions of Jewish women was as much a novelty in the late eighteenth century as were the sophisticated charms of the women they married. The changes on both the Jewish and on the Christian side which encouraged intermarriage made conversion seductively attractive to Jewish women in three ways. First, in the most literal sense, Jewish women converted partly in order to seduce gentile men into marrying them. Conversion was one of the most concrete acts undertaken by Jewish women to make themselves more desirable wives for gentiles. As we have seen, Jewish women changed their names, accents, friends, and interests to facilitate their entry into gentile society. Although this strategy of seducing gentiles by hiding Jewishness was not always successful, it by no means follows that the women's attempts to escape from Judaism were nothing

---

61. See Charlene A. Lea, *Emancipation, Assimilation and Stereotype: The Image of the Jew in German and Austrian Drama, 1800–1850* (Bonn, 1978), chap. 4. I am grateful to Marion Kaplan for bringing this volume to my attention. On gentile men's power over intermarriage decisions see John E. Mayer, "Jewish-Gentile Intermarriage Patterns: A Hypothesis," *Sociology and Social Research* 45 (1961), 188–95, and Mayer's *Jewish-Gentile Courtships: An Exploratory Study of a Social Process* (New York, 1961).

but a crass and opportunistic betrayal of their people. On the contrary, the partners in several well-documented intermarriages were complex adults who chose each other for emotional reasons. To say that subtle changes in life patterns and mutually complementary economic and status exchanges were required for Jewish women to seduce gentile men to marry them is a decidedly external view, and says nothing about the authentic love involved.

In an altogether different sense, conversion seems to have been a seductive act in and of itself, regardless of one's gender or intermarriage prospects. It was tempting in this era for Jews of both sexes to improve their personal situation by changing their faith. The absence of reform Judaism and the deistic and romantic inducements which prevailed in this setting combined to render conversion a more innocent act in this era than it was in other times and places. The intellectual and social progress toward religious equality forged in Prussia—especially in its capital city, Berlin—in the last third of the eighteenth century created an especially optimistic mood. Why bother to stay Jewish when both Jewish and gentile intellectuals argued that Judaism would soon cease to be a separate religion, when a leader of the community proposed "dry" baptism for the leading families? Rich and intellectual Jews had every reason to believe that progress toward equality would continue at the same rapid rate. To interpret conversion as "betrayal" presumes the consciousness of belonging to a people and the attachment of a positive value to ethnic solidarity. Yet the rational deism of intellectual circles in Berlin, as well as some Jews' understandable intoxication with their own experiences in cosmopolitan circles, hardly contributed to strengthening their loyalty to the Jewish people. Apostates in the eighteenth century may have felt emotionally guilty for abandoning their still-Jewish families and friends. But the evidence does not suggest that this guilt was exacerbated by feelings of "bad faith" and self-loathing voiced by converts a century later.[62]

The female conversions can also be called seductive in a third sense, and that is in terms of a specifically female path to upward mobility. Wealthy women in preindustrial estate societies often could move upward with greater ease via marriage than their brothers could via education. Families budgeted accordingly, spending their money on training and decorating their daughters. Some have even argued that the importance of maintaining the virginity of unmarried daughters was rooted in the family's attempt to preserve their (pure) daughters for the highest

---

62. For personal statements which reveal these feelings see Werner Sombart et al., eds., *Judentaufen* (Munich, 1912). See also Rozenblitt, *The Jews of Vienna*.

bidder.[63] A young woman's chances of being lifted out of her class, region, or religion by some "prince charming" from a higher status group was thus a seductive possibility. If successful, upwardly mobile marriages diluted or erased a woman's loyalty to the group into which she was born. And even if such a husband never materialized, the dreams, hopes, and plans for his arrival might have the very same effect on her relationship to her group. Thus was personal emancipation was achieved at the cost of loyalty to the class, region, or religion of her family.

Many mysteries remain about how similar the experiences of the converting women on the cards were to the experiences of the better-documented salon women. But what we do know is intriguing. Just at the time that a handful of wealthy Jewish women were hosting popular and influential salons, Jewish women outside salons were converting and intermarrying more often than Jewish men were. Moreover, the salons declined just at the time that the female conversion and intermarriage rates dropped below the male rates. All of this suggests that there was a philosemitic mood in Berlin in these years which had a particular effect on Jewish women, both inside and outside of salons. Yet if this philosemitic climate, as well as underlying social structural developments, were powerful enough to bring salons into existence, how could the Jewish salons have vanished so quickly after 1806?

63. See Sherry Ortner, "The Virgin and the State," *Feminist Studies* 4 (1978), 19–36; Pierre Bourdieu, "Marriage Strategies as Strategies of Social Reproduction," in Robert Forster and Orest Ranum, eds., *Family and Society: Selections from the Annales* (Baltimore and London, 1976), 117–44. Also useful were Lucy Mair, *Marriage* (Middlesex, England, 1971); Gayle Rubin, "The Traffic in Women: Notes on the 'Political Economy' of Sex," in Rayna R. Reiter, ed., *Toward an Anthropology of Women* (New York and London, 1975), 157–210; Karen Sacks, *Sisters and Wives: The Past and Future of Sexual Equality* (Westport, Conn., 1979); and Robin Fox, *Kinship and Marriage: An Anthropological Perspective* (Harmondsworth, England, 1967), 202.

EIGHT | *The Decline of Salons*

WILHELM VON HUMBOLDT

Flawed Friendships

On the October 24, 1806, Canvas George, then a nine-year-old living on the corner where the Friedrichstrasse met the Krausenstrasse, chanced to meet the first French soldier to enter Berlin.[1] Young Canvas George was impressed by the soldier's suntanned face, by his sable coat, by his non-chalantly smoking a clay pipe in the street, and above all, by the French-man's friendliness. But before this representative of Prussia's new occu-pying army could arrange for Canvas George's family servant to guide him to the center of town, young George was distracted by the sound of blaring trumpets. The George family gazed at the French soldier as he disappeared down the street to meet his fellow soldiers. They stood transfixed as a majestic red-clad regiment, followed by those blaring trumpets and a troop of brilliantly attired officers, all marched down the Leipzigerstrasse.

Berliners had ample chance to observe the costumes and the habits of the French troops in the weeks and months that followed. The next morning, October 25, the Halle gate was crowded with residents eager to view the official entrance of the French army. Their first surprise was the Frenchmen's wild, long hair; Prussian soldiers always wore pow-dered, stiff pigtails. Even more astonishing to the Prussian subjects were the Frenchmen's uniforms. In blatant contrast to the natty blue uniforms of their Prussian fighters, Napoleon's men sported dirty, torn linen trou-

1. This description of the occupation of Berlin is reprinted in Eckart Klessman, ed., *Deutschland unter Napoleon in Augenzeugenberichten* (Munich, 1976), 166–70; the original is Canvas George, *Erinnerungen eines Preussen aus der Napoleonischen Zeit* (Grimma, 1840).

sers. One fed his "filthy" dog from a piece of bread stuck on the end of his bayonet; a metal spoon dangled from his red hat. In the words of one Berliner, it seemed quite impossible that these "small, emaciated men should have conquered our proud warriors." But at least on this first official day of French occupation, humiliation was overshadowed by sheer turmoil and excitement. The streets were suddenly filled with cannons, powder wagons, and army forges. Hundreds of forges in operation created a noteworthy spectacle. Suddenly a veritable street fair appeared on many city streets; soldiers sold clothes, food, fabric, live cattle, and even horses "for a song."[2] The French, for their part, were more impressed with Berlin than the Berliners were with them. The wide, tree-lined avenues, elegant architecture, and gardens laid out in the English style all convinced the French army's chief surgeon that Berlin possessed "as much taste and talent" as Paris. Even when the billeted soldiers were told that their hosts could never afford the wine which they expected with their meals, the soldiers decided that the local Berlin beer was an acceptable, even a tasty substitute.[3]

Unfortunately for the Berliners, the entry of the French soldiers into their city began a new period in their lives that turned out to be more ominous than the excitement and novelty of the first days suggested. The occupation was especially problematic since Prussia had until very recently been allied with France. In 1795, early in Napoleon's struggle to export the French Revolution to the continent, Prussia had withdrawn from the anti-Napoleonic coalition, but the decision to purchase peace with submission to France was increasingly criticized by many Prussian intellectuals as spineless and unpatriotic. The patriotic intellectuals' critique of Prussian foreign policy grew sharper and more widespread after the catastrophe of October 1806. Occupation, after all, was far more humiliating than mere alliance with France. What began as a dispute among intellectuals about foreign policy became a thoroughgoing ideological upheaval that called into question the widespread French influence in Prussia, especially in its capital city, Berlin. It was an ironic turn of affairs. The decade of peace preceding the debacle of October 1806 had been necessary for a salon culture to flourish, and it was in the salons that the patriotic intellectuals had enjoyed the social mobility and the sophisticated literary environment so decisive in their lives. When they turned

2. The quote about "our proud warriors" is from Canvas George, as cited in Klessman, *Deutschland unter Napoleon*, 169; this one is also from Canvas George, as cited in Klessman, *Deutschland unter Napoleon*, 170.

3. This report is from *Gardesgrenadier* Jean-Roch Coignet, as quoted in Georg Rummler, ed., *Von Marengo bis Waterloo, Memoiren des Capitaine Coignet* (Stuttgart, 1910), and reprinted in Klessman, *Deutschland unter Napoleon*, 187.

against the Jewish salons for their French tone, these intellectuals were, as often as not, turning against friends and colleagues who had nourished them personally and intellectually. Thus the decline of the Jewish salons was at once a European-wide political story transcending individual fate and a highly personal story involving the most private experiences of key salon personalities.

The political and the personal versions of the story of how the Jewish salons disappeared were thoroughly intertwined. But how could the salons have vanished? From a far distance in time, the Jewish salons surely appear to have been a stable fixture on the Berlin scene. The historic developments which gave rise to the salons were various and deep-seated. Salons flourished in late-eighteenth-century Berlin because of a rare conjunction of social, cultural, and ideological shifts. The rise of a commercial economy led to alliances between representatives of once-distant estates and classes. A temporary vacuum in the city's cultural institutions just as the intelligentsia was expanding created a need for a face-to-face setting for informal patronage. Finally, a set of ideologies became popular which favored imitation of French high culture, the social power of educated women, and friendship with acculturated Jews. The close friendships, love affairs, and marriages among the salons' heterogeneous participants were the best demonstration of the solidity of salon society. From this same distance, the rapid decline of the Jewish salons beginning in 1806 is usually explained by pointing to a change in this third arena, ideology. As the patriotic intellectuals turned against the French occupation, they abandoned the pro-French and "philosemetic" ideologies so necessary for a thriving salon culture.

A more precise examination of salon friendships shows that the decline of the Jewish salons was more than a result of post-1806 ideological reactions to the French occupation. No, the unraveling of the delicate, complex network of salon associations was much more ironic and, one might even add, much more dialectical than it appears to have been from a distance. For a closer look at several of the friendships between key salon personalities shows that the successes of the Jewish salon women provoked resentments which contributed to the downfall of their salons. The public backlash against the Jewish salons first appeared on the printed page in 1803 and only became institutionalized in an antisemitic "counter-salon" in 1811. Yet the private backlash against the social power of the Jewish salonières was present, albeit in underground fashion, throughout the salons' most successful years. The hostility against the Jewish salon women, which became explicitly political after 1806, simmered privately in the preceding quarter-century.

The friendships between the Jews and gentiles who participated in salon culture were not randomly distributed across the two genders, but mainly bound Jewish women to gentile, usually noble men. Friendships also connected Jewish and gentile men and Jewish and gentile women, but there were no intimate relationships between gentile women and Jewish men. For the Jewish salonières, the presence of these noblemen in their drawing rooms and emotional lives was an incredible compliment; personal devotion and praise must have seemed sublime. But these same men's letters to their families and friends who did not visit Jewish homes reveal that the glamorous noble visitors were in fact intensely self-conscious about the Jewishness of their Jewish friends. There was a vast, delicate, infinitely complicated spectrum of feelings and behavior on this matter of the Jewishness of one's Jewish friends. At one end, lifelong friendships between Jews and gentiles did exist, and prominent salon guests behaved loyally toward their Jewish friends in potentially embarrassing public situations. The only tarnish on these positive relationships was that the gentile friend usually meant more to the Jewish friend than vice versa. In the middle of the spectrum, the gentile friend's face-to-face behavior may have appeared well intentioned and graceful, but snide comments about the "Jewish" qualities of the Jewish friend appeared in his letters to others. Finally, at the far end were friendships that began in the first or second category and ended with the gentile friend's withdrawing from the relationship altogether for reasons connected with the Jewish friend's Jewishness.

Using biographies and surviving letters to classify complex human relationships is a highly inexact and reductionist enterprise. The friends whose relationships are well documented are hardly a random sample of all salon participants; nor did any one individual always have the same kind of relationships with all of his or her friends of another estate. The place of any one friendship on the spectrum was obviously a combination of how gracefully the Jewish friend had mastered secular culture, the personality of both individuals, and the gentile friend's ideological stance toward Judaism and Jews. These limits on classifying friendships are not, however, very telling here. The aim of what follows is not to plot all salon participants' relationships in an abstract fashion but to use selected relationships to illustrate how a casual antisemitism poisoned the very cross-estate friendships upon which salon society was built.

Henriette Herz's relationships with gentile men tended to be on the positive pole of the spectrum. Take, for instance, her relationship with the much sought-after Wilhelm von Humboldt. In the late 1780s the two belonged to the Tugendbund, a secret and sentimental correspondence society. After von Humboldt married in 1791 and left Berlin, he distanced himself from many of his Jewish friends. But he always arranged to meet with Henriette Herz when they both happened to be visiting the same city. Toward the end of her life, when she was an impoverished widow, it was von Humboldt who arranged for the king to award her a modest pension.[4] Herz also maintained a long-term relationship with Friedrich Schleiermacher that was much deeper than her tie with von Humboldt. Herz's relative interpersonal success with men of this standing is illuminating when compared with the problems encountered by the highly controversial Rahel Levin. Herz avoided some of Levin's notoriety because she married only once, to a prominent and respected Jewish physician. Since she refused to marry a gentile before her mother died, she did not arouse the hostility such marriages could arouse. Also, Herz was a regal beauty with a rather formal temperament. She thus tended to inspire distant respect rather than the kind of complex intimacy Levin offered, an intimacy which gave the gentile friend personal knowledge that could ultimately be used against her.

While poised on the positive side of the spectrum, we cannot forget the subtly hostile public situations in which prominent noblemen defended their Jewish friends and acquaintances. In 1801 Gustav von Brinkmann recounted in a letter to his confidante Julie von Voss how he found himself at a dinner party the previous evening at the home of his superior at the embassy, the Swedish ambassador to Prussia, Herr von Engstrom. Von Brinkmann reported that "out of fear of the Christians," the von Engstroms had originally planned to exclude their Jewish friends from the event, which was planned to be only a small soupé. But at a previous gathering earlier the same evening, Frau von Engstrom forgot herself and proceeded to invite several Jews to attend the soupé. Later, von Brinkmann and his friend Friedrich Gentz amused themselves watching the lifted eyebrows of the extremely *hoffähig* (courtly) noble guests. But von Brinkmann also proudly reported that he took care to spend most of his time that evening talking to the salonière Madame Sara Levy, so that she would not feel rebuffed. In the same letter, von Brinkmann continued in the same tone, proud of his "philosemitic" attitudes. He discussed his confusion about how Henriette von Arnstein, the daughter of his friend the Viennese salonière Fanny von Arnstein, could ever find a proper mate. He deplored the "elegant commonness of her environment" and puzzled about how she could solve the contradiction between "her feelings of duty" to her family (which dictated a Jewish marriage) and her "moral cultivation" (which dictated a non-Jewish husband). Von

---

4. On von Humboldt's help with the pension see Julius Furst, ed., *Henriette Herz: Ihr Leben und ihre Erinnerungen* (Berlin, 1858), 83; on his complex relationships to his Jewish friends see Wilhelm Grau, *Wilhelm von Humboldt und das Problem des Juden* (Hamburg, 1935).

Brinkmann was full of affectionate, empathetic concern when he quoted Henriette's own troubled observation that she thought she might be happier in the end if she were a "typical Jewish girl."[5]

Most of the friendships among salon participants were more ambiguous and occupy the middle position on the spectrum. Wilhelm von Humboldt, for instance, was devoted to his friend from university days, Israel Steiglitz. The two were so close in the late 1780s and early 1790s that Wilhelm wrote Israel graphic letters expressing his deepest feelings about sensuality. One historian later complained of the "homosexual atmosphere" of their relationship. Yet this extreme intimacy did not exempt Steiglitz or his family from von Humboldt's lofty disdain. Von Humboldt wrote to another friend deriding Steiglitz's father for his "half-cultivation, his love of gossip, his vanity and his arrogance," all of which he explicitly condemned as Jewish traits.[6] Not only did von Humboldt express contempt for personal qualities he classified as Jewish; he also eyed with discomfort the distribution of wealth among those close to him, with intense consciousness of where Jews fit in this schema. Although he relied on David Friedländer as his private banker and was even on friendly personal terms with him, von Humboldt also noted with distinct displeasure that Friedländer was making more money than his own brothers, who were bankrupt.[7]

Other noblemen concerned about their family's declining fortunes were also not above profiting from their connection to wealthy Jews while criticizing them for one thing or another. Heinrich von Kleist arrived in Berlin in 1802. He led a secluded life, but on the rare occasion when he did leave his room, he attended several Jewish salons. His attendance apparently required no great love for Jews. In a letter to his sister Ulrike written in 1802 he reported that "I am seldom out in Society. Jewish [Society] would be my favorite, if [the Jews] did not act so pretentiously with their cultivation. I have made an interesting acquaintance with the Jew [Ephraim] Cohen, not so much because of he himself, as because of his impressive collection of natural science instruments, which he has allowed me to use."[8] Jewish friends, in other words, could be

---

5. This letter was written from von Brinkmann to Julie von Voss on January 21, 1802, (packet 11), and is now in the Berg-Voss Collection at the GSA.

6. Grau, *Wilhelm von Humboldt*, 30.

7. Ibid., 31 and 81. Von Humboldt mentioned his financial dealings with David Friedländer frequently in his letters to Gustav von Brinkmann; see, for instance, Albert Leitzmann, *Wilhelm von Humboldts Briefe an Karl Gustav von Brinkmann* (Leipzig, 1939), 166.

8. Von Kleist's comment is cited in Hans Karl Krüger, *Berliner Romantik und Berliner Judentum* (Bonn, 1939), 73–74; the original can be found in Kleist's *Werke*, Minde-Pouet, ed., vol. 1, 213.

useful in a variety of ways, but publicly amicable relations with them by no means meant that one liked them "for themselves."

Even Gustav von Brinkmann, the ubiquitous introducer for Rahel Levin's salon, was not immune from the occasional snide comment. His asides are all the more noteworthy since it was von Brinkmann, more than any other single individual, who brought the enlightened nobility to the Jewish salons. Even in the act of praising his special friend Rahel Levin, von Brinkmann did not forget her Jewishness. In 1802, he wrote Julie von Voss that there was more wit on Rahel Levin's "Judensopha" than in all Berlin. In another letter to von Voss, von Brinkmann went on at length about his Jewish women friends' various problems. At times he sounded concerned and sympathetic, but then he became more hostile as he attributed their problems to their "Egyptian style" and lack of "artistic completion" and "tact."[9]

At the far end of the spectrum, there were friendships that deteriorated into a one-sided antipathy on the noble side, an antipathy that was expressed in explicitly antisemitic terms. The vicious underside to some noblemen's friendships with Jewish women came to the fore as the years passed. Wilhelm von Humboldt's complex relationship with Rahel Levin is a dramatic illustration of how badly cross-estate friendships could go awry. If one initially possessed it, losing Wilhelm von Humboldt's admiration was a serious loss, especially for an ambitious Jewish woman whose avenues to official cultural power were restricted. Von Humboldt's intellectual and social prestige in Berlin was unrivaled; it was comparable to that enjoyed by Goethe within Germany as a whole. Beginning at the very end of the 1790s, after a decade of friendship with her, von Humboldt began to distance himself from Levin and make nasty pronouncements about her. His wife Caroline's dislike of Levin was one factor which influenced Wilhelm. Although in her early twenties Caroline von Dacheröden had also belonged to the Tugendbund and was close with several Jewish salon women, she withdrew from this circle after her marriage, in part because of her increasingly antisemitic views. She also came to believe that the central task for patriotic German women was procreation in service of the German nation, rather than self-education in pursuit of public cultural power.[10] Thus Caroline von Humboldt found fault both with the intellectual ambitions of several Jewish salon women and their childlessness. But whatever Caroline's behind-the-scenes influence on her husband, it was Wilhelm who tended to pub-

---

9. Gustav von Brinkmann to Julie von Voss, Letter of May 5, 1801 (packet 10), GSA.

10. On Caroline von Humboldt's changing attitudes to Jews and her influence over her husband in this regard see Grau, *Wilhelm von Humboldt*, 57.

licly voice the disdain. When their mutual friend Friedrich Gentz reminded him that Levin was "the most intellectual woman on earth," von Humboldt replied that "there are times one must forego intellect." He once referred to Rahel Levin as a "monster." When she married Karl August Varnhagen von Ense, von Humboldt queried a friend whether "there was anything a Jew could not achieve."[11]

The terms of this condemnation of Levin's marriage are fascinating, harsh as they are. Von Humboldt later earned his place in Jewish history with his public-policy intervention on behalf of the Prussian Jews, first for the 1812 edict of emancipation and subsequently at the Vienna Congress. Both his writings and his political actions justify labeling von Humboldt as a philosemite in the context of his time and place. Yet it seems that von Humboldt was not entirely pleased when individual Jews succeeded in escaping their Jewishness by upwardly mobile intermarriage.[12] The words von Humboldt chose to deride Levin's marriage to Varnhagen confirm a central theme of this book: whatever the financial or other defects of the gentile men who married the Jewish salon women, these intermarriages represented an objective achievement in terms of social history. Whether such intermarriages were heralded or denounced, and by whom, tells a great deal about various ideological interpretations of the women's successes in Berlin's high society. Von Humboldt's disdain reminds us that a Jewish-noble intermarriage was a noteworthy event which called out for special observation.

In the years after 1806, prominent Berlin intellectuals gradually became more comfortable in publicly distancing themselves from their Jewish friends and acquaintances. Antisemitic comments made discreetly in the 1790s, when the Jewish salons were still powerful institutions, could later be made nonchalantly—and even translated into highly symbolic public behavior—once the Jewish salon women had lost their glamour. This change was dramatically revealed in an incident involving Achim von Arnim in 1811; the location was Sara Levy's salon, one of the few Jewish salons still open. The episode began quietly enough when von Arnim stopped by to pick up his wife Bettina, who had always been more friendly to Jews than her husband or her brother Clemens Brentano. (Her husband had been on sufficiently good terms with the Levy family to rent an apartment at their home seven years before, but by 1811 he had become considerably cooler.) Von Arnim outraged Madame Levy and her family by appearing at the reception dressed in his street clothes in-

---

11. This quote is cited in Max Kohler, *Jewish Rights at the Congresses of Vienna (1814–1815) and Aix-La-Chapelle* (New York, 1918), 34.

12. This quote is cited in Grau, *Wilhelm von Humboldt*, 26.

stead of formal dress, and Madame Levy's nephew Moritz Itzig, sensitive about antisemitism, was so outraged by the symbolic implications of von Arnim's informal dress that he felt compelled to defend his family's and his people's honor by challenging von Arnim to a duel. Von Arnim refused, on the grounds that no Jew could possess the honor requisite to engage in a duel, while Moritz Itzig eventually sought his revenge by attacking von Arnim physically, and a protacted, notorious lawsuit ensued. Von Arnim's behavior and Moritz Itzig's response were much discussed at the time; Rahel Levin's brother Ludwig Robert wrote a controversial play about the episode. Robert's own anger was not, however, expressed openly in his play, as the Itzig character was cast as a gentile commoner, not a Jew.[13] This episode shows that by 1811, what had been discreet and casual a decade before had become open and hostile. The mood against the Jewish salons had become so strong that even in their own homes Jewish salonières were not safe from devastating symbolic attacks, attacks which became known and discussed far outside their drawing rooms.

The Pamphlet War

The snide attacks on the Jewish salonières carried on behind the scenes in the 1790s first broke into the open nine years before the von Arnim-Itzig fracas, in a spate of pamphlets published in 1803. The ongoing private derision had mainly caused personal unhappiness to individual victims—if they were unlucky enough to learn that their friends had more complex attitudes than met the eye. But the pamphlet war was altogether more disturbing, not only because of its publicity, but more importantly, because their authors attacked the achievements of which the Jewish salon women were most proud. The most controversial pamphlet was penned by Karl Wilhelm Grattenauer, who targeted the Jewish salonières as the embodiment of all that he disliked most about contemporary Jewish life. Grattenauer was a judicial official in Berlin and also a private lawyer in private practice; his closest friend among the salon guests was Friedrich Gentz.[14] Although some of Grattenauer's arguments against

13. For a summary of the Moritz Itzig–Achim von Arnim incident see Krüger, *Berliner Romantik*, 128–33. Ludwig Robert's play was entitled *Die Macht der Verhältnisse* (Stuttgart and Tübingen, 1819). For Karl Varnhagen von Ense's version of the dispute, see his *Vermischte Schriften*, vol. 2. (Leipzig, 1875). The Itzig-von Arnim correspondence on this incident was published by Ludwig Geiger, "Achim von Arnim und Moritz Itzig," *Frankfurter Zeitung*, vol. 39, no. 39 (February 8, 1895).

14. For background on the new antisemitism of this era see Eleanore Sterling, *Judenhass: Die Anfänge des politischen Antisemitismus in Deutschland 1815–1850* (Frankfurt/a.M., 1969),

the Berlin Jews were old, most of his complaints were decidedly new. Grattenauer's antisemitism was remarkable for its anti-assimilationist character, and in this regard his polemics were a more polished articulation of the offhand critiques some gentile salon participants had made about their Jewish friends. In both cases, the tone and content of the antisemitism was a reaction to the new and rapid social success of the salon women. Unlike earlier antisemites, who had mostly argued that Jews could be accepted into society if they would cease to believe and behave in a Jewish way, Grattenauer, like von Brinkmann and von Humboldt, attacked the very assimilation the salon women had so laboriously constructed.

Grattenauer's anti-assimilationist position was thus a departure both from religious antisemitism and from liberal "philosemitic" pro-assimilationism. The chief religious antisemite in eighteenth-century Germany had been Johann Eisenmenger, whose *Endecktes Judentum* ("Judaism Discovered"), first published in 1710, justified his hostility to Judaism with an interpretation of Jewish law and beliefs. The first he judged to be "wicked" and the second he judged to be "foolish." Eisenmenger was convinced that Jewish law commanded its followers to use a double moral and financial standard in relation to gentiles and concluded that these various deficiencies in Judaism were immutable, not merely the result of historic oppression. Therefore, Eisenmenger concluded that the only solution to Judaism's inferiority was Jewish conversion to Christianity.[15]

But Eisenmenger's religious and ahistorical antisemitism became increasingly difficult to maintain later in the century, as Jewish observance of a traditional way of life declined and Jewish integration in the wider society increased. The new liberal, "philosemitic" view attributed any admitted defects in Jewish behavior to history rather than to the timeless religious or legal "essence" of Judaism. Liberals argued that these defects could be overcome by political emancipation making Jews into citizens, accompanied by acculturation and social integration.[16] Religious anti-

25–26, 83–85, and Jacob Katz, *From Prejudice to Destruction: Anti-semitism, 1700–1933* (Cambridge, Mass., 1980), part 2; Katz discusses Grattenauer on 56–57. See also Henri Brunschwig, *Enlightenment and Romanticism in Eighteenth-Century Prussia* (Chicago, 1974), appendix on "The Struggle for Civic Rights of the Jews of Prussia." The pamphlet itself is *Wider die Juden* (Berlin, 1803); the third edition, which I used, includes other contemporary pamphlets originally published separately on the theme as well as Grattenauer's responses.

15. Eisenmenger's book—*Endecktes Judenthum*, 2 vols. (Königsberg [Berlin], 1710)—is discussed by Katz, *From Prejudice to Destruction*, 13–22.

16. A good summary of the liberal position can be found in Sterling, *Judenhass*, 27–30, and 82–86. The best primary source is of course Christian Wilhelm Dohm's *Über die bür-*

semites and liberals thus vigorously disagreed about whether Jewish deficiencies were the result of some essence of the Jewish religion or instead the result of historical circumstance. But in spite of this crucial difference, both traditional antisemites and liberal "philosemites" saw some kind of assimilation as the solution to the Jewish "problem." Neither group judged the existing Jewish community to be ready for acceptance without some kind of assimilation. And precisely here is where Grattenauer departed from both antisemites and philosemites with his anti-assimilationist antisemitism.

Grattenauer's original pamphlet was entitled *Wider die Juden* ("Against the Jews"). At the outset, he merely reiterated a wide variety of traditional antisemitic arguments, including an echo of Eisenmenger's religious antisemitism in his assertion that the content of Jewish law made Jews intrinsically hostile to Christians. But he quickly moved on to more avant-garde kinds of opposition to the role of Jews on the contemporary scene. He opposed citizenship for Prussian Jewry on the grounds that "the nature and essence of Judaism are bad for the goals of the state and for its public welfare, and highly dangerous" and concluded that a mutually exclusive relationship between Jews and the modern state was necessary. Grattenauer then raised another modern theme, the racial characteristics of Jews. Here, he concentrated on the "Jewish smell," which, in his view, neither wealth, elegant clothing, nor socializing with the prominent could eradicate.[17]

This juxtaposition between what Grattenauer saw as the permanent, ascribed racial status of the salon Jews and the social glory they had achieved in secular high society was at the heart of his analysis. It is startling to see both of these attacks so early in the nineteenth century. For each part of Grattenauer's double condemnation was new. It was modern for an antisemite to make race, rather than religion, the essential attribute of Jews. It was equally modern for an antisemite to condemn, rather than to praise, Jewish success at acculturation and social integration. Grattenauer's specific critiques were various. He accused the wealthy Jews of spending great sums on "frivolous enjoyment of extreme luxury," rather than using these funds to "cultivate" their poorer "brothers and sisters."[18] In a second pamphlet written in reply to one of his critics, Grattenauer again criticized the alienation of the "elegant" Jews

---

gerliche Verbesserung der Juden (Berlin, 1781). The English edition is entitled *Concerning the Amelioration of the Jews* (Cincinnati, 1957).

17. Grattenauer, *Wider die Juden* (pamphlet 1), 17. (The pagination in this volume begins anew with each pamphlet.)

18. Ibid., 17.

from the Orthodox Jews. He hoped that their lavish spending would eventually make the elegant Jews poor, which, he was confident, would surely destroy their power in society. This power, in Grattenauer's outspoken opinion, was, after all, due solely to their "unjustifiable" wealth.[19]

In this same reply to a critic of his first pamphlet, Grattenauer elaborated on why he found the local Jewish women so offensive. He complained that they "became learned in order to pretend; their femininity has become destroyed by that which they believe will make them cultivated." He continued: "they read many books, speak many languages, play many instruments, sketch in a variety of styles, paint in all colors, dance in all fashions, embroider in all patterns, and they possess every single item, that could give them a claim to charm."[20] Two contemporary satirical drawings capture Grattenauer's critique. The problem was, in Grattenauer's eyes, that in spite of these decorative accomplishments, the Jewish women were unable to "learn the art of unifying their individual talents in order to display a completely beautiful femininity." Not only did their attempts to cultivate themselves fail to coalesce into a graceful style; in Grattenauer's opinion the Jewish women's relationship to high culture was wholly opportunistic. They sought to master high culture for one reason only: to show it off to men. But Grattenauer was sure that none of this would, in the end, facilitate true assimilation, for in his view neither wealth, cultivation, nor powerful friends could erase the "stink" of Jewishness. Neither in Paris nor in Berlin nor in Vienna could the Jewish women learn "tact," "even if they go around with princes, counts, and gentlemen as long as they want."[21]

Grattenauer concluded that he was not writing his pamphlet to "improve" or "convert" the Jews. He admitted that his pessimism about whether Jews could escape Jewishness will lead some to "cry when they read these words." Grattenauer was intensely aware that he was mocking the very social and intellectual successes of which they were so proud.[22] Here, on the crucial issue of whether token exceptions to his generalizations could exist, Grattenauer was contradictory. At times he seemed ready to deny "those who cry" the token status he knew they craved, while in other passages he appeared more generous, holding out the tantalizing hope that it might be possible for a few individuals to suc-

---

19. Ibid., 16.

20. Grattenauer criticized the "jüdische Elegants" in response to the pamphlet by Johann Wilhelm Andreas Kosmann, "Für die Juden." His response to Kosmann is in his "Erklärung an das Publikum über meine Schrift: *Wider die Juden*" (pamphlet 3), 8.

21. This passage appears in the fourth pamphlet in the volume, Grattenauer's "Erster Nachtrag zu meiner Erklärung," 50.

22. Ibid., 51.

Contemporary satires of salon Jews

cessfully escape their Jewishness in some unspecified way.[23] In spite of this hint that a few token Jews might be exempted from his anti-assimilationist antisemitism, Grattenauer predicted that he would be accused of libel for his overwhelmingly negative views about the still-powerful Jewish stars of salon society. Such libel accusations would only be the result, in his opinion, of a vain hope in the coming unity of Judaism and Christianity.[24] This particular "vain hope" had, of course, been articulated by the leading Jewish liberal, David Friedländer, in his "dry baptism" proposal published four years earlier.

Grattenauer's pamphlet received an enthusiastic reception in the Berlin of 1803 and was reprinted several times. Its popularity, as well as its anti-assimilationist content, show that as early as 1803, before the salonières' power had been challenged by the new patriotism, it had become legitimate to publicly attack Jewish social and cultural successes. This hostility to assimilation festered and deepened in the coming years, exacerbated as it would become by the dramatic changes beginning in October 1806. Eventually the story came full circle, since this hostility eventually helped destroy the very salons which had generated Grattenauer's attacks in the

23. For discussion of Grattenauer's contradictions on this point see Katz, *From Prejudice to Destruction,* 56. For comments that suggest he did respect "some" Jews, see, for example, his "Erklärung an das Publikum" (pamphlet 3), 23.

m25.6   24. See Grattenauer's "Erster Nachtrag" (pamphlet 4), 23.

first place. The point is the historic novelty of Grattenauer's 1803 attack. His was anything but an eternal, timeless antisemitism which was dragged out whenever Jews attained too much prominence in society. In his pamphlet Grattenauer articulated a new kind of racial and anti-assimilationist antisemitism which was formulated in response to a new kind of Jewish prominence.

The published responses to Grattenauer's pamphlet by Jewish authors were remarkably ambivalent and show how fluid the climate of opinion was and how many ways there were to interpret the same words. One respondent tried to turn the attack upside down, suggesting that Grattenauer's views be understood as praise for the "importance" of the Berlin Jews. A second commentator concurred that Grattenauer was actually giving the Berlin Jews a "big compliment, which shows how far the local Jews had come."[25] A third Jewish respondent agreed with Grattenauer that the behavior of the Jewish daughters was a problem. Speaking for the Jewish parents, he reminded his readers how much parents tried to limit the luxury spending of their daughters, and how important it was to keep the daughters from "going around" with "persons" whom they could never marry.[26] These daughters were, indeed, moving away from the world of their parents, which disapproved of how far they had taken the project of acculturation. But they were by no means secure inside the world of the von Humboldts and the von Brinkmanns, who may have flocked to their salons and praised them to their faces, but who talked like Grattenauer behind their backs.

"Christian Patriotism"

Just as the private attacks on the salonières and Grattenauer's pamphlet both appeared while the salonières still seemed to be at the height of their power, so too the new "Christian patriotism" also grew slowly while the salons flourished.[27] But unlike the other long-simmering antagonisms which eventually destroyed the Jewish salons, the new patriotism was enacted on a far larger stage than salon society. After 1806 debate about the Jewish future necessarily became entangled with the wider problems of Prussia's national destiny and the religious character of the state.

25. The respondent who thought that Grattenauer's work should be understood as a tribute to the Berlin Jews was [Joseph Sabattja Wolff], "Sendschreiben eines Christen an einen hiesigen Juden über den Verfasser der Schrift *Wider die Juden* (pamphlet 7), 5.

26. This fascinating comment was made by [Salomon Pappenheim], "Auszug eines Schreiben von einem Juden zu B[reslau]" (pamphlet 6), 5.

27. This new patriotism is described as "Christian patriotism" in Koppel Pinson, *Modern Germany: Its History and Civilization* (New York, 1966).

Prussia's tenuous neutrality began to unravel in the fall of 1805.[28] That neutrality, so crucial for the creative achievements of the decade, could last only as long as Prussia's own territorial ambitions in northern Germany could be realized without Prussia's becoming a satellite of France or going to war. But this precarious balancing act became increasingly untenable. Patriotic sentiments grew more intense at home, not just among the intelligentsia but also within the royal family itself. Just before Austria's defeat in the Battle of Austerlitz in December 1805, Prussia had finally decided to throw in her lot with the Third Coalition opposing Napoleon. But with the defeat of Austria, fighting Napoleon without a central European ally became too quixotic a project for a still-vacillating Prussia. And so in December 1805 Prussia did a diplomatic about-face, abandoning its plan to fight Napoleon, and became an ally of France. Thus 1805 remained a year of peace for Prussia, but it was no longer a peace of neutrality. Peace had been purchased at the cost of becoming a satellite of France. Patriots at home and would-be allies abroad were outraged.

The decade of neutrality that preceded the decisive year 1806 should have left Prussia prepared for the worst. Vast new territories had been gained in the east, and maritime trade had been brisk. King Frederick William III, who came to power in 1797, attempted to reduce the deficit and administrative disarray his lazy predecessor, Frederick William II, had allowed to accumulate. But the army, on which Frederick the Great had lavished his devotion and the state's funds, had deteriorated radically. Thus when it became evident in the summer and fall of 1806 that Prussia would not be treated as an equal ally, Prussia finally declared war against France. But the Prussian army suffered a quick and bitter defeat. The beginning of the end came in early October, when French troops were mobilized in northern Thuringia. This convinced the king, who had vacillated for so long, to finally quit the alliance. And so, on October 9, Prussia issued a war manifesto. But the king's bravery on the diplomatic front was not matched by the troops' success on the field. Armies at Jena, at Auerstädt, and at fortresses along the Elbe and in the Oder valley were quickly defeated. By the end of October, Napoleon's troops had reached Berlin. The royal households and key ministers managed to escape to Königsberg. But since they left behind a largely intact administration,

28. For this summary of political and military events in the years between 1806 and 1815 I have relied upon the following standard works: Friedrich Meinecke, *The Age of German Liberation, 1795–1815* (Berkeley, 1977); H. W. Koch, *A History of Prussia* (London and New York, 1978); C. T. Atkinson, *A History of Germany, 1715–1815* (rpt. New York and London, 1969; orig. 1908); Robert Holtman, *The Napoleonic Revolution* (Philadelphia and New York, 1967), as well as on the Klessman volume (see note 2).

the occupying power could immediately begin to exact large payments from a conquered Prussia. Seeing Prussia's abject demoralization, Napoleon offered a harsh armistice. His aim was to strip Prussia of her western territories and provoke ruptures between Prussia and Russia as well as between Prussia and the smaller German states. But by now King Frederick William II was full of defiance and refused to come to terms. Prussia had finally joined the anti-Napoleonic coalition.

By the summer of 1807, Prussia's very existence was precarious. Russia had been defeated in June, and a rump Prussia was vulnerable to Napoleon's desire to transform occupation into annexation, thus demolishing Prussia altogether. It was only Russia's pressure to retain a buffer state between itself and France that kept Napoleon's intentions from becoming reality. But the rump Prussia that was allowed to survive was in economic and political chaos. In the Treaty of Tilsit in July, Prussia lost her remaining western territories and high indemnities were exacted. French troops evacuated the eastern portion of rump Prussia, where the monarchy and the most important bureaucrats had fled the previous fall, but the cash payments to France and the blockage imposed on the export of Prussian grain led to a collapse of land values. In addition, an army of 150,000 French soldiers continued to occupy much of the country.

The imperiled condition of Prussia in 1807 reinforced the political elite's new-found patriotism and their long-simmering opposition to the autocracy of the Prussian system. In early October 1807, King Frederick William III, under the influence of his wife Queen Luise and the influential Prince von Hardenberg, recalled Reichsfreiherr von Stein, who had been dismissed the previous year. In the ensuing fourteen months, Stein and his associates accomplished significant reforms. They worked to establish a practice of ministerial responsibility, which was to decrease the arbitrariness of the power of the crown. The edict of 1807 laid the legal foundation for limiting the nobility's domination over the peasantry. Thus although defeat by Napoleon caused humiliation and privation for the ordinary Prussian, it also sparked a rare openness to reform. The political elite which had "gone to sleep on the laurels of Frederick the Great" now began to awake, slowly.

In the meantime, by 1807 the Napoleonic state achieved the height of its power on the continent of Europe. But by the time that year had passed, there were accumulating indications that it was going to be difficult to maintain control over such a diverse collection of annexed provinces, satellite lands, and compulsory allies. The presence of occupying troops and conscription of the inhabitants angered local populations. Napoleon's continuing demands for cash indemnities and the economic chaos caused by the Continental System forbidding trade with England also turned local inhabitants against life in Napoleon's empire. To be sure, Napoleon's string of military victories had not yet completely run its course. In February 1808 French troops had entered Rome, but the next month the pope retaliated by excommunicating Napoleon. Next came the violent revolts in Spain in May, which led to England's entering the fray against Napoleon on the side of Spain. Nor were matters going entirely well between Napoleon and his erstwhile ally, Czar Alexander of Russia. When the two met at Erfurt during September and October 1808, Napoleon was badly in need of Alexander's help. Russia had been defeated the previous year, but Napoleon still needed Russian assistance to maintain control over the German states. War in Spain required moving his troops out of rump Prussia to fight in Spain, and Napoleon needed a friendly Russia to keep a watch on Prussia, France's increasingly compulsory ally.

In spite of Napoleon's mounting problems on the continent, Prussia benefited only minimally from his difficulties. Thanks to the Spanish revolt, the occupying troops left Prussia. But in exchange Prussia was forced to pay a new indemnity, agree to limit her army to 42,000, and enter an alliance against Austria. This last demand was unfortunate, for it came just at a time when Prussia and Austria might have acted on their common interests against Napoleon. The Prussian-Austrian alliance would have to wait until 1813. In the meantime, the real improvements in Prussia during 1808 were not in diplomacy or on the battlefield, but in domestic political and intellectual life. In November 1808 a new progressive municipal ordinance was issued. The army was reorganized; commoners could now become officers and flogging was abolished. Johann Fichte delivered his famous patriotic lectures early in the year in the lecture hall of the Royal Academy of Science. A spirit of reform and national renewal energized the Prussian elite. Prussia was still very much in chains, externally. But it looked as if defeat might become the condition for a patriotic renewal that could outlast political humiliation. The question was whether this patriotic renewal would take on a xenophobic tone that would define some Prussians and some social styles as un-Prussian, with fatal consequences for the Jewish salons.

The challenges to Napoleon's hegemony on the European continent mounted steadily in 1809. Revolts broke out in Westphalia, Hanover, Hesse, Brandenberg, and in the Tyrol. Napoleon's most serious problem, however, was with Austria. Buoyed with optimism by the departure of the French army from the continent, Austria declared herself ready to lead a pan-German revolt against Napoleon. The Austrian leadership therefore beseeched the king of Prussia to join them in a common fight. But Prussia refused, and in April, Austria declared war on France. Still involved in putting down the Spanish rebellion, Napoleon had to raise a new army to fight Austria, which was aided by England. This coalition won some important victories in the summer, but by the fall, Austria had been defeated. In October, the harsh terms of the Treaty of Schönbrunn resembled the humiliation Prussia had suffered at Tilsit in 1807. The tragedy for the future of central Europe was that Prussia and Austria had arrived separately at their military defeats, diplomatic humiliations, and status as Napoleon's compulsory allies.

The setbacks in the struggle against Napoleon on the military and diplomatic fronts in 1809 were soon accompanied by difficulties in reforming Prussia's social and legal structures. In November 1809 the king dismissed Stein from office and proceeded to sharply curtail the reform tendency in the bureaucracy. Stein's enthusiasm for radical reform had, perhaps inevitably, alienated the convervative Junkers. Ironically, it was Stein's anti-French and not his anti-noble actions which were the immediate cause of his dismissal. In a letter intercepted by Napoleon's censors, Stein described his plans to use a secret organization to build the anti-Napoleon resistance within Prussia. Napoleon then insisted that the king dismiss Stein, and Frederick William complied. After Stein's departure for Austria and then for Russia, a more moderate wing of the reform movement led by Prince Karl August von Hardenberg came into power. Napoleon's insistence that Stein be eliminated thus contributed to the Junkers' triumph against the radical reformers.

In the meantime, a unified alliance against Napoleon remained a dim hope. The compulsory allies continued to be divided among each other and were, at least officially, quiescent toward Napoleon. Relations between France and Russia were still ostensibly friendly, but tensions were building. The opportune marriage of a Hapsburg and a Bonaparte excited the jealousy of the czar, who was convinced that Napoleon had begun to favor Austria over Russia. In turn, Russia's adoption of a tariff favorable to imports from the English colonies and unfavorable to French imports angered Napoleon, who retaliated by refusing to authorize a loan to Russia. By 1811, relations had deteriorated so far as a formal breach in the alliance. In the spring of 1812, Napoleon embarked on an invasion of Russia, hoping that a swift victory would provide France with domination of a country which would connect its achieved power in western and central Europe to its new power in eastern Europe. None of this would come to be. Rather, defeat in Russia sparked the broadest anti-Napoleon coalition ever. For the first time since 1792, Prussia and Austria fought France together. Prussia's War of Liberation against France in 1813 and 1814 constituted Prussia's first popular uprising against a foreign power, an uprising which played a crucial role in transforming a dynastic collection of territories into a modern nation-state.

But in October of 1806, domestic revitalization and military victory lay far in the future. In the meantime, from that hectic fall day in October 1806 until the map of Europe was redrawn at the Vienna Congress in 1815, Prussians suffered a variety of unpleasant dislocations. A severe inflation brought financial ruin to many; friends and families were parted as government and military service required geographic moves; and military defeat by, and ultimately military resistance against revolutionary France created severe political confusions for those Prussians who had been at all sympathetic to the French Revolution. Some nobles, led by Stein and Hardenberg, resolved that the country's antiquated social structure had been one of the prime causes of military disaster. For these progressive nobles, the goal was to reform Prussia "from above" by modernizing the land's social and political structures, thereby creating a stronger state better able to expel the French invader. Other nobles reacted to occupation and defeat in precisely the opposite way. Threatened by the limits on their profits and power which would result from the reforms proposed by the Hardenberg group, these more conservative nobles argued that Prussia could regain its military strength only by strengthening its traditional social structures.[29]

Prussia's humiliation in 1806 thus set off explosive debates that went to the heart of every possible burning question of the day. Everything that had supposedly caused the revolution in France, and thus Prussia's occupation and humiliation, was called into question. Debate raged on topics ranging from reason and the irrational to French hairstyles and fashions, from cosmopolitanism and German unification to peasants' land tenure and the proper role of the Prussian woman. It was in this maelstrom of foreign occupation and the consequent ideological upheaval that the story of Berlin's Jewish salons gradually came to an end. Key personalities left the city to join the exiled Prussian government in Königsberg or to avoid the privations of life in occupied rump Prussia. In some salons, their places were taken by French officials administering the occupied city. For instance, beginning in 1806 Rebecca Friedländer's "Aesthetic Teas" seem to have been mainly attended by her French men friends, most of whom were literary types who worked for the occupying

29. Good summaries of this intra-noble debate can be found in Walter Simon, *The Failure of the Prussian Reform Movement, 1807–1819* (Ithaca, 1955); Eugene Anderson, *Nationalism and the Cultural Crisis in Prussia, 1806–1815* (New York, 1939); Barbara Vogel, "Reformpolitik in Preussen 1807–1820," in *Preussen im Rückblick,* H.-J. Puhle and H.-U. Wehler, eds. (Göttingen, 1980), 202–23.

administration. But the presence of the French at Friedländer's teas meant that the patriotic salon guests who remained in the city refused to attend, since they would never mix with Napoleon's officials.

The practical limits occupation imposed on sociability eased after 1808, when French troops departed Prussia to quell the revolt in Spain. But when more sociable conditions resumed in 1808, many former guests who returned to Berlin did not return to the Jewish salons. Levin's salon declined the most dramatically, in part because her inheritance was gradually reduced and she lacked the means to entertain in style. But her loneliness was not due only to the decline in her standard of living. Important friends, including Friedrich Gentz and Wilhelm and Caroline von Humboldt, deserted her in a rather public fashion. The consequence was that 1807 and 1808 were two of her very loneliest years. Early in 1808 she wrote to a friend complaining that "at my 'tea table' . . . I sit with nothing but dictionaries; I serve tea no oftener than every week or ten days. That is how much everything has changed! Never have I been so alone."[30]

The new isolation of the Jewish salonières was not just a result of the new patriotic mood in Berlin. Nor did the new mood close down every Jewish salon, or even completely destroy the salon as an institution. Some Jewish salons ceased to exist even before 1806, for reasons unrelated to the altered political situation. Henriette Herz closed her salon because of her poverty after her husband Markus died in 1803. Philippine Cohen's salon closed in 1804 when her husband fled Berlin because of bankruptcy. And, to be sure, a few Jewish salons remained open after 1806, notably those hosted by Sara Levy and Amalie Beer. Still, Rahel Levin described the effects of the new mood in collective, not in individual terms, later lamenting that "*our* ship went under in 1806, the ship containing the loveliest pleasures, the loveliest goods of life."[31] Although many of the Jewish salons disappeared, either for personal or for political reasons, the salon as an institution did not disappear. A circle of conservative noble families opened their homes to a far more prominent set of noble guests than had gathered in the Jewish salons of the 1780s and 1790s. Friedrich von Stägemann, a high-ranking bureaucrat, and his wife Elizabeth entertained regularly. Bettina von Arnim's sister Kunigunde and her husband, the classicist Friedrich von Savigny, hosted many for-

30. For a more detailed summary of Rebecca Friedländer's social life (discussed in the previous paragraph) and the ruptures in Friedländer's and Levin's friendships see my introduction to the collection of letters I discovered and edited: *Briefe an eine Freundin: Rahel Varnhagen an Rebecca Friedländer* (in press, Cologne, 1988). The 1808 quote from Levin is cited in Arendt, *Rahel Varnhagen: The Life of a Jewish Woman* (rpt. New York, 1974), 121.

31. Ibid., (1957 ed.).

mer salon guests. Prince Anton Radziwill and his wife Luise (the sister of Prince Louis Ferdinand) also hosted frequent open houses. A special treat at the Radziwill salon were the plays staged in the family's private theater. It was at the Radziwill home that several of Heinrich von Kleist's plays—which were usually rejected by Berlin's state theater company—were first performed. The Countess Julie von Voss, daughter of the *Hofdame* (lady-in-waiting) Caroline von Berg and a close friend of Gustav von Brinkmann, also opened an exclusive salon which was a favorite meeting place for Berlin nobles in the years after 1806.[32]

The appearance of these new noble salons shows that the French occupation and its ideological consequences did not destroy the objective social needs which salons met for their participants. Nor did the occupation destroy the subjective willingness of particular Berliners to meet their needs by attending salons. Salons emerged and endured because of social and institutional structures which were more permanent than which government was in power or which ideology was in fashion. As long as there were estates with mutually complementary amounts of status and wealth, and as long as the intellectual elite was small but lacking in opportunities for informal public socializing, the need for salons or for an institution very much like them continued to exist. Changing ideologies could, however, radically affect in whose homes salons would meet, what mix of guests would gather there, and what kind of functionally equivalent alternatives to salons would evolve. And a new patriotic, Christian, and antisemitic ideology did alter salon society in all three of these ways, contributing to a transformed social scene with new salon hosts and a new social mix of guests. By 1811, a "counter-salon" had appeared which was functionally similar to salons, but which was altogether different in its style and in the values of its participants. Called the Christlich-deutsch Tischgesellschaft (the "Christian-German Eating Club"), this counter-salon explicitly excluded Jews and even converted Jews. One of the main aims of its founders was to organize a boycott of the few Jewish salons that had survived the chaotic five years since the French first entered Berlin in October 1806.

The Tischgesellschaft was more important than its short life—it was formed in January 1811 and lasted only until 1813—might suggest. Its four

32. For discussion of von Stägemann, von Savigny, and von Voss salons see Steig, *Achim von Arnim und die ihm nahe standen*, vol. 3, (Stuttgart and Berlin, 1904), 4, 11, 179 and 431; on Iffland's reluctance to direct von Kleist's plays, see 4. For background, see Rudolf Weil, *Das Berliner Theaterpublikum unter A. W. Ifflands Direktion 1796–1814* (Berlin, 1932). Katherine Goodman's discussion of Elisabeth von Stägemann in her *Disclosures: Women's Autobiography in Germany Between 1790 and 1914* (New York, 1986), chap. 2, came to my attention too late to be used here.

central figures were Achim von Arnim, Heinrich von Kleist, Clemens
Brentano and Adam Müller, all ardent defenders of the traditional rights
of the nobility, but none born into a powerful noble family. Von Arnim
and von Kleist were sons of impoverished Junkers, Brentano the son of
a Frankfurt am Main merchant, and Müller was born into a family of
bureaucrats and preachers.[33] Despite these differences in background, by
the time they came together in the middle of the decade in Berlin, all
four young men—all were younger than thirty in 1806—had succeeded
in becoming productive intellectuals. More importantly for the formation of the Tischgesellschaft and for the demise of the Jewish salons, the
four were in passionate agreement on the burning questions of the day.
All were skittish about the cultural and economic power of Jews in Berlin, even if on occasion each dropped in at a Jewish salon. All were opposed to the French Revolution, the French occupation, and the exiled
Prussian monarchy's unwillingness to call for an armed uprising against
Napoleon. All four disagreed sharply with Stein and Hardenberg and
their followers that the way to regain Prussia's military power was to
reform its social structure.

Yet alongside their political conservatism, these four intellectuals had
anything but conservative views about art and the common people. With
their publications reconstructing ancient folk tales and songs, with their
"mass" newspaper, the *Berliner Abendblätter,* with their participation in
evening sessions of collective singing, these patriotic intellectuals and
their friends sought to share their nationalist enthusiasms with ordinary
Prussians. In the years between 1806 and 1810, the years when Jewish
salon society was falling apart, the circle which formed around these four
charismatic figures created a variety of institutions to publicize their patriotism. A favored meeting place for men "from all strata," including
some prominent noblemen, was the Liedertafel (singing club) begun in
1808 by Karl Zelter, who was a leading composer, director of the Singakademie in Berlin, and an enthusiastic patriot. The goal of the Liedertafel was to use collective singing to deepen a royalist form of nationalism. When King Frederick William III returned to Berlin in 1810 from

33. On the Tischgesellschaft see Margarete Dierks, *Die preussischen Altkonservativen und
die Judenfrage 1810–1847,* Heft 7 of *Rostocker Studien* (Rostock, 1939); Steig, *Achim von Arnim,*
vol. 3, 9–13; Philipp Eberhard, *Die politischen Anschauungen der christlich-deutschen Tischgesellschaft* (Erlangen, 1937). For von Arnim's biography I relied on Helene Riley, *Ludwig
Achim von Arnims Jugend- und Reisejahre* (Bonn, 1978) and on Roland Hoermann, *Achim
von Arnim* (Boston, 1984); on von Kleist I used Joachim Mass, *Kleist: Die Fackel Preussens*
(Vienna, 1957); on Clemens Brentano I found John Fetzer, *Clemens Brentano* (Boston, 1981),
useful; on Müller I relied on the article in the *ADB* (Leipzig, 1893), vol. 22, 587–610.

exile in Königsberg, a special welcoming celebration was organized by the Liedertafel.[34]

The short-lived daily paper edited by Kleist, the *Berliner Abenblätter,* was at once a more intellectual and a more popular organ for disseminating the new ideology than was the Liedertafel. The paper appeared for only two years, in 1810 and 1811, but it quickly became popular, and it also became most controversial with the Hardenberg government. Unlike the official twice-weekly newspapers, which contained stale foreign news, pro-French sentiments, and little reporting on culture, the *Abendblätter* ran lively satirical articles covering local culture events as well as national political issues. Authors of articles in the *Abendblätter* pleaded with the Hardenberg government to initiate a war of resistance against France, as well as to halt plans to transform the state's political structure. The regime's censors cared little about the cultural modernism of the newspaper, and even less about providing a modest income and a public voice for its talented, if still obscure editor Heinrich von Kleist. Their concern was, logically enough, with matters of state. Thus in spite of protracted negotiations by the paper's powerful noble patrons and a tenuous series of compromises, the government eventually closed down the *Abendblätter* in December 1811.[35] The timing was somewhat ironic, for there was growing sympathy in royal and ministerial circles for the radical anti-Napoleonism of the *Abendblätter.* But it would take two more years of French domination and Napoleon's attempt at conquering Russia before Prussia eventually joined with Austria in the war against France. For the time being, the *Abendblätter* circle's ardent patriotism was still too radical for the rump Prussian government.

In the same years that von Kleist, von Arnim, Brentano, and Müller worked to convince ordinary Prussians to become patriots, they also went about consolidating a committed cadre of like-minded intellectuals. To this end, in January 1811 Achim von Arnim sent out the invitations to the first meeting of the Tischgesellschaft. The proposal was sent to forty-six selected Berliners, who were anything but representative of the population at large, or even of the quite elite group of one hundred who had participated in salon society. The by-laws of the Tischgesellschaft were explicit about who was to be excluded: no Jews (including converted Jews), women, or "philistines" were to be allowed to join the lunches every other Tuesday at a local restaurant. A look at the list of those in-

34. Zelter's founding of the Liedertafel is discussed in Steig, *Achim von Arnim,* vol. 3, 14.

35. A fine summary of the history of the *Abendblätter* can be found in ibid., 39–160.

vited shows a prominent group indeed. Twenty, almost half of the forty-six men, were noble; among the commoners were some important men about town, including Friedrich von Stägemann, Karl Zelter, Hans Genelli (a leading architect), and Johann Fichte.[36]

The exclusionary rules of the Tischgesellschaft were a public pronouncement and a formal consolidation of changing trends in private friendships in the preceding years. Some of these rifts had developed in the course of common literary projects. Edward Julius Hitzig, the converted son of Isaac Daniel Itzig and an important publisher and bookseller in Berlin, was the publisher of the *Abendblätter*. Hitzig was explicitly excluded from the new club because he had converted. But Hitzig was also disliked because his political views were closer to the Hardenberg set than to the founders of the Tischgesellschaft. Ongoing financial conflicts exacerbated negative feelings toward Hitzig. For Kleist and his *Abendblätter* colleagues were convinced that Hitzig was exploiting them financially in his dealings with *Abendblätter*. Hitzig's friends, the bookseller Johann Sander and the inpoverished writer Friedrich Buchholz, were also among those not invited to join the Tischgesellschaft. The decision to exclude Buchholz (although he was a "real" gentile) was principally ideological, insofar as Buchholz was an active critic of what he called the "feudal" line taken by the *Abendblätter*. But Buchholz's exclusion was social too, insofar as he definitely did not mix in prominent circles. Another set of Hitzig's friends, the North Star circle of authors, which included Ludwig Robert and Karl August Varnhagen, were also not invited to join the Tischgesellschaft. Not only was Ludwig Robert a convert; von Arnim and Brentano declared the politics of the entire North Star circle to be "immature."[37]

The formation of the Tischgesellschaft was a direct threat to whatever power Berlin's Jewish salon women still possessed in 1811. The explicit exclusion of Jews and women cannot be compared to the rather more casual exclusion of Jews and women from the intellectual clubs of the 1770s and 1780s, at a time when Berlin's Jewish elite had not yet come into its own, culturally or socially. The Tischgesellschaft's exclusion of converted Jews shows that the targets of the patriotic intellectuals' attack were precisely those Jews pilloried by Grattenauer: those who had traveled far toward integration into the dominant society. Letters written by key participants in the Jewish salons show clearly that salon Jews and their supporters did indeed see in the formation of the Tischgesellschaft a direct assault. The time that the Tischgesellschaft met—for an early

---

36. The list of Tischgesellschaft members can be found in ibid., 21.
37. Brentano's evaluation of the North Star circle is cited in ibid., 6.

afternoon lunch on a weekday—can also be interpreted as an attack on the salons. The late evening salon gatherings were more convenient for the less privileged who worked during the day.[38]

Although the Tischgesellschaft's founders opposed the values and excluded the personalities so central to Jewish salon society, the new club did fulfill some of the same social and intellectual functions as the salons had. Members read their manuscripts at the Tuesday noon gatherings for friendly critique; it was in this way that word spread of Clemens Brentano's *Der Philister,* with its controversial antisemitic passages. The mix of noble and commoner men at the club's meetings facilitated the same kind of social mobility achieved in the intellectual clubs and in the salons. In the opinion of some, the Tischgesellschaft actually included more noble intellectuals and was the setting for more close friendships between nobles and commoners than any other association in the German past.[39] A precise comparison of salon men with the Tischgesellschaft circle necessary to test this claim lies outside the scope of this book. Although the Tischgesellschaft was in this way functionally parallel to salons, in other ways the intellectual world had changed as a result of the cataclysmic political events of the decade. Unlike many noble salon authors, whose chosen genre was mainly the novel, the noblemen affiliated with the Tischgesellschaft turned more often to treatises and satire. The tumultous political events of these years inspired talented noble intellectuals to fight for the traditional powers of their caste, and they put their pens in the service of their political passions.

In this way, the inspired polemics of an Achim von Arnim or an Alexander von der Marwitz expressed a more explicit and a more self-interested involvement in politics than the writings of the romantic intellectuals who had visited the Jewish salons a quarter century before. The early romantic circle around the Schlegel brothers, Friedrich Schleiermacher, and Ludwig Tieck wrote about politics only by way of metaphor. By lambasting the rationalism, deism, and universalism of the Enlightenment in the name of the irrational, of religious enthusiasm, of history and of subjectivity, the early romantics opened a door to the

38. See Arendt's biography of Rahel Varnhagen (1974 edition), 122–24 for a sharp analysis of the various ways that the Tischgesellschaft constituted a "direct protest against the Jewish salons of the day."

39. This claim is made by Eberhard, *Die politischen Anschauungen,* 4. Steig (*Achim von Arnim,* vol. 3, 4) makes a parallel point when he claims that patriotic activity "bonded the nobility to the *Bürgertum.*" Steig cites von Arnim's view that the nobility "could no longer relate only to itself, but needed a connection to *Bildung.*" In this sense, the noble-commoner ties developed in the Tischgesellschaft were a continuation of the same trends in salon society discussed in chap. 5, albeit involving many different individuals, whose ideology was also very different than the ideology of most salon men.

nationalism of the Tischgesellschaft circle, but it was not until the 1806 defeat that romantic intellectuals linked their enthusiasm for subjective feeling to the institutional vehicle of the nation-state. The intellectuals' new appreciation of the state was stimulated by Napoleon's ability to call his nation to arms, juxtaposed with Prussia's traumatic attempts to recover from the huge defeat at his army's hands in October 1806. But translating a diffuse patriotism into practical policy was no easy matter in the confusing geopolitical context of early-nineteenth-century Germany. The Holy Roman Empire was dead, but none of the many small states was yet hegemonic. In the same years the Jewish salons declined leading Berlin intellectuals came to believe that making Prussia into that single hegemonic state within Germany was the central project of the age for all German nationalists.

The reason that the formation of the Tischgesellschaft was such an attack on the Jewish salons was not simply that the club's founders set themselves to rebuild the Prussian state, but that they envisioned a conservative and a Christian version of that state. It was not inevitable that all these ideologies go together. There were, after all, less conservative and less Christian versions of an antisemitic, anti-French stance. It was possible to be a Prussian patriot, dislike Jews, and disdain French values without agreeing with the Tischgesellschaft's view of things. Here Friedrich Buchholz is again instructive. Buchholz was active in print pillorying the *Berliner Abendblätter's* enthusiasm for a "feudal monarchy," and defended Adam Smith against the *Abendblätter's* attacks on Smith's theories. Yet out of this radical democratic nationalism Buchholz came to oppose the personnel and the values of the same Jewish salons despised by the Tischgesellschaft circle.[40] Buchholz's position shows that more than one route could lead to antagonism against the Jewish salons. But the Buchholz line was ideiosyncratic. The conservative and Christian patriotism articulated by the Tischgesellschaft set became the increasingly dominant ideology among the city's intelligentsia. What mattered terribly was not just their German nationalism per se but the religious character of their dreamed-of state. Even though this dream would never be fully realized, it had a significant legacy. And this legacy would be telling not just for the fate of the Jewish salons but also for the politics of nineteenth-century Prussia.

The vision of the ideal Prussian state as Christian was, at one level, an

---

40. In addition to Rütger Schäfer's *Friedrich Buchholz—ein vergessener Vorläufer der Soziologie* (Göppingen, 1972), see also Otto Tschirch, "Friedrich Buchholz, Friedrich von Coelln, und Julius von Voss, drei preussische Publizisten in der Zeit der Fremdherrschaft 1806–1812," *Forschungen zur brandenburgischen und preussischen Geschichte,* N.F. 48 (Berlin, 1936), 163–81.

attack on the sensual style and the social mobility associated with Jewish salon society. King Frederick William III himself—who did eventually, with some prodding, become an ardent Christian patriot—explicitly identified "moral decay" as the cause of Prussia's military collapse in 1806. And this decay itself was caused, in the king's eyes, by the social mobility of the preceding years and the resulting "discontent."[41] Adam Müller put the matter more abstractly, asserting that the state was the essential institution which "mediated" between the lone individual and the rest of humanity. Müller added that it was only through the state that the Christian and the national "ideas" could be linked. Thus as well as being the fulfillment of pan-Germanic patriotism, in this view the state was the one institution uniquely able to integrate religion with patriotism.[42] A state that could reconcile both the individual with humanity and religion with nationalism was a powerful institution indeed. The ultimate subjectivity was merged with the ultimate objectivity, and the service of God was merged with the service of one's people. To challenge the validity of a state understood to embody so many things would be to challenge much of what matters to most people in this life.

Ultimately, because of the political victories of the Tischgesellschaft's liberal enemies, the most reactionary elements of the club's program did not become a part of the Prussian state which emerged from the reform era. But the club founders' notion that the Prussian state was intrinsically Christian came to be widely accepted by Prussian intellectuals and endured in Germany well into the twentieth century. The consequences for the fate of the Jewish community were immense. If the state was Christian in its essence, then the original liberal project of ending the Jewish community's inferior status by making Jews into citizens became problematic. The pressure on Jewish citizens to complete their integration by converting to Christianity increased radially, since to be "citizens of the Jewish faith" in a Christian state was to find oneself in an anachronistic, if not contradictory situation.

At another level, the patriotic intellectuals dreamed of a Christian state because the Jewish successes of the era challenged the assumed superiority of Christianity. These successes raised the obvious question: was the traditional charge of Jewish inferiority justified? If not, and neither Jews nor Judaism were inferior, then the superiority of Christianity was called into question. As we have learned, some deistic intellectuals, Jews as well as Christians, had pondered all of this and had come to the con-

41. King Frederick William II's views are quoted in Anderson, *Nationalism and the Cultural Crisis*, 67.
42. Steig, *Achim von Arnim*, vol. 3, 5.

clusion that Christianity was not in fact superior, that Judaism and Christianity were essentially identical and should therefore merge. But Abraham Teller's rejection of David Friedländer's 1799 "dry baptism" proposal showed that this extreme version of deism was more attractive to reform-minded Jewish intellectuals than it was to powerful Protestant ministers. The ultimate failure of the deists to synthesize Judaism and Christianity made the liberal endeavor of ending Jewish inferiority by making Jews into secular citizens all the more difficult. And even given the (perhaps inevitable) failure of the deist vision, the liberal "philosemites" still might have succeeded in the project of emnacipation, if they could manage to displace the Jewish issue from the religious to the political arena.[43] By granting unconverted Jews citizenship and declaring that sufficient, the question of the religious validity of Judaism could be avoided.

The conservative Christian patriots, in contrast, would not let go of religion. They responded to Jewish acculturation by strengthening the significance and superiority of Christianity. Here was a direct parallel to the split among the Junkers on the question of whether reforming the Prussian social structure would aid or hinder a revitalized state. The difference was that the liberal Junders were victorious on the social issue, whereas the convservatives were victorious in defining the state as Christian rather than secular. This victory had weighty consequences, not just for the salon Jews but also for successive generations of Prussian Jewry. If the nineteenth-century Prussian state had been understood by its leaders, by leading intellectuals, and by the common people to be a truly secular state, perhaps the liberal project of making Jews into "citizens of the Mosaic faith" would have been sufficient to make Jews truly equal. But since the state came to be defined as a Christian institution from the outset, becoming a "merely" secular citizen would never in itself be quite enough to make even an acculturated Jew into a real Prussian.

Epilogue

The decline of the Jewish salons was a significant loss, not only for the handful of women who enjoyed the prominence salons provided them, but also for wider sectors of Prussian society. This claim remains true in spite of the fact that only one hundred people at the very summit of society participated in salons. Even though the numbers involved were small, the symbolic import of such heterogeneous social mixing was large. To be sure, some might argue that the social glory achieved by the salonières did not constitute genuine emancipation, that the women

43. See Sterling, *Judenhass.*

achieved social integration and cultural power at the high cost of abandoning their families and their faith. But however the subjective meaning of the salonières' emancipation is interpreted, the Jewish salons were unquestionably a noteworthy achievement when measured in the objective language of social history.

As a noteworthy achievement in social history, the Jewish salons did not embody either philosemitic or antisemitic theories; such a formulation reverses the real order of influence. It would be more precise to say that both philosemitic and antisemitic treatises and policies were inspired by the different responses particular intellectuals had to Jewish salon society. For the existence of the Jewish salons in Berlin during this crucial quarter-century demonstrated just how polished, graceful, and powerful emancipated Jews could be. It was precisely the quick successes of the Jewish salonières which exposed the inconsistency between the Jews' social glory and their lack of civic rights. Thus the salonières' made a distinct contribution to Jewish political emancipation. The 1812 edict of Jewish emancipation was a policy triumph engineered by liberal philosemites. It gave wealthy Jews the right to be citizens of Berlin, allowed for Jews to move about freely, and abolished special taxes on the Jewish community. The 1812 edict has been described as the attempt to remove the discrepancy between Jewish success in society and Jewish inequality in the state.[44]

A good case can thus be made that the social glory of salons contributed to the political rights Jews achieved in 1812, and that both of these social and the political successes together were the high points in this first chapter in the story of Jewish life in modern Prussia. One might conclude then, that this first chapter was a consistently positive one for Prussian Jewry. The irony would simply be that a miniature version of the assimilationist dream had been realized so terribly early in the story. Yet as we have learned in this chapter, things Jewish were not that simple. For the decline of the Jewish salons occurred in the very decade when the 1812 edict was being formulated, and the causes of this decline were not just external events like occupation and war. Therefore, the real picture was anything but consistent and positive. No, in the same years that saw remarkable progress in Jewish social and political life, a current of antisemitism was alive within the heart of salon society, a current which undermined and eventually destroyed the very social glory which had contributed to political emancipation. As we have seen, this antisemitism was expressed on the sly by the most prominent salon men in the same years that they enjoyed themselves in Jewish salons. This antisemitism

44. See Kohler, *Jewish Rights*, 12 and 50, and Krüger, *Berliner Romantik*, 51.

broke asunder key friendships that held salon society together. Varieties of this antisemitism were expressed in the pamphlet war that began in 1803. And eventually, this antisemitism mobilized the formation of the Tischgesellschaft, the city's counter-salon.

It was a highly ironic state of affairs. For centuries traditional religious antisemites had been haranguing Jews for failing to act like gentiles and, essentially, for not being Christians. The Berlin salons were a distinctive moment early in modern European history when a sizable group of wealthy Jews mixed intimately with gentiles, converted to Christianity, and intermarried. This behavior was, objectively, precisely what traditional antisemites had long demanded. Simultaneously, this behavior was the fulfillment of the liberal pro-assimilationist vision espoused by both philosemitic gentiles and by radical Jewish reformers. Yet in the midst of this successful assimilationist institution, prominent gentile salon guests, including some who were known publicly as liberals, attacked the same acts of assimilation which both earlier antisemites and contemporary liberals had demanded. Just at the point when assimilating Jews and philosemitic gentiles together made social integration a reality, this social integration was ridiculed in private and sometimes in public as well.

Given this underside to salon culture, can the standard view that social success in the salons led to the granting of political rights in 1812 possibly be correct? A comment by Wilhelm von Humboldt, the leading liberal at the time of the Vienna Congress, suggests that the liberal position was actually riddled with contradictions. Although in principle liberals like von Humboldt were thought to be in favor of the twin goals of social integration and political emancipation, in private von Humboldt was obviously less than enthusiastic about either project. In an 1810 letter to his wife, von Humboldt wrote that he "was working with all my might to give Jews civil rights so that it would no longer be necessary, out of generosity, to go to Jewish houses."[45] Von Humboldt seems to have equated the social act of visiting Jewish salons with the political act of working for Jewish civic equality; both were gestures which fulfilled him as an enlightened, avant-garde intellectual. The implication is that these were interchangeable gestures, rather than that Jewish social success was an incentive which motivated him to work for Jewish political emancipation. To be sure, von Humboldt's underlying impulse and his public behavior both remained vaguely philosemitic. He wanted to be "generous" to Berlin's elite Jews, visited their salons, and worked on their behalf

45. This quote is cited in Kohler, *Jewish Rights*, 35. The original quote appeared in Anna von Sydow, *Wilhelm und Caroline Humboldt in ihren Briefen*, 7 vols. (Berlin, 1907–14), vol. 4, 458.

within the Prussian bureaucracy and later, at the Vienna Congress. Yet his support was tentative enough that once he had done his part for Jewish political equality, he could dispense with visiting Jewish salons.

Von Humboldt's revealing comment tells all. In these few words he summarized the historic trend which would unfold in the coming decades. As Jewish prominence in high society declined sharply, liberal gentiles and Jewish reformers both turned their attention away from society and toward politics, with the aim of expanding the limited emancipation which had been achieved in the 1812 edict. Even the most polished Jews' most ardent supporters seem to have felt that their debt to the Jewish cause was fulfilled with this political work, relieving them of the outmoded, merely metaphorical political duty of befriending individual Jews. The Jewish salons had flourished in the later eighteenth century when religious antisemitism was no longer accepted by all, yet Jewish matters had not yet come to be defined in explicitly political terms. Everything was possible, because nothing was measured by an established institutional calculus. Social gestures were politically symbolic but had no definite political implications. The old religious prejudices were ridiculed, but the new Christian vision of the state had not yet been articulated.

The reservations harbored by even the Jews' most dedicated liberal supporters were an important reason why the social glory attained by the salonières in this era did not, in fact, continue into the nineteenth century. Their reservations also help explain why the fight for the political emancipation which would consolidate social success became so protracted. But the liberals' contradictions were not the only problem. The conservative legacy was also telling. For as we have learned, even though the conservative antisemites did not succeed in imposing all of their policies on the nineteenth-century Prussian state, their definition of the state as Christian was accepted even by those who did not share their ideology completely. The notion that the state was Christian contributed to the pressures on Jews to complete their secular citizenship by converting in the next century. And even then converted Jews were not "true" Christians, and many doors, private and public, remained closed to them. This too was a legacy of the conservative antisemites, who reserved the right to condemn as insufficient the same behavior earlier antisemites—and sometimes they themselves—had called for.

The paradox that the "positive" 1812 edict should be announced just as both liberals and conservatives were undermining the salons which supposedly made the edict necessary shows how tightly the salon Jews were caught in a no-win dilemma. Their successes at assimilation made them vulnerable to double attack. Traditional antisemites might judge them as insufficiently polished at the same time that new conservative antisemites might judge the identical person or the identical behavior as *too* polished. It was extremely insulting to be reproached for trying to join the dominant society just when liberal philosemites were, at least publicly, encouraging Jews to do just this. It was a massive blow for salon Jews to be blamed not for being different, but rather for trying to be like the elegant gentiles. That they should have suffered this blow so soon after achieving a grand success must make us ponder the quality of their success.

So too must we ponder the short span of success that the salonières, Jewish and gentile alike, achieved in their roles as literary women. Just as salons offered a particular set of opportunities to Jewish women which did not continue into the nineteenth century, so too the literary scene gradually evolved in a way that made it much more difficult for wealthy women to exercise cultural power without publishing. As the intelligentsia and the reading public both grew, so too did the social and intellectual distance between the two groups increase, making communication between publishing intellectuals and their readers more formalized. The eventual disappearance of the salon as a public space was a crucial loss for the wealthy female dilettante. As the intelligentsia in big cities grew too large even for its stars to gather in the salon style—which was at once voluntaristic yet elite—an array of other intellectual institutions evolved which fulfilled some of the salon's functions. The reading public absorbed new cultural trends by increasing access to newspapers, journals, lectures, libraries, museums, theaters, and coffeehouses. The publishing intellectuals, on the other hand, participated in revitalized universities, professional societies, editorial boards, political parties, and (eventually) parliaments, where ideas could be exchanged and public power exercised. In this way intellectual life went on and flourished without salons. But women were left by the wayside, for without the salons where authors and readers could gather informally, women, even those who published, lost an idiosyncratic public stage. To be sure, certain types of male intellectuals lost out too when salons disappeared. The face-to-face casual patronage available in salons, where poor young tutors, established professors, and noble dilettantes mixed socially, was not a function often met in the various institutions that replaced salons.

Thus new intellectual institutions came into being which excluded women altogether, or at best kept them marginal. This changing institutional scene was itself affected by the retreat of the Prussian nobility from urban intellectual life, and their retreat also had consequences for literary women. A more secure, more cohesive Prussian nobility less under the sway of the French model produced fewer sensually free, literary women; commoner women, moreover, had fewer chances to mix with and imitate the nobility. A smaller, wealthier nobility with guaranteed access into the summit of officialdom in the city and larger, more profitable estates in the country was created by the reforms of 1806–14. As a result, the nineteenth-century nobility had fewer members in need of loans and diversion, and nobles lived by a more exclusive social code. As a truly bourgeois society emerged whose members had limited social contact with a more elitest nobility, the noble model of sensually free and culturally powerful women was imitated less often by non-noble women.

But the withdrawal of the nobility from the urban intellectual scene which followed from the restructuring of the Prussian nobility, important as it was, did not alone destroy the salonière's literary role. After all, the tradition of culturally powerful noblewomen was weak in Prussia to begin with, so its declining influence had limited consequences for literary women. Here again the role of ideology was decisive. For the patriotic enthusiasms of the post-1806 years which so affected the Jews also contributed to increasing difficulties for literary women. The patriots' total abhorence for the French lifestyle was particularly crucial. What the new patriots especially criticized was the salon women's tendency to shun family ties and childbearing in their pursuit of romantic love, intellectual pleasures, and public cultural power. The patriots' critique of this emancipation from the family was no isolated Prussian development. Throughout Europe and also in America, the early nineteenth century was a time when women were exhorted to return to domesticity and the raising of children. The idea was to redirect the intellectual and political enthusiasms which women had pursued in the last decades of the eighteenth century away from the public and into the private world. They could best contribute to the state by raising citizens and soldiers.[46]

The new emphasis on family and motherhood made cross-estate misalliances less acceptable, at the same time that the consolidation of the nobility removed the nobles' economic motives for entering such relationships. A decline in cross-estate misalliance did not just keep estates and classes within traditional boundaries. A social climate that discouraged misalliances also made female literary careers more difficult. After all, the salon women's major allies in getting into print were their male friends, who sometimes doubled as their own lovers or their friends' lovers. When the salons declined in importance and the few remaining salons were less heterogeneous in their composition, the salon's function

---

46. See Silvia Bovenschen, *Die imaginierte Weiblichkeit: Exemplarische Untersuchungen zu kulturgeschichtlichen und literarischen Präsentationsformen des Weiblichen* (Frankfurt a.M., 1979).

as a marriage market disappeared. Thus by the early nineteenth century, women who might have participated in salons in the previous century lost a milieu where they could meet both prominent and aspiring male writers—men who could aid in work as well as in love.

The decline of salons in Berlin was thus a loss not only to their immediate participants, but also to subsequent generations of acculturated Jews and literary women. But it is crucial that our story not end on this abstract level. We must say goodbye to the salons with a glance back not only at how the salons' demise affected Jews in general and literary women in general, but also with a look at how their demise affected Jewish women in particular. This is not to imply that Jewish women alone created salon society to Berlin. Had there been no wealthy Jews in Berlin in the last decades of the eighteenth century, no doubt there still would have been a few salons. Nine, not all fourteen of the salons reconstructed in this book were led by Jews. The social, institutional, and ideological structures which caused salons in this quarter century existed quite apart from the peculiarities of the Jewish community in Berlin.

As a wealthy surrogate bourgeoisie in an era when public banking facilities were still primitive, Jewish financiers provided an important source of capital not only for the mercantilist Prussian state, but also for individual nobles in economic distress. Without the Jewish presence in Berlin, the tiny gentile bourgeoisie would have fulfilled some of these same functions, albeit in a more modest and less conspicuous fashion. In preindustrial cities, including Berlin, where social mixing and intermarriage completed the economic exchanges binding nobles to commoners, salons—or a similar institution—would have come to life, Jews or no Jews. Had there been no wealthy Jewish financiers in Berlin, the salonières would have probably all been gentile daughters of wealthy merchants and prominent officials, as well as rebellious noble dilettantes. Attention to function and not just to personnel is key in getting beyond the mystique that without Jews there would have been no salons at all in Berlin.

Still, the Jewish elite was a surrogate bourgeoisie in late eighteenth-century Berlin, and Jewish women did dominate among the salonières. They and their successors thus had the most to lose, first when their patriotic guests deserted them, then when conservative nobles opened competitive salons and counter-salons, and finally, when salons declined altogether. Most obviously, the disappearance of salons as a marriage market affected Jewish women's chances to intermarry. Indeed, the conversion statistics shows that relative to men, Jewish women in Berlin converted and intermarried less often than Jewish men beginning in the second decade of the nineteenth century.

As the salon era came to an end, and nobles withdrew their friendship from Jewish women, the model for Jewish emancipation became more male-oriented and more oriented to the gentile middle class. The major project for Jewish reform came to be the creation of "gebildtete" (culti-vated) Jewish men, polished in their German, their clothing, their man-ners, and their behavior in the synagogue. In the eyes of the Jewish reformers, this cultivation was not to result in conversion or in intermar-riage, but in the reform of the traditional Jewish community. The news-papers, journals, clubs, and synagogues where the reform ideology was disseminated and put into practice were organized by men and open mainly to men. If the new acculturated Jews were to mix with gentiles at all, then the ideal pair would be a cultivated Jewish man and an equally upstanding middle-class gentile man, not a Jewish woman and a disso-lute nobleman.[47]

Thus it came to be that Berlin's sophisticated Jewish women and their successors lost the stage of the salon, a stage on which to perform intel-lectually, but also a stage on which to mix with powerful, elegant men. As Jews, they suffered when emancipation came to be defined as religious and political reform rather than as social integration with women as the pioneers. As literary women they suffered as the work of dilettantes be-came more private and they lost a setting in which to meet male mentors. And even within the acculturated circles of Jewry the Jewish salon women suffered in relation to Jewish men, who took over the mammoth task of designing a new and different life for Jewish Germans. Future generations could either mourn or rejoice that the salonières' style of emancipation was over, but no one could ever doubt that it had been a special time and a special institution for a special circle of women.

47. This analysis of how the reform movement involved mainly Jewish men is my inter-pretation of the splendid unpublished manuscript by David Sorkin of Oxford University: "The Invisible Community: The Subculture of German Jewry, 1780–1840, forthcoming, Oxford University Press, New York. Sorkin's dissertation on the same theme titled "Ideol-ogy and Identity: Political Emancipation and the Emergence of a Jewish Subculture in Germany, 1800–1848" (University of California at Berkeley, 1983).

Bibliographic Note

While doing the research for this book, I kept wishing that I could find a unique primary source around which the study would structure itself. But I gradually came to see that my wish was inappropriate to the subject matter. Finding the salon and placing it in the proper framework was mainly a matter of looking at the old, published sources in new ways, not finding unpublished treasures.

The exceptions to this rule were two: Gustav von Brinkmann's correspondence in the Goethe-Schiller Archive in Weimar, and the Judenkartei in the Evangelisches Zentralarchiv in West Berlin. Von Brinkmann's letters provided precious gossip from a key salon personality; the Judenkartei provided an undreamed-of statistical precision to answer the question of whether the salon women's assimilation was or was not typical of other Berlin Jews.

For chapter 1, I had to make to with rather anecdotal tales of salons in Germany and elsewhere. See, for example, Bertha Meyer, *Salon Sketches* (New York, 1938); Mary Hargrave, *Some German Women and Their Salons* (London, n.d.); Valerian Tornius, *Salons: Pictures of Society through Five Centuries* (New York, 1920); Helen Clergue, *The Salon: A Study of French Society and Personalities in the Eighteenth Century* (New York, 1907); Louis Batibfol, *The Great Literary Salons* (London, 1930); and Evelyn Hall, *The Women of the Salons* (New York 1969). Works that were more sophisticated and also more useful for deciding upon a research design for the book include: Carolyn Lougee, *Le Paradis des Femmes: Women, Salons, and Social Stratification in Seventeenth-Century France* (Princeton, 1976); Ingeborg Drewitz, *Berliner Salons: Gesellschaft und Literatur zwischen Aufklärung und Industriezeitalter* (Berlin, 1965); Chauncy Tinker, *The Salon and English Letters* (New York, 1915); Evelyn Bodek, "*Salonières* and Bluestockings," *Feminist Studies* 3 (1976), 185–99; and Peter Quennell, ed., *Affairs of the Mind: The Salon in Europe and America from the Eighteenth to the Twentieth Century* (Washington D.C., 1980). Two volumes very hostile to Berlin's Jewish salon women but indispensable as research tools were Hans Karl Krüger, *Berliner Romantik und*

Berliner Judentum (Bonn, 1939); and Kurt Fervers, *Berliner Salons: Die Geschichte einer grossen Verschwörung* (Munich, 1940).

The best source for the contemporary descriptions I used to set the scene for chapter 2 was Frank Eyssenhardt, *Berlin im Jahre 1786* (Leipzig, 1886). On the nobility, the most comprehensive works were Hans Rosenberg, *Bureaucracy, Aristocracy, Autocracy: The Prussian Experience, 1660–1815* (Cambridge, Mass., 1958); Fritz Martiny, *Die Adelsfrage in Preussen vor 1806*, Beiheft 35 of the *Vierteljahresheft für Sozial- und Wirtschaftsgeschichte* (Stuttgart, 1936); and Hanna Schissler, "Die Junker," in *Preussen im Rückblick*, H.-J. Puhle and H.-U. Wehler, eds. (Göttingen, 1980). On Berlin Jewry, I relied especially on Eugen Wolbe, *Geschichte der Juden in Berlin und der Mark Brandenburg* (Berlin, 1937); Selma Stern, *Der Preussische Staat und die Juden*, 3 vols. (Tübingen, 1971); Ismar Freund, *Die Emanzipation der Juden in Preussen* (Berlin, 1912), Stefi Jersch-Wenzel, *Juden und 'Franzosen' in der Wirtschaft des Raumes Berlin/Brandenburg* (Berlin, 1978); and Ludwig Geiger, "Vor hundert Jahren: Mitteilungen aus der Geschichte der Juden Berlins," *Zeitschrift für die Geschichte der Juden in Deutschland* 3 (1899). A stimulating brief interpretation of the Jewish legal position can be found in the indispensable Henri Brunschwig, *Enlightenment and Romanticism in Eighteenth-Century Prussia* (Chicago, 1974). My interpretation of the way in which state policy limited Jewish and gentile merchants was influenced by Hugo Rachel and Paul Wallich, *Berliner Grosskaufleute und Kapitalisten* (Berlin, 1967); two volumes by W. O. Henderson, *Studies in the Economic Policy of Frederick the Great*, (London, 1963) and *The Rise of German Industrial Power, 1834–1915* (Berkeley, 1975); and Karoline Cauer, *Oberhofbankier und Hofbaurat: Aus der Berliner Bankgeschichte des 18. Jh.* (Frankfurt a.M., 1968).

The research materials I used to uncover the Berlin intelligentsia's patterns of social mobility was the collective biography I assembled, mainly from biographical dictionaries. The single most extensive of these was G. C. Hamburger and G. J. Meusel, *Das gelehrte Teutschland* (Lemgo, 1796). On the history of the publishing industry and reading habits, the best sources were Johann Goldfriedrich, *Geschichte des Deutschen Buchhandels*, vol. 3 (Aalen, 1970); Helmut Hiller, *Zur Sozialgeschichte vom Buch und Buchhandel* (Bonn, 1966); and two books by Rolf Engelsing: *Der Bürger als Leser: Lesergeschichte in Deutschland 1500–1800* (Stuttgart, 1974) and *Analphabetentum und Lektüre: Zur Sozialgeschichte des Lesens in Deutschland zwischen feudaler und industrieller Gesellschaft* (Stuttgart, 1973). On the emergence of the freelance writing career, see H. J. Haferkorn, "Zur Entstehung der bürgerlich-literarischen Intelligenz," in *Deutsches Bürgertum und literarische Intelligenz*, B. Lutz, ed., (Stuttgart, 1974). A classic overview of the intelligentsia by a sociologist is Hans

Gerth, *Bürgerliche Intelligenz um 1800* (Gottingen, 1976). On the formal academic institutions, see Adolf Harnack, *Geschichte der königlich preussischen Akademie* (Berlin, 1900); H. Rossler and G. Franz, eds., *Universität und Gelehrtenstand 1400–1800* (Limburg/Lahn, 1970); and W. Roessler, *Die Entstehung des modernen Erziehungswesens in Deutschland* (Stuttgart, 1961).

Two lively volumes rich in telling images of the cultural world described in chapter 4 are Hans Ostwald, *Kultur- und Sittengeschichte Berlins* (Berlin, 1924); and Ludwig Geiger, *Berlin 1688–1840: Geschichte des geistigen Lebens der preussischen Hauptstadt* (Berlin, 1893–95). Jürgen Habermas's *Strukturwandel der Öffentlichkeit* (Neuwied and Berlin, 1974) and Norbert Elias's *Die höfische Gesellschaft* (Neuwied and Darmstadt, 1975) provided important conceptual and historical models for this chapter. W. H. Bruford's *Theatre and Drama in Goethe's Germany* (London, 1950) and Rudolf Weil, *Das Berliner Theaterpublikum* (Berlin, 1932) both charted the history of the theater. No one source was central for work on the intellectual clubs and on particular salons—that material was by its nature very scattered. A few of the broadest volumes used were Horst Möller, *Aufklärung in Preussen: Der Verleger, Publizist und Geschichtsschreiber Friedrich Nicolai* (Berlin, 1974); M. Kayserling, *Die jüdischen Frauen in der Geschichte, Literatur und Kunst* (Leipzig, 1879); Hannah Arendt, *Rahel Varnhagen: The Life of a Jewess* (London, 1957); Karl August Varnhagen von Ense (Karl Leutner abridged edition), *Denkwürdigkeiten des eigenen Lebens* (East Berlin, 1954); and the ideologically distasteful but useful Wilhelm Grau, *Wilhelm von Humboldt und das Problem des Juden* (Hamburg, 1935).

Research for chapter 5 provided me with an excuse to read some outstanding recent biographies, including Paul Sweet, *Wilhelm von Humboldt: A Biography* (Columbus, Oh., 1978); Alexander Altmann, *Moses Mendelssohn: A Biographical Study* (University, Ala., 1973); Joachim Mass, *Kleist: Die Fackel Preussens* (Vienna, 1957); Jacob Baxa, *Friedrich von Gentz* (Vienna, 1965); Günter de Bruyn, *Das Leben des Jean Paul Friedrich Richter* (Frankfurt a.M., 1978); and Klaus Gunzel, *König der Romantik: Das Leben des Dichters Ludwig Tieck* (Tübingen, 1981). Older works which were very useful included Reinhold Steig, *Achim von Arnim und die ihm nahe standen,* 3 vols. (Stuttgart and Berlin, 1904); Jakob Fromer, *Salomon Maimons Lebensgeschichte* (Munich, 1911); Immanuel Ritter, *Geschichte der jüdischen Reformation: David Friedländer* (Berlin, 1861); and Immanuel Fichte, *Johann Gottlieb Fichtes Leben* (Leipzig, 1862). The best primary sources were Albert Leitzmann, ed., *Wilhelm von Humboldts Briefe an Karl Gustav von Brinkmann* (Leipzig, 1939); Felix Eberty, *Jugenderinnerungen eines alten Berliners* (Berlin, 1925); Karl August Varnhagen von

Ense, ed., *Galerie von Bildnissen aus Rahels Umgang und Briefwechsel* (Leipzig, 1836); Alfons Feder Cohn, ed., *Wilhelm von Burgsdorffs Briefe* (Berlin, 1907); and Philip Miller, ed., *An Abyss Deep Enough: Letters of Heinrich von Kleist* (New York, 1982).

The richest surveys of female intellectuals in eighteenth-century Germany, on which I relied for chapter 6, are G. Jackel and M. Schlösser, eds., *Das Volk braucht Licht: Frauen aus der Zeit des Aufbruchs 1790–1848 in ihren Briefen* (Darmstadt and Zurich, 1970); Christine Touaillon, *Der deutsche Frauenroman des 18. Jahrhunderts* (Vienna and Leipzig, 1919); Adalbert von Hanstein, *Die Frauen in der Geschichte des deutschen Geisteslebens des 18. und 19. Jahrhunderts*, 2 vols. (Leipzig, 1899–1900); Silvia Bovenschen, *Die imaginierte Weiblichkeit: Exemplarische Untersuchungen zu kulturgeschichtlichen und literarischen Präsentationsformen des Weiblichen* (Frankfurt a.M., 1979); Johannes Scherr, *Geschichte der deutschen Frauenwelt* (Leipzig, 1911); and Elise Oelsner, *Die Leistungen der deutschen Frau in den letzten vierhundert Jahren auf wissenschaftlichem Gebiet* (Breslau, 1894). Excellent collective biographies are Georg Christoph Lehms, *Biographies Teutschlands galanten Poetinnen* (Frankfurt a.M., 1715); Carl von Schindel, *Die deutschen Schriftstellerinnen des 19. Jh.* (Leipzig, 1823–25, rpt. New York, 1978); and Elisabeth Friedrichs, *Die deutschsprachigen Schriftstellerinnen des 18. and 19. Jahrhunderts* (Stuttgart, 1981). Older but still useful older individual biographies are Christopher Herold, *Mistress to an Age: A Life of Madame de Staël* (London, 1959); Elisabeth Hausmann, *Die Karschin* (Frankfurt a.M., 1933); and Otto Berdrow, *Rahel Varnhagen* (Stuttgart, 1902). Excellent general studies of women and romanticism are: Helga Meise, *Die Unschuld und die Schrift: Deutsche Frauenromane im 18. Jahrhundert* (Berlin/Marburg, 1983); Paul Kluckhohn, *Die Auffassung der Liebe in der Literatur des 18. Jahrhundert und in der deutschen Romantik* (Halle, 1931); and Georg Steinhausen, *Geschichte des deutschen Briefs* (Berlin, 1889). On family life in the period, see Paul Ritterband, ed., *Modern Jewish Fertility* (Leiden, 1981); and Heidi Rosenbaum, *Formen der Familie* (Frankfurt a.M., 1982).

The best primary sources on the Jewish women's marital details discussed in chapter 7 are the two collections edited by Jacob Jacobson: *Jüdische Trauungen in Berlin, 1773–1859* (Berlin, 1968), and *Die Judenbürgerbücher der Stadt Berlin 1800–1851* (Berlin, 1962). Classic works on German-Jewish history for the period are Jacob Katz, *Out of the Ghetto* (New York, 1978); Adolf Leschnitzer, *The Magic Background of Modern Anti-Semitism: An Analysis of the German-Jewish Relationship* (New York, 1956); Heinz Moshe Graupe, *Die Entstehung des modernen Judentums* (Hamburg, 1969); and Alfred Low, *Jews in the Eyes of the Germans* (Philadelphia, 1979). Books used here on romantic attitudes toward women included Marianne Burkhardt, ed., *Gestaltet und Gestaltend: Frauen in der deutschen Kultur,* vol. 10 of *Amsterdamer Beiträge zur neueren Germanistik* (Amsterdam, 1980); Alfred Schier, *Der Liebe in der Frühromantik* (Marburg, 1913); and Genevieve Bianquis, *Love in Germany* (London, 1964). On conversion, see N. Samter, *Judentaufen im neunzehnten Jahrhundert* (Berlin, 1906); Abraham Menes, "The Conversion Movement in Prussia during the First Half of the Nineteenth Century," *YIVO Annual of Jewish Social Science* 6 (1951); and Gerhard Kessler, *Judentaufen und judenchristliche Familien in Ostpreussen,* in *Familiengeschichtliche Blätter/Deutsche Herold,* Jahrgang 36 (Leipzig, 1938).

For the antisemitic anecdotes involving salon participants reviewed in chapter 9, I relied on the same primary and secondary sources used for earlier portraits of these personalities. General works that helped me grasp the sharp change in Berlin's climate of opinion on so many matters included Max Kohler, *Jewish Rights at the Congresses of Vienna and Aix-La-Chapelle* (New York, 1918); Walter Simon, *The Failure of the Prussian Reform Movement, 1807–1819* (Ithaca, 1955); and Eugene Anderson, *Nationalism and the Cultural Crisis in Prussia, 1806–1815* (New York, 1939). The crucial primary source on anti-assimilationist antisemitism was of course Karl Wilhelm Grattenauer, *Wider die Juden* (Berlin, 1803). Broader background an antisemitism in these circles can be found in Eleanore Sterling, *Judenhass: Die Anfänge des politischen Antisemitismus in Deutschland 1815–1850* (Frankfurt a.M., 1969); Jacob Katz, *From Prejudice to Destruction: Anti-semitism, 1700–1933* (Cambridge, 1980); Margarete Dierks, *Die preussischen Altkonservativen und die Judenfrage 1810–1847,* Heft 7 of Rostocker Studien (Rostock, 1939); and Philipp Eberhard, *Die politischen Anschauungen der christlich-deutschen Tischgesellschaft* (Erlangen, 1937).

Index

Abendgesellschaften: 98
Abrahamson, Jacob: 110
Alexander of Russia, Czar: 267
Altruppin: 49
Amsterdam: 43, 99, 103
Anna Amalia, Princess of Prussia: 2, 127, 169
Arnim, Achim von: 103, 127, 137–38, 215, 258–59, 272–73, 275
Arnim, Bettina von (born Brentano): 127, 258, 270
Arnstein, Fanny von (born Itzig): 102, 126, 210, 255
Arnstein, Henriette von: 255
Arnstein, Joseph: 207
Augsburg: 28
Austria: 265, 267, 268

Bad Töplitz: 133–34, 184
Battle of Austerlitz: 265
Bauer, Hofrat: 89, 92
Becker, Sophie: 162
Beer, Amalie (born Malka Lipman): 3, 109, 186, 200–01, 210, 270
Beer, Jakob Herz: 109, 200
Behrenstrasse: 83
Bendavid, Lazarus: 92, 189
Berg, Caroline von: 181–82, 271
Berliner Abendblätter: 272–74, 276
Berlinische Monatschrift: 89, 120
Bernhard, Isaac (born Isaac Zülz): 148
Bernhard, Madame, Philippine Cohen's mother: 104

Bernhard, Samuel: 176, 207
Bernstorff, Count Christian von: 108, 131
Biester, Johann: 120, 160
Bildung: 7
Bismarck, Otto von: 1
"Bluestocking" salon women: 16
Bose, Blümchen von (born Blümchen Moses; wife of Joseph Arnstein and Kriegsrat von Bose): 204–05, 207
Bose, Kriegsrat von: 207
Boye, Frau von (born Hitzel Zülz): 104, 206–07
Boye, Major von: 207
Brandenburg, Electorate of: 26, 31, 38, 49, 267
Bremen: 27
Brentano, Clemens: 103, 174, 258, 272–73, 275
Breslau: 48, 176
Brinkmann, (Carl) Gustav von: 48, 76, 101, 112, 123–24, 132, 136–37, 139, 141, 157, 174, 181, 183, 185, 208, 216, 221, 255–56, 257, 260, 264, 271
Brumbey, K. W.: 75, 83
Brussels: 112
Buchholz, Friedrich: 49–50, 274, 276
Burgsdorff, Wilhelm von: 124, 132–36, 141, 184
Burke, Edmund: 125

Cafe "Stadt Paris": 48, 141
Cagliostro, Count Alessandro: 162

293

Casa-Valencia, Count: 131
Chamisso, Adalbert von: 137–39, 150, 165
Charlotte Sampson: 247
Chézy, Anton von: 170
Chézy, Helmina von (born von Klencke; also married von Hastfer): 167–69, 170–71
Chodowiecki, Daniel: 64
Christlich-deutsche Tischgesellschaft: 271–77, 280
Cohen, Ephraim: 103, 195, 200–01, 256
Cohen, Philippine (born Pessel Zülz): 3, 103, 151, 186, 195, 200–02, 206–07, 270
Collegium Medico-Chirurgicum: 65
Corsikan Concert Hall: 85
Cotta, Johann Friedrich: 170
Courland: 160, 162
Courland, Duchess Dorothea von (born von Medem): 81, 96, 100, 105, 114, 146, 157–58, 160, 162, 182–83
Courland, Duke of: 105, 126

Danzig: 144
Darmstadt: 17
Davidssohn, Wolf: 90
Dessau: 148
Devidel, Marianne, wife of Johann Schadow: 110, 207, 214
Dohm, Christian Wilhelm (von): 120, 140, 145, 194, 195
Dohna, Count Alexander von: 100, 124, 126, 132–33
Domeier, Wilhelm: 176
Dresden: 27, 28, 162, 176

Eberhard, a preacher: 97
Eberty, Hermann (born Ephraim): 149–50
Eckenberg, J. C. "von," a comedian: 83

Egloffstein, Count Karl von: 178, 208
Eigensatz, Christel: 185
Eisenmenger, Johann: 260
Engels, Friedrich: 50–51
England: 30, 33, 36, 71, 81, 93, 95, 176, 217, 266, 267, 268
Engstrom, Herr von, Swedish ambassador to Prussia: 255
Enlightenment: 13, 16, 51, 89, 120, 125, 164, 247
Ephraim, Adele: 198, 208
Ephraim, Benjamin Veitel: 111–12, 191, 198
Ephraim, David (converted name, Andreas Johannes Schmidt): 195, 202
Ephraim, Rebekka (born Itzig): 103, 195, 201–02
Ephraim, Veitel Heine: 111, 195, 204
Erfurt: 267

Fessler, Ignatius: 198
Fichte, Johann: 51, 104, 125, 143–47, 168, 189, 206, 267, 274
Fideicommise: 32
Finckenstein, Count Karl von: 126, 131–35, 184
Florentin: 172, 174
Forster, Georg: 24, 139
France: 36, 71, 81, 95, 120, 126, 127, 137, 138, 157, 167, 217, 265, 266, 267
Francis II, Emperor of Austria: 108
Fränkel, Rösel: 208
Frankfurt am Main: 27, 28, 38, 43, 53, 94, 190, 272
Frankfurt an der Oder: 48, 133, 138, 176
Frederick I, Elector of Brandenburg (1688–1713), King in Prussia (1701–13): 78, 80
Frederick II ("the Great"), King of Prussia (1740–86): 1, 2, 25–27, 31, 36, 40–41, 46, 54, 63–64, 75–76,

79–80, 83, 105, 111, 122, 126–27, 188, 196, 204, 265–66

Frederick William, the Great Elector of Brandenburg (1640–88): 38, 78

Frederick William I, King of Prussia (1713–40): 40, 54, 78–79, 81

Frederick William II, King of Prussia (1786–97): 31, 80, 83, 94, 96, 112, 126, 132, 140, 167–68, 181, 183, 205, 265–66

Frederick William III, King of Prussia (1797–1840): 81, 167, 265–66, 268, 272, 277

Freemasons: 93–94, 198

French Revolution: 3, 80, 101, 125, 131, 145, 183, 252, 269, 272

Friedländer, David: 92–93, 97, 109, 121, 148–49, 189, 191, 196, 215, 246, 256, 263, 278

Friedländer, Moses: 109, 178, 196, 200, 206

Friedländer, Rebecca (born Solomon; converted family name, Saaling; her converted name, Regina Frohberg): 3, 109, 177–78, 195, 200, 206–08, 269–70

Friedrichstrasse: 251

Friends of Natural Science: 88

Fromm, Henriette: 132

Gad, Esther (born Bernhard: second married name, Domeier): 167, 176–77, 206–7

Garve, Christian: 48

Gelehrtenrepublik: 87

Genelli, Hans: 274

Genlis, Count de: 166

Genlis, Félicité de (born Ducrest): 126, 166–67, 170–71, 176–77

Gentz, Friedrich: 48–50, 76, 124–25, 132, 140–42, 147, 181, 185, 215, 255, 258–59, 270

George, Canvas: 251

Gessler, Count, Saxon ambassador to the Prussian court: 108

Gleim, Johann: 168

Goethe, Johann Wolfgang von: 17, 51, 101, 108, 125, 137, 144, 146, 206, 216, 257

Göttingen: 28, 52, 53, 66, 73, 101, 120, 133, 139

Gottsched, Johann: 164

Grattenauer, Karl Wilhelm: 259–63, 274

Grotthuss, Baron von: 108, 210, 213

Grotthuss, Sara von. *See* Meyer, Sara

Gualtieri, Major Peter von: 132, 185

Gumpertz, Aron: 189

Halle: 225

Hamburg: 27, 43, 53, 94, 162, 190

Hameln, Glückel of: 188

Hanover: 267

Hapsburg, House of: 34, 38

Hardenberg, Prince Karl August von: 266, 268–69, 272

Hastfer, Freiherr Carl von: 170

Haydn, Franz Joseph: 103

Hebrew: 147, 187

Hegel, Georg Wilhelm Friedrich: 51

Heidelberg: 17

Heine, Heinrich: 150

Herder, Gottfried: 51, 108, 206

Herz, Henriette (born de Lemos): 2, 92–93, 96–97, 99, 100, 102, 104, 106, 113–14, 123, 127, 131, 146, 158, 172, 175–76, 182, 189, 197–201, 203, 207–09, 254, 269, 272

Herz, Markus: 2, 63, 92–94, 96, 99, 104, 120, 122–23, 148–49, 153, 175–76, 191, 195, 199, 200–01, 203, 207–08

Hesse: 267

Heyse, Karl: 207, 212

Heyse, Paul: 177–78, 212

Hitler, Adolf: 1

Hitzig, Julius Eduard: 149–50, 170, 191, 274

Hof, a village: 146

Hohenzollern, House of: 27, 34

Holbach, Baron D': 17
Holy Roman Empire: 276
Hotel Ville de Paris: 85
Huguenots: 25–26, 38, 48, 96, 131, 141
Humboldt, Alexander von: 2, 51, 96,
    100, 106, 123–24, 133, 137, 139–40,
    172
Humboldt, Caroline von (born von
    Dacheröden): 92, 123, 134, 181–82,
    257, 270, 280
Humboldt, Major von: 96
Humboldt, Wilhelm von: 2, 48, 51,
    67, 76, 92, 96, 100, 106, 123–24, 134,
    137, 139, 141–42, 149–50, 172, 182,
    185, 202–03, 208, 215, 221, 254–57,
    260, 264, 270, 280

Iffland, August Wilhelm: 101
Industrialization: 29, 44
Innsbruck: 94
Isaacs, Moses: 195, 202, 204–05, 214
Italy: 217
Itzig, Blümchen: 97
Itzig, Isaac Daniel: 94, 97, 102, 111,
    126, 148, 195, 204, 274
Itzig, Morris: 259
Itzig, Recha: 103
Itzig, Sara. *See* Levy, Sara

Jacobson, Isaac: 110
Jägerstrasse: 102
Jean Paul (Richter): 104–05, 124,
    145–46, 169, 177, 181, 220
Jena: 17, 107, 125, 134, 144, 145, 170,
    174, 220

Kant, Immanuel: 48, 51, 64, 99, 105,
    126, 144, 145, 148, 184, 189
Karlsbad: 134
Karsch, Anna Louise: 168, 171
Kleist, Heinrich von: 137–39, 256, 271,
    272–74
Klencke, Caroline von (born Karsch;
    first married name, Hempel): 168–
    70

Klencke, Frau Wittwe-Major: 169
Königsberg: 48, 97, 99, 105, 126, 148,
    265, 273
Koreff, David: 149–50, 170, 191
Kottwitz, Baron von: 168
Krausenstrasse: 251
Kunth, Gottlob: 100, 123, 139

Landschaft: 33
La Roche, Karl: 92, 123
La Roche, Sophie: 92, 123
Lecture Society, hosted by Dorothea
    Veit: 93, 106
Lehndorff, Count von: 24
Leibniz, Gottfried Wilhelm: 78
Leipzig: 17, 27, 28, 53, 73, 105, 146, 164
Lemos, Dr. Benjamin de: 99, 148
Lemos, Henriette de. *See* Herz, Hen-
    riette
Lessing, Gotthold: 51, 83, 108, 149
Leuchsenring, Franz von: 208
Levin, Markus: 97
Levin, Rahel (wife of Karl August
    Varnhagen von Ense): 1, 2, 7, 8, 10,
    35, 97, 100–03, 108–09, 112–14,
    120–26, 131–36, 140–42, 145, 150,
    158, 165–66, 178, 182–86, 189, 198,
    202, 208–09, 212, 215, 255, 257
Levy, Sara (born Itzig): 3, 102–04,
    126–27, 153, 186, 200–01, 210, 215,
    255, 258, 270
Levy, Solomon: 94, 103, 153, 200, 215
Liedertafel: 272–73
Ligne, Prince Karl de: 126, 136–38,
    181, 183
Liman, August (born Abraham Lieb-
    man): 202
Liman, Frederike (born Fradchen
    Marcuse; married, Liebman): 184,
    201–02
Lipman, Malka. *See* Beer, Amalie
London: 16, 19, 43, 94
Louis XIV, King of France: 16, 78,
    167

Louis Ferdinand, Prince of Prussia:
46, 126, 132–33, 135–37, 141, 185, 271
Lübeck: 27
Lucinde: 107, 172
Luise, Queen of Prussia: 81, 105, 181,
266

Maimon, Salomon: 152–54
Mannheim: 27, 28
Mansfield, an Englishman living in
Berlin: 82
Marchetti, an actress: 101, 185
Maria Theresa, Empress of Austria:
26
Marwitz, Alexander von der: 275
Matzdorf, a publisher in Berlin: 146
Meinert, Joseph: 184
Mendelssohn, Abraham: 106
Mendelssohn, Brendel. *See* Veit, Dor-
othea
Mendelssohn, Joseph: 106, 139, 172
Mendelssohn, Moses: 1–2, 40, 51, 63–
64, 88, 92, 96–98, 103, 105–06, 120,
126–27, 148–49, 153, 160, 162, 172,
189, 191, 195, 197, 208, 246
Mendelssohn-Bartholdy, Felix: 207
Mercantilism: 31, 44, 83, 284
Meyer, Marianne (married, Princess
von Reuss; as a widow, Frau von
Eybenberg): 97, 108, 126, 184, 186,
206–08, 212–13
Meyer, Sara (married, von Grot-
thuss): 97, 108, 126, 184–86, 206,
210, 213
Miltitz, Freiherr von, Johann Fichte's
patron: 144
Mirabeau, Count Honoré de: 100,
122
Molière, Jean Baptiste: 15, 16
Monday Club: 88–89, 92, 94, 123
Morino bookstore: 85
Moritz, Karl Philipp: 120
Motte Fouqué, Baron Friedrich de
la: 137, 139, 165

Motte Fouqué, Caroline de la: 165–
66
Mozart, Wolfgang: 103
Mühlendamm: 111
Müller, Adam: 272–73, 277
Müller, Johannes von: 140
Munich: 27, 28

Napoleon I (Bonaparte) of France: 7,
50, 81, 119, 132, 141, 167, 251–52, 265–
68, 273, 276
Napoleonic War: 202–03
Neumann, Wilhelm: 104, 138, 150–51
Nicolai, Friedrich: 95–98, 105, 120,
125, 135, 149, 160
Novalis (Friedrich von Hardenberg):
137
Nuremberg: 27, 28
Nuremberg Laws: 228

Oranienburg: 214
Order of Asiatic Brethren: 94
Orléans, Duke of: 167

Pachta, Josephine von: 101, 126, 183,
185
Paris: 15, 16, 17, 19, 35, 43, 94, 112, 166,
167, 183, 252, 262
Pariser Platz: 75
Parthey, Daniel Friedrich: 105
Parthey, Gustav: 105
Pascal, Jean Marc: 85
Philomatic Society: 88, 92
Poland: 39, 43, 105, 147, 152, 168, 188,
227
Polarsternbund: 150–51
Portugal: 37, 176
Potsdam: 17, 78, 79, 105, 127
Prague: 94, 184, 185

Radziwill, Prince Anton von: 126,
132, 271
Radziwill, Princess Luise von: 271
Rahn, Johann Fichte's patron: 144

Rammenau: 144
Recke, Eliza von der (born von Medem): 96–97, 105, 160, 162–63, 166, 171
Recke, Herr von der: 162
Reeve, Henry: 81–82, 85
Reform Judaism: 147
Reichardt, Johann: 120
Reichstelle für Sippenforschung: 227
Renaissance: 15, 115
Reuss, Prince Heinrich von: 108, 131, 184, 207–08, 212
Reuss, Princess Marianne von. See Meyer, Marianne
Robert, Ludwig: 145, 149–51, 189, 191, 259, 274
Romanticism: 13, 51, 220, 275
Rome: 267
Rousseau, Jean-Jacques: 16, 163, 189
Royal Academy of Art: 63, 76, 78
Royal Academy of Science: 63–65, 67, 73, 76, 78–79, 81, 87–88, 92, 120, 123, 189, 267
Runkle, Rebecca von (born Moses): 204–05
Russia: 105, 137, 266, 268

St. Petersburg: 162
Savigny, Friedrich von: 270
Savigny, Kunigunde von: 270
Saxony: 26
Schadow, Johann: 110, 207, 214
Schiller, Friedrich: 51, 134, 144
Schlabrendorf, Countess Caroline von: 120, 126, 183
Schlabrendorf, Count Gustav von: 183
Schlegel, August: 51, 63, 125, 173, 275
Schlegel, Caroline: 107
Schlegel, Dorothea. See Veit, Dorothea
Schlegel, Friedrich: 2, 51, 104, 107, 111, 124, 125, 140, 142, 170, 172–73, 175, 184, 201, 207, 201–11, 213–15, 275

Schleiermacher, Friedrich: 98–99, 104–05, 107, 124–25, 133, 139, 175–76, 184, 209, 220, 247, 255, 275
Schmerz der Liebe: 177–78
Schönemann, a comedian: 83
Schütz, Christian Gottfried: 97
Schutzbrief: 194, 237
Seiler, Mademoiselle, a singer: 201
Serfdom: 29, 34
Seven Years' War (1756–63): 26, 45, 96, 111, 195, 204, 215
Silesia: 26
Singakademie: 272
Smith, Adam: 276
Society of Friends: 93
Society of Friends of the Humanities: 88
Solomon, Julie (converted family name, Saaling; married, Heyse): 207, 212
Solomon, Rebecca. See Friedländer, Rebecca
Sophie Charlotte, Queen of Prussia: 78
Spain: 37, 267, 270
Spalding, Johann: 160
Spandauer Strasse: 36
Spree, a river: 136
Staël, Germaine de: 3, 119, 156–57, 158–59
Stägemann, Elizabeth von: 181, 270
Stägemann, Friedrich von: 140, 270, 274
Starre, von, a Swedish officer: 207
Steiglitz, Israel: 149–50, 191, 202, 256
Steiglitz, Jente (born Ephraim): 201–02
Stein, Reichsfreiherr Karl von: 266, 268–69, 272
Sulzer, Johann: 168

Teller, Abraham: 121, 246, 278
Thiergarten park: 21, 75
Thirty Years' War (1618–48): 26, 30

Tieck, Ludwig: 105, 124, 133–35, 143, 146, 168, 174, 206, 220, 275
Tilly, Count Alexander von: 126, 136, 137
Tolerance Lodge: 94
Treaty of Schönbrunn: 267
Treaty of Tilsit: 266, 268
Treitschke, Heinrich von: 10
Tugendbund: 92, 123, 182, 254, 257

Uhden, Johann: 103
Unger, Helene: 111, 163–65, 166, 171
Unger, J. H.: 111, 163
University of Berlin: 145, 207, 212
University of Halle: 49, 97, 133, 138–39, 165
University of Jena: 144
University of Königsberg: 148
Unter den Linden: 23, 36, 75, 79, 105, 160
Unzelman, Frederike: 185
Urquijo, Dan Raphael d': 131, 183

Varnhagen, Rahel. *See* Levin, Rahel
Varnhagen von Ense, Karl August: 8, 102–04, 138, 141–42, 150–51, 165–66, 177, 200, 207, 212, 258, 274
Vauxhall, Madame Schuwitz's bordello: 76
Veit, David: 101
Veit, Dorothea (born Brendel Mendelssohn): 1–2, 92–93, 106–07, 111, 113–14, 158, 165, 167, 170–76, 182, 184, 189, 195, 200–01, 206–08, 211, 213–14
Veit, Simon: 93, 106–07, 172, 175, 195, 200, 206, 213
Vienna: 17, 25, 26, 27, 94, 102, 108, 109, 126, 131, 142, 184, 190, 210, 214, 231, 262
Vienna Congress (1814–15): 17, 38, 258, 269, 280, 281
Voltaire, François Marie Arouet de: 189
Voss, Julie von: 181, 255, 257, 271
Vossische Zeitung: 84

War of Liberation (1813–14): 102, 268
Wednesday Society: 89–91, 123
Weimar: 17, 73, 146
Westphalia: 267
Wider die Juden: 261
Wiesel, Pauline (born Cesar): 132, 185
Wraxall, an English visitor to Berlin: 80

Yiddish: 147, 153, 187, 200

Zelter, Karl: 272, 274
Zülz, Pessel. *See* Cohen, Philippine
Zurich: 144